BRAVO XL CONVECTION AIR FRYER OVEN

COOKBOOK 2021

550 AMAZINGLY EASY RECIPES TO FRY, BAKE, GRILL, AND ROAST WITH YOUR NUWAVE AIR FRYER OVEN

BARBARA MARSHALL

Copyright © 2021 by Barbara Marshall All rights reserved worldwide.

No part of this book may be reproduced or transmitted in any form or by any means, electronic or mechanical, including photo- copying, recording or by any information storage and retrieval system, without written permission from the publisher, except for the inclusion of brief quotations in a review.

Warning-Disclaimer: The purpose of this book is to educate and entertain. The author or publisher does not guarantee that anyone following the techniques, suggestions, tips, ideas, or strategies will become successful. The author and publisher shall have neither liability or responsibility to anyone with respect to any loss or damage caused, or alleged to be caused, directly or indirectly by the information contained in this book.

CONTENTS

INTRODUCTION 10
What Is an Air Frying Oven? 10
The Benefits of Cooking with Your NuWave Air Fryer Oven 10
Knowing the Tips on Using Your NuWave Air Fryer Oven 11
Regularly Cleaning Your NuWave Air Fryer Oven 12

BREAKFAST 14

Southern-style Biscuits 14	Sheet-pan Hash Browns 27
Egg-loaded Potato Skins 14	Savory Breakfast Bread Pudding 27
Sesame Wafers 14	Broccoli Cornbread 28
Individual Overnight Omelets 15	Hashbrown Potatoes Lyonnaise 28
Berry Crisp 15	Coffee Cake 28
Classic Cinnamon Rolls 15	Beef And Bean Quesadillas 29
Wild Blueberry Lemon Chia Bread 16	Country Bread 29
Grilled Dagwood 16	Garlic-cheese Biscuits 29
Autumn Berry Dessert 17	Sunny-side Up Eggs 30
Buttered Poppy Seed Bread 17	Onion And Cheese Buttermilk Biscuits 30
Make-ahead Currant Cream Scones 17	Oven-baked Reuben 30
Avocado Chicken Flatbread 18	Yogurt Bread 30
Morning Glory Muffins 18	New York–style Crumb Cake 31
Blueberry Muffins 19	Freezer-ready Breakast Burritos 31
Heavenly Hash Browns 19	Cinnamon Biscuit Rolls 32
Breakfast Blueberry Peach Crisp 19	Brunch Burritos 33
Bread Boat Eggs 20	Strawberry Pie Glaze 33
Western Frittata 20	Pancake Muffins 33
Garlic Basil Bread 20	Bacon Chicken Ranch Sandwiches 34
Toasted Cheese Sandwich 21	Breakfast Pita 34
Nacho Chips 21	Crispy Bacon 34
Italian Strata 21	Honey Ham And Swiss Broiler 34
Cheddar Bacon Broiler 22	Baked Grapefruit 35
Banana Baked Oatmeal 22	Walnut Pancake 35
Homemade Biscuits 22	Baked Steel-cut Oatmeal 35
Stromboli 23	Spicy Beef Fajitas 36
Brown Sugar Grapefruit 23	Lemon Blueberry Scones 36
Apple Fritters 24	Cherries Jubilee 36
Cinnamon Rolls 24	Portobello Burgers 37
Baked Eggs With Bacon-tomato Sauce 24	Baked Macs 37
Spinach, Tomato & Feta Quiche 25	Breakfast Bars 37
Cinnamon Swirl Bread 26	Granola 38
Sweet-hot Pepperoni Pizza 26	Fry Bread 38
Cinnamon Toast 27	Strawberry Bread 38

Bacon, Broccoli And Swiss Cheese Bread Pudding ... 39

LUNCH AND DINNER 40

Miso-glazed Salmon With Broccoli 40
Roasted Vegetable Gazpacho 40
Fresh Herb Veggie Pizza 40
Pork And Brown Rice Casserole 41
Glazed Pork Tenderloin With Carrots Sheet Pan Supper 41
Lima Bean And Artichoke Casserole 41
Homemade Pizza Sauce 42
Kasha Loaf 42
Spanish Rice 42
Yeast Dough For Two Pizzas 43
Classic Beef Stew 43
Tarragon Beef Ragout 43
Quick Pan Pizza 44
Chicken Gumbo 44
Narragansett Clam Chowder 44
Cheesy Chicken–stuffed Shells 44
Green Bean Soup 45
Sage, Chicken + Mushroom Pasta Casserole 45
French Bread Pizza 46
Honey Bourbon–glazed Pork Chops With Sweet Potatoes + Apples 46
Moroccan Couscous 47
Maple Bacon 47
Individual Baked Eggplant Parmesan 47
Sheet Pan Loaded Nachos 48
Crunchy Baked Chicken Tenders 48
Chicken Tortilla Roll-ups 48
Pesto Pizza 49
Baked Picnic Pinto Beans 49
Sun-dried Tomato Pizza 49
Connecticut Garden Chowder 50
Italian Baked Stuffed Tomatoes 50
French Onion Soup 50
Italian Stuffed Zucchini Boats 51
Spicy Oven-baked Chili 51
Homemade Beef Enchiladas 52
Thai Chicken Pizza With Cauliflower Crust 52
Easy Oven Lasagne 53
Pea Soup 53
Family Favorite Pizza 53
One-step Classic Goulash 54
Sheet Pan Beef Fajitas 54
Crab Chowder 55
Baked French Toast With Maple Bourbon Syrup 55
Oven-baked Barley 55
Chicken Marengo 56
Broiled Chipotle Tilapia With Avocado Sauce 56
Baked Parsleyed Cheese Grits 56
Scalloped Corn Casserole 57
Kashaburgers 57
Couscous-stuffed Poblano Peppers 57
Creamy Roasted Pepper Basil Soup 58
Moussaka 58
Roasted Harissa Chicken + Vegetables 59
Tomato Bisque 59
Meat Lovers Pan Pizza 60
Italian Bread Pizza 60
Light Beef Stroganoff 61
Oven-baked Rice 61
Baked Tomato Casserole 61
Salad Lentils 62
Zucchini Casserole 62
Dijon Salmon With Green Beans Sheet Pan Supper 62
Oven-baked Couscous 63
Favorite Baked Ziti 63
Rosemary Lentils 63
Classic Tuna Casserole 64
Healthy Southwest Stuffed Peppers 64
Light Quiche Lorraine 65
Chicken Thighs With Roasted Rosemary Root Vegetables 65

SNACKS APPETIZERS AND SIDES 66

Cinnamon Pita Chips 66
Pork Belly Scallion Yakitori 66
Ham And Cheese Palmiers 66
Thick-crust Pepperoni Pizza 67
All-purpose Cornbread 67
Polenta Fries With Chili-lime Mayo 68
Parmesan Crisps 68
Cherry Chipotle Bbq Chicken Wings 68

Root Vegetable Crisps 69
Savory Sausage Balls 69
Middle Eastern Phyllo Rolls 69
Crispy Ravioli Bites 70
Creamy Parmesan Polenta 70
Pork Pot Stickers With Yum Yum Sauce 70
Shrimp Pirogues 71
Loaded Potato Skins 72
Caramelized Onion Dip 72
Turkey Bacon Dates 73
Cinnamon Apple Chips 73
Sheet Pan Chicken Nachos 73
Crispy Sweet Potato Fries 73
Corn Dog Muffins 74
Crispy Chili Kale Chips 74
Firecracker Bites 74
Buffalo Chicken Dip 75
Hot Mexican Bean Dip 75
Blistered Shishito Peppers 75
Italian Rice Balls 76
Spicy Pigs In A Blanket 76
Fried Mozzarella Sticks 76
Sausage Cheese Pinwheels 77
Korean "fried" Chicken Wings 77
Dill Fried Pickles With Light Ranch Dip 78
Simple Holiday Stuffing 78
Sage Butter Roasted Butternut Squash With Pepitas 79
Beet Chips 79
Grilled Ham & Muenster Cheese On Raisin Bread..79
Avocado Egg Rolls 80
Cuban Sliders 80
Spinach And Artichoke Dip 80
Sweet Or Savory Baked Sweet Potatoes 81
Turkey Burger Sliders 81
Rosemary-roasted Potatoes 81
Stuffed Mushrooms 81
Sweet And Salty Roasted Nuts 82
Baked Asparagus Fries 82
Loaded Cauliflower Casserole 82
Cauliflower "tater" Tots 83
Fried Wontons 83
Eggs In Avocado Halves 84
Parmesan Peas 84
Bagel Chips 84
Skinny Fries 84
Smoked Salmon Puffs 85
Homemade Harissa 85
Wonton Cups 86
Potato Chips 86
Bacon Bites 86
Beef Satay With Peanut Dipping Sauce 86
Mozzarella-stuffed Arancini 87
Panko-breaded Onion Rings 88
Smoked Gouda Bacon Macaroni And Cheese 88
Buffalo Cauliflower 89
Barbecue Chicken Nachos 89
Classic Cornbread 90
Beef Empanadas 90
Crispy Spiced Chickpeas 91
Cheese Arancini 91
Okra Chips 91

FISH AND SEAFOOD 92

Crab-stuffed Peppers 92
Maple-crusted Salmon 92
Fish With Sun-dried Tomato Pesto 92
Rolled Asparagus Flounder 93
Crispy Smelts 93
Crispy Pecan Fish 93
Crunchy And Buttery Cod With Ritz® Cracker Crust
....94
Better Fish Sticks 94
Maple Balsamic Glazed Salmon 94
Lobster Tails 95
Tuna Nuggets In Hoisin Sauce 95
Shrimp Po'boy With Remoulade Sauce.....................95
Popcorn Crawfish 96
Fried Scallops 96
Tilapia Teriyaki 96
Romaine Wraps With Shrimp Filling 97
Beer-battered Cod 97
Skewered Salsa Verde Shrimp 98
Tortilla-crusted Tilapia 98
Miso-rubbed Salmon Fillets 98
Shrimp With Jalapeño Dip 98
Broiled Lemon Coconut Shrimp 99
Light Trout Amandine 99

Oysters Broiled In Wine Sauce 99	Spiced Sea Bass 108
Pecan-crusted Tilapia 100	Snapper With Capers And Olives 108
Quick Shrimp Scampi 100	Chilled Clam Cake Slices With Dijon Dill Sauce ... 109
Sea Scallops 100	Capered Crab Cakes 109
Lightened-up Breaded Fish Filets 101	Flounder Fillets 109
Almond Crab Cakes 101	Horseradish Crusted Salmon 109
Stuffed Shrimp 101	Marinated Catfish 110
Fried Shrimp 102	Lemon-roasted Fish With Olives + Capers 110
Lemon-roasted Salmon Fillets 102	Fish And "chips" 110
Oven-crisped Fish Fillets With Salsa 103	Roasted Garlic Shrimp 111
Sea Bass With Potato Scales And Caper Aïoli 103	Broiled Scallops 111
Ginger Miso Calamari 103	Coconut-crusted Shrimp 111
Blackened Catfish 104	Molasses-glazed Salmon 112
Shrimp, Chorizo And Fingerling Potatoes 104	Garlic And Dill Salmon 112
Coconut Jerk Shrimp 105	Crispy Calamari 112
Roasted Pepper Tilapia 105	Fish Tacos With Jalapeño-lime Sauce 113
Fried Oysters 105	Baked Tomato Pesto Bluefish 113
Lemon-dill Salmon Burgers 106	Beer-breaded Halibut Fish Tacos 114
Garlic-lemon Shrimp Skewers 106	Crab Cakes 114
Halibut Tacos 107	Coconut Shrimp 115
Broiled Dill And Lemon Salmon 107	Pecan-topped Sole 115
Catfish Kebabs 107	Shrimp 115
Roasted Fish With Provençal Crumb Topping 108	Sesame-crusted Tuna Steaks 116

POULTRY 117

Pickle Brined Fried Chicken 117	Teriyaki Chicken Drumsticks 125
Sesame Orange Chicken 117	Harissa Lemon Whole Chicken 126
Lemon Sage Roast Chicken 118	Orange-glazed Roast Chicken 126
Honey Lemon Thyme Glazed Cornish Hen 118	Lemon Chicken 126
Buffalo Egg Rolls 119	Italian Baked Chicken 127
Oven-crisped Chicken 119	I Forgot To Thaw—garlic Capered Chicken Thighs 127
Air-fried Turkey Breast With Cherry Glaze 119	
Turkey Sausage Cassoulet 120	Crispy Duck With Cherry Sauce 127
Chicken Potpie 120	Chicken Parmesan 128
Chicken Cordon Bleu 121	Spice-rubbed Split Game Hen 128
Nacho Chicken Fries 121	Parmesan Crusted Chicken Cordon Bleu 129
Hot Thighs 122	Chicken Pot Pie 129
Pecan Turkey Cutlets 122	Coconut Chicken With Apricot-ginger Sauce 130
Crispy Fried Onion Chicken Breasts 123	Chicken Fajitas 130
Rotisserie-style Chicken 123	Chicken Chunks 131
Chicken Souvlaki Gyros 123	Chicken Ranch Roll-ups 131
Chicken Schnitzel Dogs 124	Turkey-hummus Wraps 131
Chicken Cutlets With Broccoli Rabe And Roasted Peppers 124	Marinated Green Pepper And Pineapple Chicken .. 131
	Sweet-and-sour Chicken 132
East Indian Chicken 125	Golden Seasoned Chicken Wings 132

Philly Chicken Cheesesteak Stromboli 133	Thai Chicken Drumsticks... 138
Guiltless Bacon... 133	Chicken Breast With Chermoula Sauce 139
Tandoori Chicken Legs.. 134	Fried Chicken 139
Chicken Adobo 134	Chicken In Mango Sauce... 140
Gluten-free Nutty Chicken Fingers 134	Sticky Soy Chicken Thighs 140
Pesto-crusted Chicken 135	Chicken Nuggets.. 140
Apricot Glazed Chicken Thighs 135	Quick Chicken For Filling... 141
Southwest Gluten-free Turkey Meatloaf 135	Crispy Chicken Parmesan... 141
Jerk Turkey Meatballs 136	Italian Roasted Chicken Thighs 141
Tender Chicken Meatballs 136	Tandoori Chicken 142
Tasty Meat Loaf.. 137	Roasted Game Hens With Vegetable Stuffing........ 142
Jerk Chicken Drumsticks 137	Chicken Hand Pies 142
Foiled Rosemary Chicken Breasts 137	Peanut Butter-barbeque Chicken 143
Crispy Chicken Tenders 138	Crispy Curry Chicken Tenders................................. 143
Light And Lovely Loaf 138	Sesame Chicken Breasts.. 144

BEEP PORK AND LAMB 145

Lime And Cumin Lamb Kebabs............................... 145	Spicy Little Beef Birds 155
Pork Taco Gorditas 145	Pretzel-coated Pork Tenderloin 155
Crispy Smoked Pork Chops...................................... 146	Beef, Onion, And Pepper Shish Kebab 155
Red Curry Flank Steak... 146	Perfect Strip Steaks 156
Bourbon Broiled Steak 146	Lamb Burger With Feta And Olives 156
Albóndigas... 147	Sloppy Joes.. 157
Mustard-herb Lamb Chops 147	Minted Lamb Chops 157
Glazed Meatloaf.. 148	Pork Loin 157
Barbecue-style London Broil 148	Barbecued Broiled Pork Chops................................ 158
Kielbasa Chunks With Pineapple & Peppers 148	Cilantro-crusted Flank Steak 158
Lime-ginger Pork Tenderloin 149	Beef Bourguignon 158
Italian Meatballs 149	Meatloaf With Tangy Tomato Glaze 159
Beef-stuffed Bell Peppers 149	Wasabi-coated Pork Loin Chops.............................. 160
Italian Sausage & Peppers 150	Easy Tex-mex Chimichangas 160
Perfect Pork Chops 150	Beef And Spinach Braciole 160
Stuffed Bell Peppers 150	Calzones South Of The Border 161
Almond And Sun-dried Tomato Crusted Pork Chops 151	Chinese Pork And Vegetable Non-stir-fry............. 162
	Indian Fry Bread Tacos... 162
Seasoned Boneless Pork Sirloin Chops 151	Pesto Pork Chops... 163
Extra Crispy Country-style Pork Riblets 152	Classic Pepperoni Pizza 163
Lamb Curry... 152	Beef Vegetable Stew... 163
Herbed Lamb Burgers... 152	Ribeye Steak With Blue Cheese Compound Butter 164
Calf's Liver 152	Spanish Pork Skewers 164
Orange Glazed Pork Tenderloin 153	Beef Al Carbon (street Taco Meat) 165
Tuscan Pork Tenderloin.. 153	Smokehouse-style Beef Ribs 165
Air-fried Roast Beef With Rosemary Roasted Potatoes 154	Pork Cutlets With Almond-lemon Crust................ 165
	Steak Pinwheels With Pepper Slaw And Minneapolis Potato Salad 166
Skirt Steak Fajitas... 154	

California Burritos 166	Barbeque Ribs 169
Chipotle-glazed Meat Loaf 166	Better-than-chinese-take-out Pork Ribs 169
Slow Cooked Carnitas 167	Sweet Potato–crusted Pork Rib Chops 170
Chicken Fried Steak 167	Crispy Lamb Shoulder Chops 170
Kielbasa Sausage With Pierogies And Caramelized Onions 168	Zesty London Broil 171
Lamb Koftas Meatballs 168	Beer-baked Pork Tenderloin 171
Steak With Herbed Butter 168	Traditional Pot Roast 171
Crunchy Fried Pork Loin Chops 169	Stuffed Pork Chops 172

DESSERTS 173

Black And Blue Clafoutis 173	Soft Peanut Butter Cookies 186
Midnight Nutella® Banana Sandwich 173	Wild Blueberry Sweet Empanadas 186
Donut Holes 173	Mississippi Mud Brownies 187
Warm Chocolate Fudge Cakes 174	Currant Carrot Cake 187
Mini Gingerbread Bundt Cakes 174	Make-ahead Oatmeal-raisin Cookies 188
Buttermilk Confetti Cake 175	Freezer-to-oven Chocolate Chip Cookies 188
Meringue Topping 175	Fried Snickers Bars 189
Coconut Drop Cookies 175	Dark Chocolate Banana Bread 189
Orange Almond Ricotta Cookies 176	Sour Cream Pound Cake 189
Pineapple Tartlets 176	Cowboy Cookies 190
Frozen Brazo De Mercedes 176	Mixed Berry Hand Pies 190
Blueberry Clafoutis 177	Apple Strudel 191
Coconut Cake 177	Individual Peach Crisps 191
White Chocolate Cranberry Blondies 178	Orange Glaze 192
Keto Cheesecake Cups 178	Campfire Banana Boats 192
Blackberry Pie 178	Easy Churros 192
Heavenly Chocolate Cupcakes 178	Baked Custard 193
Lemon Torte 179	Hasselback Apple Crisp 193
Maple-glazed Pumpkin Pie 179	Vegan Swedish Cinnamon Rolls (kanelbullar) 193
Peanut Butter Cup Doughnut Holes 180	Glazed Apple Crostata 194
Bourbon Bread Pudding 180	Coconut Rice Pudding 195
Chocolate And Vanilla Swirled Pudding 181	Spice Cake 195
Little Swedish Coffee Cakes 181	Chewy Brownies 196
Goat Cheese–stuffed Nectarines 181	Raspberry Hand Pies 196
Peanut Butter S'mores 182	Blueberry Crumbles 196
Make-ahead Chocolate Chip Cookies 182	Pear And Almond Biscotti Crumble 197
Blueberry Crisp 183	Cheese Blintzes 197
Sweet Potato Donut Holes 183	Brown Sugar Baked Apples 198
Cinnamon Sugar Rolls 183	Blueberry Cheesecake Tartlets 198
Giant Oatmeal–peanut Butter Cookie 184	Key Lime Pie 198
Cranapple Crisp 184	Almond Amaretto Bundt Cake 199
Carrot Cake 185	Easy Peach Turnovers 199
Orange-glazed Brownies 185	Blueberry Cookies 200
German Chocolate Cake 185	Rum-glazed Roasted Pineapple 200

Triple Chocolate Brownies 201

VEGETABLES AND VEGETARIAN 202

Cauliflower 202
Roasted Ratatouille Vegetables 202
Baked Stuffed Acorn Squash 202
Crispy, Cheesy Leeks 202
Sweet Potato Puffs 203
Oregano Zucchini 203
Quick Broccoli Quiche 204
Green Peas With Mint 204
Roasted Fennel Salad 204
Roasted Herbed Shiitake Mushrooms 204
Spicy Sweet Potatoes 205
Asparagus Fries 205
Yellow Squash 205
Marjoram New Potatoes 206
Parmesan Garlic Fries 206
Air-fried Potato Salad 206
Crunchy Roasted Potatoes 207
Zucchini Boats With Ham And Cheese 207
Classic Baked Potatoes 207
Onions 207
Sesame Carrots And Sugar Snap Peas 208
Roasted Garlic Potatoes 208
Rosemary Roasted Potatoes With Lemon ... 208
Mushrooms, Sautéed 209
Roasted Corn Salad 209
Cheesy Potato Skins 209
Empty-the-refrigerator Roasted Vegetables 210
Ratatouille 210
Broccoli With Chinese Mushrooms And Water Chestnuts 211
Roasted Heirloom Carrots With Orange And Thyme 211
Rosemary New Potatoes 211
Baked Stuffed Potatoes With Vegetables ... 211
Roasted Brussels Sprouts With Bacon 212
Yogurt Zucchini With Onion 212
Five-spice Roasted Sweet Potatoes 212
Roasted Garlic 212
Golden Grilled Cheese Tomato Sandwich 213
Broiled Tomatoes 213
Fried Green Tomatoes With Sriracha Mayo 213
Yellow Squash With Bell Peppers 214
Brown Rice And Goat Cheese Croquettes 214
Panzanella Salad With Crispy Croutons 215
Classic Falafel 215
Potato Skins 216
Fingerling Potatoes 216
Homemade Potato Puffs 216
Perfect Asparagus 216
Roasted Belgian Endive With Pistachios And Lemon 217
Salmon Salad With Steamboat Dressing ... 217
Grits Casserole 217
Steakhouse Baked Potatoes 218
Mini Hasselback Potatoes 218
Zucchini Fries 218
Roasted Vegetables 219
Brussels Sprouts 219
Blistered Tomatoes 219
Lemon-glazed Baby Carrots 220
Crispy Herbed Potatoes 220
Mushrooms 220
Brussels Sprout And Ham Salad 220
Mashed Potato Tots 221
Sweet Potato Curly Fries 221
Eggplant And Tomato Slices 222
Simple Roasted Sweet Potatoes 222
Stuffed Onions 222
Florentine Stuffed Tomatoes 223
Baked Mac And Cheese 223
Roasted Veggie Kebabs 224

RECIPE INDEX 225

INTRODUCTION

What Is an Air Frying Oven?

Air frying is a method of cooking that circulates hot air inside your oven at a high speed through the use of convection fans. This cooks food faster and creates a crispy, fried layer and even-browning on all sides using little to no oil compared to traditional deep frying.

The Benefits of Cooking with Your NuWave Air Fryer Oven

There's a lot to love about this appliance. If there weren't, people wouldn't be grabbing them off the shelves at the rate they're going. Here are some of the NuWave air fryer ovens' best qualities.

1. WORK FAST

An air fryer oven cooks much faster than any other appliances in the kitchen. Because most of the heat stays inside, it can preheat within minutes. During the actual cooking process none of the heat is expelled into the open air. In fact, it's only intensified by constant circulation, cooking even frozen foods in record time.

2. ENERGY EFFICIENT

Because of the compact nature of an air fryer oven, you won't have to worry about your kitchen turning into a sauna during the summer, like one normally would with a conventional oven. Because it's so small, it doesn't require a lot of power to run. So, not only are you cooking faster, you're also using less energy to do it.

3. HEALTHIER FOOD

Deep fried foods are slathered in oil, which isn't very healthy. Air fryers use oil but not nearly as much. A little bit of oil goes a long way when exposed to hot air. Excess oil drains away from the food, which is perfect for some of the naturally oilier snacks that have become a regular part of the American diet.

4. SAVE SPACE

Air fryer ovens could save space. It's perfect for smaller kitchens, particularly in apartments or condos. An air fryer would be perfect in an RV or camper and could be useful to cook on the go or at a camp site.

5. SIMPLE

You don't have to be a master chef to get the most out of your air fryer oven. Simply set the temperature and time, place your food in the basket and let the machine do its job.

Knowing the Tips on Using Your NuWave Air Fryer Oven

1. Don't Overcrowd
If you stuff the air fryer oven or rack, your food will steam rather than crisp. For a smaller model, this could mean cooking food in many, many batches. (If you are routinely cooking for more than two or three people, consider buying a larger-capacity model.)

2. Don't Overcook
Take care not to cook food too long: The fan may dry things out, turning ingredients from crisp to hard and leathery.

3. Use Dry Breading
Dry coating works much better than a wet batter, so cloak ingredients in flour, egg and bread crumbs, in that order, for added crunch, and to help ensure that the breading sticks. (Air fryer fans are very powerful, and if an ingredient is not well coated, the breading could fly right off.) You could also try pressing down on the crumbs so they adhere.

4. Add a Little Oil
Unless a food is inherently fatty (such as bacon, skin-on chicken or a batch of meatballs made from beef that isn't too lean) always add at least a little oil, which encourages browning. Otherwise, the fan could dry out the food before it browns.

5. Prevent Smoking
If you're cooking really greasy food like bacon, put a tablespoon of water or a piece of bread in the bottom of the air fryer to catch the grease and keep it from potentially smoking.

Regularly Cleaning Your NuWave Air Fryer Oven

Follow these steps to clean your air fryer oven:

Step 1 — Remove Power Source

Please switch off the air fryer oven, and remove the plug from the socket. If you've used it recently, let it cool down for about half an hour.

Step 2 — Initial Wipe

Use a soft damp cloth to wipe the outer body. Then use hot water along with a soft, non-abrasive sponge to clean the unit's inside.

Step 3 — Heating Element

Once satisfied with the initial wipe-down, flip the air fryer and use a cotton swab and non-abrasive sponge to brush off any residue on the heating element.

Step 4 — Eliminate Hard-To-Remove Leftovers

Time to bring some baking soda into the equation. Make a baking soda/water paste and apply it to the stubborn spots. Scrub using a soft bristle brush and then wipe off using soft cloth or cotton.

Step 5 — Let It Soak

If the basket and pan are riddled with stubborn stains, time to take your cleaning up a notch. Top the pan with hot water, and lay the basket within. Let it breathe for up to 10 minutes, use a sponge to clean loosened stains and mineral-deposits.

Step 6 — Dry Out

Before you begin frying again, make sure that each part is as dry as it can be. Firstly, wipe everything off with a clean cotton cloth and leave the air fryer for a couple of hours to air dry.

Deep Cleaning Using Vinegar

If the above steps have not done much justice, and still some stubborn baked-on grease remains present, take the following steps:

Step 1 — Initial Cleanup

Use a paper towel to wipe all grease on the inside and out. If a recent item your prepared had a considerable amount of oil or was rich in fat, put in some force to jolt anything stuck.

Step 2 — Vinegar Bath

Now, put a stopper in a tub or a sink so that the water does not move to the drainage. Keep a 9:1 ratio, i.e., nine parts water and one part vinegar or 90% water and 10% vinegar. Fill the sink or tub with this solution and submerge the flyer's basket in it for 15 minutes.

Step 3 — Scrubbing

Use a nylon-based, non-abrasive sponge to scrub the basket. It would be best to use good dish soap for better results. Keep scrubbing until you are sure that all left-behind food and grease has gone away.

Step 4 — Baking Soda Application

Despite using vinegar, still, if you spot residual food and baked-on grease, the chances are that the stubborn stains have loosened up, but they need a push to be removed. Therefore, pour a bit more than a pinch of baking soda on a non-abrasive sponge, and get to scrubbing.

Step 5 — Thorough Drying

Once satisfied with the results, thoroughly rinse the pan and basket with clean water. It would be best to keep rinsing until you can't smell any vinegar or dish soap.

Then, wipe it all with a soft cloth and paper towel, and then leave it aside for an hour or more so that the air fryer can air dry.

BREAKFAST

Southern-style Biscuits

Servings: 10
Cooking Time: 12 Minutes

Ingredients:
- 2 cups all-purpose flour
- 1 tablespoon baking powder
- 1 teaspoon table salt
- 4 tablespoons cold, unsalted butter, cut into bits
- ¾ to 1 cup buttermilk

Directions:
1. Preheat the toaster oven to 450 ºF.
2. Combine the flour, baking powder, and salt in a large bowl. Using a pastry cutter or two knives, cut the butter into the flour mixture until the mixture is crumbly throughout. Pour in the buttermilk and gently mix until just combined.
3. Turn the dough onto a lightly floured surface and knead lightly about 8 times. Roll the dough, using a rolling pin, until about ½ inch thick. Cut out rounds using a 2 ½ -inch cutter. Place on an ungreased 12 x 12-inch baking pan or 8-inch round pan.
4. Bake for 10 to 12 minutes or until golden brown. Let cool slightly before serving warm.

Egg-loaded Potato Skins

Servings: 4
Cooking Time: 55 Minutes

Ingredients:
- 2 large russet potatoes
- ½ teaspoon olive oil
- ½ cup Gruyère cheese, shredded and divided
- 4 large eggs
- ¼ cup heavy (whipping) cream, divided
- 1 scallion, both white and green parts, finely chopped
- Sea salt, for seasoning
- Freshly ground black pepper, for seasoning

Directions:
1. Preheat the toaster oven to 400°F on BAKE.
2. Prick the potatoes all over with a fork and rub with the olive oil.
3. Place the potatoes directly on the rack and bake for 40 minutes. The potatoes should be soft and tender, and the skin lightly browned. If not done, set the timer for 5 minutes more.
4. Take the potatoes out and set aside until cool enough to handle, about 10 minutes.
5. Cut the potatoes in half lengthwise and scoop out the flesh so that you have about ½-inch flesh and the intact skin. Place the potato halves in the air-fryer basket (placed on the baking tray) and sprinkle 2 tablespoons of cheese in each skin. Crack an egg into each potato half and spoon 1 tablespoon of cream over each egg. Sprinkle with scallion and lightly season with salt and pepper.
6. In position 1, bake for 15 minutes until the egg whites are set, and the yolks are still runny. If the eggs need more time, set the timer for 3 to 5 minutes more. Serve.

Sesame Wafers

Servings: 4
Cooking Time: 6 Minutes

Ingredients:
- ½ cup sesame seeds
- 1 tablespoon unbleached flour
- 1 tablespoon margarine, at room temperature
- 1 teaspoon dark brown sugar

Directions:
1. Preheat the toaster oven to 400° F.
2. Combine the sesame seeds, flour, margarine, and sugar in a small bowl, mixing well. Sprinkle equal portions into 4 individual 1-cup-size ovenproof dishes and press to cover the bottom evenly.
3. BAKE for 6 minutes, or until lightly browned.

Individual Overnight Omelets

Servings: 2
Cooking Time: 45 Minutes

Ingredients:
- 1 tablespoon unsalted butter, softened
- 2 slices hearty white sandwich bread
- 2 ounces cheddar cheese, shredded (½ cup)
- 3 large eggs
- ¾ cup whole milk
- 1 teaspoon minced fresh thyme or ¼ teaspoon dried
- ¼ teaspoon table salt
- ¼ teaspoon pepper

Directions:
1. Spray two 12-ounce ramekins with vegetable oil spray. Spread butter evenly over 1 side of bread slices, then cut into 1-inch pieces. Scatter half of bread evenly in prepared ramekins and sprinkle with half of cheddar. Repeat with remaining bread and cheese.
2. Whisk eggs, milk, thyme, salt, and pepper in bowl until well combined. Pour egg mixture evenly over bread and press lightly on bread to submerge. Wrap ramekins tightly with plastic wrap and refrigerate for at least 8 hours or up to 24 hours.
3. Adjust toaster oven rack to middle position and preheat the toaster oven to 350 degrees. Unwrap ramekins and place ramekins on small rimmed baking sheet. Bake until puffed and golden, 30 to 35 minutes, rotating sheet halfway through baking. Serve immediately.

Berry Crisp

Servings: 4
Cooking Time: 25 Minutes

Ingredients:
- 2 16-ounce packages frozen berries or 4 cups fresh berries
- 2 tablespoons lemon juice
- ½ cup rolled oats
- 1 tablespoon margarine, at room temperature
- 3 tablespoons wheat germ
- 4 ¼ cup honey
- 5 1 teaspoon vanilla extract
- Salt to taste

Directions:
1. Preheat the toaster oven to 400° F.
2. Combine the berries or fruit and lemon juice in a 1-quart-size 8½ × 8½ × 4-inch ovenproof baking dish, tossing well to mix. Set aside.
3. Combine the rolled oats, margarine, wheat germ, honey, vanilla, and salt in a small bowl and stir with a fork until the mixture is crumbly. Sprinkle evenly on top of the berries.
4. BAKE, covered, for 20 minutes, or until the berries are bubbling. Remove from the oven and uncover.
5. BROIL for 5 minutes, or until the topping is lightly browned.

Classic Cinnamon Rolls

Servings: 4
Cooking Time: 6 Minutes

Ingredients:
- 1½ cups all-purpose flour
- 1 tablespoon granulated sugar
- 2 teaspoons baking powder
- ½ teaspoon salt
- 4 tablespoons butter, divided
- ½ cup buttermilk
- 2 tablespoons brown sugar
- 1 teaspoon cinnamon
- 1 cup powdered sugar
- 2 tablespoons milk

Directions:
1. Preheat the toaster oven to 360°F.
2. In a large bowl, stir together the flour, sugar, baking powder, and salt. Cut in 3 tablespoons of the butter with a pastry blender or two knives until coarse crumbs remain. Stir in the buttermilk until a dough forms.
3. Place the dough onto a floured surface and roll out into a square shape about ½ inch thick.
4. Melt the remaining 1 tablespoon of butter in the microwave for 20 seconds. Using a pastry brush or your fingers, spread the melted butter onto the dough.
5. In a small bowl, mix together the brown sugar and cinnamon. Sprinkle the mixture across the surface of the dough. Roll the dough up, forming a long log. Using a pastry cutter or sharp knife, cut 10 cinnamon rolls.

6. Carefully place the cinnamon rolls into the air fryer oven. Then bake at 360°F for 6 minutes or until golden brown.
7. Meanwhile, in a small bowl, whisk together the powdered sugar and milk.
8. Plate the cinnamon rolls and drizzle the glaze over the surface before serving.

Wild Blueberry Lemon Chia Bread

Servings: 6
Cooking Time: 27 Minutes

Ingredients:
- ¼ cup extra-virgin olive oil
- ⅓ cup plus 1 tablespoon cane sugar
- 1 large egg
- 3 tablespoons fresh lemon juice
- 1 tablespoon lemon zest
- ⅔ cup milk
- 1 cup all-purpose flour
- ¾ teaspoon baking powder
- ⅛ teaspoon salt
- 2 tablespoons chia seeds
- 1 cup frozen wild blueberries
- ⅓ cup powdered sugar
- 2 teaspoons milk

Directions:
1. Preheat the toaster oven to 310°F.
2. In a medium bowl, mix the olive oil with the sugar. Whisk in the egg, lemon juice, lemon zest, and milk; set aside.
3. In a small bowl, combine the all-purpose flour, baking powder, and salt.
4. Slowly mix the dry ingredients into the wet ingredients. Stir in the chia seeds and wild blueberries.
5. Liberally spray a 7-inch springform pan with olive-oil spray. Pour the batter into the pan and place the pan in the air fryer oven. Bake for 25 to 27 minutes, or until a toothpick inserted in the center comes out clean.
6. Remove and let cool on a wire rack for 10 minutes prior to removing from the pan.
7. Meanwhile, in a small bowl, mix the powdered sugar with the milk to create the glaze.
8. Slice and serve with a drizzle of the powdered sugar glaze.

Grilled Dagwood

Servings: 4
Cooking Time: 20 Minutes

Ingredients:
- 4 slices whole wheat or multigrain bread
- 1 tablespoon Dijon mustard
- 2 tablespoons fresh or canned bean sprouts, washed and well drained
- 2 tablespoons chopped watercress
- 2 tablespoons chopped roasted pimientos
- 3 slices reduced-fat Swiss cheese
- 2 slices low-fat honey ham
- 2 tablespoons garlic hummus
- 6 slices sweet pickle
- 4 slices low-fat smoked turkey
- 1 tablespoon Yogurt Cheese Spread (recipe follows)
- 1 tablespoon chopped Vidalia onion
- 1 tablespoon ketchup
- 1 tablespoon pitted and chopped black olives

Directions:
1. Preheat the toaster oven to 350° F.
2. Spread the first bread slice with ½ tablespoon Dijon mustard. Add 1 tablespoon sprouts, 1 tablespoon watercress, 1 tablespoon pimientos, 1 slice Swiss cheese, and 1 slice honey ham.
3. Spread the second bread slice with ½ tablespoon Dijon mustard, turn it over, and lay it on top of the first. Spread the other side of the second slice with 1 tablespoon hummus, 1 slice honey ham, 3 pickle slices, 1 tablespoon watercress, and 2 slices smoked turkey.
4. Spread the third bread slice with the Yogurt Cheese Spread, turn it over, and lay it on top of the second slice of bread. Spread the other side of the third slice with 1 tablespoon hummus and add the chopped onion, 1 tablespoon pimientos, 3 pickle slices, 1 slice Swiss cheese, and 2 slices smoked turkey.
5. Spread the fourth bread slice with the ketchup and add 1 tablespoon sprouts, 1 tablespoon pimientos, 1 slice Swiss cheese, and the black olives. Lift up all the other bread slices together and place this one on the bottom.

Then put the slices together and wrap in aluminum foil so that the seam is on the top of the slices. Open the seam to expose the tops of the slices and place on the rack in the toaster oven, seam side up.
6. BAKE 20 minutes, or until the top is lightly browned and the cheese is melted.

Autumn Berry Dessert

Servings: 4
Cooking Time: 5 Minutes

Ingredients:
- ½ cup nonfat sour cream
- ½ cup nonfat plain yogurt
- 3 tablespoons brown sugar
- 1 16-ounce package frozen blueberries or
- 2 cups fresh blueberries, rinsed well and drained
- 1 16-ounce package frozen sliced strawberries or 2 cups sliced fresh strawberries
- 4 tablespoons ground walnuts or pecans
- Grated lemon zest

Directions:
1. Beat together the sour cream, yogurt, and brown sugar in a small bowl with an electric mixer until smooth. Set aside.
2. Combine the berries in an oiled or nonstick 8½ × 8½ × 2-inch square baking (cake) pan.
3. BROIL for 5 minutes, or until bubbling. Fill 4 individual 1-cup-size ovenproof dishes with equal portions of the berries and top with the yogurt/sour cream mixture. Serve immediately or reheat by broiling for 1 or 2 minutes prior to serving. Sprinkle each serving with a tablespoon of ground walnuts or a pinch of lemon zest.

Buttered Poppy Seed Bread

Servings: 6
Cooking Time: 25 Minutes

Ingredients:
- 3 tablespoons unsalted butter, melted
- 1 (1-pound) loaf frozen white bread dough
- 1 teaspoon poppy seeds
- ¼ teaspoon onion powder
- ¼ teaspoon garlic powder
- ¼ teaspoon freshly ground black pepper

Directions:
1. Pour about half of the melted butter into a 9 x 5-inch loaf pan. Brush the butter to cover the sides and bottom of the pan. Place the frozen bread loaf in the pan. Brush the top of the loaf with the remaining butter, covering completely. Stir the poppy seeds, onion powder, garlic powder, and pepper in a small bowl. Sprinkle the seasonings over the top of the bread. Cover with plastic wrap and refrigerate overnight.
2. Remove the bread from the refrigerator and loosen the plastic wrap so it is loosely covered. Let it rise at room temperature until the top of the bread is just over the top edge of the pan, about 2 to 4 hours.
3. Preheat the toaster oven to 350°F.
4. Bake for 20 to 25 minutes or until the bread is golden brown.
5. Let cool for 5 minutes, then remove the loaf from the pan and place on a wire rack to cool for a few minutes. Slice and serve warm.

Make-ahead Currant Cream Scones

Servings: 8
Cooking Time: 60 Minutes

Ingredients:
- 2 cups (10 ounces) all-purpose flour
- 3 tablespoons sugar
- 1 tablespoon baking powder
- ½ teaspoon table salt
- 5 tablespoons unsalted butter, cut into ¼-inch pieces and chilled
- ½ cup dried currants
- 1 cup heavy cream

Directions:
1. Adjust toaster oven rack to middle position and preheat the toaster oven to 375 degrees. Line large and small rimmed baking sheets with parchment paper.
2. Process flour, sugar, baking powder, and salt in food processor until combined, about 6 seconds. Scatter butter over top and pulse until mixture resembles coarse cornmeal with some slightly larger butter lumps, about 12 pulses. Transfer mixture to large bowl and stir in

currants. Stir in cream with rubber spatula until dough begins to form, about 30 seconds.

3. Turn dough and any floury bits onto lightly floured counter and knead until rough, slightly sticky ball forms, 5 to 10 seconds. Shape dough into 8-inch round, about ¾ inch thick. Cut dough into 8 wedges.

4. Space desired number of scones at least 1 inch apart on prepared small sheet; space remaining scones evenly on prepared large sheet. Bake small sheet of scones until scone tops are light golden brown, 18 to 23 minutes. Transfer scones to wire rack and let cool for at least 10 minutes before serving.

5. Freeze remaining large sheet of scones until firm, about 1 hour. Transfer scones to 1-gallon zipper-lock bag and freeze for up to 1 month. To bake frozen scones, increase baking time to 20 to 25 minutes; do not thaw.

Avocado Chicken Flatbread

Servings: 4
Cooking Time: 9 Minutes

Ingredients:
- 1 tablespoon olive oil
- 1 clove garlic, minced
- 1 small avocado, pitted, peeled, and thinly sliced
- 1 teaspoon fresh lime juice
- ¼ cup ranch salad dressing
- 1 tablespoon Sriracha or hot sauce
- 1 package (10.6 ounces) flatbread pizza crust
- ¾ cup chopped, cooked chicken
- 2 slices bacon, cooked until crisp and crumbled
- ¼ cup chopped red onion
- ¾ cup shredded Monterey Jack cheese
- 1 cup thinly sliced romaine or iceberg lettuce
- ½ cup cherry tomatoes, halved

Directions:
1. Preheat the toaster oven to 400°F.
2. Mix the olive oil and garlic in a small bowl; set aside.
3. Place the avocado slices in a small bowl and drizzle with the lime juice; set aside.
4. Stir the salad dressing and Sriracha in a small bowl; set aside.
5. Brush the garlic olive oil over the flatbread. Place it on a 12-inch pan and bake for 3 to 4 minutes, or until the crust is hot and lightly toasted.
6. Top the crust with the chicken, bacon, onion, and cheese. Bake for 5 minutes or until the cheese is melted. Top with the lettuce, tomatoes, and avocado slices. Drizzle with the ranch dressing mixture.

Morning Glory Muffins

Servings: 6
Cooking Time: 25 Minutes

Ingredients:
- Oil spray (hand-pumped)
- ¼ cup raisins
- 1 cup whole-wheat flour
- ½ cup packed dark brown sugar
- 1 teaspoon baking soda
- 1¼ teaspoons pumpkin pie spice
- ¼ teaspoon sea salt
- 1 cup carrot, finely shredded
- 1 small apple, peeled, cored, and shredded
- ⅓ cup shredded, sweetened coconut
- 2 large eggs
- ¼ cup canola oil
- Juice and zest of ½ orange

Directions:
1. Place the rack on position 1 and preheat the toaster oven on BAKE to 350°F for 5 minutes. Lightly spray 6 muffin cups with the oil or line them with paper liners.
2. In a small bowl, cover the raisins with hot water and set aside.
3. In a large bowl, whisk the flour, brown sugar, baking soda, pumpkin pie spice, and salt. Add the carrot, apple, and coconut, and toss to mix.
4. In a small bowl, beat the eggs, oil, orange juice, and orange zest.
5. Drain the raisins, squeezing out as much water as possible.
6. Add the wet ingredients and raisins to the dry ingredients and mix until the batter is just combined.
7. Spoon the batter into the muffin cups.
8. Bake for 25 minutes or until a knife inserted in the center comes out clean.
9. Remove from the oven and let cool before serving.

Blueberry Muffins

Servings: 8
Cooking Time: 14 Minutes

Ingredients:
- 1⅓ cups flour
- ½ cup sugar
- 2 teaspoons baking powder
- ¼ teaspoon salt
- ⅓ cup canola oil
- 1 egg
- ½ cup milk
- ⅔ cup blueberries, fresh or frozen and thawed
- 8 foil muffin cups including paper liners

Directions:
1. Preheat the toaster oven to 330°F.
2. In a medium bowl, stir together flour, sugar, baking powder, and salt.
3. In a separate bowl, combine oil, egg, and milk and mix well.
4. Add egg mixture to dry ingredients and stir just until moistened.
5. Gently stir in blueberries.
6. Spoon batter evenly into muffin cups.
7. Place 4 muffin cups in air fryer oven and bake at 330°F for 14 minutes or until tops spring back when touched lightly.
8. Repeat previous step to cook remaining muffins.

Heavenly Hash Browns

Servings: 4
Cooking Time: 50 Minutes

Ingredients:
- 2 cups raw, peeled potatoes, grated
- 2 tablespoons vegetable oil
- ½ cup grated onion
- 1 teaspoon garlic powder
- 1 teaspoon paprika
- Salt and butcher's pepper to taste

Directions:
1. Combine all the ingredients in a small bowl, mixing well. Spread the potato mixture evenly in an oiled or nonstick 6½ × 6½ × 2-inch square baking (cake) pan.
2. BROIL for 30 minutes. Remove the pan from the oven and, with a spatula, cut the potatoes into squares and carefully turn them over. Broil for another 20 minutes, or until browned and crisped to your preference.

Breakfast Blueberry Peach Crisp

Servings: 8
Cooking Time: 60 Minutes

Ingredients:
- Filling Ingredients
- 4 cups blueberries, fresh or frozen
- 2 cups peaches, sliced
- 1 teaspoon vanilla extract
- 2 teaspoons lemon juice
- 4 tablespoons pure maple syrup
- 1½ tablespoons cornstarch
- A tiny pinch of salt
- Topping Ingredients
- 2½ cups rolled oats
- 5 tablespoons almond meal (or almond flour)
- 1 teaspoon cinnamon
- 5 tablespoons pure maple syrup
- 3 tablespoons coconut sugar (or brown sugar)
- 7 tablespoons coconut oil, melted
- 1 cup sliced almonds
- 1 cup chopped walnuts
- ¼ teaspoon salt

Directions:
1. Combine the blueberries, peaches, vanilla extract, lemon juice, maple syrup, cornstarch, and salt in a bowl and toss to combine. Pour mixture into the baking dish.
2. Combine all the topping ingredients in a separate bowl and stir until clumps form, then spread evenly over the fruit mixture.
3. Preheat the toaster Oven to 350°F.
4. Place the baking dish on the wire rack, then insert rack at low position in the preheated oven.
5. Select the Bake function, adjust time to 1 hour, then press
6. Start/Pause.
7. Remove crisp when golden on top and fruit is bubbly.
8. Serve with yogurt for breakfast or vanilla ice cream for dessert.

Bread Boat Eggs

Servings: 4
Cooking Time: 10 Minutes

Ingredients:
- 4 pistolette rolls
- 1 teaspoon butter
- ¼ cup diced fresh mushrooms
- ½ teaspoon dried onion flakes
- 4 eggs
- ½ teaspoon salt
- ¼ teaspoon dried dill weed
- ¼ teaspoon dried parsley
- 1 tablespoon milk

Directions:
1. Cut a rectangle in the top of each roll and scoop out center, leaving ½-inch shell on the sides and bottom.
2. Place butter, mushrooms, and dried onion in air fryer oven baking pan and air-fry for 1 minute. Stir and cook 3 more minutes.
3. In a medium bowl, beat together the eggs, salt, dill, parsley, and milk. Pour mixture into pan with mushrooms.
4. Air-fry at 390°F for 2 minutes. Stir. Continue cooking for 3 or 4 minutes, stirring every minute, until eggs are scrambled to your liking.
5. Remove baking pan from air fryer oven and fill rolls with scrambled egg mixture.
6. Place filled rolls in air fryer oven and air-fry at 390°F for 2 to 3 minutes or until rolls are lightly browned.

Western Frittata

Servings: 1
Cooking Time: 19 Minutes

Ingredients:
- ½ red or green bell pepper, cut into ½-inch chunks
- 1 teaspoon olive oil
- 3 eggs, beaten
- ¼ cup grated Cheddar cheese
- ¼ cup diced cooked ham
- salt and freshly ground black pepper, to taste
- 1 teaspoon butter
- 1 teaspoon chopped fresh parsley

Directions:
1. Preheat the toaster oven to 400°F.
2. Toss the peppers with the olive oil and air-fry for 6 minutes, redistribute the ingredients once or twice during the process.
3. While the vegetables are cooking, beat the eggs well in a bowl, stir in the Cheddar cheese and ham, and season with salt and freshly ground black pepper. Add the air-fried peppers to this bowl when they have finished cooking.
4. Place a 6- or 7-inch non-stick metal cake pan into the air fryer oven with the butter using an aluminum sling to lower the pan into the air fryer oven. (Fold a piece of aluminum foil into a strip about 2-inches wide by 24-inches long.) Air-fry for 1 minute at 380°F to melt the butter. Remove the cake pan and rotate the pan to distribute the butter and grease the pan. Pour the egg mixture into the cake pan and return the pan to the air fryer oven, using the aluminum sling.
5. Air-fry at 380°F for 12 minutes, or until the frittata has puffed up and is lightly browned. Let the frittata sit in the air fryer oven for 5 minutes to cool to an edible temperature and set up. Remove the cake pan from the air fryer oven, sprinkle with parsley and serve immediately.

Garlic Basil Bread

Servings: 6
Cooking Time: 18 Minutes

Ingredients:
- Mixture:
- 3 tablespoons olive oil
- 2 garlic cloves
- ¼ cup pine nuts (pignoli)
- ½ cup fresh basil leaves
- 2 plum tomatoes, chopped
- Salt to taste
- 1 French baguette, cut diagonally into 1-inch slices

Directions:
1. Preheat the toaster oven to 400° F.
2. Process the mixture ingredients in a blender or food processor until smooth.

3. Spread the mixture on both sides of each bread slice, reassemble into a loaf, and wrap in aluminum foil.
4. BAKE for 12 minutes, or until the bread is thoroughly heated. Peel back the aluminum foil to expose the top of the bread.
5. BAKE again for 5 minutes, or until the top is lightly browned.

Toasted Cheese Sandwich

Servings: 1
Cooking Time: 8 Minutes

Ingredients:
- 2 slices bread, country, sourdough, white, or your choice
- 2 teaspoons salted butter, softened
- 2 to 3 slices cheese such as Colby Jack or cheddar

Directions:
1. Place a baking pan into the toaster oven and preheat with the baking pan in the oven to 450°F (not the Toast setting).
2. Spread one side of each slice of bread with the butter. Place one piece of bread, buttered side down, on a plate and top with the cheese slices. (Do not allow any cheese to hang over the edge of the bread.) Top with the second slice bread, buttered side up.
3. Carefully remove the hot baking pan from the toaster oven and place the sandwich in the middle of the pan. Bake for 4 minutes. Carefully remove the pan and flip the sandwich, using a spatula. Bake for an additional 3 to 4 minutes, or until the sandwich is golden brown and the cheese is melted.
4. Cool slightly and cut in half for serving.

Nacho Chips

Servings: 12
Cooking Time: 20 Minutes

Ingredients:
- 3 jalapeño peppers
- 4 6-inch flour tortillas
- 1 cup shredded low-fat Cheddar cheese

Directions:
1. Seed and cut the jalapeño peppers into thin rings. Arrange one-fourth of the rings on the tortilla. It's a good idea to wear gloves, since the peppers can sometimes cause skin irritation.
2. Place the tortilla in an oiled or nonstick 8½ × 8½ × 2-inch square baking (cake) pan. Sprinkle evenly with ¼ cup cheese.
3. BROIL for 5 minutes, or until the cheese is melted. Repeat the process for the remaining tortillas. Cut each into 6 wedges with a sharp knife or scissors.

Italian Strata

Servings: 6
Cooking Time: 55 Minutes

Ingredients:
- 1 cup boiling water
- 3 tablespoons chopped sun-dried tomatoes (dry-packed)
- 5 cups cubed French bread or country bread (cut into 1-inch cubes)
- Nonstick cooking spray
- 1 ½ ounces sliced turkey pepperoni, cut into fourths (about ¾ cup)
- 2 tablespoons chopped pepperoncini peppers
- 1 cup coarsely chopped fresh spinach
- 1 cup shredded Italian blend cheese or mozzarella cheese
- 4 large eggs
- 1 ½ cups whole milk
- 1 teaspoon Italian seasoning
- ¼ teaspoon kosher salt
- 2 tablespoons shredded Parmesan cheese

Directions:
1. Pour the boiling water the over sun-dried tomatoes in a small, deep bowl; set aside.
2. Preheat the toaster oven to 350 °F. Place the bread cubes on a 12 x 12-inch baking pan. Bake for 10 minutes, stirring once.
3. Spray an 8 x 8-inch square baking pan with nonstick cooking spray. Drain the sun-dried tomatoes and pat dry with paper towels. Arrange half the bread cubes evenly in the prepared pan. Top with half the pepperoni, half the pepperoncini, all the spinach, and all of the

reconstituted tomatoes. Sprinkle with ½ cup of the Italian cheese. Repeat layers with the remaining bread, pepperoni, pepperoncini, and ½ cup cheese.

4. Whisk the eggs, milk, Italian seasoning, and salt in a large bowl. Pour the egg mixture over the bread layers. Press down lightly with the back of a large spoon. Sprinkle with the Parmesan cheese. Cover and chill for at least 2 hours or overnight.

5. Preheat the toaster oven to 350°F. Bake the strata, uncovered, for 35 to 45 minutes, or until a knife inserted into the center comes out clean. Let stand for 10 minutes before serving.

Cheddar Bacon Broiler

Servings: 4
Cooking Time: 8 Minutes

Ingredients:
- 4 slices pumpernickel bread
- 4 strips lean turkey bacon, cut in half
- 4 tablespoons shredded Cheddar cheese
- 4 tablespoons grated Parmesan cheese
- 4 tablespoons finely chopped bell pepper
- 1 medium tomato, chopped
- 2 tablespoons finely chopped onion
- Salt and freshly ground black pepper
- 2 tablespoons chopped fresh parsley or cilantro

Directions:
1. Layer the bread slices with 2 half strips turkey bacon and 1 tablespoon each Cheddar cheese, Parmesan cheese, and bell pepper. Sprinkle each with equal portions of tomato and onion. Season to taste with salt and pepper.
2. BROIL on a broiling rack with a pan underneath for 8 minutes, or until the cheese is well melted. Before serving, sprinkle with parsley or cilantro.

Banana Baked Oatmeal

Servings: 4
Cooking Time: 35 Minutes

Ingredients:
- Oil spray (hand-pumped)
- 1 cup rolled gluten-free oats
- ¾ teaspoon baking powder
- ¾ teaspoon ground cinnamon
- ¼ teaspoon sea salt
- ¾ cup whole milk
- ¼ cup maple syrup
- 1 large egg
- 2 tablespoons unsalted butter, melted
- 1 teaspoon vanilla extract
- 1 banana, chopped

Directions:
1. Place the rack on position 1 and preheat the toaster oven on BAKE to 375°F for 5 minutes.
2. Lightly spray an 8-inch-square baking dish with oil and set aside.
3. In a large bowl, stir the oats, baking powder, cinnamon, and salt until well combined.
4. In a small bowl, whisk the milk, maple syrup, egg, butter, and vanilla until blended.
5. Add the wet ingredients to the dry and stir until well mixed. Stir in the banana.
6. Spoon the batter into the baking dish and place the wire rack on position 1.
7. Place the baking dish on the rack and bake for 35 minutes. The oatmeal should look just set in the middle; if not, add 5 minutes more.
8. Cool the baked oatmeal for 5 minutes and serve with desired toppings.

Homemade Biscuits

Servings: 12
Cooking Time: 28 Minutes

Ingredients:
- 1 1/2 cups milk
- 1 tablespoon white vinegar
- 4 cups all-purpose flour
- 1/4 cup sugar
- 1 tablespoon plus 1 1/2 teaspoons baking powder
- 1 teaspoon salt
- 1 cup unsalted butter, cut into pieces
- Sausage Gravy

Directions:
1. Preheat the toaster oven to 375°F. Line a cookie sheet with parchment paper.

2. In a small bowl, stir milk and vinegar until blended. Set aside.
3. In a large bowl, combine flour, sugar, baking powder and salt. Cut in butter with a fork or a pastry blender until coarse crumbs form. Stir in the milk mixture until moistened (dough will be slightly moist).
4. On a well floured surface, roll dough to 3/4-inch thickness. Cut with a 3-inch round cookie cutter and arrange 2-inches apart on cookie sheet. Repeat with remaining dough.
5. Bake 26 to 28 minutes or until lightly browned.
6. Serve with Sausage Gravy, if desired.

Stromboli

Servings: 4
Cooking Time: 30 Minutes

Ingredients:
- CRUST
- 2 cups all-purpose flour
- 2 tablespoons unsalted butter, cut into small pieces
- 1 teaspoon table salt
- 2 teaspoons active dry yeast
- 2 teaspoons sugar
- TOPPINGS
- ½ cup marinara or pizza sauce
- ½ teaspoon Italian seasoning
- 2 ounces pepperoni slices
- 2 ounces salami slices
- 2 ounces thin ham slices
- 1 ½ cups shredded mozzarella cheese
- 3 tablespoons shredded Parmesan cheese
- 1 large egg
- ½ teaspoon granulated garlic
- 1 teaspoon sesame seeds

Directions:
1. Make the crust: Place the flour in a large bowl and create a well. Place ⅔ cup water, the butter, and salt in a small microwave-safe bowl and microwave on High (100 percent) power for 30 seconds or until warm. (The temperature of the mixture should not be above 110 ºF.) Pour the liquid into the well. Sprinkle the yeast and sugar over the water mixture and allow to stand for 5 minutes. Mix the flour mixture until a dough forms. Oil a medium bowl and place the dough in the bowl. Cover and let rise for 1 hour.
2. Preheat the toaster oven to 375 ºF. Line a 12 x 12-inch baking pan with parchment paper.
3. Flour a clean surface and roll the dough into a 15 x 13 ½-inch rectangle. Place the dough diagonally on the prepared pan. Spread the marinara sauce over the surface of the dough to within ½ inch of all four edges. Sprinkle with the Italian seasoning. Layer the pepperoni, salami, and ham slices on top of the marinara. Sprinkle with the cheeses. Roll up as tightly as possible and pinch the seams to make sure nothings seeps out.
4. Whisk the egg, 1 tablespoon of water, and the garlic in a small bowl. Brush the egg wash over the stromboli and sprinkle with the sesame seeds. Bake for 25 to 30 minutes or until golden brown.

Brown Sugar Grapefruit

Servings: 2
Cooking Time: 4 Minutes

Ingredients:
- 1 grapefruit
- 2 to 4 teaspoons brown sugar

Directions:
1. Preheat the toaster oven to 400°F.
2. While the air fryer oven is Preheating, cut the grapefruit in half horizontally (in other words not through the stem or blossom end of the grapefruit). Slice the bottom of the grapefruit to help it sit flat on the counter if necessary. Using a sharp paring knife (serrated is great), cut around the grapefruit between the flesh of the fruit and the peel. Then, cut each segment away from the membrane so that it is sitting freely in the fruit.
3. Sprinkle 1 to 2 teaspoons of brown sugar on each half of the prepared grapefruit. Set up a rack in the air fryer oven (use an air fryer oven rack or make your own rack with some crumpled up aluminum foil). You don't have to use a rack, but doing so will get the grapefruit closer to the element so that the brown sugar can caramelize a little better. Transfer the grapefruit half to the rack in the air fryer oven. Depending on how big your grapefruit are and what size air fryer oven you have,

you may need to do each half separately to make sure they sit flat.
4. Air-fry at 400°F for 4 minutes.
5. Remove and let it cool for just a minute before enjoying.

Apple Fritters

Servings: 6
Cooking Time: 12 Minutes

Ingredients:
- 1 cup all-purpose flour
- 1½ teaspoons baking powder
- ¼ teaspoon salt
- 2 tablespoon brown sugar
- 1 teaspoon vanilla extract
- ¾ cup plain Greek yogurt
- 1 tablespoon cinnamon
- 1 large Granny Smith apple, cored, peeled, and finely chopped
- ¼ cup chopped walnuts
- ½ cup powdered sugar
- 1 tablespoon milk

Directions:
1. Preheat the toaster oven to 320°F.
2. In a medium bowl, combine the flour, baking powder, and salt.
3. In a large bowl, add the brown sugar, vanilla, yogurt, cinnamon, apples, and walnuts. Mix the dry ingredients into the wet, using your hands to combine, until all the ingredients are mixed together. Knead the mixture in the bowl about 4 times.
4. Lightly spray the air fryer oven with olive oil spray.
5. Divide the batter into 6 equally sized balls; then lightly flatten them and place inside the air fryer oven. Repeat until all the fritters are formed.
6. Place in the air fryer oven and air-fry for 6 minutes, flip, and then cook another 6 minutes.
7. While the fritters are cooking, in a small bowl, mix the powdered sugar with the milk. Set aside.
8. When the cooking completes, remove the air fryer oven and allow the fritters to cool on a wire rack. Drizzle with the homemade glaze and serve.

Cinnamon Rolls

Servings: 12
Cooking Time: 10 Minutes

Ingredients:
- Buttermilk Biscuit dough
- Cinnamon mixture:
- 3 tablespoons dark brown sugar
- 3 tablespoons chopped pecans
- 2 tablespoons margarine
- 1 teaspoon ground cinnamon
- Salt to taste
- Icing:
- 1 cup confectioners' sugar, sifted
- 1 tablespoon fat-free half-and-half
- ½ teaspoon vanilla extract
- Salt to taste

Directions:
1. Preheat the toaster oven to 400° F.
2. Make the buttermilk biscuit dough.
3. Roll out or pat the dough to ½ inch thick. In a small bowl, combine the cinnamon mixture ingredients. Spread the dough evenly with the cinnamon mixture and roll up like a jelly roll. With a sharp knife, cut the roll into 1-inch slices. Place on an oiled or nonstick 6½ × 10-inch baking sheet.
4. BAKE for 15 minutes, or until lightly browned. Let cool before frosting.
5. Combine the icing ingredients in a small bowl, adding more half-and-half or confectioners' sugar until the consistency is like thick cream. Drizzle over the tops of the cinnamon rolls and serve.

Baked Eggs With Bacon-tomato Sauce

Servings: 1
Cooking Time: 12 Minutes

Ingredients:
- 1 teaspoon olive oil
- 2 tablespoons finely chopped onion
- 1 teaspoon chopped fresh oregano
- pinch crushed red pepper flakes
- 1 (14-ounce) can crushed or diced tomatoes

- salt and freshly ground black pepper
- 2 slices of bacon, chopped
- 2 large eggs
- ¼ cup grated Cheddar cheese
- fresh parsley, chopped

Directions:
1. Start by making the tomato sauce. Preheat a medium saucepan over medium heat on the stovetop. Add the olive oil and sauté the onion, oregano and pepper flakes for 5 minutes. Add the tomatoes and bring to a simmer. Season with salt and freshly ground black pepper and simmer for 10 minutes.
2. Meanwhile, preheat the toaster oven to 400°F and pour a little water into the bottom of the air fryer oven. (This will help prevent the grease that drips into the bottom drawer from burning and smoking.) Place the bacon in the air fryer oven and air-fry at 400°F for 5 minutes.
3. When the bacon is almost crispy, remove it to a paper-towel lined plate and rinse out the air fryer oven, draining away the bacon grease.
4. Transfer the tomato sauce to a shallow 7-inch pie dish. Crack the eggs on top of the sauce and scatter the cooked bacon back on top. Season with salt and freshly ground black pepper and transfer the pie dish into the air fryer oven. You can use an aluminum foil sling to help with this by taking a long piece of aluminum foil, folding it in half lengthwise twice until it is roughly 26-inches by 3-inches. Place this under the pie dish and hold the ends of the foil to move the pie dish in and out of the air fryer oven. Tuck the ends of the foil beside the pie dish while it cooks in the air fryer oven.
5. Air-fry at 400°F for 5 minutes, or until the eggs are almost cooked to your liking. Sprinkle cheese on top and air-fry for an additional 2 minutes. When the cheese has melted, remove the pie dish from the air fryer oven, sprinkle with a little chopped parsley and let the eggs cool for a few minutes – just enough time to toast some buttered bread in your air fryer oven!

Spinach, Tomato & Feta Quiche

Servings: 8
Cooking Time: 60 Minutes

Ingredients:
- Pie Crust Ingredients
- 1½ cups all-purpose flour, plus more for dusting
- ½ teaspoon kosher salt
- 3 tablespoons unsalted butter, chilled and cubed
- 6 tablespoons vegetable shortening, chilled
- 3 tablespoons ice water
- Dry beans or uncooked rice, for filling
- Filling Ingredients
- 1½ ounces frozen spinach, thawed and squeezed dry
- 9 cherry tomatoes, halved
- 1½ ounces crumbled feta cheese 4 large eggs
- ½ cup heavy cream
- ½ teaspoon kosher salt
- ¼ teaspoon freshly ground black pepper
- Extra virgin olive oil, for drizzling

Directions:
1. Combine the flour and salt in a food processor and pulse once to combine.
2. Add the butter and shortening, then pulse until the mixture creates fine crumbs.
3. Pour the water in slowly and pulse until it forms a dough.
4. Form the dough into a square, wrap with plastic wrap, and place in the fridge for 6 hours or overnight.
5. Remove the dough from the fridge, unwrap it, and place onto a lightly floured work surface.
6. Roll out the dough into a 10-inch diameter circle. You may need to use additional flour to keep the dough from sticking to the rolling pin.
7. Place the dough into the tart pan and use your fingers to form the dough to fit the pan.
8. Trim the edges and prick the bottom of the tart shell all over.
9. Cover with plastic wrap and place in the freezer for 30 minutes.
10. Remove from the freezer, unwrap, and top with parchment paper that covers all the edges.
11. Fill the tart shell with dry beans or uncooked rice until the dough is fully covered. Set aside.
12. Preheat the toaster Oven to 350°F.
13. Place the tart shell on the wire rack, then insert the rack at low position in the preheated oven.

14. Select the Bake function, press the Fan/Light button to start the fan, then press Start/Pause.
15. Remove the tart shell from the oven and let it cool for 1 hour.
16. Arrange the spinach, tomatoes, and feta cheese evenly inside the empty tart shell.
17. Whisk together the eggs, heavy cream, salt, and pepper until well combined.
18. Pour the egg mixture into the filled tart shell and lightly drizzle with extra-virgin olive oil. You may have some extra filling left over.
19. Preheat the toaster Oven to 350°F.
20. Place the quiche on the wire rack, then insert the rack at low position in the preheated oven.
21. Select the Bake function, then press Start/Pause.
22. Remove the quiche from the oven and let it cool for 5 minutes.
23. Cut into slices and serve.

Cinnamon Swirl Bread

Servings: 4
Cooking Time: 50 Minutes

Ingredients:
- 2 cups all-purpose flour
- 1 cup granulated sugar
- 1 teaspoon baking soda
- ½ teaspoon table salt
- 1 teaspoon cider vinegar
- 1 cup whole milk
- 1 large egg
- ¼ cup canola or vegetable oil
- FILLING
- ½ cup granulated sugar
- 1 tablespoon ground cinnamon
- GLAZE
- ¼ cup confectioners' sugar
- 2 teaspoons whole milk

Directions:
1. Preheat the toaster oven to 350 °F. Grease the bottom of a 9 x 5-inch loaf pan.
2. Combine the flour, granulated sugar, baking soda, and salt in a large bowl. Place the vinegar in a 1-cup liquid measuring cup and add the milk; stir to combine. Whisk the milk mixture, egg, and oil in a medium bowl. Stir into the flour mixture, blending until combined.
3. Make the filling: Combine the granulated sugar and cinnamon in a small bowl.
4. Pour half of the batter into the prepared pan. Sprinkle half the cinnamon-sugar mixture over the batter in the loaf pan. Top with the remaining batter and sprinkle with remaining cinnamon-sugar mixture. Using a butter knife, make deep swirls in the batter. Make sure most of the cinnamon-sugar mixture from the top is covered in batter.
5. Bake for 45 to 50 minutes, or until a wooden pick inserted into the center comes out clean. Cool on a wire rack for 10 minutes. Run a knife around the edges of the bread, then remove the bread from the pan. Cool for an additional 10 minutes.
6. Meanwhile, make the glaze: Whisk the confectioners' sugar and milk in a small bowl until smooth. Drizzle the glaze over the partially cooled loaf. Serve warm or at room temperature.

Sweet-hot Pepperoni Pizza

Servings: 2
Cooking Time: 18 Minutes

Ingredients:
- 1 (6- to 8-ounce) pizza dough ball
- olive oil
- ½ cup pizza sauce
- ¾ cup grated mozzarella cheese
- ½ cup thick sliced pepperoni
- ⅓ cup sliced pickled hot banana peppers
- ¼ teaspoon dried oregano
- 2 teaspoons honey

Directions:
1. Preheat the toaster oven to 390°F.
2. Cut out a piece of aluminum foil the same size as the bottom of the air fryer oven. Brush the foil circle with olive oil. Shape the dough into a circle and place it on top of the foil. Dock the dough by piercing it several times with a fork. Brush the dough lightly with olive oil and transfer it into the air fryer oven with the foil on the bottom.

3. Air-fry the plain pizza dough for 6 minutes. Turn the dough over, remove the aluminum foil and brush again with olive oil. Air-fry for an additional 4 minutes.
4. Spread the pizza sauce on top of the dough and sprinkle the mozzarella cheese over the sauce. Top with the pepperoni, pepper slices and dried oregano. Lower the temperature of the air fryer oven to 350°F and air-fry for 8 minutes, until the cheese has melted and lightly browned. Transfer the pizza to a cutting board and drizzle with the honey. Slice and serve.

Cinnamon Toast

Servings: 2
Cooking Time: 2 Minutes

Ingredients:
- 1 tablespoon brown sugar
- 2 teaspoons margarine, at room temperature
- ¼ teaspoon ground cinnamon
- 2 slices whole wheat or multigrain bread

Directions:
1. Combine the sugar, margarine, and cinnamon in a small bowl with a fork until well blended. Spread each bread slice with equal portions of the mixture.
2. TOAST once, or until the sugar is melted and the bread is browned to your preference.

Sheet-pan Hash Browns

Servings: 2
Cooking Time: 60 Minutes

Ingredients:
- 1½ pounds Yukon Gold potatoes, unpeeled, shredded
- 3 tablespoons extra-virgin olive oil
- ½ teaspoon table salt
- ⅛ teaspoon pepper

Directions:
1. Adjust toaster oven rack to lowest position, select air-fry or convection function, and preheat the toaster oven to 450 degrees. Place potatoes in large bowl and cover with cold water. Let sit for 5 minutes.
2. Lift potatoes out of water, one handful at a time, and transfer to colander; discard water. Rinse and dry bowl. Place half of shredded potatoes in center of clean dish towel. Gather ends of towel and twist tightly to wring out excess moisture from potatoes. Transfer dried potatoes to now-empty bowl. Repeat with remaining potatoes.
3. Add oil, salt, and pepper to potatoes and toss to combine. Distribute potatoes in even layer on small rimmed baking sheet, but do not pack down. Cook until top of potatoes is spotty brown, 30 to 40 minutes, rotating sheet halfway through baking.
4. Remove sheet from oven. Using spatula, flip hash browns in sections. Return sheet to oven and continue to cook until spotty brown and dry, 10 to 15 minutes. Season with salt and pepper to taste. Serve.

Savory Breakfast Bread Pudding

Servings: 4
Cooking Time: 30 Minutes

Ingredients:
- Oil spray (hand-pumped)
- 4 slices whole-wheat bread, cubed
- 1 cup frozen potato hash browns, thawed
- 5 large eggs
- 1 cup whole milk
- ½ cup diced ham
- ½ cup shredded cheddar cheese
- 1 teaspoon fresh parsley, chopped
- ⅛ teaspoon sea salt
- ⅛ teaspoon freshly ground black pepper

Directions:
1. Place the baking tray on position 1 and preheat the toaster oven on BAKE to 350°F for 5 minutes.
2. Lightly oil an 8-inch-square baking dish with spray.
3. Spread the bread cubes and potatoes in the baking dish evenly.
4. In a medium bowl, combine the eggs, milk, ham, cheese, parsley, salt, and pepper.
5. Pour the egg mixture over the bread and potatoes in the dish.
6. Bake for 30 minutes. The bread pudding should be lightly golden, the eggs set, and a knife inserted in the center should come out clean.
7. Cool the pudding for 5 minutes and serve.

Broccoli Cornbread

Servings: 6
Cooking Time: 18 Minutes

Ingredients:
- 1 cup frozen chopped broccoli, thawed and drained
- ¼ cup cottage cheese
- 1 egg, beaten
- 2 tablespoons minced onion
- 2 tablespoons melted butter
- ½ cup flour
- ½ cup yellow cornmeal
- 1 teaspoon baking powder
- ½ teaspoon salt
- ¼ cup milk, plus 2 tablespoons
- cooking spray

Directions:
1. Place thawed broccoli in colander and press with a spoon to squeeze out excess moisture.
2. Stir together all ingredients in a large bowl.
3. Spray 6 x 6-inch baking pan with cooking spray.
4. Spread batter in pan and air-fry at 330°F for 18 minutes or until cornbread is lightly browned and loaf starts to pull away from sides of pan.

Hashbrown Potatoes Lyonnaise

Servings: 4
Cooking Time: 33 Minutes

Ingredients:
- 1 Vidalia (or other sweet) onion, sliced
- 1 teaspoon butter, melted
- 1 teaspoon brown sugar
- 2 large russet potatoes (about 1 pound), sliced ½-inch thick
- 1 tablespoon vegetable oil
- salt and freshly ground black pepper

Directions:
1. Preheat the toaster oven to 370°F.
2. Toss the sliced onions, melted butter and brown sugar together in the air fryer oven. Air-fry for 8 minutes, help the onions cook evenly.
3. While the onions are cooking, bring a 3-quart saucepan of salted water to a boil on the stovetop. Par-cook the potatoes in boiling water for 3 minutes. Drain the potatoes and pat them dry with a clean kitchen towel.
4. Add the potatoes to the onions in the air fryer oven and drizzle with vegetable oil. Toss to coat the potatoes with the oil and season with salt and freshly ground black pepper.
5. Increase the air fryer oven temperature to 400°F and air-fry for 22 minutes tossing the vegetables a few times during the cooking time to help the potatoes brown evenly. Season to taste again with salt and freshly ground black pepper and serve warm.

Coffee Cake

Servings: 6
Cooking Time: 40 Minutes

Ingredients:
- Cake:
- 2 cups unbleached flour
- 2 teaspoons baking powder
- 2 tablespoons vegetable oil
- 1 egg
- 1¼ cups skim milk
- Topping:
- ½ cup brown sugar
- 1 tablespoon margarine, at room temperature
- 1 teaspoon ground cinnamon
- ¼ teaspoon grated nutmeg
- ¼ cup chopped pecans
- Salt to taste

Directions:
1. Preheat the toaster oven to 375° F.
2. Combine the ingredients for the cake in a medium bowl and mix thoroughly. Pour the batter into an oiled or 8½ × 8½ × 2inch square baking (cake) pan and set aside.
3. Combine the topping ingredients in a small bowl, mashing the margarine into the dry ingredients with a fork until the mixture is crumbly. Sprinkle evenly on top of the batter.
4. BAKE for 40 minutes, or until a toothpick inserted in the center comes out clean. Cool and cut into squares.

Beef And Bean Quesadillas

Servings: 2
Cooking Time: 30 Minutes

Ingredients:
- Quesadilla filling:
- 1 8-ounce flank steak, trimmed and cut into thin ⅛ × 2-inch strips
- 1 jalapeño pepper, seeded and minced
- 2 plum tomatoes, chopped
- 1 small onion, cut into thin strips
- 1 bell pepper, seeded and cut into thin strips
- 2 garlic cloves, minced
- 1 15-ounce can black beans, rinsed and drained
- 2 tablespoons chopped fresh cilantro
- ½ cup reduced-fat Monterey Jack cheese
- 4 6-inch flour tortillas
- Low-fat or fat-free sour cream

Directions:
1. Combine the filling ingredients in an oiled or nonstick 8½ × 8½ × 2-inch square baking (cake) pan, mixing well to blend.
2. BROIL for 10 minutes, remove from the oven, and turn the pieces with tongs. Broil for 10 minutes, or until the pepper, onion, and beef are cooked and tender. Remove from the oven and transfer to a bowl. Add the beans and cilantro and mix well.
3. Spread one quarter of the tortilla mixture in the center of each tortilla. Sprinkle each tortilla with 2 tablespoons cheese. Roll up the edges and lay each, seam side down, in the pan.
4. BROIL for 10 minutes, or until the tortillas are lightly browned and the cheese is melted. Serve with sour cream.

Country Bread

Servings: 2
Cooking Time: 30 Minutes

Ingredients:
- Yeast mixture:
- 1¼-ounce package active dry yeast
- ¼ cup skim milk, at room temperature
- 1 teaspoon brown sugar
- Flour mixture:
- ¾ cup tepid water
- 2½ cups unbleached flour
- 1 egg
- 2 teaspoons granulated sugar
- 2 tablespoons vegetable oil
- 2 tablespoons wheat germ
- Salt to taste
- Vegetable oil
- 1 egg, beaten, to brush the top

Directions:
1. Combine the yeast mixture ingredients in a large bowl and let stand for 10 minutes, or until the yeast is dissolved and foamy.
2. Add the flour mixture ingredients to the yeast mixture, blending well. Turn out the mixture on a lightly floured surface.
3. KNEAD the dough for 6 minutes, or until smooth and elastic. Return the dough to the large bowl, cover with a clean damp towel, and put in a warm place for 1 hour, or until doubled in size.
4. Punch down the dough and turn out onto a lightly floured surface. Knead for 2 minutes, then place the dough in an oiled or nonstick regular size 8½ × 4½ × 2¼-inch loaf pan. Brush the loaf with vegetable oil, cover the pan with a damp towel, and place in a warm place for 1 hour, or until doubled in size. Brush the loaf with the beaten egg.
5. Preheat the toaster oven to 375° F.
6. BAKE for 30 minutes, or until a toothpick inserted in the middle comes out clean and the top is browned. Sharply tap the pan to loosen the loaf, invert, and place on a rack to cool.

Garlic-cheese Biscuits

Servings: 8
Cooking Time: 8 Minutes

Ingredients:
- 1 cup self-rising flour
- 1 teaspoon garlic powder
- 2 tablespoons butter, diced
- 2 ounces sharp Cheddar cheese, grated
- ½ cup milk
- cooking spray

Directions:
1. Preheat the toaster oven to 330°F.
2. Combine flour and garlic in a medium bowl and stir together.
3. Using a pastry blender or knives, cut butter into dry ingredients.
4. Stir in cheese.
5. Add milk and stir until stiff dough forms.
6. If dough is too sticky to handle, stir in 1 or 2 more tablespoons of self-rising flour before shaping. Biscuits should be firm enough to hold their shape. Otherwise, they'll stick to the air fryer oven.
7. Divide dough into 8 portions and shape into 2-inch biscuits about ¾-inch thick.
8. Spray air fryer oven with nonstick cooking spray.
9. Place all 8 biscuits in air fryer oven and air-fry at 330°F for 8 minutes.

Sunny-side Up Eggs

Servings: 2
Cooking Time: 3 Minutes

Ingredients:
- 2 large eggs
- Salt and freshly ground black pepper

Directions:
1. Crack the eggs into an oiled or nonstick small 4 × 8 × 2¼-inch loaf pan. Sprinkle with salt and pepper to taste.
2. TOAST once, or until the eggs are done to your preference.

Onion And Cheese Buttermilk Biscuits

Servings: 4
Cooking Time: 15 Minutes

Ingredients:
- 2 cups unbleached flour
- 3 tablespoons margarine, at room temperature
- ¾ cup low-fat buttermilk
- 4 teaspoons baking powder
- 1 teaspoon garlic powder
- ¼ cup grated Parmesan cheese
- 3 tablespoons finely chopped onion
- 2 tablespoons chopped fresh parsley
- Salt to taste

Directions:
1. Preheat the toaster oven to 400° F.
2. Blend all the ingredients in a medium bowl with a fork, then press together to form a dough ball.
3. KNEAD the dough on a lightly floured surface just until smooth.
4. Roll the dough to ½-inch thickness and cut with a round 3-inch cookie cutter. Place on an oiled or nonstick 6½ × 10-inch baking sheet or in an oiled or nonstick 8½ × 8½ × 2-inch square baking (cake) pan.
5. BAKE for 15 minutes, or until lightly browned.

Oven-baked Reuben

Servings: 2
Cooking Time: 3 Minutes

Ingredients:
- 4 slices rye bread
- 2 tablespoons Dijon mustard
- 6 slices reduced-fat Swiss cheese
- 1 6-ounce package sliced corned beef
- ½ cup sauerkraut, drained
- Russian Dressing (recipe follows)

Directions:
1. Spread each slice of bread with mustard. Layer 2 slices with 3 slices each of Swiss cheese and equal portions of corned beef and sauerkraut. Top with the remaining bread slices and place on a broiling rack with the pan underneath.
2. TOAST twice, or until the cheese is melted. Serve with Russian Dressing.

Yogurt Bread

Servings: 2
Cooking Time: 40 Minutes

Ingredients:
- 3 cups unbleached flour
- 4 teaspoons baking powder
- 5 2 teaspoons sugar
- Salt to taste

- 1 cup plain nonfat yogurt
- ¼ cup vegetable oil
- 1 egg, beaten, to brush the top

Directions:
1. Preheat the toaster oven to 375° F.
2. Combine the flour, baking powder, sugar, and salt in a large bowl. Make a hole in the center and spoon in the yogurt and oil.
3. Stir the flour into the center. When the dough is well mixed, turn it out onto a lightly floured surface and knead for 8 minutes, until the dough is smooth and elastic. Place the dough in an oiled or nonstick regular-size 8½ × 4½ × 2¼-inch loaf pan. Brush the top with the beaten egg.
4. BAKE for 40 minutes, or until a toothpick inserted in the center comes out clean and the loaf is browned. Invert on a wire rack to cool.

New York–style Crumb Cake

Servings: 8
Cooking Time: 90 Minutes

Ingredients:
- CRUMB TOPPING
- 8 tablespoons unsalted butter, melted
- ⅓ cup (2⅓ ounces) granulated sugar
- ⅓ cup packed (2⅓ ounces) dark brown sugar
- ¾ teaspoon ground cinnamon
- ⅛ teaspoon table salt
- 1¾ cups (7 ounces) cake flour
- CAKE
- 1¼ cups (5 ounces) cake flour
- ½ cup (3½ ounces) granulated sugar
- ¼ teaspoon baking soda
- ¼ teaspoon table salt
- 6 tablespoons unsalted butter, cut into 6 pieces and softened
- ⅓ cup buttermilk
- 1 large egg plus 1 large yolk
- 1 teaspoon vanilla extract
- Confectioners' sugar

Directions:
1. Adjust toaster oven rack to middle position and preheat the toaster oven to 325 degrees. Make foil sling for 8-inch square baking pan by folding 2 long sheets of aluminum foil so each is 8 inches wide. Lay sheets of foil in pan perpen-dicular to each other, with extra foil hanging over edges of pan. Push foil into corners and up sides of pan, smoothing foil flush to pan.
2. FOR THE CRUMB TOPPING: Whisk melted butter, granulated sugar, brown sugar, cinnamon, and salt in medium bowl until combined. Add flour and stir with rubber spatula or wooden spoon until mixture resembles thick, cohesive dough; set aside to cool to room temperature, 10 to 15 minutes.
3. FOR THE CAKE: Using stand mixer fitted with paddle, mix flour, sugar, baking soda, and salt on low speed to combine. With mixer running, add softened butter 1 piece at a time. Continue beating until mixture resembles moist crumbs with no visible butter pieces remaining, 1 to 2 minutes. Add buttermilk, egg and yolk, and vanilla and beat on medium-high speed until light and fluffy, about 1 minute, scraping down bowl as needed.
4. Transfer batter to prepared pan. Using rubber spatula, spread batter into even layer. Break apart crumb topping into large pea-size pieces and sprinkle in even layer over batter, beginning with edges and then working toward center. (Assembled cake can be wrapped tightly with plastic wrap and refrigerated for up to 24 hours; increase baking time to 40 to 45 minutes.)
5. Bake until crumbs are golden and toothpick inserted in center of cake comes out clean, 35 to 40 minutes, rotating pan halfway through baking. Let cool on wire rack for at least 30 minutes. Using foil overhang, lift cake out of pan. Dust with confectioners' sugar before serving.

Freezer-ready Breakast Burritos

Servings: 8
Cooking Time: 28 Minutes

Ingredients:
- 8 large eggs
- 2 tablespoons whole milk
- Kosher salt and freshly ground black pepper
- 1 tablespoon unsalted butter
- 1 pound bulk breakfast sausage

- 1 medium russet potato, peeled and finely chopped
- 2 green onions, white and green portions, chopped
- 8 flour tortillas, about 8 inches in diameter
- 1 cup shredded sharp cheddar cheese
- Salsa
- Optional toppings: guacamole, chopped avocado, chopped tomato

Directions:
1. Whisk the eggs and milk in a large bowl and season with salt and pepper. Melt the butter in a large skillet over medium heat. Add the eggs and cook, stirring occasionally, until the eggs are softly set. Spoon the cooked eggs into a medium bowl; set aside.
2. Cook the sausage in the same skillet over medium heat until lightly browned, stirring to crumble. Add the potato and cook, stirring frequently, until the sausage is fully cooked and the potato is tender. Stir in the green onions and cook for 2 minutes. Drain.
3. Wrap the tortillas in a clean towel and microwave on High (100 percent power) for 90 seconds or until warm.
4. Spoon the sausage-vegetable mixture, eggs, and cheese evenly into each tortilla. Fold in the sides of the tortilla, then roll gently to form a burrito. Wrap each burrito in aluminum foil, then seal in a freezer bag or container. Label and freeze for up to 1 month.
5. The night before serving, place the number of wrapped burritos you wish to serve in the refrigerator to partially thaw.
6. Preheat the toaster oven to 375°F. Place the foil-wrapped burrito on the rack in the toaster oven. Bake for 20 to 25 minutes or until heated through. Carefully unwrap the burrito and place on a plate. Top with salsa and any of the suggested toppings.

Cinnamon Biscuit Rolls

Servings: 12
Cooking Time: 5 Minutes

Ingredients:
- Dough
- ¼ cup warm water (105–115°F)
- 1 teaspoon active dry yeast
- 1 tablespoon sugar
- ½ cup buttermilk, lukewarm
- 2 cups flour, plus more for dusting
- 1 teaspoon baking powder
- ½ teaspoon salt
- 3 tablespoons cold butter
- Filling
- 1 tablespoon butter, melted
- 1 teaspoon cinnamon
- 2 tablespoons sugar
- Icing
- ⅔ cup powdered sugar
- ¼ teaspoon vanilla
- 2–3 teaspoons milk

Directions:
1. Dissolve yeast and sugar in warm water. Add buttermilk, stir, and set aside.
2. In a large bowl, sift together flour, baking powder, and salt. Using knives or a pastry blender, cut in butter until mixture is well combined and crumbly.
3. Pour in buttermilk mixture and stir with fork until a ball of dough forms.
4. Knead dough on a lightly floured surface for 5 minutes. Roll into an 8 x 11-inch rectangle.
5. For the filling, spread the melted butter over the dough.
6. In a small bowl, stir together the cinnamon and sugar, then sprinkle over dough.
7. Starting on a long side, roll up dough so that you have a roll about 11 inches long. Cut into 12 slices with a serrated knife and sawing motion so slices remain round.
8. Place rolls on a plate or cookie sheet about an inch apart and let rise for 30 minutes.
9. For icing, mix the powdered sugar, vanilla, and milk. Stir and add additional milk until icing reaches a good spreading consistency.
10. Preheat the toaster oven to 360°F.
11. Place 6 cinnamon rolls in baking pan and cook 5 minutes or until top springs back when lightly touched. Repeat to cook remaining 6 rolls.
12. Spread icing over warm rolls and serve.

Brunch Burritos

Servings: 4
Cooking Time: 14 Minutes

Ingredients:
- Egg mixture:
- 4 medium eggs, lightly beaten
- 3 tablespoons finely chopped bell pepper
- 2 tablespoons finely chopped onion
- 4 strips lean turkey bacon, uncooked and cut into small ¼ × ¼-inch pieces
- 1 tablespoon chopped fresh cilantro
- ½ teaspoon ground cumin
- ½ teaspoon chili powder
- Salt and red pepper flakes to taste
- 4 6-inch flour tortillas
- 4 tablespoons salsa
- 4 tablespoons shredded part-skim, low-moisture mozzarella

Directions:
1. Combine the egg mixture ingredients in an oiled or nonstick 8½ × 8½ × 2-inch square baking (cake) pan.
2. TOAST twice, or until the mixture is firm and cooked.
3. Spoon the egg mixture in equal portions onto the center of each tortilla. Add 1 tablespoon salsa and 1 tablespoon mozzarella cheese to each. Roll each tortilla around the filling and lay, seam side down, in an oiled or nonstick 8½ × 8½ × 2-inch square baking (cake) pan.
4. BROIL for 8 minutes, or until lightly browned.

Strawberry Pie Glaze

Servings: 2
Cooking Time: 15 Minutes

Ingredients:
- ½ cup apple juice
- 2 tablespoons sugar
- 1 teaspoon lemon or lime juice

Directions:
1. Combine all the ingredients in an oiled or nonstick 8½ × 8½ × 2-inch square baking (cake) pan.
2. BROIL for 6 minutes, or until the sugar is melted. Carefully remove from the oven using oven mitts, stir to blend, then broil again for 6 minutes, or until the liquid is reduced and clear. Remove from the oven and brush the strawberries immediately with the glaze. Chill before serving.

Pancake Muffins

Servings: 4
Cooking Time: 8 Minutes

Ingredients:
- 1 cup flour
- 2 tablespoons sugar (optional)
- ½ teaspoon baking soda
- 1 teaspoon baking powder
- ¼ teaspoon salt
- 1 egg, beaten
- 1 cup buttermilk
- 2 tablespoons melted butter
- 1 teaspoon pure vanilla extract
- 24 foil muffin cups
- cooking spray
- Suggested Fillings
- 1 teaspoon of jelly or fruit preserves
- 1 tablespoon or less fresh blueberries; chopped fresh strawberries; chopped frozen cherries; dark chocolate chips; chopped walnuts, pecans, or other nuts; cooked, crumbled bacon or sausage

Directions:
1. In a large bowl, stir together flour, optional sugar, baking soda, baking powder, and salt.
2. In a small bowl, combine egg, buttermilk, butter, and vanilla. Mix well.
3. Pour egg mixture into dry ingredients and stir to mix well but don't overbeat.
4. Double up the muffin cups and remove the paper liners from the top cups. Spray the foil cups lightly with cooking spray.
5. Place 6 sets of muffin cups in air fryer oven. Pour just enough batter into each cup to cover the bottom. Sprinkle with desired filling. Pour in more batter to cover the filling and fill the cups about ¾ full.
6. Air-fry at 330°F for 8 minutes.
7. Repeat steps 5 and 6 for the remaining 6 pancake muffins.

Bacon Chicken Ranch Sandwiches

Servings: 2
Cooking Time: 23 Minutes

Ingredients:
- Nonstick cooking spray
- ½ pound chicken tenders (about 4)
- 4 slices country or sourdough bread
- 2 tablespoons unsalted or salted butter, softened
- 2 tablespoons ranch dressing
- 2 slices sliced Colby Jack or cheddar cheese
- 6 slices bacon, cooked until crisp

Directions:
1. Preheat the toaster oven to 375°F. Spray a small baking sheet with nonstick cooking spray.
2. Place the chicken tenders on the prepared baking sheet. Bake, uncovered, for 12 to 15 minutes or until the chicken is done and a meat thermometer registers 165°F. Carefully remove from the oven and allow the chicken tenders to cool slightly.
3. Increase the toaster oven temperature to 450°F. Place a 12 x 12-inch baking pan in the toaster oven while it is preheating.
4. Spread one side of each slice of bread with butter. Place two pieces of bread, buttered side down, on a sheet of parchment or wax paper. Spread each slice with 1 tablespoon ranch dressing. Divide the chicken tenders among the two slices. Cut the cheese to fit on the chicken tenders and within the bread perimeter. Fold the slices of bacon to fit within the bread perimeter. Top with the second slice of bread, butter side up.
5. Carefully remove the hot baking pan from the toaster oven and place the sandwiches on the baking sheet. Place the baking sheet in the toaster oven and bake for 4 minutes. Carefully remove the pan and flip the sandwich, using a spatula. Bake for an additional 3 to 4 minutes, or until the sandwich is golden brown and the cheese is melted.
6. Cool slightly and cut in half for serving.

Breakfast Pita

Servings: 2
Cooking Time: 3 Minutes

Ingredients:
- 1 5-inch whole wheat pita loaf
- 1 teaspoon olive oil
- 1 egg, well beaten
- 2 tablespoons shredded low-fat mozzarella cheese
- Garlic powder
- Salt and freshly ground black pepper

Directions:
1. Cut a circle out of the top layer of one pita bread loaf and remove the disk-shaped layer, leaving the bottom intact. Brush the pita loaf with the olive oil. Carefully pour the beaten egg into the cavity. Sprinkle with cheese and season with garlic powder and salt and pepper to taste.
2. TOAST once on the oven rack, or until the egg is cooked thoroughly and the cheese is lightly browned.

Crispy Bacon

Servings: 6
Cooking Time: 20 Minutes

Ingredients:
- 12 ounces bacon

Directions:
1. Preheat the toaster oven to 350°F for 3 minutes.
2. Lay out the bacon in a single layer, slightly overlapping the strips of bacon.
3. Air fry for 10 minutes or until desired crispness.
4. Repeat until all the bacon has been cooked.

Honey Ham And Swiss Broiler

Servings: 2
Cooking Time: 5 Minutes

Ingredients:
- 4 slices pumpernickel bread
- 1 tablespoon olive oil
- 1 tablespoon spicy brown mustard
- 1 tablespoon horseradish
- 4 slices reduced-fat honey ham
- 4 slices reduced-fat Swiss cheese
- 2 tablespoons finely chopped fresh parsley

Directions:

1. Brush one side of the 4 bread slices with oil and lay, oil side down, in an oiled or nonstick 8½ × 8½ × 2-inch square baking (cake) pan.
2. Spread 2 slices with mustard and 2 slices with horseradish.
3. Layer each with 1 slice honey ham and 1 slice Swiss cheese.
4. BROIL for 5 minutes, or until the cheese is melted. Sprinkle with equal portions of parsley and serve.

Baked Grapefruit

Servings: 4
Cooking Time: 20 Minutes

Ingredients:
- 1 grapefruit, cut in half
- 2 tablespoons currant jelly
- 2 tablespoons ground almonds, walnuts, or pecans
- 2 tablespoons chopped raisins

Directions:
1. Preheat the toaster oven to 350° F.
2. Section the grapefruit halves with a serrated knife. Place them in an oiled or nonstick 8½ × 8½ × 2-inch square baking (cake) pan. Spread 1 tablespoon currant jelly on each half and sprinkle each with 1 tablespoon ground nuts and 1 tablespoon chopped raisins.
3. BAKE for 20 minutes, or until the grapefruit is lightly browned.

Walnut Pancake

Servings: 4
Cooking Time: 20 Minutes

Ingredients:
- 3 tablespoons butter, divided into thirds
- 1 cup flour
- 1½ teaspoons baking powder
- ¼ teaspoon salt
- 2 tablespoons sugar
- ¾ cup milk
- 1 egg, beaten
- 1 teaspoon pure vanilla extract
- ½ cup walnuts, roughly chopped
- maple syrup or fresh sliced fruit, for serving

Directions:
1. Place 1 tablespoon of the butter in air fryer oven baking pan. Air-fry at 330°F for 3 minutes to melt.
2. In a small dish or pan, melt the remaining 2 tablespoons of butter either in the microwave or on the stove.
3. In a medium bowl, stir together the flour, baking powder, salt, and sugar. Add milk, beaten egg, the 2 tablespoons of melted butter, and vanilla. Stir until combined but do not beat. Batter may be slightly lumpy.
4. Pour batter over the melted butter in air fryer oven baking pan. Sprinkle nuts evenly over top.
5. Air-fry for 20 minutes or until toothpick inserted in center comes out clean. Turn air fryer oven off, close the machine, and let pancake rest for 2 minutes.
6. Remove pancake from pan, slice, and serve with syrup or fresh fruit.

Baked Steel-cut Oatmeal

Servings: 2
Cooking Time: 60 Minutes

Ingredients:
- ½ cup steel-cut oats
- 1 tablespoon unsalted butter, cut into 2 pieces
- 2 cups boiling water, plus extra as needed
- ⅛ teaspoon table salt

Directions:
1. Adjust toaster oven rack to middle position and preheat the toaster oven to 450 degrees. Place oats and butter in 8-inch square baking dish or pan and bake until oats are golden brown and fragrant, 5 to 7 minutes, stirring thoroughly halfway through baking to incorporate butter into oats.
2. Remove pan from oven and reduce oven temperature to 325 degrees. Carefully stir boiling water and salt into oats and bake until oats are softened but still retain some chew and mixture thickens and resembles warm pudding, 40 to 45 minutes, rotating pan halfway through baking. Remove pan from oven, cover, and let sit for 5 minutes. Stir oatmeal to recombine and adjust consistency with extra boiling water as needed. Serve.

Spicy Beef Fajitas

Servings: 4
Cooking Time: 40 Minutes

Ingredients:
- Mixture:
- 1 pound flank steak, cut into thin strips 2 inches long
- 1 bell pepper, seeded and cut into thin strips
- 2 tablespoons chopped onion
- 1 tablespoon chopped fresh cilantro
- ¼ teaspoon hot sauce
- 1 teaspoon garlic powder
- ½ teaspoon cumin
- 1 teaspoon chili powder
- Salt and freshly ground black pepper to taste
- 4 8-inch flour tortillas

Directions:
1. Combine all the mixture ingredients in an oiled or nonstick 8½ × 8½ × 2-inch square baking (cake) pan.
2. BROIL for 20 minutes, turning every 5 minutes, or until the pepper and onion are tender and the meat is beginning to brown. Remove from the oven and place equal portions of the mixture in the center of each tortilla. Roll the tortilla around the mixture and lay, seam side down, in a shallow baking pan.
3. BAKE at 350° F. for 20 minutes, or until the tortillas are lightly browned.

Lemon Blueberry Scones

Servings: 6
Cooking Time: 25 Minutes

Ingredients:
- 1 ½ cups all-purpose flour
- 2 tablespoons granulated sugar
- 2 ¼ teaspoons baking powder
- 1 teaspoon grated lemon zest
- ¼ teaspoon table salt
- ¼ cup unsalted butter, cut into 1-tablespoon pieces
- ¾ cup fresh or frozen blueberries
- ¾ cup plus 1 tablespoon heavy cream, plus more for brushing
- Coarse white sugar
- LEMON GLAZE
- 1 cup confectioners' sugar
- 2 to 3 tablespoons fresh lemon juice

Directions:
1. Line a 12 x 12-inch baking pan with parchment paper.
2. Whisk the flour, granulated sugar, baking powder, lemon zest, and salt in a large bowl. Cut in the butter using a pastry cutter or two knives until the mixture is crumbly throughout. Gently stir in the blueberries, taking care not to mash them. Add ¾ cup cream and gently stir until a soft dough forms. If needed, stir in an additional tablespoon of cream so all of the flour is moistened.
3. Turn the dough onto a lightly floured board. Pat the dough into a circle about ¾ inch thick and 6 inches in diameter. Cut into 6 triangles. Arrange the triangles on the prepared pan. Freeze for 15 minutes.
4. Preheat the toaster oven to 400°F. Brush the scones lightly with cream and sprinkle with coarse sugar. Bake for 20 to 25 minutes or until golden brown. Let cool for 5 minutes.
5. Meanwhile, make the glaze: Stir the confectioners' sugar and lemon juice in a small bowl, blending until smooth. Drizzle the glaze over the scones. Let stand for about 5 minutes. These taste best served freshly made and slightly warm.

Cherries Jubilee

Servings: 4
Cooking Time: 10 Minutes

Ingredients:
- 1 15-ounce can cherries, pitted and drained, with 2 tablespoons juice reserved
- 1 tablespoon orange juice
- 1 tablespoon sugar
- 1 tablespoon cornstarch
- ¼ cup warmed Kirsch or Cognac
- Vanilla yogurt or fat-free half-and-half

Directions:
1. Combine the reserved juice, orange juice, sugar, and cornstarch in a shallow baking pan, blending well.
2. BROIL for 5 minutes, or until the juice clarifies and thickens slightly. Add the cherries and heat, broiling for

5 minutes more and stirring to blend. Remove from the oven and transfer to a flameproof serving dish.

3. Spoon the Kirsch over the cherries and ignite. Top with vanilla yogurt or drizzle with warm fat-free half-and-half and serve.

Portobello Burgers

Servings: 4
Cooking Time: 12 Minutes

Ingredients:
- 4 multigrain hamburger buns Dijon mustard
- 4 large portobello mushroom caps, stemmed and brushed clean
- 2 tablespoons olive oil
- Garlic powder
- Salt and butcher's pepper
- 4 thin onion slices
- 4 tomato slices

Directions:
1. TOAST the split hamburger buns and spread each slice with mustard. Set aside.
2. Brush both sides of the mushroom caps with olive oil and sprinkle with garlic powder and salt and pepper to taste.
3. BROIL the caps on a broiling rack with a pan underneath, ribbed side up, for 6 minutes. Turn the mushrooms carefully with tongs and broil again for 6 minutes, or until lightly browned. Place the mushroom caps on the bottom buns and layer each with an onion and tomato slice. Top with the remaining bun halves and serve.

Baked Macs

Servings: 2
Cooking Time: 30 Minutes

Ingredients:
- 2 tablespoons rolled oats
- 2 tablespoons applesauce
- 1 tablespoon honey
- 1 teaspoon ground cinnamon
- Pinch of ground allspice
- Pinch of salt
- 2 McIntosh apples, cored
- Maple Yogurt Sauce (recipe follows)

Directions:
1. Preheat the toaster oven to 375° F.
2. Mix together the oatmeal, applesauce, honey, and seasonings in a small bowl. Spoon the mixture into the cavities of the apples and place the apples in an oiled or nonstick 8½ × 8½ × 2-inch square baking (cake) pan.
3. BAKE the apples for 30 minutes, or until tender. Serve chilled or warm with Maple Yogurt Sauce.

Breakfast Bars

Servings: 6
Cooking Time: 35 Minutes

Ingredients:
- 1 cup unsweetened applesauce
- 1 carrot, peeled and grated
- ½ cup raisins
- 1 egg
- 1 tablespoon vegetable oil
- 2 tablespoons molasses
- 2 tablespoons brown sugar
- ¼ cup chopped walnuts
- 2 cups rolled oats
- 2 tablespoons sesame seeds
- 1 teaspoon ground cinnamon
- ¼ teaspoon grated nutmeg
- ¼ teaspoon ground ginger
- Salt to taste

Directions:
1. Preheat the toaster oven to 375° F.
2. Combine all the ingredients in a bowl, stirring well to blend. Press the mixture into an oiled or nonstick 8½ × 8½ × 2inch square baking (cake) pan.
3. BAKE for 35 minutes, or until golden brown. Cool and cut into squares.

Granola

Servings: 4
Cooking Time: 18 Minutes

Ingredients:
- 2 cups old-fashioned oats
- ⅔ cup sliced almonds or chopped pecans, walnuts, or cashews
- 1 tablespoon flax seeds
- 2 teaspoons white sesame seeds
- ½ teaspoon kosher salt
- ½ teaspoon ground cinnamon
- 3 tablespoons olive oil
- 3 tablespoons maple syrup
- 1 ⅓ cups dried fruit such as raisins, cherries, or chopped apricots

Directions:
1. Preheat the toaster oven to 350°F.
2. Combine the oats, nuts, flax seeds, sesame seeds, salt, and cinnamon in a large bowl. Place the olive oil and maple syrup in a small bowl and stir. Pour the oil-syrup mixture over the oat mixture and stir until coated well.
3. Spread the granola in a 12 x 12-inch baking pan. Bake, uncovered, for 10 minutes. Stir and continue to bake for an additional 6 to 8 minutes, or until the oats are golden brown. Remove from the oven and stir in the dried fruit. Set on a wire rack to cool. Store in a sealed jar or container for up to two weeks.

Fry Bread

Servings: 4
Cooking Time: 5 Minutes

Ingredients:
- 1 cup flour
- 2 teaspoons baking powder
- ¼ teaspoon salt
- ¼ cup lukewarm milk
- 1 teaspoon oil
- 2–3 tablespoons water
- oil for misting or cooking spray

Directions:
1. Stir together flour, baking powder, and salt. Gently mix in the milk and oil. Stir in 1 tablespoon water. If needed, add more water 1 tablespoon at a time until stiff dough forms. Dough shouldn't be sticky, so use only as much as you need.
2. Divide dough into 4 portions and shape into balls. Cover with a towel and let rest for 10 minutes.
3. Preheat the toaster oven to 390°F.
4. Shape dough as desired:
5. a. Pat into 3-inch circles. This will make a thicker bread to eat plain or with a sprinkle of cinnamon or honey butter. You can cook all 4 at once.
6. b. Pat thinner into rectangles about 3 x 6 inches. This will create a thinner bread to serve as a base for dishes such as Indian tacos. The circular shape is more traditional, but rectangles allow you to cook 2 at a time in your air fryer oven.
7. Spray both sides of dough pieces with oil or cooking spray.
8. Place the 4 circles or 2 of the dough rectangles in the air fryer oven and air-fry at 390°F for 3 minutes. Spray tops, turn, spray other side, and air fry for 2 more minutes. If necessary, repeat to cook remaining bread.
9. Serve piping hot as is or allow to cool slightly and add toppings to create your own Native American tacos.

Strawberry Bread

Servings: 6
Cooking Time: 28 Minutes

Ingredients:
- ½ cup frozen strawberries in juice, completely thawed (do not drain)
- 1 cup flour
- ½ cup sugar
- 1 teaspoon cinnamon
- ½ teaspoon baking soda
- ⅛ teaspoon salt
- 1 egg, beaten
- ⅓ cup oil
- cooking spray

Directions:
1. Cut any large berries into smaller pieces no larger than ½ inch.

2. Preheat the toaster oven to 330°F.
3. In a large bowl, stir together the flour, sugar, cinnamon, soda, and salt.
4. In a small bowl, mix together the egg, oil, and strawberries. Add to dry ingredients and stir together gently.
5. Spray 6 x 6-inch baking pan with cooking spray.
6. Pour batter into prepared pan and air-fry at 330°F for 28 minutes.
7. When bread is done, let cool for 10 minutes before removing from pan.

Bacon, Broccoli And Swiss Cheese Bread Pudding

Servings: 2
Cooking Time: 48 Minutes

Ingredients:
- ½ pound thick cut bacon, cut into ¼-inch pieces
- 3 cups brioche bread or rolls, cut into ½-inch cubes
- 3 eggs
- 1 cup milk
- ½ teaspoon salt
- freshly ground black pepper
- 1 cup frozen broccoli florets, thawed and chopped
- 1½ cups grated Swiss cheese

Directions:

1. Preheat the toaster oven to 400°F.
2. Air-fry the bacon for 6 minutes until crispy, rotate a few times while it cooks to help it cook evenly. Remove the bacon and set it aside on a paper towel.
3. Air-fry the brioche bread cubes for 2 minutes to dry and toast lightly. (If your brioche is a few days old and slightly stale, you can omit this step.)
4. Butter a 6- or 7-inch cake pan. Combine all the ingredients in a large bowl and toss well. Transfer the mixture to the buttered cake pan, cover with aluminum foil and refrigerate the bread pudding overnight, or for at least 8 hours.
5. Remove the casserole from the refrigerator an hour before you plan to cook, and let it sit on the countertop to come to room temperature.
6. Preheat the toaster oven to 330°F. Transfer the covered cake pan, to the air fryer oven, lowering the dish into the air fryer oven using a sling made of aluminum foil (fold a piece of aluminum foil into a strip about 2-inches wide by 24-inches long). Fold the ends of the aluminum foil over the top of the dish before returning to the air fryer oven. Air-fry for 20 minutes. Remove the foil and air-fry for an additional 20 minutes. If the top starts to brown a little too much before the custard has set, simply return the foil to the pan. The bread pudding has cooked through when a skewer inserted into the center comes out clean.

LUNCH AND DINNER

Miso-glazed Salmon With Broccoli

Servings: 2
Cooking Time: 25 Minutes

Ingredients:
- Nonstick cooking spray
- 2 tablespoons miso, preferably yellow
- 2 tablespoons mirin
- 1 tablespoon packed dark brown sugar
- 2 teaspoons minced fresh ginger
- 1 ½ teaspoons sesame oil
- 8 ounces fresh broccoli, cut into spears
- 1 tablespoon canola or vegetable oil
- Kosher salt and freshly ground black pepper
- 2 salmon fillets (5 to 6 ounces each)

Directions:
1. Preheat the toaster oven to 425°F. Spray a 12 x 12-inch baking pan with nonstick cooking spray.
2. Stir the miso, mirin, brown sugar, ginger, and sesame oil in a small bowl; set aside.
3. Toss the broccoli spears with the canola oil and season with salt and pepper. Place the broccoli on the pan. Bake, uncovered, for 10 minutes. Stir the broccoli and move to one side of the pan.
4. Place the salmon, skin side down, on the other end of the pan. Brush lightly with olive oil and season with salt and pepper. Bake for 10 minutes.
5. Brush the fish generously with the miso sauce. Bake for an additional 3 to 5 minutes, or until the fish flakes easily with a fork and a meat thermometer registers 145°F.

Roasted Vegetable Gazpacho

Servings: 4
Cooking Time: 35 Minutes

Ingredients:
- Vegetables and seasonings:
- 1 bell pepper, thinly sliced
- ½ cup chopped celery
- ½ cup frozen or canned corn
- 1 medium onion, thinly sliced
- 1 small yellow squash, cut into 1-inch slices
- 1 small zucchini, cut into 1-inch slices
- 3 garlic cloves, chopped
- ½ teaspoon ground cumin
- 2 tablespoons olive oil
- Salt and freshly ground black pepper to taste
- 1 quart tomato juice
- 1 tablespoon lemon juice
- 3 tablespoons chopped fresh cilantro

Directions:
1. Preheat the toaster oven to 400°F.
2. Combine the vegetables and seasonings in an oiled or nonstick 8½ × 8½ × 2-inch square baking (cake) pan, mixing well.
3. BAKE, covered, for 25 minutes, or until the onions and celery are tender. Remove from the oven, uncover, and turn the vegetable pieces with tongs.
4. BROIL for 10 minutes, or until the vegetables are lightly browned. Remove from the oven and cool. Transfer to a large nonaluminum container and add the tomato juice, lemon juice, and cilantro. Adjust the seasonings.
5. Chill, covered, for several hours, preferably a day or two to enrich the flavor of the stock.

Fresh Herb Veggie Pizza

Servings: 4
Cooking Time: 25 Minutes

Ingredients:
- 1 9-inch ready-made pizza crust
- 1 tablespoon olive oil
- 1 4-ounce can tomato paste
- 2 tablespoons shredded part-skim mozzarella
- 2 tablespoons grated Parmesan cheese
- 2 tablespoons crumbled feta cheese
- ½ bell pepper, chopped
- 1 tablespoon chopped fresh parsley
- 1 tablespoon chopped fresh oregano
- 1 tablespoon chopped fresh basil
- ½ teaspoon red pepper flakes
- Salt and freshly ground black pepper to taste

- Pizza mixture:
- 2 garlic cloves, minced
- 1 plum tomato, chopped

Directions:
1. Preheat the toaster oven to 400° F.
2. Brush the pizza crust with olive oil and spread the tomato paste evenly to cover.
3. Combine the ingredients for the pizza mixture and spread evenly on top of the tomato paste layer. Sprinkle the cheeses over all and season to taste. Place the pizza on the toaster oven rack.
4. BAKE for 25 minutes, or until the vegetables are cooked and the cheese is melted.

Pork And Brown Rice Casserole

Servings: 4
Cooking Time: 45 Minutes

Ingredients:
- 2 very lean 6-ounce boneless pork chops, cut into 1-inch cubes
- ½ cup brown rice
- 1 cup chunky tomato sauce
- ½ cup dry white wine
- 3 tablespoons finely chopped onion
- 2 small zucchini squashes, finely chopped
- 2 plum tomatoes, chopped
- ½ teaspoon ground cumin
- ½ teaspoon ground ginger
- 1 teaspoon garlic powder
- 2 bay leaves
- Salt and freshly ground black pepper

Directions:
1. Preheat the toaster oven to 400° F.
2. Combine all the ingredients in a 1-quart 8½ × 8½ × 4-inch ovenproof baking dish. Cover with aluminum foil.
3. BAKE, covered, for 45 minutes, or until the rice is cooked to your preference. Discard the bay leaves before serving.

Glazed Pork Tenderloin With Carrots Sheet Pan Supper

Servings: 4-6
Cooking Time: 20 Minutes

Ingredients:
- 1 pound pork tenderloin
- 1 teaspoon steak seasoning blend
- 2 large carrots, sliced 1/2-inch thick
- 2 large parsnips, sliced 1/2-inch thick
- 1/2 small sweet onion, cut in thin wedges
- 1 tablespoon olive oil
- Salt and pepper to taste
- 1/2 cup apricot jam
- 1 tablespoon balsamic vinegar

Directions:
1. Place rack on bottom position of toaster oven. Heat the toaster oven to 425°F. Spray the toaster oven baking pan with nonstick cooking spray or line the pan with nonstick aluminum foil.
2. Place pork tenderloin diagonally in center of pan. Sprinkle pork with seasoning blend.
3. In a large bowl, combine carrots, parsnips and onion. Add olive oil, salt and black pepper and stir until vegetables are coated. Arrange vegetables evenly in pan around pork.
4. Bake 20 minutes. Stir vegetables.
5. Meanwhile, in a small bowl, combine apricot jam and balsamic vinegar. Spoon about half of mixture over pork.
6. Continue baking until pork reaches reaches 160°F when tested with a meat thermometer and vegetables are roasted, about 10 minutes. Slice pork and serve with remaining sauce, if desired.

Lima Bean And Artichoke Casserole

Servings: 4
Cooking Time: 40 Minutes

Ingredients:
- 1 15-ounce can lima beans, drained
- 1 6-ounce jar artichokes, marinated in olive oil (include the oil)
- ½ cup dry white wine

- 1 small onion, thinly sliced
- 2 medium carrots, thinly sliced
- 1 5-ounce can roasted peppers, drained and chopped
- ¼ teaspoon paprika
- ½ teaspoon ground cumin
- 1 teaspoon curry powder
- Salt and freshly ground black pepper to taste

Directions:
1. Preheat the toaster oven to 350° F.
2. Combine all the ingredients in a 1-quart 8½ × 8½ × 4-inch ovenproof baking dish, blending well. Adjust the seasonings to taste. Cover with aluminum foil.
3. BAKE, covered, for 40 minutes, or until the carrots and onion are tender.

Homemade Pizza Sauce

Servings: 1
Cooking Time: 20 Minutes

Ingredients:
- 1 9-inch ready-made pizza crust or 1 homemade pizza crust
- 2 plum tomatoes, chopped
- 1 tablespoon olive oil
- 3 garlic cloves, peeled and chopped ¼ cup chopped onion
- 2 tablespoons tomato paste
- 2 tablespoons dry red wine
- 1 tablespoon chopped fresh basil or 1 teaspoon dried basil
- 1 tablespoon chopped fresh oregano or 1 teaspoon dried oregano
- 1 bay leaf
- Salt and freshly ground black pepper to taste

Directions:
1. Combine all ingredients in an 8½ × 8½ × 2-inch square baking (cake) pan. Adjust the seasonings to taste.
2. BROIL for 20 minutes, or until the onions and tomatoes are tender. Remove the bay leaf and cool before spreading on the pizza crust. Bake the pizza according to instructions on the ready-made crust package or in the homemade pizza crust recipe.

Kasha Loaf

Servings: 4
Cooking Time: 30 Minutes

Ingredients:
- 1 cup whole grain kasha
- 2 cups tomato sauce or 3 2 8-ounce cans tomato sauce (add a small amount of water to make 4 2 cups)
- 3 tablespoons minced onion or scallions
- 1 tablespoon minced garlic
- 1 cup multigrain bread crumbs
- 1 egg
- 1 teaspoon paprika
- 1 teaspoon chili powder
- 1 teaspoon sesame oil

Directions:
1. Preheat the toaster oven to 400° F.
2. Combine all the ingredients in a bowl and transfer to an oiled or nonstick regular-size 4½ × 8½ × 2/4-inch loaf pan.
3. BAKE, uncovered, for 30 minutes, or until lightly browned.

Spanish Rice

Servings: 4
Cooking Time: 45 Minutes

Ingredients:
- ¾ cup rice
- 2 tablespoons dry white wine
- 3 tablespoons olive oil
- 1 15-ounce can whole tomatoes
- ¼ cup thinly sliced onions
- 3 tablespoons chopped fresh cilantro
- 4 ½ cup chopped bell pepper
- 5 2 bay leaves
- Salt and a pinch of red pepper flakes to taste

Directions:
1. Preheat the toaster oven to 375° F.
2. Combine all the ingredients with 1 cup water in a 1-quart 8½ × 8½ × 4-inch ovenproof baking dish and adjust the seasonings. Cover with aluminum foil.
3. BAKE, covered, for 45 minutes, or until the rice is cooked, removing the cover after 30 minutes.

Yeast Dough For Two Pizzas

Servings: 8
Cooking Time: 20 Minutes

Ingredients:
- ¼ cup tepid water
- 1 cup tepid skim milk
- ½ teaspoon sugar
- 1 1¼-ounce envelope dry yeast
- 2 cups unbleached flour
- 1 tablespoon olive oil

Directions:
1. Preheat the toaster oven to 400° F.
2. Combine the water, milk, and sugar in a bowl. Add the yeast and set aside for 3 to 5 minutes, or until the yeast is dissolved.
3. Stir in the flour gradually, adding just enough to form a ball of the dough.
4. KNEAD on a floured surface until the dough is satiny, and then put the dough in a bowl in a warm place with a damp towel over the top. In 1 hour or when the dough has doubled in bulk, punch it down and divide it in half. Flatten the dough and spread it out to the desired thickness on an oiled or nonstick 9¾-inch-diameter pie pan. Spread with Homemade Pizza Sauce (recipe follows) and add any desired toppings.
5. BAKE for 20 minutes, or until the topping ingredients are cooked and the cheese is melted.

Classic Beef Stew

Servings: 4
Cooking Time: 50 Minutes

Ingredients:
- 1½ cups dark beer
- 4 tablespoons unbleached flour
- 2 cups (approximately 1 pound) lean top round steak, cut into 1-inch cubes
- 1 cup peeled and coarsely chopped carrots
- 1 cup peeled and coarsely chopped potatoes
- ½ cup coarsely chopped onion
- 1 cup fresh or frozen peas
- 2 plum tomatoes, chopped
- 3 garlic cloves, minced
- 4 3 bay leaves
- ¼ teaspoon ground cumin
- Salt and butcher's pepper to taste

Directions:
1. Preheat the toaster oven to 400° F.
2. Whisk together the beer and flour in a 1-quart 8½ × 8½ × 4-inch ovenproof baking dish. Add all the other ingredients and seasonings and mix well, adjusting the seasonings to taste. Cover the dish with aluminum foil.
3. BAKE, covered, for 50 minutes, or until the meat is cooked and the vegetables are tender. Remove the bay leaves before serving.

Tarragon Beef Ragout

Servings: 6
Cooking Time: 53 Minutes

Ingredients:
- 1 pound lean round steak, cut across the grain of the meat into thin strips, approximately ¼ × 2 inches
- ½ cup dry red wine
- 1 small onion, chopped
- 2 carrots, peeled and thinly sliced
- 3 2 plum tomatoes, chopped
- 1 celery stalk, chopped
- 1 10-ounce package frozen peas
- 3 garlic gloves, minced
- 1 tablespoon Dijon mustard
- ½ teaspoon ground cumin
- ½ teaspoon dried tarragon
- Salt and freshly ground black pepper to taste

Directions:
1. Preheat the toaster oven to 375° F.
2. Combine all the ingredients with ½ cup water in an 8½ × 8½ × 4-inch ovenproof baking dish. Adjust the seasonings. Cover with aluminum foil.
3. BAKE, covered, for 45 minutes, or until the beef, onion, and celery are tender. Remove the cover.
4. BROIL 8 minutes to reduce the liquid and lightly brown the top.

Quick Pan Pizza

Servings: 8
Cooking Time: 22 Minutes

Ingredients:
- 1 can (13.8 oz.) refrigerator pizza crust, cut in half
- 2 tablespoons oil, divided
- 2/3 cup Slow Cooker Marinara Sauce, divided
- 2 cups shredded mozzarella cheese, divided
- 18 slices pepperoni, divided
- 1 small green pepper, sliced into rings, divided
- 2 large mushrooms, sliced, divided

Directions:
1. Preheat the toaster oven to 425°F. Spray baking pan with nonstick cooking spray.
2. Press half of dough into pan. Brush with 1 tablespoon oil.
3. Bake 8 to 9 minutes or until light brown.
4. Top baked crust with 1/3 cup sauce, 1 cup shredded mozzarella cheese and half of the pepperoni, green pepper and mushrooms.
5. Bake an additional 11 to 13 minutes or until cheese is melted and crust is brown. Repeat to make second pizza.

Chicken Gumbo

Servings: 4
Cooking Time: 40 Minutes

Ingredients:
- 2 skinless, boneless chicken breast halves, cut into 1-inch cubes
- ½ cup dry red wine
- 1 small onion, finely chopped
- 1 celery stalk, finely chopped
- 2 plum tomatoes, chopped
- 3 1 bell pepper, chopped
- 1 tablespoon minced fresh garlic
- 2 okra pods, stemmed, seeded, and finely chopped
1 bay leaf
- ½ teaspoon hot sauce
- ½ teaspoon dried thyme
- Salt and freshly ground black pepper to taste

Directions:
1. Preheat the toaster oven to 400° F.
2. Combine all the ingredients in a 1-quart 8½ × 8½ × 4-inch ovenproof baking dish. Adjust the seasonings to taste. Cover with aluminum foil.
3. BAKE, covered, for 40 minutes, or until the onion, pepper, and celery are tender. Discard the bay leaf before serving.

Narragansett Clam Chowder

Servings: 4
Cooking Time: 35 Minutes

Ingredients:
- 1 cup fat-free half-and-half
- 2 tablespoons unbleached flour
- 3 ½ cup chopped onion
- 1 cup peeled and diced potato
- 1 tablespoon vegetable oil
- 1 tablespoon chopped fresh parsley
- 1 6-ounce can clams, drained and chopped
- 1 15-ounce can fat-free low-sodium chicken broth
- Salt and freshly ground black pepper

Directions:
1. Whisk together the half-and-half and flour in a small bowl. Set aside.
2. Combine the onion, potato, and oil in an 8½ × 8½ × 2-inch square baking (cake) pan.
3. BROIL 15 minutes, turning every 5 minutes with tongs, or until the potato is tender and the onion is cooked. Transfer to a 1-quart baking dish. Add the parsley, clams, broth, and half-and-half/flour mixture. Stir well and season to taste with salt and pepper.
4. BAKE, uncovered, at 375° F. for 20 minutes, stirring after 10 minutes, or until the stock is reduced and thickened. Ladle into bowls and serve with Yogurt Bread.

Cheesy Chicken–stuffed Shells

Servings: 4
Cooking Time: 40 Minutes

Ingredients:
- Nonstick cooking spray
- 16 jumbo pasta shells
- 1 cup finely diced cooked chicken

- 1 cup whole milk ricotta cheese
- 1 ¼ cups shredded mozzarella cheese
- 1 large egg, slightly beaten
- ⅓ cup grated Parmesan cheese
- 1 teaspoon Italian seasoning
- 2 cloves garlic, minced
- ¼ teaspoon kosher salt
- ¼ teaspoon freshly ground black pepper
- 1 ½ cups marinara sauce

Directions:

1. Preheat the toaster oven to 350 ºF. Spray an 8 x 8-inch square baking pan with nonstick cooking spray.
2. Cook the shells according to the package directions, drain, and rinse with cool water.
3. Combine the chicken, ricotta, ¾ cup of the mozzarella, egg, Parmesan, Italian seasoning, garlic, salt, and pepper in a large bowl.
4. Spread about ¾ cup of the marinara sauce in the prepared pan. Fill each shell with a heaping tablespoon of the chicken-cheese mixture. Place the prepared shells, stuffed side up, in the pan. Pour the remaining marinara over the shells.
5. Cover and bake for 25 to 30 minutes. Sprinkle with the remaining ½ cup mozzarella and bake, uncovered, for an additional 5 to 10 minutes or until the cheese is melted. Remove from the oven and let stand for 5 to 10 minutes before serving.

Green Bean Soup

Servings: 4
Cooking Time: 47 Minutes

Ingredients:

- Roux mixture:
- 2 tablespoons unbleached flour
- 1 tablespoon margarine
- 3 cups water or low-sodium vegetable stock
- 1 cup (½ pound) fresh string beans, trimmed and cut into 1-inch pieces
- ½ teaspoon dried oregano
- ½ teaspoon ground cumin
- Salt and freshly ground black pepper to taste

Directions:

1. Combine the roux mixture in an 8½ × 8½ × 2-inch baking (cake) pan.
2. BROIL for 5 minutes, or until the margarine is melted. Remove from the oven and stir, then broil again for 2 minutes, or until the mixture is brown but not burned. Remove from the oven and stir to mix well. Set aside.
3. Combine the water or broth, string beans, and seasonings in a 1-quart 8½ × 8½ × 4-inch ovenproof baking dish. Stir in the roux mixture, blending well. Adjust the seasonings to taste.
4. BAKE, covered, at 375°F. for 40 minutes, or until the string beans are tender.

Sage, Chicken + Mushroom Pasta Casserole

Servings: 6
Cooking Time: 35 Minutes

Ingredients:

- Nonstick cooking spray
- 8 ounces bow-tie pasta, uncooked
- 4 tablespoons unsalted butter
- 8 ounces button or white mushrooms, sliced
- 3 tablespoons all-purpose flour
- Kosher salt and freshly ground black pepper
- 2 cups whole milk
- ½ cup dry white wine
- 2 tablespoons minced fresh sage
- 1 ½ cups chopped cooked chicken
- 1 cup shredded fontina, Monterey Jack, or Swiss cheese
- ½ cup shredded Parmesan cheese

Directions:

1. Preheat the toaster oven to 350°F. Spray a 2-quart baking pan with nonstick cooking spray.
2. Cook the pasta according to the package directions; drain and set aside.
3. Melt the butter in a large skillet over medium-high heat. Add the mushrooms and cook, stirring frequently, until the liquid has evaporated, 7 to 10 minutes. Blend in the flour and cook, stirring constantly, for 1 minute. Season with salt and pepper. Gradually stir in the milk and wine. Cook, stirring constantly, until the mixture

bubbles and begins to thicken. Remove from the heat. Stir in the sage, cooked pasta, chicken, and fontina. Season with salt and pepper.

4. Spoon into the prepared pan. Cover and bake for 25 to 30 minutes. Uncover, sprinkle with the Parmesan, and bake for an additional 5 minutes or until the cheese is melted.

5. Remove from the oven and let stand for 5 to 10 minutes before serving.

French Bread Pizza

Servings: 6
Cooking Time: 8 Minutes

Ingredients:
- 2 tablespoons unsalted butter, melted
- 2 cloves garlic, minced
- ½ teaspoon Italian seasoning
- 1 tablespoon olive oil
- ½ cup chopped onion
- ½ cup chopped green pepper
- 1 cup sliced button or white mushrooms
- 1 (10- to 12-ounce) loaf French or Italian bread, about 12 inches long, split in half lengthwise
- ½ cup pizza sauce
- 6 to 8 slices Canadian bacon or ¼ cup pepperoni slices
- ¼ cup sliced ripe olives, drained
- 1 cup shredded mozzarella cheese
- 3 tablespoons shredded Parmesan cheese

Directions:
1. Preheat the toaster oven to 450°F.
2. Stir the melted butter, garlic, and Italian seasoning in a small bowl; set aside.
3. Heat the oil in a small skillet over medium-high heat. Add the onion and green pepper and sauté, stirring frequently, for 3 minutes. Add the mushrooms and cook, stirring frequently, for 7 to 10 minutes or until the liquid has evaporated. Remove from the heat; set aside.
4. Gently pull a little of the soft bread out of the center of the loaf, making a well. (Take care not to tear the crust.) Brush the garlic butter over the cut sides of the bread.
5. Place both halves of the bread, side by side, cut side up, on a 12 x 12-inch baking pan. Bake for 3 minutes or until heated through. Carefully remove the bread from the oven.
6. Spoon the pizza sauce evenly over the cut sides of the bread. Top evenly with the Canadian bacon, the onion-mushroom mixture, and the olives. Top with the mozzarella and Parmesan cheeses. Return to the oven and bake for 3 to 5 minutes or until the cheese is melted.
7. Cut the French bread pizza crosswise into slices.

Honey Bourbon–glazed Pork Chops With Sweet Potatoes + Apples

Servings: 2
Cooking Time: 42 Minutes

Ingredients:
- Nonstick cooking spray
- 2 medium sweet potatoes, peeled and quartered
- 2 tablespoons bourbon
- 2 tablespoons honey
- 1 tablespoon canola or vegetable oil
- ½ teaspoon onion powder
- ½ teaspoon dry mustard
- ¼ teaspoon dried thyme leaves
- Kosher salt and freshly ground black pepper
- 2 bone-in pork chops, cut about ¾ inch thick
- 1 Granny Smith apple, not peeled, cored and cut into ½-inch wedges

Directions:
1. Preheat the toaster oven to 375°F. Spray a 12 x 12-inch baking pan with nonstick cooking spray.
2. Place the sweet potatoes on one side of the prepared pan. Spray with nonstick cooking spray. Bake, uncovered, for 20 minutes.
3. Meanwhile, stir the bourbon, honey, oil, onion powder, mustard, and thyme in a small bowl. Season with salt and pepper and set aside.
4. Turn the potatoes over. Place the pork chops on the other end of the pan in a single layer. Arrange the apple wedges around the potatoes and pork chops, stacking the apples as needed. Brush the bourbon mixture generously over all. Bake for 15 to 18 minutes or until

the pork is done as desired and a meat thermometer registers a minimum of 145°F.
5. For additional browning, set the toaster oven to Broil and broil for 2 to 4 minutes, or until the edges are brown as desired.
6. Transfer to a serving platter. Spoon any drippings over the meat and vegetables. Let stand for 5 minutes before serving.

Moroccan Couscous

Servings: 4
Cooking Time: 22 Minutes

Ingredients:
- 1 cup couscous
- 2 tablespoons finely chopped scallion
- 2 tablespoons finely chopped bell pepper
- 1 plum tomato, finely chopped
- 2 tablespoons chopped pitted black olives
- 1 tablespoon olive oil
- ¼ teaspoon ground cumin
- ¼ teaspoon ground cinnamon
- ¼ teaspoon turmeric Pinch of cayenne
- Salt and freshly ground black pepper to taste

Directions:
1. Preheat the toaster oven to 400° F.
2. Combine all the ingredients with ¼ cups water in a 1-quart 8½ × 8½ × 4-inch ovenproof baking dish. Adjust the seasonings to taste. Cover with aluminum foil.
3. BAKE, covered, for 12 minutes. Remove from the heat and fluff with a fork. Cover again and let stand for 10 minutes. Fluff once more before serving.

Maple Bacon

Servings: 6
Cooking Time: 16 Minutes

Ingredients:
- 12 slices bacon
- ½ cup packed dark brown sugar
- 2 tablespoons maple syrup
- 1 teaspoon Dijon mustard
- 2 tablespoons red or white wine

Directions:

1. Preheat the toaster oven to 350°F. Line a 12 x 12-inch baking pan with aluminum foil.
2. Place 6 bacon strips on the prepared pan, leaving space between the strips. Bake for 10 minutes or until the bacon is almost crisp. Carefully drain the bacon and return it to the pan.
3. Combine the brown sugar, maple syrup, mustard, and wine in a small bowl. Blend until smooth. Brush the glaze over the bacon. Bake for 8 minutes. Turn the bacon and brush with the glaze. Continue to bake for an additional 6 to 8 minutes, or until golden brown.
4. Repeat with the remaining bacon strips.

Individual Baked Eggplant Parmesan

Servings: 5
Cooking Time: 55 Minutes

Ingredients:
- 1 medium eggplant, cut into 1/2-inch thick slices
- 1 1/2 teaspoons salt
- 1 cup Slow Cooker Marinara Sauce
- 1 package (8 oz.) fresh mozzarella, cut into 8 slices, divided
- 1 package (0.75 oz.) fresh basil, leaves only, divided
- 1/4 cup grated Parmesan cheese, divided

Directions:
1. Sprinkle eggplant with salt and place in a colander to drain for 1 hour.
2. Preheat the toaster oven to 375°F. Spray baking pan and 5 (4-inch) ramekins with nonstick cooking spray.
3. Rinse eggplant thoroughly with water to remove salt. Press each slice between paper towels to remove extra water and salt. Place on papertowels to dry. Arrange a single layer of eggplant slices in baking pan.
4. Bake 25 to 30 minutes or until eggplant is tender. Remove slices to cooking rack. Repeat baking remaining eggplant. Reduce oven temperature to 350°F.
5. In each ramekin, layer 1 slice eggplant, 1 tablespoon sauce, 1 slice mozzarella, 1 basil leaf, 1 additional tablespoon sauce and sprinkle with Parmesan cheese. Repeat layers ending with a sprinkle of Parmesan cheese.
6. Bake 20 to 25 minutes or until cheese is melted and eggplant layers are heated through.

Sheet Pan Loaded Nachos

Servings: 4
Cooking Time: 13 Minutes

Ingredients:
- 1 tablespoon canola or vegetable oil
- ½ pound lean ground beef
- ½ cup chopped onion
- 2 cloves garlic, minced
- 1 teaspoon chili powder
- ½ teaspoon ground cumin
- Kosher salt and freshly ground black pepper
- 6 ounces tortilla chips
- ½ cup canned black beans, rinsed and drained
- 1 ½ cups shredded sharp cheddar cheese or Mexican blend cheese
- ½ cup salsa
- Optional toppings: sliced jalapeño peppers, chopped bell peppers, sliced ripe olives, chopped tomatoes, minced fresh cilantro, sour cream, chopped avocado, guacamole, or chopped onion.

Directions:
1. Preheat the toaster oven to 400°F. Line a 12 x 12-inch baking pan with nonstick aluminum foil. (Or if lining the pan with regular foil, spray it with nonstick cooking spray.)
2. Heat the oil in a large skillet over medium-high heat. Add the ground beef and onion and cook, stirring frequently, until the beef is almost done. Add the garlic, chili powder, cumin, season with salt and pepper, and cook, stirring frequently, until the beef is fully cooked; drain.
3. Arrange the tortilla chips in an even layer in the prepared pan. Top with the beef-onion mixture, then top with the beans. Bake, uncovered, for 6 to 8 minutes. Top with the cheese and bake for 5 minutes more, or until the cheese is melted.
4. Drizzle with the salsa. Top as desired with any of the various toppings.

Crunchy Baked Chicken Tenders

Servings: 3-4
Cooking Time: 18 Minutes

Ingredients:
- 2/3 cup seasoned panko breadcrumbs
- 2/3 cup cheese crackers, crushed
- 2 teaspoons melted butter
- 2 large eggs, beaten
- Salt and pepper
- 1 1/2 pounds chicken tenders
- Barbecue sauce

Directions:
1. Preheat the toaster oven to 450°F. Spray the toaster oven baking pan with nonstick cooking spray.
2. In medium bowl, combine breadcrumbs, cheese cracker crumbs and butter.
3. In another medium bowl, mix eggs, salt and pepper.
4. Dip chicken tenders in eggs and dredge in breadcrumb mixture.
5. Place on pan.
6. Bake for 15 to 18 minutes, turning once. Serve with barbecue sauce for dipping.

Chicken Tortilla Roll-ups

Servings: 4
Cooking Time: 10 Minutes

Ingredients:
- Nonstick cooking spray
- ¼ cup olive oil
- 2 cloves garlic, minced
- 1 ½ cups shredded cooked chicken
- 1 cup shredded Mexican blend or cheddar cheese
- ½ cup frozen corn, thawed
- ⅓ cup salsa verde
- 1 green onion, white and green portions, chopped
- 2 tablespoons minced fresh cilantro
- 1 tablespoon fresh lime juice
- ½ teaspoon ground cumin
- ¼ teaspoon Sriracha or hot sauce
- Kosher salt and freshly ground black pepper
- 8 flour tortillas, about 8 inches in diameter
- Optional toppings: minced cilantro, salsa, guacamole, sour cream

Directions:
1. Preheat the toaster oven to 375°F. Spray a 12 x 12-inch baking pan with nonstick cooking spray.
2. Stir the oil and garlic in a small bowl; set aside.

3. Stir the chicken, cheese, corn, salsa verde, green onion, cilantro, lime juice, cumin, and Sriracha in a large bowl. Season with salt and pepper.
4. Brush both sides of a tortilla very lightly with the garlic oil. Spoon about ⅓ cup chicken filling on the lower side of the tortilla. Roll the tortilla over the filling. Place the filled tortilla, seam side down, in the prepared baking pan. Repeat with the remaining tortillas and filling.
5. Brush the tops of each filled tortilla with the remaining garlic oil, coating them evenly and especially covering the edges of the tortillas.
6. Bake, uncovered, for 10 minutes or until the tortillas are crisp and the filling is hot. Serve with your choice of any of the various toppings.

Pesto Pizza

Servings: 1
Cooking Time: 20 Minutes

Ingredients:
- Topping:
- ½ cup chopped fresh basil
- 1 tablespoon pine nuts (pignoli)
- 1 tablespoon olive oil
- 2 tablespoons shredded Parmesan cheese
- 1 garlic clove, minced
- ½ teaspoon dried oregano or 1 tablespoon chopped fresh oregano
- 1 plum tomato, chopped
- Salt and pepper to taste
- 1 9-inch ready-made pizza crust
- 2 tablespoons shredded low-fat mozzarella

Directions:
1. Preheat the toaster oven to 375° F.
2. Combine the topping ingredients in a small bowl.
3. Process the mixture in a blender or food processor until smooth. Spread the mixture on the pizza crust, then sprinkle with the mozzarella cheese. Place the pizza crust on the toaster oven rack.
4. BAKE for 20 minutes, or until the cheese is melted and the crust is brown.

Baked Picnic Pinto Beans

Servings: 4
Cooking Time: 40 Minutes

Ingredients:
- 1 tomato, peeled and finely chopped
- 2 15-ounce cans pinto beans, drained
- 6 lean turkey bacon strips, cooked, drained, and crumbled
- 1 cup good-quality dark beer or ale
- 3 tablespoons finely chopped onion
- 1 tablespoon ketchup
- 2 tablespoons molasses
- 1 teaspoon Dijon mustard
- 1 teaspoon Worcestershire sauce
- 1 teaspoon garlic powder
- Salt and butcher's pepper to taste

Directions:
1. Preheat the toaster oven to 375° F.
2. Peel the tomato by immersing it in boiling water for 1 minute. Remove with tongs and when cool enough to handle, pull the skin away with a sharp paring knife. Chop and place in a 1-quart 8½ × 8½ × 4-inch ovenproof baking dish. Add all the other ingredients, stirring to mix well. Adjust the seasonings to taste. Cover with aluminum foil.
3. BAKE, covered, for 40 minutes.

Sun-dried Tomato Pizza

Servings: 4
Cooking Time: 25 Minutes

Ingredients:
- Tomato mixture:
- 1 cup chopped sun-dried tomatoes
- 2 tablespoons tomato paste
- 2 tablespoons olive oil
- 2 tablespoons chopped onion
- 2 garlic cloves, minced
- 1 teaspoon dried oregano
- 1 teaspoon dried basil
- Salt and red pepper flakes to taste
- 1 9-inch ready-made pizza crust
- 1 5-ounce can mushrooms
- ¼ cup pitted and sliced black olives

- ½ cup shredded low-fat mozzarella cheese

Directions:

1. Combine the tomato mixture ingredients with ½ cup water in an 8½ × 8½ × 2-inch square baking (cake) pan.
2. BROIL for 8 minutes, or until the tomatoes are softened. Remove from the oven and cool for 5 minutes.
3. Process the mixture in a blender or food processor until well blended. Spread on the pizza crust and layer with the mushrooms, olives, and cheese.
4. BAKE at 400° F. for 25 minutes, or until the cheese is melted.

Connecticut Garden Chowder

Servings: 4
Cooking Time: 60 Minutes

Ingredients:

- Soup:
- ½ cup peeled and shredded potato
- ½ cup shredded carrot
- ½ cup shredded celery 2 plum tomatoes, chopped
- 1 small zucchini, shredded
- 2 bay leaves
- ¼ teaspoon sage
- 1 teaspoon garlic powder
- Salt and butcher's pepper to taste
- Chowder base:
- 2 tablespoons reduced-fat cream cheese, at room temperature
- ½ cup fat-free half-and-half
- 2 tablespoons unbleached flour
- 2 tablespoons chopped fresh parsley

Directions:

1. Preheat the toaster oven to 375° F.
2. Combine the soup ingredients in a 1-quart 8½ × 8½ × 4-inch ovenproof baking dish, mixing well. Adjust the seasonings to taste.
3. BAKE, covered, for 40 minutes, or until the vegetables are tender.
4. Whisk the chowder mixture ingredients together until smooth. Add the mixture to the cooked soup ingredients and stir well to blend.
5. BAKE, uncovered for 20 minutes, or until the stock is thickened. Ladle the soup into individual soup bowls and garnish with the parsley.

Italian Baked Stuffed Tomatoes

Servings: 4
Cooking Time: 30 Minutes

Ingredients:

- 4 large tomatoes
- 1 cup shredded chicken
- 1 1/2 cup shredded mozzarella, divided
- 1 1/2 cup cooked rice
- 2 tablespoon minced onion
- 1/4 cup grated parmesan cheese
- 1 tablespoon dried Italian seasoning
- salt
- pepper
- Basil

Directions:

1. Preheat the toaster oven to 350°F. Spray toaster oven pan with nonstick cooking spray.
2. Cut the top off each tomato and scoop centers out. Place bottoms on prepared pan. Chop 3 tomatoes (about 1 1/2 cup, chopped) and add to large bowl.
3. Add shredded chicken, 1 cup shredded mozzarella cheese, rice, onion, Parmesan cheese, Italian seasoning, salt and pepper to large bowl and stir until blended. Divide between tomatoes, about 1 cup per tomato. Top with remaining mozzarella and tomato top.
4. Bake 25 to 30 minutes until cheese is melted and mixture is heated through.
5. Garnish with basil before serving.

French Onion Soup

Servings: 4
Cooking Time: 46 Minutes

Ingredients:

- 1 cup finely chopped onions
- 1 teaspoon toasted sesame oil
- 1 tablespoon vegetable oil
- 2 ½ cup dry white wine
- 3 teaspoons soy sauce
- ½ teaspoon garlic powder

- Freshly ground black pepper to taste
- 4 French bread rounds, sliced 1 inch thick
- 4 tablespoons grated Parmesan cheese
- 1 tablespoon chopped fresh parsley

Directions:
1. Place the onions, sesame oil, and vegetable oil in an 8½ × 8½ × 2-inch square baking (cake) pan.
2. BROIL for 10 minutes, stirring every 3 minutes until the onions are tender. Remove from the oven and transfer to a 1-quart 8½ × 8½ × 4-inch ovenproof baking dish. Add 2 cups water, the wine, and the soy sauce. Add the garlic powder and pepper and adjust the seasonings.
3. BAKE, covered, at 400° F. for 30 minutes. Remove from the oven, uncover, and add the 4 bread rounds, letting them float on top of the soup. Sprinkle each with 1 tablespoon Parmesan cheese.
4. BROIL, uncovered, for 6 minutes, or until the cheese is lightly browned. With tongs, transfer the bread rounds to 4 individual soup bowls. Ladle the soup on top of the bread rounds. Garnish with the parsley and serve immediately.

Italian Stuffed Zucchini Boats

Servings: 6
Cooking Time: 26 Minutes

Ingredients:
- 6 small zucchini, halved lengthwise
- 1 pound bulk hot sausage
- 1 small onion, chopped
- 2 cloves garlic, minced
- 1 small Roma tomato, seeded and chopped
- 1/4 cup Parmesan cheese
- 3 tablespoons tomato paste
- 2 teaspoons dried Italian seasoning
- 1 teaspoon salt
- 1/2 teaspoon coarse black pepper
- 1 cup shredded mozzarella cheese
- Sliced fresh basil

Directions:
1. Preheat the toaster oven to 350°F. Spray a 13x9-inch baking pan with nonstick cooking spray.
2. Scoop out center of zucchini halves. Reserve 1 1/2 cups. Place zucchini boats in baking pan.
3. In a large skillet over medium-high heat, cook sausage, stirring to crumble, about 6 minutes or until browned. Remove sausage to a medium bowl.
4. Add onion and garlic to skillet, cook until onion is translucent. Stir in reserved zucchini, sausage, tomatoes, Parmesan cheese, tomato paste, Italian seasoning, salt and black pepper.
5. Spoon mixture into the zucchini boats.
6. Bake for 20 minutes. Remove from oven and top with mozzarella cheese.
7. Bake an additional 5 to 6 minutes or until cheese is melted.
8. Sprinkle with sliced fresh basil before serving.

Spicy Oven-baked Chili

Servings: 6
Cooking Time: 30 Minutes

Ingredients:
- 1 pound lean ground turkey or ground chicken breast or 1 pound lean ground sirloin or round steak
- 1 15-ounce can black beans, drained
- 1 8-ounce can tomato sauce
- ¾ cup chopped onion
- ¼ cup dry white wine
- 1 cup tomato salsa
- 1 tablespoon garlic powder
- 1 tablespoon chili powder
- 2 ⅛ teaspoon cayenne
- 3 teaspoons unsweetened cocoa
- Salt and butcher's pepper to taste

Directions:
1. Preheat the toaster oven to 375° F.
2. Combine all the ingredients in a 1-quart 8½ × 8½ × 4-inch ovenproof baking dish and mix well. Adjust the seasonings to taste. Cover with aluminum foil.
3. BAKE, covered, for 30 minutes.

Homemade Beef Enchiladas

Servings: 4
Cooking Time: 20 Minutes

Ingredients:
- 1 tablespoon canola or vegetable oil
- 1 tablespoon plus 1 teaspoon all-purpose flour
- 2 tablespoons chili powder
- ½ teaspoon ground cumin
- ½ teaspoon garlic powder
- ¼ teaspoon kosher salt
- 1 ¼ cups chicken or vegetable broth
- ¾ pound lean ground beef
- Nonstick cooking spray
- 8 flour or corn tortillas
- ¼ cup finely chopped onion
- 1 ½ cups shredded Mexican-blend or cheddar cheese

Directions:
1. Heat the oil in a small saucepan over medium-high heat. Add the flour and whisk for about a minute. Stir in the chili powder, cumin, garlic powder, and salt. Gradually stir in the broth, whisking until smooth. Reduce the heat to a simmer and cook the sauce for 10 to 12 minutes.
2. Cook the ground beef in a medium skillet over medium-high heat until browned and cooked through, stirring to crumble into a fine texture. Remove from the heat and drain.
3. Preheat the toaster oven to 350°F. Spray an 11 x 7 x 2 ½-inch baking dish with nonstick cooking spray. Place about ½ cup sauce over the bottom of the dish. Lay a tortilla on a large plate and spread about 2 tablespoons of sauce over the surface of the tortilla. Spoon 2 tablespoons of the ground beef down the center of the tortilla. Sprinkle with some onion and cheese (amount is up to you). Roll up and place in the baking dish. Repeat with the remaining tortillas. Pour the remaining sauce over the top. Sprinkle with remaining cheese. Bake, uncovered, for 20 minutes or until the tortillas are heated through and slightly crisp on the outside.

Thai Chicken Pizza With Cauliflower Crust

Servings: 6
Cooking Time: 20 Minutes

Ingredients:
- Nonstick cooking spray
- ½ large head cauliflower (about 1 pound), cut into florets (3 ½ to 4 cups)
- 2 large eggs, lightly beaten
- ⅓ cup shredded mozzarella cheese
- 3 tablespoons shredded Parmesan cheese
- 2 teaspoons Italian seasoning
- ½ teaspoon garlic powder
- Kosher salt and freshly ground black pepper
- SAUCE
- ¼ cup creamy peanut butter
- 1 ½ tablespoons reduced-sodium soy sauce
- 1 ½ tablespoons fresh lime juice
- 1 tablespoon honey
- 1 tablespoon unseasoned rice vinegar
- ½ teaspoon chili garlic sauce
- TOPPINGS
- 1 cup chopped or shredded cooked chicken
- 1 carrot, shredded
- 2 green onions, white and green portions, thinly sliced
- 1 cup shredded Monterey Jack cheese

Directions:
1. Preheat the toaster oven to 425°F. Line a 12-inch pizza pan with parchment paper. Spray with nonstick cooking spray.
2. Place the cauliflower in the work bowl of a food processor. Pulse until finely chopped. (Work in batches, as necessary, so as not to overload the food processor.) Transfer the cauliflower rice to a large, microwave-safe bowl. Add 1 tablespoon water. Cover and microwave on High (100 percent) power for 3 minutes or until the cauliflower is tender. Uncover and let the cauliflower cool to room temperature.
3. Spoon the cauliflower into a clean kitchen towel and twist to drain the cauliflower well. Return the drained cauliflower to the bowl. Stir in the eggs, mozzarella,

Parmesan, Italian seasoning, and garlic powder and season with salt and pepper. Stir well.

4. Spoon the cauliflower mixture onto the prepared pan. Gently spread or pat the mixture into an even circle, about 11 inches in diameter. Bake for 12 to 15 minutes or until the crust is set and beginning to brown.

5. Meanwhile, make the sauce: Stir the peanut butter, soy sauce, lime juice, honey, vinegar, and chili garlic sauce in a small bowl.

6. Remove the cauliflower crust from the toaster oven. Spread the peanut sauce over the crust. Top with the chicken, carrot, green onions, and Monterey Jack cheese. Bake for 5 minutes or until hot and the cheese is melted.

Easy Oven Lasagne

Servings: 4
Cooking Time: 60 Minutes

Ingredients:
- 6 uncooked lasagna noodles, broken in half
- 1 15-ounce jar marinara sauce
- ½ pound ground turkey or chicken breast
- ½ cup part-skim ricotta cheese
- ½ cup shredded part-skim mozzarella cheese
- 2 tablespoons chopped fresh oregano leaves or 1 teaspoon dried oregano
- 2 tablespoons chopped fresh basil leaves or 1 teaspoon dried basil
- 1 tablespoon garlic cloves, minced
- ¼ cup grated Parmesan cheese
- Salt and freshly ground black pepper to taste

Directions:
1. Preheat the toaster oven to 375° F.
2. Layer in a 1-quart 8½ × 8½ × 4-inch ovenproof baking dish in this order: 6 lasagna noodle halves, ½ jar of the marinara sauce, ½ cup water, half of the ground meat, half of the ricotta and mozzarella cheeses, half of the oregano and basil leaves, and half of the minced garlic. Repeat the layer, starting with the noodles. Cover the dish with aluminum foil.
3. BAKE, covered, for 50 minutes, or until the noodles are tender. Uncover, sprinkle the top with Parmesan cheese and bake for another 10 minutes, or until the liquid is reduced and the top is browned.

Pea Soup

Servings: 6
Cooking Time: 55 Minutes

Ingredients:
- 1 cup dried split peas, ground in a blender to a powderlike consistency
- 3 strips lean turkey bacon, uncooked and chopped
- ¼ cup grated carrots
- ¼ cup grated celery
- 2 tablespoons grated onion
- ½ teaspoon garlic powder
- Salt and freshly ground black pepper to taste
- Garnish:
- 2 tablespoons chopped fresh chives

Directions:
1. Preheat the toaster oven to 400° F.
2. Combine all the ingredients in a 1-quart 8½ × 8½ × 4-inch ovenproof baking dish, mixing well. Adjust the seasonings.
3. BAKE, covered, for 35 minutes. Remove from the oven and stir.
4. BAKE, covered, for another 20 minutes, or until the soup is thickened. Ladle the soup into individual soup bowls and garnish each with chopped fresh chives.

Family Favorite Pizza

Servings: 6
Cooking Time: 22 Minutes

Ingredients:
- CRUST
- ½ cup warm water (about 110 °F)
- 1 teaspoon active dry yeast
- 1 ½ cups all-purpose flour, plus more for kneading
- 1 teaspoon kosher salt
- ½ teaspoon olive oil
- TOPPINGS
- Pizza sauce
- 2 cups shredded Italian blend cheese or mozzarella cheese
- ¼ cup grated Parmesan cheese
- Optional toppings: pepperoni slices, cooked crumbled or sliced sausage, vegetables, or other favorite pizza toppings

Directions:
1. Make the Crust: Pour the water into a medium bowl and sprinkle with the yeast. Let stand for 5 minutes until the yeast is foamy. Add the flour, salt, and olive oil. Mix until a dough forms. Turn the dough out on a floured surface and knead until a ball forms that springs back when you poke a finger into it, about 5 minutes. If the dough is too sticky, add a tablespoon of flour and knead into the dough. Cover the dough and allow to rest for 10 minutes.
2. Preheat the toaster oven to 450°F. Place a 12-inch pizza pan in the toaster oven while it is preheating.
3. Stretch and roll the dough into an 11 ½-inch round. If the dough starts to shrink back, let it rest for 5 to 10 more minutes and then continue to roll. Carefully remove the hot pan from the toaster oven and place the pizza crust on the hot pan. Top with the desired amount of sauce. Layer cheese and any of your favorite pizza toppings over the pizza.
4. Bake for 18 to 22 minutes, or until the crust is golden brown and the cheese is melted. Let stand for 5 minutes before cutting.

One-step Classic Goulash

Servings: 4
Cooking Time: 56 Minutes

Ingredients:
- 1 cup elbow macaroni
- 1 cup (8-ounce can) tomato sauce
- 1 cup very lean ground round or sirloin
- 1 cup peeled and chopped fresh tomato
- ½ cup finely chopped onion
- 1 teaspoon garlic powder
- Salt and freshly ground black pepper
- Topping:
- 1 cup homemade bread crumbs
- 1 tablespoon margarine

Directions:
1. Preheat the toaster oven to 400° F.
2. Combine all the ingredients, except the topping, with 2 cups water in a 1-quart 8½ × 8½ × 4-inch ovenproof baking dish and mix well. Adjust the seasonings to taste. Cover with aluminum foil.
3. BAKE, covered, for 50 minutes, or until the macaroni is cooked, stirring after 25 minutes to distribute the liquid. Uncover, sprinkle with bread crumbs, and dot with margarine.
4. BROIL for 6 minutes, or until the topping is lightly browned.

Sheet Pan Beef Fajitas

Servings: 3
Cooking Time: 10 Minutes

Ingredients:
- Nonstick cooking spray
- 3 tablespoons olive oil
- 1 ½ teaspoons chili powder
- 2 teaspoons ground cumin
- 1 teaspoon kosher salt
- 1 onion, halved and sliced into ¼-inch strips
- 1 large red or green bell pepper, cut into thin strips
- ¾-pound flank steak, cut across the grain into thin strips
- 3 tablespoons fresh lime juice
- 3 cloves garlic, minced
- 6 flour or corn tortillas, warmed

Directions:
1. Position the rack to broil. Preheat the toaster oven on the Broil setting. Spray a 12 x 12-inch baking pan with nonstick cooking spray.
2. Combine the olive oil, chili powder, cumin, and salt in a small bowl. Add the onion and bell pepper and toss to coat them evenly with the mixture. Use a slotted spoon to remove the vegetables from the seasoned oil mixture. Reserve the seasoned oil mixture. Place the vegetables in a single layer on the prepared pan. Broil for about 5 minutes or until the vegetables are beginning to brown.
3. Meanwhile, toss the steak strips in the reserved seasoned oil mixture. Push the vegetables to one side of the pan and add the steak in a single layer on the other side of the pan. Broil for 5 minutes.
4. When the meat is done, remove the meat from the pan and toss with the lime juice and garlic. Serve the meat and vegetables in warm tortillas.

Crab Chowder

Servings: 4
Cooking Time: 40 Minutes

Ingredients:

- 1 6-ounce can lump crabmeat, drained and chopped, or ½ pound fresh crabmeat, cleaned and chopped
- 1 cup skim milk or low-fat soy milk
- 1 cup fat-free half-and-half
- 2 tablespoons unbleached flour
- ¼ cup chopped onion
- ½ cup peeled and diced potato
- 1 carrot, peeled and chopped
- 1 celery stalk, chopped
- 2 garlic cloves, minced
- 2 tablespoons chopped fresh parsley
- ½ teaspoon ground cumin
- 1 teaspoon paprika
- Salt and butcher's pepper to taste

Directions:

1. Preheat the toaster oven to 400° F.
2. Whisk together the milk, half-and-half, and flour in a bowl. Transfer the mixture to a 1-quart 8½ × 8½ × 4-inch ovenproof baking dish. Add all the other ingredients, mixing well. Adjust the seasonings to taste.
3. BAKE, covered, for 40 minutes, or until the vegetables are tender.

Baked French Toast With Maple Bourbon Syrup

Servings: 6
Cooking Time: 40 Minutes

Ingredients:

- Nonstick cooking spray
- 4 tablespoons unsalted butter, melted
- ½ cup packed dark brown sugar
- ⅔ cup chopped pecans, toasted
- 6 (1-inch-thick) slices crusty artisan, brioche, or firm country bread
- 3 large eggs
- 1 cup milk
- 1 teaspoon pure vanilla extract
- ⅓ cup maple syrup
- 2 tablespoons bourbon

Directions:

1. Spray an 11 x 7 x 2 ½-inch baking dish with nonstick cooking spray. Pour the butter into the dish. Stir in the brown sugar and pecans. Arrange the bread at an angle in the dish, overlapping the bottom of the slices as necessary.
2. Whisk the eggs, milk, and vanilla in a medium bowl. Drizzle the milk mixture over the bread, taking care to pour slowly and moisten the edges of the bread. Cover and refrigerate overnight.
3. When ready to bake, preheat the toaster oven to 350°F. Bake, uncovered, for 30 to 35 minutes or until golden and set.
4. Mix the maple syrup and bourbon in a small bowl. Drizzle the syrup over the French toast. Bake for 3 to 5 minutes. Let stand for 2 to 3 minutes, then serve warm.

Oven-baked Barley

Servings: 2
Cooking Time: 60 Minutes

Ingredients:

- ⅓ cup barley, toasted
- Seasonings:
- 1 tablespoon sesame oil
- 1 tablespoon sesame seeds
- ¼ teaspoon ground cumin
- ¼ teaspoon turmeric
- ½ teaspoon garlic powder
- Salt and freshly ground black pepper to taste

Directions:

1. Combine the barley and 1½ cups water in a 1-quart 8½ × 8½ × 4-inch ovenproof baking dish. Cover with aluminum foil.
2. BAKE, covered, for 50 minutes, or until almost cooked, testing the grains after 30 minutes for softness.
3. Add the oil and seasonings and fluff with a fork to combine. Cover and let the barley sit for 10 minutes to finish cooking and absorb the flavors of the seasonings. Fluff once more before serving.

Chicken Marengo

Servings: 4
Cooking Time: 30 Minutes

Ingredients:
- Chicken mixture:
- 2 skinless, boneless chicken breast halves, cut into 1 × 1-inch pieces
- 6 large shrimp, peeled, deveined, and cut into 1 × 1-inch pieces
- 2 plum tomatoes, chopped
- 1 tablespoon olive oil
- ½ cup dry white wine
- 3 garlic cloves, chopped
- 6 fresh mushrooms, rinsed quickly, patted dry, and thinly sliced
- 1 teaspoon dried tarragon
- 1 tablespoon chopped fresh parsley
- Salt and freshly ground black pepper to taste
- 2 hard-boiled eggs, peeled and sliced
- ½ cup pitted and sliced black olives
- 2 tablespoons chopped fresh parsley

Directions:
1. Preheat the toaster oven to 375° F.
2. Combine the chicken mixture ingredients in a 1-quart 8½ × 8½ × 4-inch ovenproof baking dish and adjust the seasonings to taste. Cover with aluminum foil.
3. BAKE, covered, for 30 minutes, or until the chicken and shrimp are tender.
4. Garnish with slices of hard-boiled eggs, black olives, and parsley.

Broiled Chipotle Tilapia With Avocado Sauce

Servings: 2
Cooking Time: 10 Minutes

Ingredients:
- 1 small avocado, halved, pitted and peeled
- 3 tablespoons sour cream
- 1 teaspoon lime juice
- 2 1/2 teaspoons chipotle and roasted garlic seasoning, divided
- 1 tablespoon mayonnaise
- 1/2 pound tilapia fillets
- Chopped cilantro

Directions:
1. Using a chopper or small food processor, blend avocado, sour cream, lime juice and 1 1/2 teaspoons seasoning until smooth. Cover and refrigerate.
2. Spray toaster oven baking pan with nonstick cooking spray.
3. in small bowl, mix mayonnaise and remaining 1 teaspoon seasoning.
4. Brush mayonnaise mixture on both sides of tilapia fillets.
5. Place coated fish in pan.
6. Set toaster oven to BROIL. Broil fish for 10 minutes or until fish flakes with a fork.
7. Serve with avocado sauce and garnish with lime slices and cilantro, if desired.

Baked Parsleyed Cheese Grits

Servings: 4
Cooking Time: 30 Minutes

Ingredients:
- 4 strips lean uncooked turkey bacon, cut in half
- 1 cup grits
- 2 cups skim or low-fat soy milk
- 1 egg
- ½ cup shredded Parmesan cheese
- 1 tablespoon chopped fresh parsley
- ½ teaspoon garlic powder
- Salt and butcher's pepper to taste

Directions:
1. Preheat the toaster oven to 350° F.
2. Layer an 8½ × 8½ × 2-inch square baking (cake) pan with the bacon strips.
3. Combine the remaining ingredients in a medium bowl and pour the mixture over the strips.
4. BAKE, uncovered, for 30 minutes, or until the grits are cooked. Cut into squares with a spatula and serve.

Scalloped Corn Casserole

Servings: 4
Cooking Time: 38 Minutes

Ingredients:

- Casserole mixture:
- 2 15-ounce cans corn
- 1 red bell pepper, chopped
- ¼ cup chopped scallions
- ½ cup fat-free half-and-half
- 2 tablespoons unbleached flour
- 2 eggs
- ½ teaspoon chili powder
- 1 teaspoon ground cumin
- 1 teaspoon garlic powder
- Salt and freshly ground black pepper to taste
- ¼ cup multigrain seasoned bread Crumbs
- 1 tablespoon margarine

Directions:

1. Preheat the toaster oven to 400° F.
2. Combine all the casserole mixture ingredients in a 1-quart 8½ × 8½ × 4-inch ovenproof baking dish, mixing well. Adjust the seasonings to taste. Cover with aluminum foil.
3. BAKE, covered, for 30 minutes, or until the pepper and onions are tender. Remove from the oven and uncover. Sprinkle with the bread crumbs and dot with the margarine.
4. BROIL for 8 minutes, or until the bread crumb topping is lightly browned.

Kashaburgers

Servings: 4
Cooking Time: 50 Minutes

Ingredients:

- 1 cup kasha
- 2 tablespoons minced onion or scallions
- 1 tablespoon minced garlic
- ½ cup multigrain bread crumbs
- 1 egg
- ¼ teaspoon paprika
- ½ teaspoon chili powder
- ¼ teaspoon sesame oil
- 1 tablespoon vegetable oil
- Salt and freshly ground black pepper to taste

Directions:

1. Preheat the toaster oven to 400° F.
2. Combine 2 cups water and the kasha in a 1-quart 8½ × 8½ × 4-inch ovenproof baking dish.
3. BAKE, uncovered, for 30 minutes, or until the grains are cooked. Remove from the oven and add all the other ingredients, stirring to mix well. When the mixture is cooled, shape into 4 to 6 patties and place on a rack with a broiling pan underneath.
4. BROIL for 20 minutes, turn with a spatula, then broil for another 10 minutes, or until browned.

Couscous-stuffed Poblano Peppers

Servings: 6
Cooking Time: 35 Minutes

Ingredients:

- 2 tablespoons olive oil
- ⅔ cup Israeli couscous
- 1 ¼ cups vegetable broth or water
- Kosher salt and freshly ground black pepper
- ½ medium onion, chopped
- 2 cloves garlic, minced
- 1 teaspoon dried oregano leaves
- ½ teaspoon ground cumin
- 1 (14.5-ounce) can fire-roasted diced tomatoes, with liquid
- Nonstick cooking spray
- 3 large poblano peppers, halved lengthwise, seeds and stem removed
- 1 ½ cups shredded Mexican blend, pepper Jack, or sharp cheddar cheese
- Optional toppings: minced fresh cilantro, sliced jalapeño peppers, diced tomatoes, sliced green onions (white and green portions)

Directions:

1. Heat 1 tablespoon oil in a medium saucepan over medium heat. Add the couscous and cook, stirring frequently, until golden brown, 2 to 3 minutes. Stir in the broth and season with salt and pepper. Cover, reduce the heat to a simmer, and cook, stirring occasionally, for about 10 minutes or until the liquid is absorbed. Remove

from the heat and let stand, covered, for 5 minutes. Remove the cover, stir, and set aside to cool.

2. Heat the remaining 1 tablespoon oil in a small saucepan over medium heat. Add the onion, and cook, stirring frequently, for 3 to 5 minutes or until tender. Stir in the garlic and cook for 30 seconds. Stir in the oregano and cumin and season with salt and pepper. Stir in the tomatoes and simmer for 5 minutes.

3. Preheat the toaster oven to 400°F. Spray a 9-inch square baking pan with nonstick cooking spray. Spoon about one-third of the tomato mixture into the prepared pan. Arrange the peppers, cut side up, in the pan.

4. Stir 1 cup of the cheese into the couscous. Spoon the couscous mixture into the peppers, mounding slightly. Spoon the remaining tomato mixture over the peppers. Cover the pan and bake for 30 minutes.

5. Uncover the pan and sprinkle with the remaining cheese. Bake for 5 minutes or until the cheese is melted.

6. Top as desired with any of the various topping choices.

Creamy Roasted Pepper Basil Soup

Servings: 4
Cooking Time: 35 Minutes

Ingredients:
- 1 5-ounce jar roasted peppers, drained ½ cup fresh basil leaves
- 1 cup fat-free half-and-half
- 1 cup skim milk
- 2 tablespoons reduced-fat cream cheese
- 1 teaspoon garlic powder
- 1 teaspoon paprika
- Salt and freshly ground black pepper to taste
- 2 tablespoons chopped fresh basil leaves (garnish for cold soup)
- 2 tablespoons grated Parmesan cheese (topping for hot soup)

Directions:
1. Preheat the toaster oven to 400° F.
2. Process all the ingredients in a blender or food processor until smooth. Transfer the mixture to a 1-quart 8½ × 8½ × 4-inch ovenproof baking dish.

3. BAKE, covered, for 35 minutes. Ladle into individual soup bowls and serve.

Moussaka

Servings: 6
Cooking Time: 50 Minutes

Ingredients:
- 2 cups eggplant, peeled and cut into 1-inch cubes
- Beef mixture:
- 1 pound very lean ground beef
- 2 tablespoons finely chopped onion
- 3 4 tablespoons tomato paste
- ¼ cup dry red wine
- 2 tablespoons finely chopped fresh parsley
- ¼ teaspoon ground cinnamon
- Salt and freshly ground black pepper to taste
- Cheese mixture:
- 2 eggs, beaten
- 1 tablespoon unbleached flour
- ½ cup fat-free half-and-half
- ¼ teaspoon grated nutmeg
- 1 cup low-fat ricotta cheese
- Bread crumb mixture:
- 1 cup multigrain bread crumbs
- 1 cup freshly grated Parmesan cheese
- Olive oil

Directions:
1. Preheat the toaster oven to 375° F.
2. Dissolve 1 tablespoon salt in 2 cups water. Add the eggplant cubes and let soak for 10 minutes. Rinse well, drain, and pat with paper towel to remove any excess moisture. Set aside.
3. Combine the beef mixture ingredients in a medium bowl and set aside.
4. Whisk together the cheese mixture ingredients in a medium bowl and set aside.
5. Combine the bread crumb mixture in a medium bowl and set aside.
6. Layer half the eggplant cubes in a 1-quart 8½ × 8½ × 4-inch ovenproof baking dish that has been brushed with olive oil.
7. Sprinkle the eggplant with half the bread crumb mixture.

8. Add a layer of half the beef mixture. Repeat the layering process, using up the remaining eggplant, beef, and bread crumb mixtures.
9. Pour the cheese mixture over the top.
10. BAKE, uncovered, for 50 minutes, or until the eggplant is tender and the top is golden.

Roasted Harissa Chicken + Vegetables

Servings: 4
Cooking Time: 30 Minutes

Ingredients:
- Nonstick cooking spray
- 1 medium zucchini, halved lengthwise and sliced crosswise ½ inch thick
- ½ large red onion, sliced ¼ inch thick
- 2 tablespoons olive oil
- Kosher salt and freshly ground black pepper
- 1 pound boneless, skinless chicken breasts, cut into 1-inch cubes
- ½ teaspoon ground cumin
- 1 clove garlic, minced
- 2 tablespoons harissa sauce or paste
- 1 tablespoon honey
- 2 tablespoons minced fresh cilantro
- 2 cups hot cooked rice
- Optional toppings: plain Greek yogurt or sour cream, sesame seeds (toasted or chopped), or dry-roasted peanuts

Directions:
1. Preheat the toaster oven to 400°F. Spray a 12 x 12-inch baking pan with nonstick cooking spray.
2. Place the zucchini and red onion in a medium bowl. Drizzle with 1 tablespoon olive oil and season with salt and pepper. Stir to coat the vegetables evenly. Arrange the vegetables in a single layer in the prepared baking pan. Roast, uncovered, for 10 minutes.
3. Place the chicken cubes in that same bowl. Drizzle with the remaining 1 tablespoon olive oil. Season with the cumin, garlic, salt, and pepper. Stir to coat the chicken evenly.
4. Stir the vegetables and move to one side of the pan. Arrange the chicken in a single layer on the other side of the pan. Roast for 10 minutes.
5. Blend the harissa and honey in a small bowl. Drizzle the sauce over the chicken and vegetables. Using a pastry brush, coat the chicken and vegetables evenly. Roast, uncovered, for an additional 8 to 10 minutes, or until the vegetables are tender and the chicken registers 165°F on a meat thermometer.
6. Spoon the chicken, vegetables, and any collected liquid onto a serving platter. Sprinkle with the cilantro. Serve the chicken and vegetables with the rice and, if desired, a dollop of plain Greek yogurt and a sprinkling of sesame seeds.

Tomato Bisque

Servings: 4
Cooking Time: 25 Minutes

Ingredients:
- 1 8-ounce can tomato sauce
- 1 7-ounce jar diced pimientos, drained
- 1 tablespoon finely chopped onion
- 2 cups low-fat buttermilk
- 1 cup fat-free half-and-half
- 1 tablespoon low-fat cream cheese
- 1 teaspoon garlic powder
- ½ teaspoon paprika
- ½ teaspoon ground bay leaf
- 1 teaspoon hot sauce (optional)
- Salt and white pepper to taste
- 2 tablespoons minced fresh basil leaves

Directions:
1. Preheat the toaster oven to 350° F.
2. Process all the ingredients except the basil in a blender or food processor until smooth. Pour into a 1-quart 8½ × 8½ × 4-inch ovenproof baking dish. Adjust the seasonings to taste.
3. BAKE, covered, for 25 minutes. Ladle into small soup bowls and garnish each with fresh basil leaves before serving.

Meat Lovers Pan Pizza

Servings: 9
Cooking Time: 15 Minutes

Ingredients:
- Dough
- ¾ cup plus 1½ tablespoons warm water, 100°-110°F
- 1¾ teaspoons instant yeast
- 2 cups all-purpose flour, plus more for dusting
- 1 teaspoon kosher salt
- 1 tablespoon extra virgin olive oil, plus more for drizzling
- Toppings
- 6 tablespoons pizza sauce
- 8 ounces shredded low-moisture mozzarella
- Pepperoni slices
- 8 ounces cooked Italian sausage
- Crushed red pepper, for sprinkling
- Dried oregano, for sprinkling
- Black pepper, for sprinkling

Directions:
1. Pour water into a large mixing bowl, then whisk in the yeast. Allow to bloom for 10 minutes.
2. Add the flour and salt and mix with your hands until no dry flour remains.
3. Cover the dough tightly with plastic wrap and allow to rest at room temperature for 15 hours.
4. Add the olive oil and form into a ball.
5. Drizzle extra-virgin olive oil generously on the food tray and use your hands to coat evenly.
6. Place the dough on the food tray and spread it out slightly toward the corners of the pan.
7. Drizzle some more extra-virgin olive oil on top and use your hands to evenly coat the top of the dough.
8. Cover the dough and allow it to rest for 90 minutes.
9. Spread the dough out further so that it covers the bottom of the pan, then pop any bubbles that formed in the dough.
10. Spread pizza sauce on the dough, followed by cheese, then pepperoni and sausage.
11. Sprinkle the pizza with crushed red pepper, dried oregano, and black pepper.
12. Preheat the toaster Oven to 450°F.
13. Insert the pizza at low position in the preheated oven.
14. Select the Pizza function, adjust time to 15 minutes, and press Start/Pause.
15. Remove when done and allow to rest for 5 minutes before cutting.
16. Cut the pizza into squares and serve.

Italian Bread Pizza

Servings: 4
Cooking Time: 30 Minutes

Ingredients:
- 1 loaf Italian or French bread, unsliced
- Filling:
- ½ cup tomato sauce
- 2 tablespoons tomato paste
- 2 tablespoons olive oil
- ½ cup grated zucchini
- ½ cup grated onion
- 2 tablespoons grated bell pepper
- 1 teaspoon garlic powder
- 2 tablespoons chopped pitted black olives
- 1 teaspoon dried oregano or 1 tablespoon chopped fresh oregano
- Salt to taste
- ¼ cup mozzarella cheese

Directions:
1. Preheat the toaster oven to 375° F.
2. Cut the loaf of bread in half lengthwise, then in quarters crosswise. Remove some of the bread from the center to make a cavity for the pizza topping.
3. Combine all the topping ingredients and spoon equal portions into the cavities in the bread. Sprinkle with mozzarella cheese. Place the bread quarters on the toaster oven rack.
4. BAKE for 30 minutes, or until the cheese is melted and the crust is lightly browned.

Light Beef Stroganoff

Servings: 4
Cooking Time: 40 Minutes

Ingredients:
- Sauce:
- 1 cup skim milk
- 1 cup fat-free half-and-half
- 2 tablespoons reduced-fat cream cheese, at room temperature
- 4 tablespoons unbleached flour
- 2 pounds lean round or sirloin steak, cut into strips 2 inches long and ½ inch thick
- Browning mixture:
- 1 tablespoon soy sauce
- 2 tablespoons spicy brown mustard
- 1 tablespoon olive oil
- 2 teaspoons garlic powder
- Salt and freshly ground black pepper to taste

Directions:
1. Whisk together the sauce ingredients in a medium bowl until smooth. Set aside.
2. Combine the beef strips and browning mixture ingredients in an oiled or nonstick 8½ × 8½ × 2-inch square baking (cake) pan.
3. BROIL for 8 minutes, or until the strips are browned, turning with tongs after 4 minutes. Transfer to a 1-quart 8½ × 8½ × 4-inch ovenproof baking dish. Add the sauce and mix well. Adjust the seasonings to taste. Cover with aluminum foil.
4. BAKE, covered, for 40 minutes, or until the meat is tender.

Oven-baked Rice

Servings: 2
Cooking Time: 40 Minutes

Ingredients:
- ¼ cup regular rice (not parboiled or precooked)
- Seasonings:
- 1 tablespoon olive oil
- 1 teaspoon dried parsley or
- 1 tablespoon chopped fresh parsley
- 1 teaspoon garlic powder or roasted garlic
- Salt and freshly ground black pepper to taste

Directions:
1. Preheat the toaster oven to 400° F.
2. Combine ¼ cups water and the rice in a 1-quart 8½ × 8½ × 4-inch ovenproof baking dish. Stir well to blend. Cover with aluminum foil.
3. BAKE, covered, for 30 minutes, or until the rice is almost cooked. Add the seasonings, fluff with a fork to combine the seasonings well, then let the rice sit, covered, for 10 minutes. Fluff once more before serving.

Baked Tomato Casserole

Servings: 4
Cooking Time: 45 Minutes

Ingredients:
- Casserole mixture:
- 1 medium onion, coarsely chopped
- 3 medium tomatoes, coarsely chopped
- 1 medium green pepper, coarsely chopped
- 2 garlic cloves, minced
- ½ teaspoon crushed oregano
- ½ teaspoon crushed basil
- 1 tablespoon extra virgin olive oil
- 2 tablespoons chopped fresh cilantro
- Salt and freshly ground black pepper
- 3 4 tablespoons grated Parmesan cheese
- ¼ cup multigrain bread crumbs

Directions:
1. Preheat the toaster oven to 400° F.
2. Combine the casserole mixture ingredients in a 1-quart 8½ × 8½ × 4-inch ovenproof baking dish. Adjust the seasonings to taste and cover with aluminum foil.
3. BAKE, covered, for 35 minutes, or until the tomatoes and pepper are tender. Remove from the oven, uncover, and sprinkle with the bread crumbs and Parmesan cheese.
4. BROIL for 10 minutes, or until the topping is lightly browned.

Salad Lentils

Servings: 4
Cooking Time: 35 Minutes

Ingredients:
- ¼ cup lentils
- 1 tablespoon olive oil
- Salad ingredients:
- 1 celery stalk, trimmed and Chopped
- 1 plum tomato, chopped
- 1 cucumber, peeled, seeded, and chopped
- 1½ cups spinach leaves, pulled into small pieces
- 1 tablespoon balsamic vinegar
- 1 tablespoon olive oil
- ½ teaspoon dried oregano
- 1 tablespoon chopped scallions
- 2 tablespoons sliced pitted black olives
- 1 teaspoon minced roasted garlic

Directions:
1. Preheat the toaster oven to 400° F.
2. Combine the lentils, ¼ cups water, and olive oil in a 1-quart 8½ × 8½ × 4-inch ovenproof baking dish. Cover with aluminum foil.
3. BAKE, covered, for 35 minutes, or until the lentils are tender. When cool, combine with all the salad ingredients in a serving bowl and toss well. Adjust the seasonings, chill, and serve.

Zucchini Casserole

Servings: 4
Cooking Time: 37 Minutes

Ingredients:
- 4 small zucchini squashes, halved and quartered
- 2 plum tomatoes, quartered
- 1 8-ounce can tomato sauce
- 2 tablespoons chopped onion
- 2 garlic cloves, minced
- 1 tablespoon olive oil
- 1 tablespoon chopped fresh oregano
- 1 tablespoon chopped fresh basil
- 2 tablespoons pine nuts (pignoli)
- Salt and freshly ground black pepper to taste
- ½ cup shredded low-fat mozzarella cheese

Directions:
1. Preheat the toaster oven to 400° F.
2. Combine all the ingredients, except the mozzarella cheese, in a 1-quart 8½ × 8½ × 4-inch ovenproof baking dish. Cover with aluminum foil.
3. BAKE, covered, for 30 minutes, or until the zucchini is tender. Uncover and sprinkle the top with the cheese.
4. BROIL for 7 minutes, or until the cheese is melted and lightly browned.

Dijon Salmon With Green Beans Sheet Pan Supper

Servings: 2-3
Cooking Time: 15 Minutes

Ingredients:
- 3/4 pound salmon fillets, cut in portion-size pieces
- 2 tablespoons olive oil
- 1 tablespoon soy sauce
- 1 tablespoon Dijon mustard
- 2 cloves garlic
- 6 ounces thin green beans, trimmed
- 1/2 small red bell pepper, thinly sliced
- 1/2 small yellow bell pepper, thinly sliced
- 1 small leek, white part only, thinly sliced
- Dash coarse black pepper

Directions:
1. Place rack on bottom position of toaster oven. Preheat the toaster oven to 400°F. Spray the toaster oven baking pan with nonstick cooking spray or line the pan with nonstick aluminum foil. Place salmon skin-side down in center of pan.
2. In a food chopper, process olive oil, soy sauce, mustard and garlic until blended and garlic is chopped. Set aside.
3. In a large bowl, combine green beans, bell peppers and leeks. Add 2 tablespoons olive oil mixture and stir until vegetables are coated. Arrange vegetables evenly in pan around salmon.
4. Drizzle salmon with remaining olive oil mixture.
5. Bake until salmon is done to medium-well and vegetables are crisp-tender, about 15 minutes.

Oven-baked Couscous

Servings: 4
Cooking Time: 10 Minutes

Ingredients:

- 1 10-ounce package couscous
- 2 tablespoons olive oil
- 2 tablespoons canned chickpeas
- 2 tablespoons canned or frozen green peas
- 1 tablespoon chopped fresh parsley
- 3 scallions, chopped
- Salt and pepper to taste

Directions:

1. Preheat the toaster oven to 400° F.
2. Mix together all the ingredients with 2 cups water in a 1-quart 8½ × 8½ × 4-inch ovenproof baking dish. Adjust the seasonings to taste. Cover with aluminum foil.
3. BAKE, covered, for 10 minutes, or until the couscous and vegetables are tender. Adjust the seasonings to taste and fluff with a fork before serving.

Favorite Baked Ziti

Servings: 4
Cooking Time: 30 Minutes

Ingredients:

- 2 tablespoons olive oil
- 1 small onion, diced
- 3 cloves garlic, minced
- ¼ teaspoon red pepper flakes
- 1 pound lean ground beef
- ½ teaspoon kosher salt
- ¼ cup dry red wine
- 1 (14.5-ounce) can crushed tomatoes
- 1 tablespoon tomato paste
- 16 ounces ziti, uncooked
- Nonstick cooking spray
- ⅓ cup grated Parmesan cheese
- 1 ½ cups shredded mozzarella cheese
- 2 ounces fresh mozzarella cheese, cut into cubes (about ½ cup)

Directions:

1. Heat the olive oil in a large skillet over medium-high heat. Add the onion and cook, stirring frequently, until tender, 3 to 4 minutes. Stir in the garlic and red pepper flakes. Add the ground beef and salt. Cook, breaking up the ground beef, until the meat is brown and cooked through. Drain well, if needed, and return to the skillet.
2. Add the wine and cook for 2 minutes. Add the tomatoes, tomato paste, and ¾ cup water. Reduce the heat and simmer, uncovered, for 20 to 25 minutes, stirring occasionally.
3. Cook the ziti according to the package directions, except reduce the cooking time to 7 minutes. The ziti will be harder than Al Dente, which is what you want. Drain and rinse under cold water. Transfer to a large bowl.
4. Preheat the toaster oven to 425 °F. Spray an 11 x 7 x 2 ½-inch baking dish with nonstick cooking spray. Spoon about 1 cup of the meat sauce into the prepared dish. Add half of the ziti in an even layer. Spoon about half of the remaining sauce over the ziti. Sprinkle with half the Parmesan and all the shredded mozzarella. Add the remaining half of ziti and cover with the remaining sauce. Sprinkle the remaining Parmesan on top.
5. Bake, covered, for 20 minutes. Remove from the oven and add the cubes of fresh mozzarella. Bake, uncovered, for an additional 10 minutes. If desired, turn to broil for a few minutes to make the top crispy and brown.
6. Remove from the oven and let stand for 10 minutes before serving.

Rosemary Lentils

Servings: 2
Cooking Time: 35 Minutes

Ingredients:

- ¼ cup lentils
- 1 tablespoon mashed Roasted Garlic
- 1 rosemary sprig
- 1 bay leaf
- Salt and freshly ground black pepper
- 2 tablespoons low-fat buttermilk
- 2 tablespoons tomato sauce

Directions:
1. Preheat the toaster oven to 400° F.
2. Combine the lentils, 1¼ cups water, garlic, rosemary sprig, and bay leaf in a 1-quart 8½ × 8½ × 4-inch ovenproof baking dish, stirring to blend well. Add the salt and pepper to taste. Cover with aluminum foil.
3. BAKE, covered, for 35 minutes, or until the lentils are tender. Remove the rosemary sprig and bay leaf and stir in the buttermilk and tomato sauce. Serve immediately.

Classic Tuna Casserole

Servings: 4
Cooking Time: 65 Minutes

Ingredients:
- 1 cup elbow macaroni
- 2 6-ounce cans tuna packed in water, drained well and crumbled
- 1 cup frozen peas 1 6-ounce can button mushrooms, drained
- 1 tablespoon margarine
- Salt and freshly ground black pepper
- 1 cup fat-free half-and-half
- 4 tablespoons unbleached flour
- 1 teaspoon garlic powder
- 1 cup multigrain bread crumbs

Directions:
1. Preheat the toaster oven to 400° F.
2. Combine the macaroni and 3 cups water in a 1-quart 8½ × 8½ × 4-inch ovenproof baking dish, stirring to blend well. Cover with aluminum foil.
3. BAKE, covered, for 35 minutes, or until the macaroni is tender. Remove from the oven and drain well. Return to the baking dish and add the tuna, peas, and mushrooms. Add salt and pepper to taste.
4. Whisk together the half-and-half, flour, and garlic powder in a small bowl until smooth. Add to the macaroni mixture and stir to blend well.
5. BAKE, covered, for 25 minutes. Remove from the oven, sprinkle the top with the bread crumbs, and dot with the margarine. Bake, uncovered, for 10 minutes, or until the top is browned.

Healthy Southwest Stuffed Peppers

Servings: 6
Cooking Time: 30 Minutes

Ingredients:
- 1 tablespoon oil
- 1 small onion, chopped
- 1 garlic clove, minced
- 1/2 pound ground turkey
- 1/2 cup drained black beans
- 1/2 cup whole kernel corn
- 1 jar (16 oz.) medium salsa, divided
- 1/2 cup cooked white rice
- 1/2 teaspoon chili powder
- 1/2 teaspoon salt
- 1/4 teaspoon ground cumin
- 1/4 teaspoon black pepper
- 3 medium peppers, halved lengthwise leaving stem on, seeded
- 1/3 cup shredded Monterey Jack cheese, divided
- Sour cream
- Chopped fresh cilantro

Directions:
1. Preheat the toaster oven to 350°F. Spray baking pan with nonstick cooking spray.
2. In a large skillet over medium-high, heat oil. Add onion and garlic, cook for 2 to 3 minutes.
3. Add turkey to skillet, cook, stirring frequently, for 6 to 8 minutes or until turkey is cooked through.
4. Stir black beans, corn, 1/2 cup salsa, rice, chili powder, salt, cumin and pepper into turkey mixture.
5. Fill each pepper half with turkey mixture, dividing mixture evenly among peppers.
6. Top each pepper half with remaining salsa.
7. Bake 20 minutes. Sprinkle with cheese and bake an additional 10 minutes or until heated through.
8. Top with sour cream and cilantro.

Light Quiche Lorraine

Servings: 4
Cooking Time: 35 Minutes

Ingredients:
- Crust:
- 1½ cups bread crumbs
- 1 tablespoon olive oil
- Filling:
- 4 eggs
- ½ cup plain nonfat yogurt
- 2 tablespoons finely chopped scallions
- ¼ cup shredded low-fat mozzarella
- 4 strips lean turkey bacon, broiled, blotted with paper towels, and chopped
- Salt and freshly ground black pepper to taste

Directions:
1. Preheat the toaster oven to 350° F.
2. Combine the bread crumbs, 1 tablespoon water, and the oil in a small bowl and transfer to a pie pan, pressing the mixture flat, starting at the center and working out to the sides. Chill for at least 5 minutes in the refrigerator.
3. Combine the filling ingredients and pour into the chilled bread crumb mixture in the pie pan.
4. BAKE for 40 minutes, or until the center is firm and springy to the touch.

Chicken Thighs With Roasted Rosemary Root Vegetables

Servings: 2
Cooking Time: 70 Minutes

Ingredients:
- 2 sprigs fresh rosemary
- 1 small turnip, peeled and cut into 1 1/2-inch cubes
- 1 parsnip, peeled and cut into 1/2-inch slices
- 1 small onion, quartered
- 1 large sweet potato, peeled and cut into 1-inch cubes
- 2 cloves garlic, peeled
- 2 tablespoons olive oil
- 1 teaspoon salt, divided
- 1/2 teaspoon coarse pepper, divided
- 1/2 teaspoon rotisserie chicken seasoning
- 4 chicken thighs with bone and skin

Directions:
1. Place rack on bottom position of toaster oven. Preheat the toaster oven to 425°F.
2. Spray the toaster oven baking pan with nonstick cooking spray. Place rosemary sprigs on pan.
3. In a large bowl, mix turnip. parsnip, onion, sweet potato, garlic, oil, 1/2 teaspoon salt and 1/4 teaspoon pepper until vegetables are coated with oil. Add to baking pan.
4. Bake 30 minutes. Stir vegetables.
5. Sprinkle remaining salt, pepper and rotisserie chicken seasoning over chicken pieces.
6. Place chicken on top of vegetables in pan. Continue baking for an additional 35 to 40 minutes or until chicken reaches 165°F when tested with a meat thermometer and vegetables are roasted.

SNACKS APPETIZERS AND SIDES

Cinnamon Pita Chips

Servings: 4
Cooking Time: 6 Minutes

Ingredients:
- 2 tablespoons sugar
- 2 teaspoons cinnamon
- 2 whole 6-inch pitas, whole grain or white
- oil for misting or cooking spray

Directions:
1. Mix sugar and cinnamon together.
2. Cut each pita in half and each half into 4 wedges. Break apart each wedge at the fold.
3. Mist one side of pita wedges with oil or cooking spray. Sprinkle them all with half of the cinnamon sugar.
4. Turn the wedges over, mist the other side with oil or cooking spray, and sprinkle with the remaining cinnamon sugar.
5. Place pita wedges in air fryer oven and air-fry at 330°F for 2 minutes.
6. Cook 2 more minutes. If needed cook 2 more minutes, until crisp. Watch carefully because at this point they will cook very quickly.

Pork Belly Scallion Yakitori

Servings: 3
Cooking Time: 10 Minutes

Ingredients:
- ¼ cup soy sauce
- 1 tablespoons sake
- 2 tablespoons mirin
- 2 teaspoons rice wine vinegar
- 2 tablespoons dark brown sugar
- ½ teaspoon onion powder
- ¼ teaspoon garlic powder
- ¼ teaspoon kosher salt
- 1½ inch piece of ginger, peeled and roughly sliced
- 1 pound of ½-inch thick sliced pork belly, cut into 2-inch pieces
- 6 scallions
- Lemon wedges, for serving

Directions:
1. Combine soy sauce, sake, mirin, rice wine vinegar, dark brown sugar, onion powder, garlic powder, kosher salt, and ginger in a bowl.
2. Add the pork belly to the marinade and massage the marinade into the meat.
3. Cover and place into the refrigerator for 5 hours.
4. Remove from the fridge and pat the pork belly dry with paper towels. Set aside and allow to sit at room temperature for 1 hour.
5. Cut off the thinner dark green part of the scallion and discard.
6. Cut the trimmed scallions into thirds.
7. Skewer a piece of pork belly, followed by a piece of scallion, then repeat until the skewer is filled. Place the skewers onto the food tray.
8. Preheat the toaster oven to 450°F.
9. Insert the food tray with yakitori at top position in the preheated oven.
10. Select the Broil and Shake functions, then press Start/Pause.
11. Flip the yakitori halfway through cooking. The Shake Reminder will let you know when.
12. Remove when done and serve with a wedge of lemon.

Ham And Cheese Palmiers

Servings: 30
Cooking Time: 60 Minutes

Ingredients:
- 1 (9½ by 9-inch) sheet puff pastry, thawed
- 2 tablespoons Dijon mustard
- 2 teaspoons minced fresh thyme
- 2 ounces Parmesan cheese, grated (1 cup)
- 4 ounces thinly sliced deli ham

Directions:
1. Roll puff pastry into 12-inch square on lightly floured counter. Brush evenly with mustard; sprinkle with thyme and Parmesan; pressing gently to adhere, and lay ham evenly over top. Roll up opposite sides of

pastry until they meet in middle. Wrap pastry log in plastic wrap and refrigerate until firm, about 1 hour.

2. Adjust toaster oven rack to middle position, select air-fry or convection setting, and preheat the toaster oven to 400 degrees. Line large and small rimmed baking sheets with parchment paper. Using sharp knife, trim ends of log, then slice into ⅓-inch-thick pieces. Space desired number of palmiers at least 1 inch apart on prepared small sheet; space remaining palmiers evenly on prepared large sheet. Re-shape palmiers as needed.

3. Bake small sheet of palmiers until golden brown and crisp, 15 to 25 minutes. Transfer palmiers to wire rack and let cool for 15 minutes before serving. (Palmiers can be held at room temperature for up to 6 hours before serving.)

4. Freeze remaining large sheet of palmiers until firm, about 1 hour. Transfer palmiers to 1-gallon zipper-lock bag and freeze for up to 1 month. Cook frozen palmiers as directed; do not thaw.

Thick-crust Pepperoni Pizza

Servings: 2
Cooking Time: 10 Minutes

Ingredients:
- 10 ounces Purchased fresh pizza dough (not a prebaked crust)
- Olive oil spray
- ¼ cup Purchased pizza sauce
- 10 slices Sliced pepperoni
- ⅓ cup Purchased shredded Italian 3- or 4-cheese blend

Directions:
1. Preheat the toaster oven to 400°F.
2. Generously coat the inside of a 6-inch round cake pan for a small air fryer oven, a 7-inch round cake pan for a medium air fryer oven, or an 8-inch round cake pan for a large model with olive oil spray.
3. Set the dough in the pan and press it to fill the bottom in an even, thick layer. Spread the sauce over the dough, then top with the pepperoni and cheese.
4. When the machine is at temperature, set the pan in the air fryer oven and air-fry undisturbed for 10 minutes, or until puffed, brown, and bubbling.

5. Use kitchen tongs to transfer the cake pan to a wire rack. Cool for only a minute or so. Use a spatula to loosen the pizza from the pan and lift it out and onto the rack. Continue cooling for a few minutes before cutting into wedges to serve.

All-purpose Cornbread

Servings: 6
Cooking Time: 60 Minutes

Ingredients:
- 1½ cups (7½ ounces) all-purpose flour
- 1 cup (5 ounces) cornmeal
- 2 teaspoons baking powder
- ¼ teaspoon baking soda
- ¾ teaspoon table salt
- ¼ cup packed (1¾ ounces) light brown sugar
- ¾ cup frozen corn, thawed
- 1 cup buttermilk
- 2 large eggs
- 8 tablespoons unsalted butter, melted and cooled

Directions:
1. Adjust toaster oven rack to middle position and preheat the toaster oven to 400 degrees. Spray 8-inch square baking dish or pan with vegetable oil spray. Whisk flour, cornmeal, baking powder, baking soda, and salt together in medium bowl; set aside.
2. Process sugar, corn, and buttermilk in food processor until combined, about 5 seconds. Add eggs and process until well combined (corn lumps will remain), about 5 seconds.
3. Using rubber spatula, make well in center of dry ingredients; pour wet ingredients into well. Begin folding dry ingredients into wet, giving mixture only a few turns to barely combine. Add melted butter and continue to fold until dry ingredients are just moistened. Transfer batter to prepared dish and smooth top.
4. Bake until deep golden brown and toothpick inserted in center comes out clean, 25 to 35 minutes. Let cornbread cool in dish on wire rack for 10 minutes. Remove bread from dish and let cool until just warm, about 10 minutes longer. Serve. (Cornbread can be wrapped in aluminum foil and reheated in 350-degree oven for 10 to 15 minutes.)

Polenta Fries With Chili-lime Mayo

Servings: 4
Cooking Time: 28 Minutes

Ingredients:
- 2 teaspoons vegetable or olive oil
- ¼ teaspoon paprika
- 1 pound prepared polenta, cut into 3-inch x ½-inch sticks
- salt and freshly ground black pepper
- Chili-Lime Mayo
- ½ cup mayonnaise
- 1 teaspoon chili powder
- ¼ teaspoon ground cumin
- juice of half a lime
- 1 teaspoon chopped fresh cilantro
- salt and freshly ground black pepper

Directions:
1. Preheat the toaster oven to 400°F.
2. Combine the oil and paprika and then carefully toss the polenta sticks in the mixture.
3. Air-fry the polenta fries at 400°F for 15 minutes. Rotate the fries and continue to air-fry for another 13 minutes or until the fries have browned nicely. Season to taste with salt and freshly ground black pepper.
4. To make the chili-lime mayo, combine all the ingredients in a small bowl and stir well.
5. Serve the polenta fries warm with chili-lime mayo on the side for dipping.

Parmesan Crisps

Servings: 6
Cooking Time: 7 Minutes

Ingredients:
- 6 tablespoons shredded Parmesan cheese

Directions:
1. Preheat the toaster oven to 350°F on BAKE for 10 minutes.
2. Line the baking tray with a silicone mat or parchment paper.
3. Place the Parmesan by tablespoons about 2 inches apart on the tray, spreading the cheese out in an even layer about 2½ inches in diameter.
4. Place the try in position 2 and bake for 7 minutes until the edges are browned, and the cheese is no longer bubbling.
5. Remove from the oven and allow to cool on the rack for 10 minutes before serving.

Cherry Chipotle Bbq Chicken Wings

Servings: 2
Cooking Time: 12 Minutes

Ingredients:
- 1 teaspoon smoked paprika
- ½ teaspoon dry mustard powder
- 1 teaspoon dried oregano
- 1 teaspoon dried thyme
- ½ teaspoon chili powder
- 1 teaspoon salt
- 2 pounds chicken wings
- vegetable oil or spray
- salt and freshly ground black pepper
- 1 to 2 tablespoons chopped chipotle peppers in adobo sauce
- ⅓ cup cherry preserves ¼ cup tomato ketchup

Directions:
1. Combine the first six ingredients in a large bowl. Prepare the chicken wings by cutting off the wing tips and discarding (or freezing for chicken stock). Divide the drumettes from the win-gettes by cutting through the joint. Place the chicken wing pieces in the bowl with the spice mix. Toss or shake well to coat.
2. Preheat the toaster oven to 400°F.
3. Spray the wings lightly with the vegetable oil and air-fry the wings in two batches for 10 minutes per batch. When both batches are done, toss all the wings back into the air fryer oven for another 2 minutes to heat through and finish cooking.
4. While the wings are air-frying, combine the chopped chipotle peppers, cherry preserves and ketchup in a bowl.
5. Remove the wings from the air fryer oven, toss them in the cherry chipotle BBQ sauce and serve with napkins!

Root Vegetable Crisps

Servings: 4
Cooking Time: 8 Minutes

Ingredients:
- 1 small taro root, peeled and washed
- 1 small yucca root, peeled and washed
- 1 small purple sweet potato, washed
- 2 cups filtered water
- 2 teaspoons extra-virgin olive oil
- ½ teaspoon salt

Directions:
1. Using a mandolin, slice the taro root, yucca root, and purple sweet potato into ⅛-inch slices.
2. Add the water to a large bowl. Add the sliced vegetables and soak for at least 30 minutes.
3. Preheat the toaster oven to 370°F.
4. Drain the water and pat the vegetables dry with a paper towel or kitchen cloth. Toss the vegetables with the olive oil and sprinkle with salt. Liberally spray the air fryer oven with olive oil mist.
5. Place the vegetables into the air fryer oven, making sure not to overlap the pieces.
6. Air-fry for 8 minutes, stir every 2 minutes, until the outer edges start to turn up and the vegetables start to brown. Remove from the air fryer oven and serve warm. Repeat with the remaining vegetable slices until all are cooked.

Savory Sausage Balls

Servings: 10
Cooking Time: 8 Minutes

Ingredients:
- 2 cups all-purpose flour
- 1 tablespoon baking powder
- ½ teaspoon garlic powder
- ¼ teaspoon onion powder
- ½ teaspoon salt
- 3 tablespoons milk
- 2½ cups grated pepper jack cheese
- 1 pound fresh sausage, casing removed

Directions:
1. Preheat the toaster oven to 370°F.
2. In a large bowl, whisk together the flour, baking powder, garlic powder, onion powder, and salt. Add in the milk, grated cheese, and sausage.
3. Using a tablespoon, scoop out the sausage and roll it between your hands to form a rounded ball. You should end up with approximately 32 balls. Place them in the air fryer oven in a single layer and working in batches as necessary.
4. Air-fry for 8 minutes, or until the outer coating turns light brown.
5. Carefully remove, repeating with the remaining sausage balls.

Middle Eastern Phyllo Rolls

Servings: 6
Cooking Time: 5 Minutes

Ingredients:
- 6 ounces Lean ground beef or ground lamb
- 3 tablespoons Sliced almonds
- 1 tablespoon Chutney (any variety), finely chopped
- ¼ teaspoon Ground cinnamon
- ¼ teaspoon Ground coriander
- ¼ teaspoon Ground cumin
- ¼ teaspoon Ground dried turmeric
- ¼ teaspoon Table salt
- ¼ teaspoon Ground black pepper
- 6 18 × 14-inch phyllo sheets (thawed, if necessary)
- Olive oil spray

Directions:
1. Set a medium skillet over medium heat for a minute or two, then crumble in the ground meat. Air-fry for 3 minutes, stirring often, or until well browned. Stir in the almonds, chutney, cinnamon, coriander, cumin, turmeric, salt, and pepper until well combined. Remove from the heat, scrape the cooked ground meat mixture into a bowl, and cool for 15 minutes.
2. Preheat the toaster oven to 400°F.
3. Place one sheet of phyllo dough on a clean, dry work surface. (Keep the others covered.) Lightly coat it with olive oil spray, then fold it in half by bringing the short ends together. Place about 3 tablespoons of the ground meat mixture along one of the longer edges, then fold both of the shorter sides of the dough up and over the

meat to partially enclose it (and become a border along the sheet of dough). Roll the dough closed, coat it with olive oil spray on all sides, and set it aside seam side down. Repeat this filling and spraying process with the remaining phyllo sheets.

4. Set the rolls seam side down in the air fryer oven in one layer with some air space between them. Air-fry undisturbed for 5 minutes, or until very crisp and golden brown.

5. Use kitchen tongs to transfer the rolls to a wire rack. Cool for only 2 or 3 minutes before serving hot.

Crispy Ravioli Bites

Servings: 5
Cooking Time: 7 Minutes

Ingredients:
- ⅓ cup All-purpose flour
- 1 Large egg(s), well beaten
- ⅔ cup Seasoned Italian-style dried bread crumbs
- 10 ounces (about 20) Frozen mini ravioli, meat or cheese, thawed
- Olive oil spray

Directions:
1. Preheat the toaster oven to 400°F.
2. Pour the flour into a medium bowl. Set up and fill two shallow soup plates or small pie plates on your counter: one with the beaten egg(s) and one with the bread crumbs.
3. Pour all the ravioli into the flour and toss well to coat. Pick up 1 ravioli, gently shake off any excess flour, and dip the ravioli in the egg(s), coating both sides. Let any excess egg slip back into the rest, then set the ravioli in the bread crumbs, turning it several times until lightly and evenly coated on all sides. Set aside on a cutting board and continue on with the remaining ravioli.
4. Lightly coat the ravioli on both sides with olive oil spray, then set them in the air fryer oven in as close to a single layer as you can. Some can lean up against the side of the air fryer oven. Air-fry for 7 minutes, tossing the air fryer oven at the 4-minute mark to rearrange the pieces, until brown and crisp.
5. Pour the contents of the air fryer oven onto a wire rack. Cool for 5 minutes before serving.

Creamy Parmesan Polenta

Servings: 4
Cooking Time: 60 Minutes

Ingredients:
- 2½ cups boiling water, divided, plus extra as needed
- ½ cup coarse-ground cornmeal
- ½ teaspoon table salt
- Pinch baking soda
- 1 ounce Parmesan cheese, grated (½ cup)
- 1 tablespoon unsalted butter

Directions:
1. Adjust toaster oven rack to middle position and preheat the toaster oven to 325 degrees. Combine 2 cups boiling water, cornmeal, salt, and baking soda in greased 8-inch square baking dish or pan. Transfer dish to oven and bake until water is absorbed and polenta is thickened, 35 to 40 minutes, rotating dish halfway through baking.
2. Remove baking dish from oven. Stir in remaining ½ cup boiling water, then stir in Parmesan and butter until polenta is smooth and creamy. Adjust consistency with extra boiling water as needed. Serve.

Pork Pot Stickers With Yum Yum Sauce

Servings: 48
Cooking Time: 8 Minutes

Ingredients:
- 1 pound ground pork
- 2 cups shredded green cabbage
- ¼ cup shredded carrot
- ½ cup finely chopped water chestnuts
- 2 teaspoons minced fresh ginger
- ¼ cup hoisin sauce
- 2 tablespoons soy sauce
- 1 tablespoon sesame oil
- freshly ground black pepper
- 3 scallions, minced
- 48 round dumpling wrappers (or wonton wrappers with the corners cut off to make them round)
- 1 tablespoon vegetable oil
- soy sauce, for serving

- Yum Yum Sauce:
- 1½ cups mayonnaise
- 2 tablespoons sugar
- 3 tablespoons rice vinegar
- 1 teaspoon soy sauce
- 2 tablespoons ketchup
- 1½ teaspoons paprika
- ¼ teaspoon ground cayenne pepper
- ¼ teaspoon garlic powder

Directions:
1. Preheat a large sauté pan over medium-high heat. Add the ground pork and brown for a few minutes. Remove the cooked pork to a bowl using a slotted spoon and discard the fat from the pan. Return the cooked pork to the sauté pan and add the cabbage, carrots and water chestnuts. Sauté for a minute and then add the fresh ginger, hoisin sauce, soy sauce, sesame oil, and freshly ground black pepper. Sauté for a few more minutes, just until cabbage and carrots are soft. Then stir in the scallions and transfer the pork filling to a bowl to cool.
2. Make the pot stickers in batches of 1 Place 12 dumpling wrappers on a flat surface. Brush a little water around the perimeter of the wrappers. Place a rounded teaspoon of the filling into the center of each wrapper. Fold the wrapper over the filling, bringing the edges together to form a half moon, sealing the edges shut. Brush a little more water on the top surface of the sealed edge of the pot sticker. Make pleats in the dough around the sealed edge by pinching the dough and folding the edge over on itself. You should have about 5 to 6 pleats in the dough. Repeat this three times until you have 48 pot stickers. Freeze the pot stickers for 2 hours (or as long as 3 weeks in an airtight container).
3. Preheat the toaster oven to 400°F.
4. Air-fry the pot stickers in batches of 16. Brush or spray the pot stickers with vegetable oil just before putting them in the air fryer oven. Air-fry for 8 minutes, turning the pot stickers once or twice during the cooking process.
5. While the pot stickers are cooking, combine all the ingredients for the Yum Yum sauce in a bowl. Serve the pot stickers warm with the Yum Yum sauce and soy sauce for dipping.

Shrimp Pirogues

Servings: 8
Cooking Time: 5 Minutes

Ingredients:
- 12 ounces small, peeled, and deveined raw shrimp
- 3 ounces cream cheese, room temperature
- 2 tablespoons plain yogurt
- 1 teaspoon lemon juice
- 1 teaspoon dried dill weed, crushed
- salt
- 4 small hothouse cucumbers, each approximately 6 inches long

Directions:
1. Pour 4 tablespoons water in bottom of air fryer oven.
2. Place shrimp in air fryer oven in single layer and air-fry at 390°F for 5 minutes, just until done. Watch carefully because shrimp cooks quickly, and overcooking makes it tough.
3. Chop shrimp into small pieces, no larger than ½ inch. Refrigerate while mixing the remaining ingredients.
4. With a fork, mash and whip the cream cheese until smooth.
5. Stir in the yogurt and beat until smooth. Stir in lemon juice, dill weed, and chopped shrimp.
6. Taste for seasoning. If needed, add ¼ to ½ teaspoon salt to suit your taste.
7. Store in refrigerator until serving time.
8. When ready to serve, wash and dry cucumbers and split them lengthwise. Scoop out the seeds and turn cucumbers upside down on paper towels to drain for 10 minutes.
9. Just before filling, wipe centers of cucumbers dry. Spoon the shrimp mixture into the pirogues and cut in half crosswise. Serve immediately.

Loaded Potato Skins

Servings: 8
Cooking Time: 8 Minutes

Ingredients:
- 12 round baby potatoes
- 3 ounces cream cheese
- 4 slices cooked bacon, crumbled or chopped
- 2 green onions, finely chopped
- ½ cup grated cheddar cheese, divided
- ¼ cup sour cream
- 1 tablespoon milk
- 2 teaspoons hot sauce

Directions:
1. Preheat the toaster oven to 320°F.
2. Poke holes into the baby potatoes with a fork. Place the potatoes onto a microwave-safe plate and microwave on high for 4 to 5 minutes, or until soft to squeeze. Let the potatoes cool until they're safe to handle, about 5 minutes.
3. Meanwhile, in a medium bowl, mix together the cream cheese, bacon, green onions, and ¼ cup of the cheddar cheese; set aside.
4. Slice the baby potatoes in half. Using a spoon, scoop out the pulp, leaving enough pulp on the inside to retain the shape of the potato half. Place the potato pulp into the cream cheese mixture and mash together with a fork. Using a spoon, refill the potato halves with filling.
5. Place the potato halves into the air fryer oven and top with the remaining ¼ cup of cheddar cheese.
6. Cook the loaded baked potato bites in batches for 8 minutes.
7. Meanwhile, make the sour cream sauce. In a small bowl, whisk together the sour cream, milk, and hot sauce. Add more hot sauce if desired.
8. When the potatoes have all finished cooking, place them onto a serving platter and serve with sour cream sauce drizzled over the top or as a dip.

Caramelized Onion Dip

Servings: 2
Cooking Time: 20 Minutes

Ingredients:
- 1 tablespoon unsalted butter
- 1 tablespoon olive oil
- 1 large sweet onion, quartered and very thinly sliced crosswise
- Kosher salt
- 1 clove garlic, minced
- 3 tablespoons dry white wine
- ½ teaspoon dried thyme leaves
- ½ teaspoon freshly ground black pepper
- 1 baguette, thinly sliced
- Nonstick cooking spray
- 1 cup shredded Gruyère or Swiss cheese
- ½ cup sour cream
- ½ cup mayonnaise
- ¼ cup shredded Parmesan cheese
- 3 strips bacon, cooked until crisp and crumbled

Directions:
1. Melt the butter and olive oil in a large skillet over medium heat. Add the onion and season with salt. Cook, stirring frequently, for 3 minutes. Reduce the heat to low and cook, stirring occasionally, for 20 to 25 minutes, or until the onions are a deep golden brown color.
2. Increase the heat to medium. Stir in the garlic, wine, thyme, and pepper. Cook, stirring frequently, for 3 minutes or until the wine has mostly evaporated. Remove from the heat.
3. Meanwhile, toast the baguette slices in the toaster oven until golden brown and crisp; set aside.
4. Preheat the toaster oven to 350°F. Spray a 1-quart casserole with nonstick cooking spray.
5. Stir the Gruyère, sour cream, mayonnaise, Parmesan, and bacon into the onions. Spoon the mixture into the prepared casserole dish. Cover and bake for 20 minutes or until hot and the cheese is melted. Allow to stand for 5 to 10 minutes before serving. To serve, spoon the warm onion-cheese mixture onto the toast.

Turkey Bacon Dates

Servings: 16
Cooking Time: 7 Minutes

Ingredients:
- 16 whole, pitted dates
- 16 whole almonds
- 6 to 8 strips turkey bacon

Directions:
1. Stuff each date with a whole almond.
2. Depending on the size of your stuffed dates, cut bacon strips into halves or thirds. Each strip should be long enough to wrap completely around a date.
3. Wrap each date in a strip of bacon with ends overlapping and secure with toothpicks.
4. Place in air fryer oven and air-fry at 390°F for 7 minutes, until bacon is as crispy as you like.
5. Drain on paper towels or wire rack. Serve hot or at room temperature.

Cinnamon Apple Chips

Servings: 4
Cooking Time: 480 Minutes

Ingredients:
- 1 apple
- 1 tablespoon lemon juice
- ¼ teaspoon cinnamon

Directions:
1. Slice the apple into ⅛-inch-thick slices, preferably by using a mandoline slicer.
2. Place slices in a bowl of water mixed with the lemon juice to prevent browning. Remove after 2 minutes and dry thoroughly with paper towels.
3. Sprinkle the apple slices with cinnamon and place on the food tray.
4. Insert the food tray at mid position in the preheated oven.
5. Preheat the toaster oven to 130°F.
6. Remove when apple chips are crispy.

Sheet Pan Chicken Nachos

Servings: 2
Cooking Time: 20 Minutes

Ingredients:
- Tortilla chips
- 2 cups shredded chicken
- 1 3/4 cup Fresh & Spicy Salsa, divided
- 1 cup drained black beans
- 1 package (2 cups) shredded colby and Monterey Jack cheese, divided
- 1 fresh jalapeno, sliced
- Guacamole

Directions:
1. Heat toaster oven to 350°F. Line a toaster oven pan with aluminum foil and spray foil with nonstick cooking spray.
2. Arrange tortilla chips in an even layer in pan.
3. In a small bowl, combine chicken, 3/4 cup salsa, black beans and 1 cup shredded cheese.
4. Spoon chicken mixture over chips. Top with remaining cheese and jalapeno slices.
5. Bake until cheese is melted and mixture is heated through, 18 to 20 minutes
6. Serve with remaining salsa and guacamole.

Crispy Sweet Potato Fries

Servings: 4
Cooking Time: 18 Minutes

Ingredients:
- 1 tablespoon white vinegar
- A pinch of salt, plus more for sprinkling
- 1 large sweet potato, peeled and sliced into ⅓-inch strips
- 2½ tablespoons cornstarch
- 2 tablespoons cold water
- Avocado oil or olive oil spray (or 1 tablespoon light flavored oil)

Directions:
1. Bring a medium-sized pot of water to a boil. Add the vinegar and a large pinch of salt.
2. Add the sweet potato and boil for 6 minutes. Drain sweet potatoes when done.
3. Whisk the cornstarch and water in a large bowl until smooth. Add the drained sweet potatoes and toss to evenly coat.
4. Preheat the toaster oven to 430°F.

5. Place the sweet potatoes in the fry basket in an even layer, then insert the basket at mid position in the preheated oven.
6. Select the Air Fry and Shake functions, adjust time to 18 minutes, and press Start/Pause.
7. Flip sweet potatoes halfway through cooking. The Shake Reminder will let you know when.
8. Remove when sweet potato fries are crispy and golden, then sprinkle with salt and serve.

Corn Dog Muffins

Servings: 8
Cooking Time: 10 Minutes

Ingredients:
- 1¼ cups sliced kosher hotdogs (3 or 4, depending on size)
- ½ cup flour
- ½ cup yellow cornmeal
- 2 teaspoons baking powder
- ½ cup skim milk
- 1 egg
- 2 tablespoons canola oil
- 8 foil muffin cups, paper liners removed
- cooking spray
- mustard or your favorite dipping sauce

Directions:
1. Slice each hot dog in half lengthwise, then cut in ¼-inch half-moon slices. Set aside.
2. Preheat the toaster oven to 390°F.
3. In a large bowl, stir together flour, cornmeal, and baking powder.
4. In a small bowl, beat together the milk, egg, and oil until just blended.
5. Pour egg mixture into dry ingredients and stir with a spoon to mix well.
6. Stir in sliced hot dogs.
7. Spray the foil cups lightly with cooking spray.
8. Divide mixture evenly into muffin cups.
9. Place 4 muffin cups in the air fryer oven and air-fry for 5 minutes.
10. Reduce temperature to 360°F and cook 5 minutes or until toothpick inserted in center of muffin comes out clean.
11. Repeat steps 9 and 10 to bake remaining corn dog muffins.
12. Serve with mustard or other sauces for dipping.

Crispy Chili Kale Chips

Servings: 4
Cooking Time: 10 Minutes

Ingredients:
- 2 cups kale, stemmed and torn into 2-inch pieces
- 1 tablespoon extra-virgin olive oil
- ½ teaspoon chipotle chili powder
- Sea salt, for seasoning

Directions:
1. Preheat the toaster oven to 350°F on AIR FRY for 5 minutes.
2. Dry the kale with paper towels. Transfer the kale to a medium bowl and add the olive oil and chili powder. Toss the kale using your hands to evenly coat the leaves with the oil.
3. Place the air-fryer basket in the baking sheet and spread the kale in a single layer in the basket. You might have to cook two batches.
4. Air fry in position 2 for 5 minutes, until the leaves are crispy.
5. Transfer the kale chips to a large bowl and repeat with the remaining kale. Season the chips with salt and serve immediately.

Firecracker Bites

Servings: 20
Cooking Time: 15 Minutes

Ingredients:
- 1 sleeve saltine crackers (about 43)
- ¼ cup canola or vegetable oil
- 1 tablespoon dried parsley flakes
- 1 teaspoon dried dill
- 1 teaspoon garlic powder or granulated garlic
- 1 teaspoon onion powder
- ½ teaspoon freshly ground black pepper
- ½ teaspoon seasoned salt
- 2 teaspoons red pepper flakes

Directions:

1. Place the crackers in a zip-top bag.
2. Combine the canola oil, parsley, dill, garlic powder, onion powder, pepper, salt, and red pepper flakes in a small bowl. Pour the oil-seasoning mixture over the crackers and turn the bag over to allow the mixture to permeate all the crackers. Turn the bag frequently for about 15 minutes.
3. Preheat the toaster oven to 250°F.
4. Place the crackers evenly in a 12 x 12-inch baking pan. Bake for 15 minutes. Let the crackers cool completely. These will keep for several weeks in a sealed container.

Buffalo Chicken Dip

Servings: 6
Cooking Time: 60 Minutes

Ingredients:

- 1 pound cream cheese
- ¾ cup Frank's RedHot Original Cayenne Pepper Sauce
- 3 cups shredded cooked chicken
- 1 cup ranch dressing
- 4 ounces blue cheese, crumbled (1 cup)
- 2 teaspoons Worcestershire sauce
- 4 ounces sharp cheddar cheese, shredded (1 cup)
- 2 scallions, sliced thin

Directions:

1. Adjust toaster oven rack to middle position and preheat the toaster oven to 350 degrees. Combine cream cheese and hot sauce in medium bowl and microwave until cream cheese is very soft, about 2 minutes, whisking halfway through microwaving. Whisk until smooth and no lumps of cream cheese remain. Stir in chicken, dressing, blue cheese, and Worcestershire until combined (visible bits of blue cheese are OK).
2. Transfer mixture to 2-quart baking dish and smooth top with rubber spatula. Bake for 20 minutes. Remove dish from toaster oven, stir dip, and sprinkle with cheddar. Return dish to oven and continue to bake until cheddar is melted and dip is bubbling around edges, 15 to 20 minutes longer. Transfer dish to wire rack and let cool for 10 minutes. Sprinkle with scallions and serve.

Hot Mexican Bean Dip

Servings: 8-10
Cooking Time: 15 Minutes

Ingredients:

- 2 cans (15 oz. each) black beans, well-drained
- 8 oz. Monterey Jack cheese or Cheddar cheese, shredded
- 1/2 cup sour cream
- 1/2 cup salsa
- 1 teaspoon hot pepper sauce

Directions:

1. Preheat the toaster oven to 350°F.
2. Place black beans, half of the cheese, sour cream, salsa and hot pepper sauce in food processor bowl. Process until slightly chunky.
3. Spoon into shallow 1-quart casserole dish.
4. Sprinkle remaining cheese on top.
5. Bake 15 minutes or until bubbly.
6. Top with additional cheese, salsa and sour cream, if desired. Serve with tortilla chips.

Blistered Shishito Peppers

Servings: 3
Cooking Time: 5 Minutes

Ingredients:

- 6 ounces (about 18) Shishito peppers
- Vegetable oil spray
- For garnishing Coarse sea or kosher salt and lemon wedges

Directions:

1. Preheat the toaster oven to 400°F.
2. Put the peppers in a bowl and lightly coat them with vegetable oil spray. Toss gently, spray again, and toss until the peppers are glistening but not drenched.
3. Pour the peppers into the pan, spread them into as close to one layer as you can, and air-fry for 5 minutes, tossing and rearranging the peppers at the 2- and 4-minute marks, until the peppers are blistered and even blackened in spots.
4. Pour the peppers into a bowl, add salt to taste, and toss gently. Serve the peppers with lemon wedges to squeeze over them.

Italian Rice Balls

Servings: 8
Cooking Time: 10 Minutes

Ingredients:
- 1½ cups cooked sticky rice
- ½ teaspoon Italian seasoning blend
- ¾ teaspoon salt
- 8 pitted black olives
- 1 ounce mozzarella cheese cut into tiny sticks (small enough to stuff into olives)
- 2 eggs, beaten
- ⅓ cup Italian breadcrumbs
- ¾ cup panko breadcrumbs
- oil for misting or cooking spray

Directions:
1. Preheat the toaster oven to 390°F.
2. Stir together the cooked rice, Italian seasoning, and ½ teaspoon of salt.
3. Stuff each black olive with a piece of mozzarella cheese.
4. Shape the rice into a log and divide into 8 equal pieces. Using slightly damp hands, mold each portion of rice around an olive and shape into a firm ball. Chill in freezer for 10 to 15 minutes or until the outside is cold to the touch.
5. Set up 3 shallow dishes for dipping: beaten eggs in one dish, Italian breadcrumbs in another dish, and in the third dish mix the panko crumbs and remaining salt.
6. Roll each rice ball in breadcrumbs, dip in beaten egg, and then roll in the panko crumbs.
7. Spray all sides with oil.
8. Air-fry for 10 minutes, until outside is light golden brown and crispy.

Spicy Pigs In A Blanket

Servings: 20
Cooking Time: 15 Minutes

Ingredients:
- 6 tablespoons unsalted butter, melted
- 1 teaspoon poppy seeds
- 1 teaspoon dry minced onion
- ½ teaspoon granulated garlic
- ½ teaspoon dry mustard
- ¼ teaspoon red pepper flakes
- 1 (8-ounce) tube refrigerated crescent dough sheets
- 1 (12-ounce) package cocktail smoked sausages

Directions:
1. Combine the butter, poppy seeds, onion, garlic, dry mustard, and red pepper flakes in a small bowl.
2. Lightly flour a clean surface and unroll the crescent roll sheet. Cut the sheet in half down the center, then cut those pieces in half the other way. Continue to make vertical and horizontal cuts until you have 32 strips of dough.
3. Preheat the toaster oven to 375°F.
4. Drain and pat dry the cocktail sausages using paper towels. Wrap each sausage in a strip of dough. Place about half on a 12 x 12-inch baking pan, seam side down.
5. Stir the butter mixture again to distribute all the spices and brush generously over the pastry-wrapped sausages. Bake for 14 to 15 minutes, or until they are golden brown. Repeat with the remaining half of the ingredients. Allow to cool slightly before serving.

Fried Mozzarella Sticks

Servings: 7
Cooking Time: 5 Minutes

Ingredients:
- 7 1-ounce string cheese sticks, unwrapped
- ½ cup All-purpose flour or tapioca flour
- 2 Large egg(s), well beaten
- 2¼ cups Seasoned Italian-style dried bread crumbs (gluten-free, if a concern)
- Olive oil spray

Directions:
1. Unwrap the string cheese and place the pieces in the freezer for 20 minutes (but not longer, or they will be too frozen to soften in the time given in the air fryer oven).
2. Preheat the toaster oven to 400°F.
3. Set up and fill three shallow soup plates or small pie plates on your counter: one for the flour, one for the egg(s), and one for the bread crumbs.
4. Dip a piece of cold string cheese in the flour until well coated (keep the others in the freezer). Gently tap off any excess flour, then set the stick in the egg(s). Roll

it around to coat, let any excess egg mixture slip back into the rest, and set the stick in the bread crumbs. Gently roll it around to coat it evenly, even the ends. Now dip it back in the egg(s), then again in the bread crumbs, rolling it to coat well and evenly. Set the stick aside on a cutting board and coat the remaining pieces of string cheese in the same way.

5. Lightly coat the sticks all over with olive oil spray. Place them in the air fryer oven in one layer and air-fry undisturbed for 5 minutes, or until golden brown and crisp.

6. Remove from the machine and cool for 5 minutes. Use a nonstick-safe spatula to transfer the mozzarella sticks to a serving platter. Serve hot.

Sausage Cheese Pinwheels

Servings: 16
Cooking Time: 22 Minutes

Ingredients:
- 1 sheet frozen puff pastry, about 9 inches square, thawed (½ of a 17.3-ounce package)
- ½ pound bulk sausage
- ¾ cup shredded cheddar cheese

Directions:
1. Preheat the toaster oven to 400°F. Grease a 12 x 12-inch baking pan.
2. Unfold the puff pastry on a lightly floured surface and roll into a 10 x 12-inch rectangle. Carefully spread the sausage over the surface of the rectangle to within ½ inch of all four edges. Sprinkle the cheese evenly over the sausage. Starting with the long side, roll up tightly and press the edges to seal.
3. Using a serrated knife, slice the roll into ½-inch-thick pieces. You will get about 16 slices. Place the slices, cut side up, in the prepared baking pan. Bake for 18 to 22 minutes or until golden and the sausage is cooked through.
4. Serve warm or at room temperature.

Korean "fried" Chicken Wings

Servings: 4
Cooking Time: 25 Minutes

Ingredients:
- Wings Ingredients
- 2 pounds chicken wings
- 1 teaspoon kosher salt
- ½ teaspoon black pepper
- 1½ teaspoons onion powder
- 1½ teaspoons garlic powder
- ¾ teaspoons ground mustard
- 1 teaspoon gochugaru
- 2 tablespoons cornstarch
- 1 tablespoon water
- Cooking spray
- Toasted sesame seeds, for sprinkling
- Sauce Ingredients
- 3 tablespoons Korean gojuchang red pepper paste
- 2 tablespoon white distilled vinegar
- 1 tablespoon hot water
- 2 tablespoons honey
- 1 tablespoon soy sauce

Directions:
1. Combine all the ingredients for the wings except the cooking spray and sesame seeds in a large bowl. Mix well.
2. Preheat the toaster oven to 400°F.
3. Spray both sides of the wings with cooking spray.
4. Place the wings into the fry basket, then insert the basket at mid position in the preheated oven.
5. Select the Air Fry function, adjust time to 25 minutes, then press Start/Pause.
6. Mix together sauce ingredients until well combined, then microwave on high for 30 seconds. Set aside.
7. Remove wings when done, then place the wings and sauce in a large bowl and toss together until the wings are well coated.
8. Sprinkle the wings with toasted sesame seeds and serve.

Dill Fried Pickles With Light Ranch Dip

Servings: 4
Cooking Time: 8 Minutes

Ingredients:
- 4 to 6 large dill pickles, sliced in half or quartered lengthwise
- ½ cup all-purpose flour
- 2 eggs, lightly beaten
- 1 cup plain breadcrumbs
- 1 teaspoon salt
- ⅛ teaspoon cayenne pepper
- 2 tablespoons fresh dill leaves, dried well
- vegetable oil, in a spray bottle
- Light Ranch Dip
- ¼ cup reduced-fat mayonnaise
- ¼ cup buttermilk
- ¼ cup non-fat Greek yogurt
- 1 tablespoon chopped fresh chives
- 1 tablespoon chopped fresh parsley
- 1 tablespoon lemon juice
- salt and freshly ground black pepper

Directions:
1. Dry the dill pickle spears very well with a clean kitchen towel.
2. Set up a dredging station using three shallow dishes. Place the flour in the first shallow dish. Place the eggs into the second dish. Combine the breadcrumbs, salt, cayenne and fresh dill in a food processor and process until everything is combined and the crumbs are very fine. Place the crumb mixture in the third dish.
3. Preheat the toaster oven to 400°F.
4. Coat the pickles by dredging them first in the flour, then the egg, and then the breadcrumbs, pressing the crumbs on gently with your hands. Set the coated pickles on a tray and spray them on all sides with vegetable oil.
5. Air-fry one layer of pickles at a time at 400°F for 8 minutes, turning them over halfway through the cooking process and spraying lightly again if necessary. The crumbs should be nicely browned on all sides.
6. While the pickles are air-frying, make the light ranch dip by mixing everything together in a bowl. Serve the pickles warm with the dip on the side.

Simple Holiday Stuffing

Servings: 4
Cooking Time: 120 Minutes

Ingredients:
- 12 ounces hearty white sandwich bread, cut into ½-inch pieces (8 cups)
- 1 onion, chopped fine
- 1 celery rib, chopped fine
- 1 tablespoon unsalted butter, plus 5 tablespoons, melted
- 1 tablespoon minced fresh thyme or 1 teaspoon dried
- 2 teaspoons minced fresh sage or ½ teaspoon dried
- ¾ teaspoon table salt
- ¼ teaspoon pepper
- 1¼ cups chicken broth

Directions:
1. Adjust toaster oven rack to middle position and preheat the toaster oven to 300 degrees. Spread bread into even layer on small rimmed baking sheet and bake until light golden brown, 35 to 45 minutes, tossing halfway through baking. Let bread cool completely on sheet.
2. Increase oven temperature to 375 degrees. Microwave onion, celery, 1 tablespoon butter, thyme, sage, salt, and pepper in covered large bowl, stirring occasionally, until vegetables are softened, 2 to 4 minutes.
3. Stir in broth, then add bread and toss to combine. Let mixture sit for 10 minutes, then toss mixture again until broth is fully absorbed. Transfer bread mixture to 8-inch square baking dish or pan and distribute evenly but do not pack down. (Stuffing can be covered and refrigerated for up to 24 hours; increase covered baking time to 15 minutes.)
4. Drizzle melted butter evenly over top of stuffing. Cover dish tightly with aluminum foil and bake for 10 minutes. Uncover and continue to bake until top is golden brown and crisp, 15 to 25 minutes. Transfer dish to wire rack and let cool for 10 minutes. Serve.

Sage Butter Roasted Butternut Squash With Pepitas

Servings: 4
Cooking Time: 20 Minutes

Ingredients:
- Nonstick cooking spray
- 1 medium butternut squash, peeled
- 2 tablespoons unsalted butter, melted
- 2 tablespoons minced fresh sage, plus more leaves for garnish (optional)
- 1 teaspoon honey
- ¼ cup shelled pumpkin seeds, or pepitas
- Kosher salt and freshly ground black pepper

Directions:
1. Preheat the toaster oven to 375°F. Spray a 12 x 12-inch baking pan with nonstick cooking spray.
2. Cut the squash crosswise into ¾-inch slices. Use a teaspoon to remove the seeds, as needed, from the center of the slices. Arrange the slices in a single layer on the baking sheet.
3. Stir the butter, sage, honey, and pumpkin seeds in a small bowl. Season with salt and pepper. Spoon the butter mixture over the squash slices, then brush to coat each slice of squash evenly.
4. Roast for 20 minutes or until the squash is tender. Transfer to a serving platter and spoon the seeds and any drippings over the squash. Garnish with extra sage leaves, if desired.

Beet Chips

Servings: 4
Cooking Time: 20 Minutes

Ingredients:
- 2 large red beets, washed and skinned
- 1 tablespoon avocado oil
- ¼ teaspoon salt

Directions:
1. Preheat the toaster oven to 330°F.
2. Using a mandolin or sharp knife, slice the beets in ⅛-inch slices. Place them in a bowl of water and let them soak for 30 minutes. Drain the water and pat the beets dry with a paper towel or kitchen cloth.
3. In a medium bowl, toss the beets with avocado oil and sprinkle them with salt.
4. Lightly spray the air fryer oven with olive oil mist and place the beet chips into the air fryer oven. To allow for even cooking, don't overlap the beets; cook in batches if necessary.
5. Cook the beet chips 15 to 20 minutes, rotate every 5 minutes, until the outer edges of the beets begin to flip up like a chip. Remove from the air fryer oven and serve warm. Repeat with the remaining chips until they're all cooked.

Grilled Ham & Muenster Cheese On Raisin Bread

Servings: 1
Cooking Time: 10 Minutes

Ingredients:
- 2 slices raisin bread
- 2 tablespoons butter, softened
- 2 teaspoons honey mustard
- 3 slices thinly sliced honey ham (about 3 ounces)
- 4 slices Muenster cheese (about 3 ounces)
- 2 toothpicks

Directions:
1. Preheat the toaster oven to 370°F.
2. Spread the softened butter on one side of both slices of raisin bread and place the bread, buttered side down on the counter. Spread the honey mustard on the other side of each slice of bread. Layer 2 slices of cheese, the ham and the remaining 2 slices of cheese on one slice of bread and top with the other slice of bread. Remember to leave the buttered side of the bread on the outside.
3. Transfer the sandwich to the air fryer oven and secure the sandwich with toothpicks.
4. Air-fry at 370°F for 5 minutes. Flip the sandwich over, remove the toothpicks and air-fry for another 5 minutes. Cut the sandwich in half and enjoy!!

Avocado Egg Rolls

Servings: 8
Cooking Time: 8 Minutes

Ingredients:
- 8 full-size egg roll wrappers
- 1 medium avocado, sliced into 8 pieces
- 1 cup cooked black beans, divided
- ½ cup mild salsa, divided
- ½ cup shredded Mexican cheese, divided
- ⅓ cup filtered water, divided
- ½ cup sour cream
- 1 teaspoon chipotle hot sauce

Directions:
1. Preheat the toaster oven to 400°F.
2. Place the egg roll wrapper on a flat surface and place 1 strip of avocado down in the center.
3. Top the avocado with 2 tablespoons of black beans, 1 tablespoon of salsa, and 1 tablespoon of shredded cheese.
4. Place two of your fingers into the water, and then moisten the four outside edges of the egg roll wrapper with water (so the outer edges will secure shut).
5. Fold the bottom corner up, covering the filling. Then secure the sides over the top, remembering to lightly moisten them so they stick. Tightly roll the egg roll up and moisten the final flap of the wrapper and firmly press it into the egg roll to secure it shut.
6. Repeat Steps 2–5 until all 8 egg rolls are complete.
7. When ready to cook, spray the air fryer oven with olive oil spray and place the egg rolls into the air fryer oven. Depending on the size and type of air fryer oven you have, you may need to do this in two sets.
8. Air-fry for 4 minutes, flip, and then cook the remaining 4 minutes.
9. Repeat until all the egg rolls are cooked. Meanwhile, mix the sour cream with the hot sauce to serve as a dipping sauce.
10. Serve warm.

Cuban Sliders

Servings: 8
Cooking Time: 8 Minutes

Ingredients:
- 8 slices ciabatta bread, ¼-inch thick
- cooking spray
- 1 tablespoon brown mustard
- 6–8 ounces thin sliced leftover roast pork
- 4 ounces thin deli turkey
- ⅓ cup bread and butter pickle slices
- 2–3 ounces Pepper Jack cheese slices

Directions:
1. Spray one side of each slice of bread with butter or olive oil cooking spray.
2. Spread brown mustard on other side of each slice.
3. Layer pork roast, turkey, pickles, and cheese on 4 of the slices. Top with remaining slices.
4. Air-fry at 390°F for approximately 8 minutes. The sandwiches should be golden brown.
5. Cut each slider in half to make 8 portions.

Spinach And Artichoke Dip

Servings: 6
Cooking Time: 45 Minutes

Ingredients:
- 6 ounces cream cheese, softened
- ½ cup mayonnaise
- 2 tablespoons water
- 1 tablespoon lemon juice
- 3 garlic cloves, minced
- ¼ teaspoon table salt
- ¼ teaspoon pepper
- 3 cups jarred whole baby artichokes packed in water, rinsed, patted dry, and chopped
- 10 ounces frozen spinach, thawed and squeezed dry
- 2 tablespoons minced fresh chives

Directions:
1. Adjust toaster oven rack to middle position and preheat the toaster oven to 400 degrees. Whisk cream cheese, mayonnaise, water, lemon juice, garlic, salt, and pepper in large bowl until well combined. Gently fold in artichokes and spinach. Transfer mixture to 2-quart baking dish and smooth top with rubber spatula.
2. Bake until spotty golden brown and bubbling around edges, 20 to 25 minutes. Transfer dish to wire rack and let cool for 10 minutes. Sprinkle with chives and serve.

Sweet Or Savory Baked Sweet Potatoes

Servings: 6
Cooking Time: 60 Minutes

Ingredients:
- 6 medium sweet potatoes, scrubbed
- Cinnamon Butter
- Salted Garlic Herb Butter

Directions:
1. Preheat the toaster oven to 450ºF. Line a 15x10-inch baking pan with foil.
2. Prick each sweet potato several times with a fork and place on baking pan.
3. Bake 45 to 1 hour or until fork tender. Serve with Cinnamon Butter or Salted Garlic Herb Butter.

Turkey Burger Sliders

Servings: 8
Cooking Time: 7 Minutes

Ingredients:
- 1 pound ground turkey
- ¼ teaspoon curry powder
- 1 teaspoon Hoisin sauce
- ½ teaspoon salt
- 8 slider buns
- ½ cup slivered red onions
- ½ cup slivered green or red bell pepper
- ½ cup fresh chopped pineapple (or pineapple tidbits from kids' fruit cups, drained)
- light cream cheese, softened

Directions:
1. Combine turkey, curry powder, Hoisin sauce, and salt and mix together well.
2. Shape turkey mixture into 8 small patties.
3. Place patties in air fryer oven and air-fry at 360°F for 7 minutes, until patties are well done and juices run clear.
4. Place each patty on the bottom half of a slider bun and top with onions, peppers, and pineapple. Spread the remaining bun halves with cream cheese to taste, place on top, and serve.

Rosemary-roasted Potatoes

Servings: 4
Cooking Time: 40 Minutes

Ingredients:
- 1 pound russet potatoes, or baby potatoes, cut into 1-inch chunks
- 2 tablespoons olive oil
- 1 teaspoon garlic powder
- 1 teaspoon dried rosemary
- Sea salt, for seasoning
- Freshly ground black pepper, for seasoning

Directions:
1. Preheat the toaster oven on AIR FRY to 400°F for 5 minutes.
2. In a large bowl, toss the potatoes with the oil, garlic powder, and rosemary. Season with salt and pepper.
3. Place the air-fryer basket in the baking tray and spread the potatoes in a single layer in the basket. You may have to do two batches. Cover the first batch loosely with foil to keep it warm while you cook the second batch.
4. In position 2, AIR FRY on 400°F for 20 minutes, shaking the basket at 10 minutes, until the potatoes are tender and golden brown. Repeat with the remaining potatoes and serve.

Stuffed Mushrooms

Servings: 10
Cooking Time: 8 Minutes

Ingredients:
- 8 ounces white mushroom caps, stems removed
- salt
- 6 fresh mozzarella cheese balls
- ground dried thyme
- ¼ roasted red pepper cut into small pieces (about ½ inch)

Directions:
1. Sprinkle inside of mushroom caps with salt to taste.
2. Cut mozzarella balls in half.
3. Stuff each cap with half a mozzarella cheese ball. Sprinkle very lightly with thyme.

4. Top each mushroom with a small strip of roasted red pepper, lightly pressing it into the cheese.
5. Air-fry at 390°F for 8 minutes or longer if you prefer softer mushrooms.

Sweet And Salty Roasted Nuts

Servings: 4
Cooking Time: 20 Minutes

Ingredients:
- 1 large egg white
- 1 tablespoon water
- 3 cups raw mixed nuts (almonds, cashews, hazelnuts, pecan halves, or walnut halves)
- ¼ cup granulated sugar
- ½ teaspoon chili powder
- ¼ teaspoon ground cinnamon
- ⅛ teaspoon cayenne powder

Directions:
1. Preheat the toaster oven to 325°F on AIR FRY for 5 minutes.
2. In a medium bowl, whisk the egg white and the water until frothy.
3. Add the nuts to the bowl and toss to coat.
4. In a small bowl, stir the sugar, chili powder, cinnamon, and cayenne until well mixed. Add the sugar mixture to the nuts and toss to coat them thoroughly.
5. Place the air-fryer basket in the baking tray and spread the nuts out evenly in a single layer. Air fry in position 2 for 20 minutes, shaking the basket after 10 minutes until the nuts are golden brown and dry.
6. Cool the nuts completely on the tray and serve.

Baked Asparagus Fries

Servings: 2-3
Cooking Time: 14 Minutes

Ingredients:
- 1 1/2 cups mayonnaise
- 3/4 cup grated Parmesan cheese
- 2 cloves garlic, minced
- 1 tablespoon dried parsley
- 1 tablespoon Italian seasoning
- 1 teaspoon salt
- 1/2 teaspoon coarse black pepper
- 1/2 pound thick asparagus, trimmed
- 1 cup panko crumbs

Directions:
1. Heat the oven to 425°F.
2. In a small bowl, combine mayonnaise, Parmesan cheese, garlic, parsley, Italian seasoning, salt and black pepper.
3. Brush asparagus with 3 tablespoons mayonnaise mixture and roll in crumbs. Place asparagus on the baking pan.
4. Bake 12 to 14 minutes or until lightly browned and asparagus are cooked.
5. Serve asparagus with the remaining mayonnaise mixture.

Loaded Cauliflower Casserole

Servings: 6
Cooking Time: 35 Minutes

Ingredients:
- Nonstick cooking spray
- 1 cup heavy cream
- 4 tablespoons unsalted butter
- 3 cloves garlic, minced
- 1 teaspoon fresh thyme leaves
- ¾ teaspoon kosher salt
- ¼ teaspoon freshly ground black pepper
- 6 cups cauliflower florets (a medium head)
- ½ cup finely chopped sweet or yellow onion
- 2 cups shredded white cheddar cheese
- 1 ½ cups fresh coarse bread crumbs
- 2 tablespoons sesame seeds
- 3 tablespoons unsalted butter, melted

Directions:
1. Preheat the toaster oven to 425 °F. Spray a 9-inch deep-dish pie plate or 9-inch cake pan with nonstick cooking spray.
2. Bring the cream, butter, garlic, thyme, salt, and pepper to a simmer in a small saucepan over medium heat. Remove from the heat.
3. Place half of the cauliflower into the prepared pan. Sprinkle with half of the onion and half of the cheese. Repeat with the remaining cauliflower, onion, and cheese. Pour the cream mixture over all. Cover and bake

until the cauliflower is tender and cooked through, about 20 minutes.

4. Remove the foil and bake for an additional 15 minutes, or until the top is bubbly and beginning to turn golden.

5. Combine the bread crumbs, sesame seeds, and melted butter in a small bowl. Sprinkle over the top and bake for an additional 15 minutes or until golden.

Cauliflower "tater" Tots

Servings: 6
Cooking Time: 10 Minutes

Ingredients:
- 1 head of cauliflower
- 2 eggs
- ¼ cup all-purpose flour
- ½ cup grated Parmesan cheese
- 1 teaspoon salt
- freshly ground black pepper
- vegetable or olive oil, in a spray bottle

Directions:
1. Grate the head of cauliflower with a box grater or finely chop it in a food processor. You should have about 3½ cups. Place the chopped cauliflower in the center of a clean kitchen towel and twist the towel tightly to squeeze all the water out of the cauliflower. (This can be done in two batches to make it easier to drain all the water from the cauliflower.)

2. Place the squeezed cauliflower in a large bowl. Add the eggs, flour, Parmesan cheese, salt and freshly ground black pepper. Shape the cauliflower into small cylinders or "tater tot" shapes, rolling roughly one tablespoon of the mixture at a time. Place the tots on a cookie sheet lined with paper towel to absorb any residual moisture. Spray the cauliflower tots all over with oil.

3. Preheat the toaster oven to 400°F.

4. Air-fry the tots at 400°F, one layer at a time for 10 minutes, turning them over for the last few minutes of the cooking process for even browning. Season with salt and black pepper. Serve hot with your favorite dipping sauce.

Fried Wontons

Servings: 24
Cooking Time: 6 Minutes

Ingredients:
- 6 ounces Lean ground beef, pork, or turkey
- 1 tablespoon Regular or reduced-sodium soy sauce or tamari sauce
- 1½ teaspoons Minced garlic
- ¾ teaspoon Ground dried ginger
- ½ teaspoon Ground white pepper
- 24 Wonton wrappers (thawed, if necessary)
- Vegetable oil spray

Directions:
1. Preheat the toaster oven to 350°F.

2. Stir the ground meat, soy or tamari sauce, garlic, ginger, and white pepper in a bowl until the spices are uniformly distributed in the mixture.

3. Set a small bowl of water on a clean, dry surface or next to a clean, dry cutting board. Set one wonton wrapper on the surface. Dip your clean finger in the water, then run it along the edges of the wrapper. Set 1 teaspoon of the ground meat mixture in the center of the wrapper. Fold it over, corner to corner, to create a filled triangle. Press to seal the edges, then pull the corners on the longest side up and together over the filling to create the classic wonton shape. Press the corners together to seal. Set aside and continue filling and making more filled wontons.

4. Generously coat the filled wontons on all sides with vegetable oil spray. Arrange them in the air fryer oven in one layer and air-fry for 6 minutes, at the 2- and 4- minute marks to rearrange the wontons (but always making sure they're still in one layer), until golden brown and crisp.

5. Pour the wontons in the pan onto a wire rack or even into a serving bowl. Cool for 2 or 3 minutes (but not much longer) and serve hot.

Eggs In Avocado Halves

Servings: 3
Cooking Time: 23 Minutes

Ingredients:
- 3 Hass avocados, halved and pitted but not peeled
- 6 Medium eggs
- Vegetable oil spray
- 3 tablespoons Heavy or light cream (not fat-free cream)
- To taste Table salt
- To taste Ground black pepper

Directions:
1. Preheat the toaster oven to 350°F.
2. Slice a small amount off the (skin) side of each avocado half so it can sit stable, without rocking. Lightly coat the skin of the avocado half (the side that will now sit stable) with vegetable oil spray.
3. Arrange the avocado halves open side up on a cutting board, then crack an egg into the indentation in each where the pit had been. If any white overflows the avocado half, wipe that bit of white off the cut edge of the avocado before proceeding.
4. Remove the pan (or its attachment) from the machine and set the filled avocado halves in it in one layer. Return it to the machine without pushing it in. Drizzle each avocado half with about 1½ teaspoons cream, a little salt, and a little ground black pepper.
5. Air-fry undisturbed for 10 minutes for a soft-set yolk, or air-fry for 13 minutes for more-set eggs.
6. Use a nonstick-safe spatula and a flatware fork for balance to transfer the avocado halves to serving plates. Cool a minute or two before serving.

Parmesan Peas

Servings: 3
Cooking Time: 15 Minutes

Ingredients:
- 3 tablespoons olive oil
- 1 clove garlic, minced
- 1 1/2 cups frozen peas, thawed and drained
- 1/2 cup shredded Parmesan cheese
- 1/2 teaspoon coarse pepper

Directions:
1. Heat the toaster oven to 350°F.
2. In toaster oven baking pan, add oil and garlic.
3. Bake for 5 minutes or until garlic is lightly browned.
4. Add peas to the pan.
5. Bake an additional 8 to 10 minutes or until peas are heated.
6. Sprinkle with cheese and pepper before serving.

Bagel Chips

Servings: 2
Cooking Time: 4 Minutes

Ingredients:
- Sweet
- 1 large plain bagel
- 2 teaspoons sugar
- 1 teaspoon ground cinnamon
- butter-flavored cooking spray
- Savory
- 1 large plain bagel
- 1 teaspoon Italian seasoning
- ½ teaspoon garlic powder
- oil for misting or cooking spray

Directions:
1. Preheat the toaster oven to 390°F.
2. Cut bagel into ¼-inch slices or thinner.
3. Mix the seasonings together.
4. Spread out the slices, mist with oil or cooking spray, and sprinkle with half of the seasonings.
5. Turn over and repeat to coat the other side with oil or cooking spray and seasonings.
6. Place in air fryer oven and air-fry for 2 minutes. Stir a little and continue cooking for 2 minutes or until toasty brown and crispy.

Skinny Fries

Servings: 2
Cooking Time: 15 Minutes

Ingredients:
- 2 to 3 russet potatoes, peeled and cut into ¼-inch sticks
- 2 to 3 teaspoons olive or vegetable oil
- salt

Directions:
1. Cut the potatoes into ¼-inch strips. (A mandolin with a julienne blade is really helpful here.) Rinse the potatoes with cold water several times and let them soak in cold water for at least 10 minutes or as long as overnight.
2. Preheat the toaster oven to 380°F.
3. Drain and dry the potato sticks really well, using a clean kitchen towel. Toss the fries with the oil in a bowl and then air-fry the fries in two batches at 380°F for 15 minutes.
4. Add the first batch of French fries back into the air fryer oven with the finishing batch and let everything warm through for a few minutes. As soon as the fries are done, season them with salt and transfer to a plate. Serve them warm with ketchup or your favorite dip.

Smoked Salmon Puffs

Servings: 2
Cooking Time: 8 Minutes

Ingredients:
- Two quarters of one thawed sheet (that is, a half of the sheet; wrap and refreeze the remainder) A 17.25-ounce box frozen puff pastry
- 4 ½-ounce smoked salmon slices
- 2 tablespoons Softened regular or low-fat cream cheese (not fat-free)
- Up to 2 teaspoons Drained and rinsed capers, minced
- Up to 2 teaspoons Minced red onion
- 1 Large egg white
- 1 tablespoon Water

Directions:
1. Preheat the toaster oven to 400°F.
2. For a small air fryer oven, roll the piece of puff pastry into a 6 x 6-inch square on a clean, dry work surface.
3. For a medium or larger air fryer oven, roll each piece of puff pastry into a 6 x 6-inch square.
4. Set 2 salmon slices on the diagonal, corner to corner, on each rolled-out sheet. Smear the salmon with cream cheese, then sprinkle with capers and red onion. Fold the sheet closed by picking up one corner that does not have an edge of salmon near it and folding the dough across the salmon to its opposite corner. Seal the edges closed by pressing the tines of a flatware fork into them.
5. Whisk the egg white and water in a small bowl until uniform. Brush this mixture over the top(s) of the packet(s).
6. Set the packet(s) in the air fryer oven (if you're working with more than one, they cannot touch). Air-fry undisturbed for 8 minutes, or until golden brown and flaky.
7. Use a nonstick-safe spatula to transfer the packet(s) to a wire rack. Cool for 5 minutes before serving.

Homemade Harissa

Servings: 20
Cooking Time: 20 Minutes

Ingredients:
- 2 red bell peppers, halved, cored, and seeded
- 1 teaspoon cumin seeds
- 1 teaspoon coriander seeds
- 4 tablespoons olive oil
- 1 cup onions, chopped
- 5 garlic cloves, minced
- 1 serrano chile, chopped (remove seeds to make less spicy)
- 1 lemon, juiced
- ½ teaspoon salt

Directions:
1. Select the Preheat function on the Cosori Smart Air Fryer Toaster Oven, adjust temperature to 450°F, and press Start/Pause.
2. Line the food tray with foil and place the bell pepper halves on the tray.
3. Insert the food tray at mid position in the preheated oven.
4. Select the Roast function, adjust time to 20 minutes, and press Start/Pause.
5. Remove when bell peppers are charred. Immediately place bell peppers into a bowl and cover tightly with plastic wrap. Allow peppers to steam for 15 minutes. Remove plastic wrap, peel the skin off the peppers, and place into a food processor.

6. Place cumin and coriander seeds in a dry skillet. Toast over medium heat for 4-5 minutes or until fragrant.
7. Place seeds into a mortar and pestle or spice grinder and grind to a powder. Place into the food processor.
8. Heat olive oil in a pan over medium heat. Add the onion and garlic and saute for 10 minutes or until they begin to soften and caramelize. Place into the food processor.
9. Place the remaining ingredients into the food processor and blend until smooth. Taste and add additional lemon juice, salt, or olive oil if needed.
10. Store harissa in a sealed jar for up to 2 weeks.

Wonton Cups

Servings: 6
Cooking Time: 10 Minutes

Ingredients:
- 6 wonton wrappers (3-inch squares)
- 2 Tablespoons melted butter
- Filling of choice

Directions:
1. Preheat toaster oven to 350°F.
2. Carefully press and fold one wonton wrapper in each cup of a 6-cup muffin pan.
3. Very lightly brush edges of wrappers with butter.
4. Bake 8 to 10 minutes or until golden brown.

Potato Chips

Servings: 2
Cooking Time: 15 Minutes

Ingredients:
- 2 medium potatoes
- 2 teaspoons extra-light olive oil
- oil for misting or cooking spray
- salt and pepper

Directions:
1. Peel the potatoes.
2. Using a mandoline or paring knife, shave potatoes into thin slices, dropping them into a bowl of water as you cut them.
3. Dry potatoes as thoroughly as possible with paper towels or a clean dish towel. Toss potato slices with the oil to coat completely.
4. Spray air fryer oven with cooking spray and add potato slices.
5. Stir and separate with a fork.
6. Cook 390°F for 5 minutes. Stir and separate potato slices. Cook 5 more minutes. Stir and separate potatoes again. Cook another 5 minutes.
7. Season to taste.

Bacon Bites

Servings: 6
Cooking Time: 20 Minutes

Ingredients:
- ½ cup packed dark brown sugar
- 6 slices bacon
- 6 very thin breadsticks from a 3-ounce package

Directions:
1. Preheat the toaster oven to 350°F. Line a 12 x 12-inch baking pan with aluminum foil.
2. Spread the brown sugar on a large plate. Wrap a bacon slice around each breadstick. Roll the bacon-wrapped breadstick in the brown sugar and press to adhere to the bacon. Place on the prepared pan.
3. Bake for 18 to 20 minutes, or until the bacon is cooked through. Immediately remove and place the warm sticks on wax paper (to prevent sticking). Let cool to room temperature before serving.

Beef Satay With Peanut Dipping Sauce

Servings: 4
Cooking Time: 60 Minutes

Ingredients:
- SKEWERS
- 1 pound flank steak, trimmed
- 2 tablespoons soy sauce
- 2 tablespoons vegetable oil
- 2 tablespoons packed dark brown sugar
- 2 tablespoons minced fresh cilantro
- 2 scallions, sliced thin

- 1½ tablespoons ketchup
- 1 garlic clove, minced
- ½ teaspoon sriracha
- SPICY PEANUT DIPPING SAUCE
- ¼ cup peanut butter (creamy or chunky)
- 2 tablespoons hot water, plus extra as needed
- 1½ tablespoons lime juice
- 1 scallion, sliced thin
- 1 tablespoon ketchup
- 1½ teaspoons soy sauce
- 1½ teaspoons packed dark brown sugar
- 1½ teaspoons minced fresh cilantro
- ¾ teaspoon sriracha
- 1 garlic clove, minced

Directions:

1. FOR THE SKEWERS: Slice beef against grain ¼ inch thick (you should have at least 20 slices).
2. Combine soy sauce, oil, sugar, cilantro, scallions, ketchup, garlic, and sriracha in medium bowl; add beef; and toss to combine. Cover and refrigerate for 15 minutes. Weave 1 beef slice evenly onto each skewer, leaving at least 1 inch at bottom of skewer exposed (Skewers can be refrigerated for up to 24 hours.)
3. FOR THE SPICY PEANUT DIPPING SAUCE: Whisk peanut butter and hot water together in medium bowl. Stir in lime juice, scallion, ketchup, soy sauce, sugar, cilantro, sriracha, and garlic. Adjust consistency with extra hot water as needed; set aside for serving.
4. Adjust toaster oven rack to middle position, select broiler function, and heat broiler. Set small wire rack in aluminum foil–lined small rimmed baking sheet and spray rack with vegetable oil spray. Arrange skewers in two rows across width of prepared rack with all exposed skewer ends facing center of rack. Cover skewer ends in center of sheet with strip of foil and secure by crimping tightly at edges. Broil skewers until beef is no longer pink on top, 2 to 3 minutes. Flip skewers and continue to broil until beef is fully cooked and spotty brown, 4 to 6 minutes. Serve with peanut sauce.

Mozzarella-stuffed Arancini

Servings: 14
Cooking Time: 20 Minutes

Ingredients:
- Pie Crust
- 3½ cups low sodium chicken stock
- 4 tablespoons unsalted butter, divided
- 1 medium onion, finely chopped
- 2 garlic cloves, minced
- 1 cup arborio rice
- 1½ teaspoons kosher salt, plus more to taste
- ½ cup dry white wine
- 2 ounces finely grated Parmesan
- ¼ cup heavy cream
- 1 teaspoon freshly ground black pepper, plus more to taste
- 3 ounces low-moisture mozzarella, cut into ⅓-inch pieces
- 1½ cups panko breadcrumbs
- 2 tablespoons melted salted butter
- ½ cup all-purpose flour 2 large eggs, beaten Cooking spray
- Marinara sauce, for serving

Directions:

1. Simmer chicken stock in a pot, then keep warm on low heat.
2. Heat 2 tablespoons of unsalted butter in a medium saucepan over medium heat.
3. Add onions to the saucepan and cook for 5 minutes or until softened.
4. Add garlic and cook for 1 minute or until softened.
5. Add rice and 1½ teaspoons of kosher salt to the saucepan.
6. Cook the rice for 3 minutes or until the edges turn translucent.
7. Pour in the wine, stir, and cook for 3 minutes or until the wine is all evaporated and the rice looks dry.
8. Ladle in 1 cup of the warm chicken stock and bring to a simmer. Stirring often, cook the rice for 5 minutes or until liquid is absorbed. Repeat this process with another cup of chicken stock.
9. Add the remaining 1½ cups of chicken stock and cook, stirring often, for 10 minutes or until the rice is cooked through but toothsome and the liquid is mostly absorbed.

10. Remove the risotto from the heat and mix in Parmesan, heavy cream, black pepper, and the remaining two tablespoons of unsalted butter.
11. Season the risotto to taste with salt and black pepper.
12. Spread risotto in an even layer on a parchment-lined baking sheet and cover with plastic wrap.
13. Place the risotto in the fridge and chill for 4 hours.
14. Seperate the chilled risotto into 14 even pieces and form them into round patties about 2½ inches in diameter.
15. Place a piece of mozzarella in the center of a patty, pinch and shape the risotto so it completely encases the cheese, then roll into a ball. Repeat with each risotto patty.
16. Place the balls onto the baking sheet lined with fresh parchment paper, cover with plastic wrap, and place in the freezer for 15 minutes.
17. Place the panko breadcrumbs into a food processor and pulse until finely ground, then place into a bowl.
18. Mix the panko breadcrumbs with the melted salted butter until well combined.
19. Remove the risotto balls from the freezer and dredge in flour, dip in beaten eggs, then cover with breadcrumbs. Repeat this process with the rest of the balls. Set aside.
20. Preheat the toaster oven to 400°F.
21. Place the balls into the fry basket, spray them liberally with cooking spray, then insert the basket at mid position in the preheated oven.
22. Select the Air Fry function, adjust time to 20 minutes, and press Start/Pause.
23. Remove the arancini from the oven and serve with marinara sauce.

Panko-breaded Onion Rings

Servings: 4
Cooking Time: 12 Minutes

Ingredients:

- 1 large sweet onion, cut into ½-inch slices and rings separated
- 2 cups ice water
- ½ cup all-purpose flour
- 1 teaspoon paprika
- 1 teaspoon salt
- ½ teaspoon black pepper
- ½ teaspoon garlic powder
- ¼ teaspoon onion powder
- 1 egg, whisked
- 2 tablespoons milk
- 1 cup breadcrumbs

Directions:

1. Preheat the toaster oven to 400°F.
2. In a large bowl, soak the onion rings in the water for 5 minutes. Drain and pat dry with a towel.
3. In a medium bowl, place the flour, paprika, salt, pepper, garlic powder, and onion powder.
4. In a second bowl, whisk together the egg and milk.
5. In a third bowl, place the breadcrumbs.
6. To bread the onion rings, dip them first into the flour mixture, then into the egg mixture (shaking off the excess), and then into the breadcrumbs. Place the coated onion rings onto a plate while you bread all the rings.
7. Place the onion rings into the air fryer oven in a single layer, sometimes nesting smaller rings into larger rings. Spray with cooking spray. Air-fry for 3 minutes, turn the rings over, and spray with more cooking spray. Air-fry for another 3 to 5 minutes. Cook the rings in batches; you may need to do 2 or 3 batches, depending on the size of your air fryer oven.

Smoked Gouda Bacon Macaroni And Cheese

Servings: 10-12
Cooking Time: 30 Minutes

Ingredients:

- 1 (4 oz.) French baguette, torn
- 6 slices cooked bacon, chopped
- 1/4 cup loosely packed parsley
- 2 Tablespoons butter, melted
- 1 package (16 oz.) corkscrew or elbow pasta
- 1/3 cup butter
- 1/4 cup flour
- 4 cups milk
- 1 package (8 oz.) extra sharp Cheddar cheese, shredded
- 1 package (8 oz.) smoked Gouda cheese, shredded

- 2 1/2 teaspoons Creole seasoning

Directions:
1. Preheat the toaster oven to 400°F.
2. Using S-blade with food processor running, drop bread, 1/2 of the bacon and parsley into food chute. Process until finely chopped. Gradually add melted butter; process until crumbs form. Set aside.
3. Cook pasta according to package directions for al dente. Drain and rinse with cold water. Set aside.
4. Melt 1/3 cup butter in Dutch oven over medium-high heat. Gradually add flour, whisking until smooth, about 1 minute. Slowly add milk, stirring 8 to 10 minutes until mixture is thickened and smooth. Remove from heat.
5. Stir in cheeses, remaining bacon and Creole seasoning until cheese is melted. Fold in pasta.
6. Pour mixture into 11x7-inch baking dish sprayed with nonstick cooking spray. Sprinkle with breadcrumb mixture.
7. Bake 25 to 30 minutes or until crumbs are browned and mixture is heated through.

Buffalo Cauliflower

Servings: 4
Cooking Time: 30 Minutes

Ingredients:
- 1 cup gluten free panko breadcrumbs
- 1 teaspoon ground paprika
- ½ teaspoon garlic powder
- ¼ teaspoon onion powder
- ½ teaspoon cayenne pepper
- 1 teaspoon kosher salt
- ½ teaspoon freshly ground black pepper
- 1 head cauliflower, cut into florets
- 2 tablespoons cornstarch
- 3 eggs, beaten
- Cooking spray
- ¾ cup buffalo wing sauce, warm
- Ranch or bleu cheese dressing, for serving

Directions:
1. Combine panko breadcrumbs, paprika, garlic powder, onion powder, cayenne pepper, kosher salt, and black pepper in a large bowl. Set aside.
2. Toss together cauliflower and cornstarch until the cauliflower is lightly coated.
3. Shake any excess cornstarch off the cauliflower, then dip into beaten eggs, then into seasoned breadcrumbs.
4. Spray the breaded cauliflower with cooking spray, place into the fry basket, and set aside. You may need to work in batches.
5. Preheat the toaster oven to 380°F.
6. Insert the fry basket with the cauliflower at top position in the preheated oven.
7. Select the Air Fry and Shake functions, adjust time to 30 minutes, and press Start/Pause.
8. Flip the cauliflower halfway through cooking. The Shake Reminder will let you know when.
9. Remove when done and place into a large bowl.
10. Toss the cauliflower in the buffalo wing sauce until they are well coated.
11. Serve with a side of ranch or blue cheese dressing.

Barbecue Chicken Nachos

Servings: 3
Cooking Time: 5 Minutes

Ingredients:
- 3 heaping cups (a little more than 3 ounces) Corn tortilla chips (gluten-free, if a concern)
- ¾ cup Shredded deboned and skinned rotisserie chicken meat (gluten-free, if a concern)
- 3 tablespoons Canned black beans, drained and rinsed
- 9 rings Pickled jalapeño slices
- 4 Small pickled cocktail onions, halved
- 3 tablespoons Barbecue sauce (any sort)
- ¾ cup (about 3 ounces) Shredded Cheddar cheese

Directions:
1. Preheat the toaster oven to 400°F.
2. Cut a circle of parchment paper to line a 6-inch round cake pan for a small air fryer oven, a 7-inch round cake pan for a medium air fryer oven, or an 8-inch round cake pan for a large machine.
3. Fill the pan with an even layer of about two-thirds of the chips. Sprinkle the chicken evenly over the chips.

Set the pan in the air fryer oven and air-fry undisturbed for 2 minutes.

4. Remove the pan from the machine. Scatter the beans, jalapeño rings, and pickled onion halves over the chicken. Drizzle the barbecue sauce over everything, then sprinkle the cheese on top.

5. Return the pan to the machine and air-fry undisturbed for 3 minutes, or until the cheese has melted and is bubbly. Remove the pan from the machine and cool for a couple of minutes before serving.

Classic Cornbread

Servings: 4
Cooking Time: 25 Minutes

Ingredients:
- Oil spray (hand-pumped)
- ¾ cup all-purpose flour
- ¾ cup yellow cornmeal
- ¼ cup granulated sugar
- 2 teaspoons baking powder
- ½ teaspoon sea salt
- ¾ cup buttermilk
- ¼ cup salted butter, melted
- 1 large egg

Directions:
1. Place the rack on position 1 and preheat the toaster oven on BAKE to 400°F for 5 minutes.
2. Lightly oil a 7-inch-round cake pan with the oil spray and set aside.
3. In a medium bowl, stir the flour, cornmeal, sugar, baking powder, and salt until well blended.
4. Make a well in the center and add the buttermilk, melted butter, and egg. Stir until just combined.
5. Spoon the batter into the cake pan and bake for 25 minutes until the cornbread is golden brown and a knife inserted in the center comes out clean. If not ready at 25 minutes, increase the time by 5-minute intervals until baked through. Serve.

Beef Empanadas

Servings: 8
Cooking Time: 75 Minutes

Ingredients:
- 8 ounces 93 percent lean ground beef
- 3 garlic cloves, minced
- 2 teaspoons chili powder
- 1 teaspoon ground cumin
- 1 teaspoon minced fresh oregano or ¼ teaspoon dried
- 4 ounces Monterey Jack cheese, shredded (1 cup)
- 1 cup mild tomato salsa, drained
- 2 tablespoons chopped fresh cilantro
- 1 package store-bought pie dough
- 1 large egg, lightly beaten

Directions:
1. Microwave beef, garlic, chili powder, cumin, and oregano in bowl, stirring occasionally and breaking up meat with wooden spoon, until beef is no longer pink, about 3 minutes. Transfer beef mixture to fine-mesh strainer set over large bowl and let drain for 10 minutes; discard juices. Return drained beef mixture to now-empty bowl and stir in Monterey Jack, salsa, and cilantro.
2. Adjust toaster oven rack to middle position, select air-fry or convection setting, and preheat the toaster oven to 350 degrees. Line large and small rimmed baking sheets with parchment paper. Roll 1 dough round into 12-inch circle on lightly floured counter. Using 5-inch round biscuit cutter, stamp out 4 rounds; discard dough scraps. Repeat with remaining dough round. Mound beef mixture evenly in center of each stamped round. Fold dough over filling and crimp edges together with fork to seal.
3. Space desired number of empanadas at least 1 inch apart on prepared small sheet; space remaining empanadas evenly on prepared large sheet. Brush all empanadas with egg.
4. Cook small sheet of empanadas until golden brown and crisp, 15 to 25 minutes. Transfer empanadas to wire rack and let cool for 15 minutes before serving.
5. Freeze remaining large sheet of empanadas until firm, about 1 hour. Transfer empanadas to 1-gallon zipper-lock bag and freeze for up to 1 month. Cook frozen empanadas as directed; do not thaw.

Crispy Spiced Chickpeas

Servings: 4
Cooking Time: 12 Minutes

Ingredients:
- 1 (15 ounce) can chickpeas, drained, rinsed, and patted dry
- 1 tablespoon olive oil
- ½ teaspoon cumin
- ¼ teaspoon paprika
- ½ teaspoon ground fennel seeds
- ⅛ teaspoon cayenne pepper

Directions:
1. Combine all ingredients in a large bowl and stir to combine.
2. Preheat the toaster oven to 430°F.
3. Place chickpeas on the food tray, then insert the tray at mid position in the preheated oven.
4. Select the Air Fry function, adjust time to 12 minutes, and press Start/Pause.
5. Remove when chickpeas are crispy and golden.

Cheese Arancini

Servings: 8
Cooking Time: 12 Minutes

Ingredients:
- 1 cup Water
- ½ cup Raw white Arborio rice
- 1½ teaspoons Butter
- ¼ teaspoon Table salt
- 8 ¾-inch semi-firm mozzarella cubes (not fresh mozzarella)
- 2 Large egg(s), well beaten
- 1 cup Seasoned Italian-style dried bread crumbs (gluten-free, if a concern)
- Olive oil spray

Directions:
1. Combine the water, rice, butter, and salt in a small saucepan. Bring to a boil over medium-high heat, stirring occasionally. Cover, reduce the heat to very low, and simmer very slowly for 20 minutes.
2. Take the saucepan off the heat and let it stand, covered, for 10 minutes. Uncover it and fluff the rice. Cool for 20 minutes. (The rice can be made up to 1 hour in advance; keep it covered in its saucepan.)
3. Preheat the toaster oven to 375°F.
4. Set up and fill two shallow soup plates or small bowls on your counter: one with the beaten egg(s) and one with the bread crumbs.
5. With clean but wet hands, scoop up about 2 tablespoons of the cooked rice and form it into a ball. Push a cube of mozzarella into the middle of the ball and seal the cheese inside. Dip the ball in the egg(s) to coat completely, letting any excess egg slip back into the rest. Roll the ball in the bread crumbs to coat evenly but lightly. Set aside and continue making more rice balls.
6. Generously spray the balls with olive oil spray, then set them in the air fryer oven in one layer. They must not touch. Air-fry undisturbed for 10 minutes, or until crunchy and golden brown. If the machine is at 360°F, you may need to add 2 minutes to the cooking time.
7. Use a nonstick-safe spatula, and maybe a flatware spoon for balance, to gently transfer the balls to a wire rack. Cool for at least 5 minutes or up to 20 minutes before serving.

Okra Chips

Servings: 4
Cooking Time: 16 Minutes

Ingredients:
- 1¼ pounds Thin fresh okra pods, cut into 1-inch pieces
- 1½ tablespoons Vegetable or canola oil
- ¾ teaspoon Coarse sea salt or kosher salt

Directions:
1. Preheat the toaster oven to 400°F.
2. Toss the okra, oil, and salt in a large bowl until the pieces are well and evenly coated.
3. When the machine is at temperature, pour the contents of the bowl into the air fryer oven. Air-fry, tossing several times, for 16 minutes, or until crisp and quite brown (maybe even a little blackened on the thin bits).
4. Pour the contents of the air fryer oven onto a wire rack. Cool for a couple of minutes before serving.

FISH AND SEAFOOD

Crab-stuffed Peppers

Servings: 4
Cooking Time: 45 Minutes

Ingredients:
- Filling:
- 1½ cups fresh crabmeat, chopped, or 2 6-ounce cans lump crabmeat, drained
- 4 plum tomatoes, chopped
- 2 4-ounce cans sliced mushrooms, drained well
- 4 tablespoons pitted and sliced black olives
- 2 tablespoons olive oil
- 2 garlic cloves, minced
- ½ teaspoon ground cumin
- Salt and freshly ground black pepper to taste
- 4 large bell peppers, tops cut off, seeds and membrane removed
- ½ cup shredded low-fat mozzarella cheese

Directions:
1. Preheat the toaster oven to 375° F.
2. Combine the filling ingredients in a bowl and adjust the seasonings. Spoon the mixture to generously fill each pepper. Place the peppers upright in an 8½ × 8½ × 2-inch oiled or nonstick square (cake) pan.
3. BAKE for 40 minutes, or until the peppers are tender. Remove from the oven and sprinkle the cheese in equal portions on top of the peppers.
4. BROIL 5 minutes, or until the cheese is melted.

Maple-crusted Salmon

Servings: 2
Cooking Time: 8 Minutes

Ingredients:
- 12 ounces salmon filets
- ⅓ cup maple syrup
- 1 teaspoon Worcestershire sauce
- 2 teaspoons Dijon mustard or brown mustard
- ½ cup finely chopped walnuts
- ½ teaspoon sea salt
- ½ lemon
- 1 tablespoon chopped parsley, for garnish

Directions:
1. Place the salmon in a shallow baking dish. Top with maple syrup, Worcestershire sauce, and mustard. Refrigerate for 30 minutes.
2. Preheat the toaster oven to 350°F.
3. Remove the salmon from the marinade and discard the marinade.
4. Place the chopped nuts on top of the salmon filets, and sprinkle salt on top of the nuts. Place the salmon, skin side down, in the air fryer oven. Air-fry for 6 to 8 minutes or until the fish flakes in the center.
5. Remove the salmon and plate on a serving platter. Squeeze fresh lemon over the top of the salmon and top with chopped parsley. Serve immediately.

Fish With Sun-dried Tomato Pesto

Servings: 4
Cooking Time: 31 Minutes

Ingredients:
- Tomato sauce:
- ¼ cup chopped sun-dried tomatoes
- 2 tablespoons chopped fresh basil
- ⅔ cup dry white wine
- 2 tablespoons grated Parmesan cheese
- 2 tablespoons olive oil
- 1 tablespoon pine nuts
- 2 garlic cloves
- Salt and freshly ground black pepper to taste
- 4 6-ounce fish fillets (trout, catfish, flounder, or tilapia)
- 1 tablespoon reduced-fat mayonnaise
- 2 tablespoons chopped fresh cilantro Olive oil

Directions:
1. Preheat the toaster oven to 400° F.
2. Process the tomato sauce ingredients in a blender or food processor until smooth.
3. Layer the fish fillets in an oiled or nonstick 8½ × 8½ × 2-inch square baking (cake) pan. Spoon the sauce over the fish, spreading evenly.
4. BAKE, uncovered, for 25 minutes, or until the fish flakes easily with a fork. Remove from the oven, spread the mayonnaise on top of the fish, and garnish with the cilantro.
5. BROIL for 6 minutes, or until lightly browned.

Rolled Asparagus Flounder

Servings: 4
Cooking Time: 30 Minutes

Ingredients:
- 1 dozen asparagus stalks, tough stem part cut off
- 4 6-ounce flounder fillets
- 4 tablespoons chopped scallions
- 4 tablespoons shredded carrots
- 4 tablespoons finely chopped
- Almonds
- 1 teaspoon dried dill weed
- Salt and freshly ground black pepper
- 1 lemon, cut into wedges

Directions:
1. Preheat the toaster oven to 400° F.
2. Place 3 asparagus stalks lengthwise on a flounder fillet. Add 1 tablespoon scallions, 1 tablespoon carrots, 1 tablespoon almonds, and a sprinkling of dill. Season to taste with salt and pepper and roll the fillet together so that the long edges overlap. Secure the edges with toothpicks or tie with cotton string. Carefully place the rolled fillet in an oiled or nonstick 8½ × 8½ × 2-inch square baking (cake) pan. Repeat the process for the remaining ingredients. Cover the pan with aluminum foil.
3. BAKE, covered, for 20 minutes, or until the asparagus is tender. Remove the cover.
4. BROIL, uncovered, for 10 minutes, or until the fish is lightly browned. Remove and discard the toothpicks or string. Serve the rolled filets with lemon wedges.

Crispy Smelts

Servings: 3
Cooking Time: 20 Minutes

Ingredients:
- 1 pound Cleaned smelts
- 3 tablespoons Tapioca flour
- Vegetable oil spray
- To taste Coarse sea salt or kosher salt

Directions:
1. Preheat the toaster oven to 400°F.
2. Toss the smelts and tapioca flour in a large bowl until the little fish are evenly coated.
3. Lay the smelts out on a large cutting board. Lightly coat both sides of each fish with vegetable oil spray.
4. When the machine is at temperature, set the smelts close together in the air fryer oven, with a few even overlapping on top. Air-fry undisturbed for 20 minutes, until lightly browned and crisp.
5. Remove from the machine and turn out the fish onto a wire rack. The smelts will most likely come out as one large block, or maybe in a couple of large pieces. Cool for a minute or two, then sprinkle the smelts with salt and break the block(s) into much smaller sections or individual fish to serve.

Crispy Pecan Fish

Servings: 4
Cooking Time: 20 Minutes

Ingredients:
- 3 tablespoons multigrain bread crumbs
- 3 tablespoons ground pecans
- 4 6-ounce fish fillets, approximately ¼ inch thick
- 1 egg white, whisked until frothy
- 1 tablespoon olive oil
- Salt and freshly ground black pepper to taste

Directions:
1. Combine the bread crumbs and pecans in a small bowl and transfer to a platter or plate.
2. Brush both sides of the fillets with egg white and dredge in the bread crumb/pecan mixture. Transfer the fillets to an oiled or nonstick 8½ × 8½ × 2-inch square baking (cake) pan.
3. BROIL for 10 minutes. Remove from the oven and carefully turn the fillets with a spatula. Broil again for 10 minutes, or until the fillets are lightly browned. Season to taste with the salt and pepper.

Crunchy And Buttery Cod With Ritz® Cracker Crust

Servings: 2
Cooking Time: 10 Minutes

Ingredients:
- 4 tablespoons butter, melted
- 8 to 10 RITZ® crackers, crushed into crumbs
- 2 (6-ounce) cod fillets
- salt and freshly ground black pepper
- 1 lemon

Directions:
1. Preheat the toaster oven to 380°F.
2. Melt the butter in a small saucepan on the stovetop or in a microwavable dish in the microwave, and then transfer the butter to a shallow dish. Place the crushed RITZ® crackers into a second shallow dish.
3. Season the fish fillets with salt and freshly ground black pepper. Dip them into the butter and then coat both sides with the RITZ® crackers.
4. Place the fish into the air fryer oven and air-fry at 380°F for 10 minutes, flipping the fish over halfway through the cooking time.
5. Serve with a wedge of lemon to squeeze over the top.

Better Fish Sticks

Servings: 3
Cooking Time: 8 Minutes

Ingredients:
- ¾ cup Seasoned Italian-style dried bread crumbs (gluten-free, if a concern)
- 3 tablespoons (about ½ ounce) Finely grated Parmesan cheese
- 10 ounces Skinless cod fillets, cut lengthwise into 1-inch-wide pieces
- 3 tablespoons Regular or low-fat mayonnaise (not fat-free; gluten-free, if a concern)
- Vegetable oil spray

Directions:
1. Preheat the toaster oven to 400°F.
2. Mix the bread crumbs and grated Parmesan in a shallow soup bowl or a small pie plate.
3. Smear the fish fillet sticks completely with the mayonnaise, then dip them one by one in the breadcrumb mixture, turning and pressing gently to make an even and thorough coating. Coat each stick on all sides with vegetable oil spray.
4. Set the fish sticks in the air fryer oven with at least ¼ inch between them. Air-fry undisturbed for 8 minutes, or until golden brown and crisp.
5. Use a nonstick-safe spatula to gently transfer them from the air fryer oven to a wire rack. Cool for only a minute or two before serving.

Maple Balsamic Glazed Salmon

Servings: 4
Cooking Time: 10 Minutes

Ingredients:
- 4 (6-ounce) fillets of salmon
- salt and freshly ground black pepper
- vegetable oil
- ¼ cup pure maple syrup
- 3 tablespoons balsamic vinegar
- 1 teaspoon Dijon mustard

Directions:
1. Preheat the toaster oven to 400°F.
2. Season the salmon well with salt and freshly ground black pepper. Spray or brush the bottom of the air fryer oven with vegetable oil and place the salmon fillets inside. Air-fry the salmon for 5 minutes.
3. While the salmon is air-frying, combine the maple syrup, balsamic vinegar and Dijon mustard in a small saucepan over medium heat and stir to blend well. Let the mixture simmer while the fish is cooking. It should start to thicken slightly, but keep your eye on it so it doesn't burn.
4. Brush the glaze on the salmon fillets and air-fry for an additional 5 minutes. The salmon should feel firm to the touch when finished and the glaze should be nicely browned on top. Brush a little more glaze on top before removing and serving with rice and vegetables, or a nice green salad.

Lobster Tails

Servings: 4
Cooking Time: 10 Minutes

Ingredients:
- Brushing mixture:
- 2 tablespoons lemon juice
- 2 tablespoons olive oil
- ½ teaspoon garlic powder
- ¼ teaspoon ground thyme
- 4 6-ounce lobster tails

Directions:
1. Whisk together the brushing mixture ingredients in a small bowl and set aside. CUT the top of each lobster shell lengthwise from the top edge to the tail with a sharp scissors. Place the lobster tails, cut side down, on a broiling rack with a pan underneath. Brush with the brushing mixture.
2. BROIL for 5 minutes. Remove from the oven and brush again. Broil for 5 minutes, or until the lobster flesh turns from translucent to opaque.

Tuna Nuggets In Hoisin Sauce

Servings: 4
Cooking Time: 7 Minutes

Ingredients:
- ½ cup hoisin sauce
- 2 tablespoons rice wine vinegar
- 2 teaspoons sesame oil
- 1 teaspoon garlic powder
- 2 teaspoons dried lemongrass
- ¼ teaspoon red pepper flakes
- ½ small onion, quartered and thinly sliced
- 8 ounces fresh tuna, cut into 1-inch cubes
- cooking spray
- 3 cups cooked jasmine rice

Directions:
1. Mix the hoisin sauce, vinegar, sesame oil, and seasonings together.
2. Stir in the onions and tuna nuggets.
3. Spray air fryer oven baking pan with nonstick spray and pour in tuna mixture.
4. Air-fry at 390°F for 3 minutes. Stir gently.
5. Cook 2 minutes and stir again, checking for doneness. Tuna should be barely cooked through, just beginning to flake and still very moist. If necessary, continue cooking and stirring in 1-minute intervals until done.
6. Serve warm over hot jasmine rice.

Shrimp Po'boy With Remoulade Sauce

Servings: 6
Cooking Time: 8 Minutes

Ingredients:
- ½ cup all-purpose flour
- ½ teaspoon paprika
- 1 teaspoon garlic powder
- ½ teaspoon black pepper
- ¼ teaspoon salt
- 2 eggs, whisked
- 1½ cups panko breadcrumbs
- 1 pound small shrimp, peeled and deveined
- Six 6-inch French rolls
- 2 cups shredded lettuce
- 12 ⅛-inch tomato slices
- ¾ cup Remoulade Sauce (see the following recipe)

Directions:
1. Preheat the toaster oven to 360°F.
2. In a medium bowl, mix the flour, paprika, garlic powder, pepper, and salt.
3. In a shallow dish, place the eggs.
4. In a third dish, place the panko breadcrumbs.
5. Covering the shrimp in the flour, dip them into the egg, and coat them with the breadcrumbs. Repeat until all shrimp are covered in the breading.
6. Liberally spray the metal trivet that fits inside the air fryer oven with olive oil spray. Place the shrimp onto the trivet, leaving space between the shrimp to flip. Air-fry for 4 minutes, flip the shrimp, and cook another 4 minutes. Repeat until all the shrimp are cooked.
7. Slice the rolls in half. Stuff each roll with shredded lettuce, tomato slices, breaded shrimp, and remoulade sauce. Serve immediately.

Popcorn Crawfish

Servings: 4
Cooking Time: 18 Minutes

Ingredients:
- ½ cup flour, plus 2 tablespoons
- ½ teaspoon garlic powder
- 1½ teaspoons Old Bay Seasoning
- ½ teaspoon onion powder
- ½ cup beer, plus 2 tablespoons
- 12-ounce package frozen crawfish tail meat, thawed and drained
- oil for misting or cooking spray
- Coating
- 1½ cups panko crumbs
- 1 teaspoon Old Bay Seasoning
- ½ teaspoon ground black pepper

Directions:
1. In a large bowl, mix together the flour, garlic powder, Old Bay Seasoning, and onion powder. Stir in beer to blend.
2. Add crawfish meat to batter and stir to coat.
3. Combine the coating ingredients in food processor and pulse to finely crush the crumbs. Transfer crumbs to shallow dish.
4. Preheat the toaster oven to 390°F.
5. Pour the crawfish and batter into a colander to drain. Stir with a spoon to drain excess batter.
6. Working with a handful of crawfish at a time, roll in crumbs and place on a cookie sheet. It's okay if some of the smaller pieces of crawfish meat stick together.
7. Spray breaded crawfish with oil or cooking spray and place all at once into air fryer oven.
8. Air-fry at 390°F for 5 minutes. Stir and mist again with olive oil or spray. Cook 5 more minutes, stir again, and mist lightly again. Continue cooking 5 more minutes, until browned and crispy.

Fried Scallops

Servings: 3
Cooking Time: 6 Minutes

Ingredients:
- ½ cup All-purpose flour or tapioca flour
- 1 Large egg(s), well beaten
- 2 cups Corn flake crumbs (gluten-free, if a concern)
- Up to 2 teaspoons Cayenne
- 1 teaspoon Celery seeds
- 1 teaspoon Table salt
- 1 pound Sea scallops
- Vegetable oil spray

Directions:
1. Preheat the toaster oven to 400°F.
2. Set up and fill three shallow soup plates or small pie plates on your counter: one for the flour; one for the beaten egg(s); and one for the corn flake crumbs, stirred with the cayenne, celery seeds, and salt until well combined.
3. One by one, dip a scallop in the flour, turning it every way to coat it thoroughly. Gently shake off any excess flour, then dip the scallop in the egg(s), turning it again to coat all sides. Let any excess egg slip back into the rest, then set the scallop in the corn flake mixture. Turn it several times, pressing gently to get an even coating on the scallop all around. Generously coat the scallop with vegetable oil spray, then set it aside on a cutting board. Coat the remaining scallops in the same way.
4. Set the scallops in the air fryer oven with as much air space between them as possible. They should not touch. Air-fry undisturbed for 6 minutes, or until lightly browned and firm.
5. Use kitchen tongs to gently transfer the scallops to a wire rack. Cool for only a minute or two before serving.

Tilapia Teriyaki

Servings: 3
Cooking Time: 10 Minutes

Ingredients:
- 4 tablespoons teriyaki sauce
- 1 tablespoon pineapple juice
- 1 pound tilapia fillets
- cooking spray
- 6 ounces frozen mixed peppers with onions, thawed and drained
- 2 cups cooked rice

Directions:

1. Mix the teriyaki sauce and pineapple juice together in a small bowl.
2. Split tilapia fillets down the center lengthwise.
3. Brush all sides of fish with the sauce, spray air fryer oven with nonstick cooking spray, and place fish in the air fryer oven.
4. Stir the peppers and onions into the remaining sauce and spoon over the fish. Save any leftover sauce for drizzling over the fish when serving.
5. Air-fry at 360°F for 10 minutes, until fish flakes easily with a fork and is done in center.
6. Divide into 3 or 4 servings and serve each with approximately ½ cup cooked rice.

Romaine Wraps With Shrimp Filling

Servings: 4
Cooking Time: 8 Minutes

Ingredients:
- Filling:
- 1 6-ounce can tiny shrimp, drained, or 1 cup fresh shrimp, peeled, cooked, and chopped
- ¾ cup canned chickpeas, mashed into 1 tablespoon olive oil
- 2 tablespoons chopped fresh parsley
- 2 tablespoons grated carrot
- 2 tablespoons chopped bell pepper
- 2 tablespoons minced onion
- 2 tablespoons lemon juice
- 1 teaspoon soy sauce
- Freshly ground black pepper to taste
- 4 large romaine lettuce leaves Olive oil
- 3 tablespoons lemon juice
- 1 teaspoon paprika

Directions:
1. Combine the filling ingredients in a bowl, adjusting the seasonings to taste. Spoon equal portions of the filling into the centers of the romaine leaves. Fold the leaves in half, pressing the filling together, overlap the leaf edges, and skewer with toothpicks to fasten. Carefully place the leaves in an oiled or nonstick 8½ × 8½ × 2-inch square baking (cake) pan. Lightly spray or brush the lettuce rolls with olive oil.
2. BROIL for 8 minutes, or until the filling is cooked and the leaves are lightly browned. Remove from the oven, remove the toothpicks, and drizzle with the lemon juice and sprinkle with paprika.

Beer-battered Cod

Servings: 3
Cooking Time: 12 Minutes

Ingredients:
- 1½ cups All-purpose flour
- 3 tablespoons Old Bay seasoning
- 1 Large egg(s)
- ¼ cup Amber beer, pale ale, or IPA
- 3 4-ounce skinless cod fillets
- Vegetable oil spray

Directions:
1. Preheat the toaster oven to 400°F.
2. Set up and fill two shallow soup plates or small pie plates on your counter: one with the flour, whisked with the Old Bay until well combined; and one with the egg(s), whisked with the beer until foamy and uniform.
3. Dip a piece of cod in the flour mixture, turning it to coat on all sides (not just the top and bottom). Gently shake off any excess flour and dip the fish in the egg mixture, turning it to coat. Let any excess egg mixture slip back into the rest, then set the fish back in the flour mixture and coat it again, then back in the egg mixture for a second wash, then back in the flour mixture for a third time. Coat the fish on all sides with vegetable oil spray and set it aside. "Batter" the remaining piece(s) of cod in the same way.
4. Set the coated cod fillets in the air fryer oven with as much space between them as possible. They should not touch. Air-fry undisturbed for 12 minutes, or until brown and crisp.
5. Use kitchen tongs to gently transfer the fish to a wire rack. Cool for only a couple of minutes before serving.

Skewered Salsa Verde Shrimp

Servings: 4
Cooking Time: 8 Minutes

Ingredients:
- 1½ pounds large fresh shrimp, peeled and deveined
- Brushing mixture:
- 1 7-ounce can salsa verde
- 1 teaspoon ground cumin
- ½ teaspoon chopped fresh cilantro or parsley
- 1 teaspoon garlic powder
- 3 tablespoons plain yogurt
- 1 tablespoon olive oil
- Lemon wedges

Directions:
1. Thread the shrimp onto the skewers.
2. Combine the brushing mixture ingredients in a small bowl. Adjust the seasonings and brush the shrimp with the mixture.
3. BROIL the shrimp for 4 minutes. Turn the skewers, brush the shrimp again, and broil for another 4 minutes, or until the shrimp are firm and cooked. Remove the shrimp from the skewers and serve with lemon wedges.

Tortilla-crusted Tilapia

Servings: 4
Cooking Time: 12 Minutes

Ingredients:
- 4 (5-ounce) tilapia fillets
- ½ teaspoon ground cumin
- Sea salt, for seasoning
- 1 cup tortilla chips, coarsely crushed
- Oil spray (hand-pumped)
- 1 lime, cut into wedges

Directions:
1. Preheat the toaster oven to 375°F on BAKE for 5 minutes.
2. Line the baking tray with parchment paper.
3. Lightly season the fish with the cumin and salt.
4. Press the tortilla chips onto the top of the fish fillets and place them on the baking sheet.
5. Lightly spray the fish with oil.
6. In position 2, bake until golden and just cooked through, about 12 minutes in total.
7. Serve with the lime wedges.

Miso-rubbed Salmon Fillets

Servings: 3
Cooking Time: 5 Minutes

Ingredients:
- ¼ cup White (shiro) miso paste (usually made from rice and soy beans)
- 1½ tablespoons Mirin or a substitute
- 2½ teaspoons Unseasoned rice vinegar
- Vegetable oil spray
- 3 6-ounce skin-on salmon fillets

Directions:
1. Preheat the toaster oven to 400°F.
2. Mix the miso, mirin, and vinegar in a small bowl until uniform.
3. Remove from the machine. Generously spray the skin side of each fillet. Pick them up one by one with a nonstick-safe spatula and set them in the baking pan skin side down with as much air space between them as possible. Coat the top of each fillet with the miso mixture, dividing it evenly between them.
4. Return the baking pan to the machine. Air-fry undisturbed for 5 minutes, or until lightly browned and firm.
5. Use a nonstick-safe spatula to transfer the fillets to serving plates. Cool for only a minute or so before serving.

Shrimp With Jalapeño Dip

Servings: 4
Cooking Time: 10 Minutes

Ingredients:
- Seasonings:
- 1 teaspoon ground cumin
- 1 tablespoon minced garlic
- 1 teaspoon paprika
- 1 teaspoon chili powder
- Pinch of cayenne
- Salt to taste
- 1½ pounds large shrimp, peeled and deveined

Directions:

1. Combine the seasonings in a plastic bag, add the shrimp, and shake well to coat. Transfer the shrimp to an oiled or nonstick 8½ × 8½ × 2-inch square baking (cake) pan.
2. BROIL for 5 minutes. Remove the pan from the oven and turn the shrimp with tongs. Broil 5 minutes again, or until the shrimp are cooked (they should be firm but not rubbery.) Serve with Jalapeño Dip.

Broiled Lemon Coconut Shrimp

Servings: 4
Cooking Time: 10 Minutes

Ingredients:

- Brushing mixture:
- 2 tablespoons lemon juice
- 4 tablespoons olive oil
- 1 tablespoon grated lemon zest
- Salt to taste
- 1 pound fresh shrimp, peeled, deveined, and butterflied
- ½ cup grated unsweetened coconut

Directions:

1. Combine the brushing mixture ingredients in a small bowl. Add the shrimp and toss to coat well. Set aside.
2. Place the coconut on a plate, spreading it out evenly.
3. Press each shrimp into the coconut, coating well on all sides. Place the shrimp in an 8½ × 8½ × 2-inch oiled or nonstick square (cake) pan.
4. BROIL the shrimp for 5 minutes, turn with tongs, and broil for 5 more minutes, or until browned lightly.

Light Trout Amandine

Servings: 4
Cooking Time: 15 Minutes

Ingredients:

- 1 tablespoon margarine
- ½ cup sliced almonds
- 1 tablespoon lemon juice
- 1 teaspoon Worcestershire sauce
- Salt and freshly ground black pepper
- 4 6-ounce trout fillets
- 2 tablespoons chopped fresh parsley

Directions:

1. Combine the margarine and almonds in an oiled or nonstick 8½ × 8½ × 2-inch square baking (cake) pan.
2. BROIL for 5 minutes, or until the margarine is melted. Remove the pan from the oven and add the lemon juice and Worcestershire sauce. Season to taste with salt and pepper, and stir again to blend well. Add the trout fillets and spoon the mixture over them to coat well.
3. BROIL for 10 minutes, or until the almonds and fillets are lightly browned. Garnish with the chopped parsley before serving.

Oysters Broiled In Wine Sauce

Servings: 2
Cooking Time: 20 Minutes

Ingredients:

- Sauce:
- 2 tablespoons margarine, at room temperature
- 1 cup dry white wine
- 3 garlic cloves, minced
- Salt and freshly ground black pepper to taste
- 24 fresh oysters, shucked and drained

Directions:

1. Combine the sauce ingredients in a 1-quart 8½ × 8½ × 4-inch ovenproof baking dish and adjust the seasonings to taste.
2. BROIL the sauce for 5 minutes, remove the pan from the oven, and stir. Return to the oven and broil for another 5 minutes, or until the sauce begins to bubble. Remove from the oven and cool for 5 minutes. Add the oysters, spooning the sauce over them to cover thoroughly.
3. BROIL for 5 minutes, or until the oysters are just cooked.

Pecan-crusted Tilapia

Servings: 4
Cooking Time: 8 Minutes

Ingredients:
- 1 pound skinless, boneless tilapia filets
- ¼ cup butter, melted
- 1 teaspoon minced fresh or dried rosemary
- 1 cup finely chopped pecans
- 1 teaspoon sea salt
- ¼ teaspoon paprika
- 2 tablespoons chopped parsley
- 1 lemon, cut into wedges

Directions:
1. Pat the tilapia filets dry with paper towels.
2. Pour the melted butter over the filets and flip the filets to coat them completely.
3. In a medium bowl, mix together the rosemary, pecans, salt, and paprika.
4. Preheat the toaster oven to 350°F.
5. Place the tilapia filets into the air fryer oven and top with the pecan coating. Air-fry for 6 to 8 minutes. The fish should be firm to the touch and flake easily when fully cooked.
6. Remove the fish from the air fryer oven. Top the fish with chopped parsley and serve with lemon wedges.

Quick Shrimp Scampi

Servings: 2
Cooking Time: 5 Minutes

Ingredients:
- 16 to 20 raw large shrimp, peeled, deveined and tails removed
- ½ cup white wine
- freshly ground black pepper
- ¼ cup + 1 tablespoon butter, divided
- 1 clove garlic, sliced
- 1 teaspoon olive oil
- salt, to taste
- juice of ½ lemon, to taste
- ¼ cup chopped fresh parsley

Directions:
1. Start by marinating the shrimp in the white wine and freshly ground black pepper for at least 30 minutes, or as long as 2 hours in the refrigerator.
2. Preheat the toaster oven to 400°F.
3. Melt ¼ cup of butter in a small saucepan on the stovetop. Add the garlic and let the butter simmer, but be sure to not let it burn.
4. Pour the shrimp and marinade into the air fryer oven, letting the marinade drain through to the bottom drawer. Drizzle the olive oil on the shrimp and season well with salt. Air-fry at 400°F for 3 minutes. Turn the shrimp over and pour the garlic butter over the shrimp. Air-fry for another 2 minutes.
5. Remove the shrimp from the air fryer oven and transfer them to a bowl. Squeeze lemon juice over all the shrimp and toss with the chopped parsley and remaining tablespoon of butter. Season to taste with salt and serve immediately.

Sea Scallops

Servings: 4
Cooking Time: 8 Minutes

Ingredients:
- 1½ pounds sea scallops
- salt and pepper
- 2 eggs
- ½ cup flour
- ½ cup plain breadcrumbs
- oil for misting or cooking spray

Directions:
1. Rinse scallops and remove the tough side muscle. Sprinkle to taste with salt and pepper.
2. Beat eggs together in a shallow dish. Place flour in a second shallow dish and breadcrumbs in a third.
3. Preheat the toaster oven to 390°F.
4. Dip scallops in flour, then eggs, and then roll in breadcrumbs. Mist with oil or cooking spray.
5. Place scallops in air fryer oven in a single layer, leaving some space between. You should be able to cook about a dozen at a time.
6. Air-fry at 390°F for 8 minutes, watching carefully so as not to overcook. Scallops are done when they turn opaque all the way through. They will feel slightly firm when pressed with tines of a fork.
7. Repeat step 6 to cook remaining scallops.

Lightened-up Breaded Fish Filets

Servings: 4
Cooking Time: 10 Minutes

Ingredients:
- ½ cup all-purpose flour
- ½ teaspoon cayenne pepper
- 1 teaspoon garlic powder
- ½ teaspoon black pepper
- ¼ teaspoon salt
- 2 eggs, whisked
- 1½ cups panko breadcrumbs
- 1 pound boneless white fish filets
- 1 cup tartar sauce
- 1 lemon, sliced into wedges

Directions:
1. In a medium bowl, mix the flour, cayenne pepper, garlic powder, pepper, and salt.
2. In a shallow dish, place the eggs.
3. In a third dish, place the breadcrumbs.
4. Cover the fish in the flour, dip them in the egg, and coat them with panko. Repeat until all fish are covered in the breading.
5. Liberally spray the metal trivet that fits inside the air fryer oven with olive oil mist. Place the fish onto the trivet, leaving space between the filets to flip. Air-fry for 5 minutes, flip the fish, and cook another 5 minutes. Repeat until all the fish is cooked.
6. Serve warm with tartar sauce and lemon wedges.

Almond Crab Cakes

Servings: 4
Cooking Time: 10 Minutes

Ingredients:
- 1 pound cooked lump crabmeat, drained and picked over
- ¼ cup ground almonds
- 1 tablespoon Dijon mustard
- 1 scallion, white and green parts, finely chopped
- ½ red bell pepper, finely chopped
- 1 large egg
- 1 teaspoon lemon zest
- Oil spray (hand-pumped)
- 3 tablespoons almond flour

Directions:
1. Preheat the toaster oven to 375°F on AIR FRY for 5 minutes.
2. In a medium bowl, mix the crab meat, almonds, mustard, scallion, bell pepper, egg, and lemon zest until well combined and the mixture holds together when pressed. If the crab cakes do not stick together, add more ground almond.
3. Divide the crab mixture into 8 patties and press them to about 1 inch thick. Place them on a plate, cover, and chill for 30 minutes.
4. Place the air-fryer basket in the baking tray and generously spray with the oil.
5. Place the almond flour on a plate and dredge the crab cakes until they are lightly coated.
6. Place them in the basket and lightly spray both sides with the oil.
7. In position 2, air fry for 10 minutes, turning halfway through, until golden brown. Serve.

Stuffed Shrimp

Servings: 4
Cooking Time: 12 Minutes

Ingredients:
- 16 tail-on shrimp, peeled and deveined (last tail section intact)
- ¾ cup crushed panko breadcrumbs
- oil for misting or cooking spray
- Stuffing
- 2 6-ounce cans lump crabmeat
- 2 tablespoons chopped shallots
- 2 tablespoons chopped green onions
- 2 tablespoons chopped celery
- 2 tablespoons chopped green bell pepper
- ½ cup crushed saltine crackers
- 1 teaspoon Old Bay Seasoning
- 1 teaspoon garlic powder
- ¼ teaspoon ground thyme
- 2 teaspoons dried parsley flakes
- 2 teaspoons fresh lemon juice
- 2 teaspoons Worcestershire sauce
- 1 egg, beaten

Directions:

1. Rinse shrimp. Remove tail section (shell) from 4 shrimp, discard, and chop the meat finely.
2. To prepare the remaining 12 shrimp, cut a deep slit down the back side so that the meat lies open flat. Do not cut all the way through.
3. Preheat the toaster oven to 360°F.
4. Place chopped shrimp in a large bowl with all of the stuffing ingredients and stir to combine.
5. Divide stuffing into 12 portions, about 2 tablespoons each.
6. Place one stuffing portion onto the back of each shrimp and form into a ball or oblong shape. Press firmly so that stuffing sticks together and adheres to shrimp.
7. Gently roll each stuffed shrimp in panko crumbs and mist with oil or cooking spray.
8. Place 6 shrimp in air fryer oven and air-fry at 360°F for 10 minutes. Mist with oil or spray and cook 2 minutes longer or until stuffing cooks through inside and is crispy outside.
9. Repeat step 8 to cook remaining shrimp.

Fried Shrimp

Servings: 3
Cooking Time: 7 Minutes

Ingredients:
- 1 Large egg white
- 2 tablespoons Water
- 1 cup Plain dried bread crumbs (gluten-free, if a concern)
- ¼ cup All-purpose flour or almond flour
- ¼ cup Yellow cornmeal
- 1 teaspoon Celery salt
- 1 teaspoon Mild paprika
- Up to ½ teaspoon Cayenne (optional)
- ¾ pound Large shrimp (20–25 per pound), peeled and deveined
- Vegetable oil spray

Directions:
1. Preheat the toaster oven to 400°F.
2. Set two medium or large bowls on your counter. In the first, whisk the egg white and water until foamy. In the second, stir the bread crumbs, flour, cornmeal, celery salt, paprika, and cayenne (if using) until well combined.
3. Pour all the shrimp into the egg white mixture and stir gently until all the shrimp are coated. Use kitchen tongs to pick them up one by one and transfer them to the bread-crumb mixture. Turn each in the bread-crumb mixture to coat it evenly and thoroughly on all sides before setting it on a cutting board. When you're done coating the shrimp, coat them all on both sides with the vegetable oil spray.
4. Set the shrimp in as close to one layer in the air fryer oven as you can. Some may overlap. Air-fry for 7 minutes, gently rearranging the shrimp at the 4-minute mark to get covered surfaces exposed, until golden brown and firm but not hard.
5. Use kitchen tongs to gently transfer the shrimp to a wire rack. Cool for only a minute or two before serving.

Lemon-roasted Salmon Fillets

Servings: 3
Cooking Time: 7 Minutes

Ingredients:
- 3 6-ounce skin-on salmon fillets
- Olive oil spray
- 9 Very thin lemon slices
- ¾ teaspoon Ground black pepper
- ¼ teaspoon Table salt

Directions:
1. Preheat the toaster oven to 400°F.
2. Generously coat the skin of each of the fillets with olive oil spray. Set the fillets skin side down on your work surface. Place three overlapping lemon slices down the length of each salmon fillet. Sprinkle them with the pepper and salt. Coat lightly with olive oil spray.
3. Use a nonstick-safe spatula to transfer the fillets one by one to the air fryer oven, leaving as much air space between them as possible. Air-fry undisturbed for 7 minutes, or until cooked through.
4. Use a nonstick-safe spatula to transfer the fillets to serving plates. Cool for only a minute or two before serving.

Oven-crisped Fish Fillets With Salsa

Servings: 4
Cooking Time: 14 Minutes

Ingredients:
- Coating ingredients:
- 1 cup cornmeal
- 1 teaspoon garlic powder
- 1 teaspoon ground cumin
- 1 teaspoon paprika
- Salt to taste
- 4 6-ounce fish fillets, approximately
- ¼ to ½ inch thick
- 2 tablespoons vegetable oil

Directions:
1. Combine the coating ingredients in a small bowl, blending well. Transfer to a large plate, spreading evenly over the surface. Brush the fillets with vegetable oil and press both sides of each fillet into the coating.
2. BROIL an oiled or nonstick 8½ × 8½ × 2-inch square baking (cake) pan for 1 or 2 minutes to preheat. Remove the pan and place the fillets in the hot pan, laying them flat.
3. BROIL for 7 minutes, then remove the pan from the oven and carefully turn the fillets with a spatula. Broil for another 7 minutes, or until the fish flakes easily with a fork and the coating is crisped to your preference. Serve immediately.

Sea Bass With Potato Scales And Caper Aïoli

Servings: 2
Cooking Time: 10 Minutes

Ingredients:
- 2 (6- to 8-ounce) fillets of sea bass
- salt and freshly ground black pepper
- ¼ cup mayonnaise
- 2 teaspoons finely chopped lemon zest
- 1 teaspoon chopped fresh thyme
- 2 fingerling potatoes, very thinly sliced into rounds
- olive oil
- ½ clove garlic, crushed into a paste
- 1 tablespoon capers, drained and rinsed
- 1 tablespoon olive oil
- 1 teaspoon lemon juice, to taste

Directions:
1. Preheat the toaster oven to 400°F.
2. Season the fish well with salt and freshly ground black pepper. Mix the mayonnaise, lemon zest and thyme together in a small bowl. Spread a thin layer of the mayonnaise mixture on both fillets. Start layering rows of potato slices onto the fish fillets to simulate the fish scales. The second row should overlap the first row slightly. Dabbing a little more mayonnaise along the upper edge of the row of potatoes where the next row overlaps will help the potato slices stick. Press the potatoes onto the fish to secure them well and season again with salt. Brush or spray the potato layer with olive oil.
3. Transfer the fish to the air fryer oven and air-fry for 8 to 10 minutes, depending on the thickness of your fillets. 1-inch of fish should take 10 minutes at 400°F.
4. While the fish is cooking, add the garlic, capers, olive oil and lemon juice to the remaining mayonnaise mixture to make the caper aïoli.
5. Serve the fish warm with a dollop of the aïoli on top or on the side.

Ginger Miso Calamari

Servings: 4
Cooking Time: 10 Minutes

Ingredients:
- 15 ounces calamari, cleaned
- Sauce:
- 2 tablespoons dry white wine
- 2 tablespoons white miso
- 1 tablespoon balsamic vinegar
- 1 teaspoon honey
- 1 teaspoon toasted sesame oil
- 1 teaspoon olive oil
- 1 tablespoon grated fresh ginger
- Salt and white pepper to taste

Directions:
1. Slice the calamari bodies into ½-inch rings, leaving the tentacles uncut. Set aside.

2. Whisk together the sauce ingredients in a bowl. Transfer the mixture to a baking pan and add the calamari, mixing well to coat.
3. BROIL for 20 minutes, turning with tongs every 5 minutes, or until cooked but not rubbery. Serve with the sauce.

Blackened Catfish

Servings: 4
Cooking Time: 8 Minutes

Ingredients:
- 1 teaspoon paprika
- 1 teaspoon garlic powder
- 1 teaspoon onion powder
- 1 teaspoon ground dried thyme
- ½ teaspoon ground black pepper
- ⅛ teaspoon cayenne pepper
- ½ teaspoon dried oregano
- ⅛ teaspoon crushed red pepper flakes
- 1 pound catfish filets
- ½ teaspoon sea salt
- 2 tablespoons butter, melted
- 1 tablespoon extra-virgin olive oil
- 2 tablespoons chopped parsley
- 1 lemon, cut into wedges

Directions:
1. In a small bowl, stir together the paprika, garlic powder, onion powder, thyme, black pepper, cayenne pepper, oregano, and crushed red pepper flakes.
2. Pat the fish dry with paper towels. Season the filets with sea salt and then coat with the blackening seasoning.
3. In a small bowl, mix together the butter and olive oil and drizzle over the fish filets, flipping them to coat them fully.
4. Preheat the toaster oven to 350°F.
5. Place the fish in the air fryer oven and air-fry for 8 minutes, checking the fish for doneness after 4 minutes. The fish will flake easily when cooked.
6. Remove the fish from the air fryer oven. Top with chopped parsley and serve with lemon wedges.

Shrimp, Chorizo And Fingerling Potatoes

Servings: 4
Cooking Time: 16 Minutes

Ingredients:
- ½ red onion, chopped into 1-inch chunks
- 8 fingerling potatoes, sliced into 1-inch slices or halved lengthwise
- 1 teaspoon olive oil
- salt and freshly ground black pepper
- 8 ounces raw chorizo sausage, sliced into 1-inch chunks
- 16 raw large shrimp, peeled, deveined and tails removed
- 1 lime
- ¼ cup chopped fresh cilantro
- chopped orange zest (optional)

Directions:
1. Preheat the toaster oven to 380°F.
2. Combine the red onion and potato chunks in a bowl and toss with the olive oil, salt and freshly ground black pepper.
3. Transfer the vegetables to the air fryer oven and air-fry for 6 minutes.
4. Add the chorizo chunks and continue to air-fry for another 5 minutes.
5. Add the shrimp, season with salt and continue to air-fry for another 5 minutes.
6. Transfer the tossed shrimp, chorizo and potato to a bowl and squeeze some lime juice over the top to taste. Toss in the fresh cilantro, orange zest and a drizzle of olive oil, and season again to taste.
7. Serve with a fresh green salad.

Coconut Jerk Shrimp

Servings: 3
Cooking Time: 8 Minutes

Ingredients:
- 1 Large egg white(s)
- 1 teaspoon Purchased or homemade jerk dried seasoning blend
- ¾ cup Plain panko bread crumbs (gluten-free, if a concern)
- ¾ cup Unsweetened shredded coconut
- 12 Large shrimp (20–25 per pound), peeled and deveined
- Coconut oil spray

Directions:
1. Preheat the toaster oven to 375°F.
2. Whisk the egg white(s) and seasoning blend in a bowl until foamy. Add the shrimp and toss well to coat evenly.
3. Mix the bread crumbs and coconut on a dinner plate until well combined. Use kitchen tongs to pick up a shrimp, letting the excess egg white mixture slip back into the rest. Set the shrimp in the bread-crumb mixture. Turn several times to coat evenly and thoroughly. Set on a cutting board and continue coating the remainder of the shrimp.
4. Lightly coat all the shrimp on both sides with the coconut oil spray. Set them in the air fryer oven in one layer with as much space between them as possible. (You can even stand some up along the air fryer oven's wall in some models.) Air-fry undisturbed for 6 minutes, or until the coating is lightly browned. If the air fryer oven is at 360°F, you may need to add 2 minutes to the cooking time.
5. Use clean kitchen tongs to transfer the shrimp to a wire rack. Cool for only a minute or two before serving.

Roasted Pepper Tilapia

Servings: 6
Cooking Time: 20 Minutes

Ingredients:
- 6 5-ounce tilapia fillets
- 2 tablespoons olive oil
- Filling:
- 1 cucumber, peeled, seeds scooped out and discarded, and chopped
- ½ cup chopped roasted peppers, drained
- 2 tablespoons lemon juice
- 2 tablespoons chopped fresh parsley or cilantro
- 1 teaspoon garlic powder
- 1 teaspoon paprika
- Salt and freshly ground black pepper to taste
- Dip mixture:
- 1 cup nonfat sour cream
- 2 tablespoons low-fat mayonnaise
- 3 tablespoons Dijon mustard
- 1 teaspoon Worcestershire sauce
- 1 teaspoon dried dill

Directions:
1. Combine the filling ingredients in a bowl, adjusting the seasonings to taste.
2. Spoon equal portions of filling in the centers of the tilapia filets. Roll up the fillets, starting at the smallest end. Secure each roll with toothpicks and place the rolls in an oiled or nonstick baking pan. Carefully brush the fillets with oil and place them in an oiled or nonstick 8½ × 8½ × 2-inch square baking (cake) pan.
3. BROIL for 20 minutes, or until the fillets are lightly browned. Combine the dip mixture ingredients in a small bowl and serve with the fish.

Fried Oysters

Servings: 12
Cooking Time: 8 Minutes

Ingredients:
- 1½ cups All-purpose flour
- 1½ cups Yellow cornmeal
- 1½ tablespoons Cajun dried seasoning blend
- 1¼ cups, plus more if needed Amber beer, pale ale, or IPA
- 12 Large shucked oysters, any liquid drained off
- Vegetable oil spray

Directions:
1. Preheat the toaster oven to 400°F.
2. Whisk ⅔ cup of the flour, ½ cup of the cornmeal, and the seasoning blend in a bowl until uniform. Set aside.

3. Whisk the remaining ⅓ cup flour and the remaining ½ cup cornmeal with the beer in a second bowl, adding more beer in dribs and drabs until the mixture is the consistency of pancake batter.

4. Using a fork, dip a shucked oyster in the beer batter, coating it thoroughly. Gently shake off any excess batter, then set the oyster in the dry mixture and turn gently to coat well and evenly. Set the coated oyster on a cutting board and continue dipping and coating the remainder of the oysters.

5. Coat the oysters with vegetable oil spray, then set them in the air fryer oven with as much air space between them as possible. Air-fry undisturbed for 8 minutes, or until lightly browned and crisp.

6. Use a nonstick-safe spatula to transfer the oysters to a wire rack. Cool for a couple of minutes before serving.

Lemon-dill Salmon Burgers

Servings: 4
Cooking Time: 8 Minutes

Ingredients:
- 2 (6-ounce) fillets of salmon, finely chopped by hand or in a food processor
- 1 cup fine breadcrumbs
- 1 teaspoon freshly grated lemon zest
- 2 tablespoons chopped fresh dill weed
- 1 teaspoon salt
- freshly ground black pepper
- 2 eggs, lightly beaten
- 4 brioche or hamburger buns
- lettuce, tomato, red onion, avocado, mayonnaise or mustard, to serve

Directions:
1. Preheat the toaster oven to 400°F.
2. Combine all the ingredients in a bowl. Mix together well and divide into four balls. Flatten the balls into patties, making an indentation in the center of each patty with your thumb (this will help the burger stay flat as it cooks) and flattening the sides of the burgers so that they fit nicely into the air fryer oven.
3. Transfer the burgers to the air fryer oven and air-fry for 4 minutes. Flip the burgers over and air-fry for another 3 to 4 minutes, until nicely browned and firm to the touch.
4. Serve on soft brioche buns with your choice of topping – lettuce, tomato, red onion, avocado, mayonnaise or mustard.

Garlic-lemon Shrimp Skewers

Servings: 2
Cooking Time: 8 Minutes

Ingredients:
- Juice and zest of 1 lemon
- 1 tablespoon olive oil
- ½ teaspoon garlic puree
- ¼ teaspoon smoked paprika
- 12 large shrimp, peeled and deveined
- Oil spray (hand-pumped)
- Sea salt, for seasoning
- Freshly ground black pepper, for seasoning
- 1 tablespoon chopped fresh parsley

Directions:
1. Preheat the toaster oven to 350°F on AIR FRY for 5 minutes.
2. In a medium bowl, stir the lemon juice, lemon zest, olive oil, garlic, and paprika.
3. Add the shrimp and toss to combine. Cover, refrigerate, and let marinate for 30 minutes.
4. Soak 4 wooden skewers in water while the shrimp marinate.
5. Place the air-fryer basket in the baking tray and spray it generously with the oil.
6. Thread 3 shrimp on each skewer and place them in the basket. Discard any remaining marinade.
7. In position 2, air fry for 8 minutes, turning halfway through, until just cooked.
8. Season with the salt and pepper and serve topped with the parsley.

Halibut Tacos

Servings: 4
Cooking Time: 15 Minutes

Ingredients:
- Oil spray (hand-pumped)
- 1 teaspoon ground cumin
- ¼ teaspoon sea salt
- ⅛ teaspoon freshly ground black pepper
- 4 (4-ounce) halibut fillets
- 1 tablespoon olive oil
- 1 cup red cabbage, shredded
- 1 carrot, shredded
- 1 scallion, white and green parts, finely chopped
- ¼ cup sour cream
- Juice of 1 lime
- ⅛ teaspoon chili powder
- 4 (8-inch) corn tortillas, room temperature

Directions:
1. Preheat the toaster oven to 350°F on CONVECTION BAKE for 5 minutes.
2. Place the air-fryer basket in the baking tray and spray it generously with the oil.
3. In a small bowl, stir the cumin, salt, and pepper until well blended.
4. Season the fish all over with the seasoning mixture.
5. Place the fish in the basket and drizzle with the olive oil.
6. In position 2, bake for 15 minutes until cooked through and lightly browned.
7. While the fish is cooking, in a medium bowl, toss together the cabbage, carrot, scallion, sour cream, lime juice, and chili powder until very well mixed. Set aside.
8. Divide the fish among the tortillas and top with the slaw. Serve.

Broiled Dill And Lemon Salmon

Servings: 25
Cooking Time: 2 Minutes

Ingredients:
- Brushing mixture:
- 2 tablespoons lemon juice
- 2 tablespoons olive oil
- 1 tablespoon soy sauce
- 1 teaspoon dried dill or dill weed
- ½ teaspoon garlic powder
- 1 teaspoon soy sauce
- 2 6-ounce salmon steaks

Directions:
1. Combine the brushing mixture ingredients in a small bowl and brush the salmon steak tops, skin side down, liberally, reserving the remaining mixture. Let the steaks sit at room temperature for 10 minutes, then place on a broiling rack with a pan underneath.
2. BROIL 15 minutes, remove from the oven, and brush the steaks with the remaining mixture. Broil again for 5 minutes, or until the meat flakes easily with a fork.

Catfish Kebabs

Servings: 4
Cooking Time: 20 Minutes

Ingredients:
- Marinade:
- 3 tablespoons lemon juice
- 3 tablespoons tomato juice
- 2 garlic cloves, minced
- 2 tablespoons olive oil
- 1 teaspoon soy sauce
- 4 5-ounce catfish fillets
- 4 9-inch metal skewers
- 2 plum tomatoes, quartered
- 1 onion, cut into 1 × 1-inch pieces

Directions:
1. Combine the marinade ingredients in a small bowl. Set aside.
2. Cut the fillets into 2 by 3-inch strips and place in a shallow glass or ceramic dish. Add the marinade and refrigerate, covered, for at least 20 minutes. Remove the strips from the marinade, roll, and skewer, alternating the rolled strips with the tomatoes and onion.
3. Brush the kebabs with marinade, reserving the remaining marinade for brushing again later. Place the skewers on a broiling rack with a pan underneath.
4. Broil for 10 minutes, then remove the pan from the oven and carefully turn the skewers. Brush the kebabs with the marinade and broil again for 10 minutes, or until browned.

Roasted Fish With Provençal Crumb Topping

Servings: 3
Cooking Time: 25 Minutes

Ingredients:
- 1 tablespoon olive oil, plus more for greasing
- ⅓ cup finely chopped onion
- 1 clove garlic, minced
- ¾ cup fresh bread crumbs
- 2 tablespoons chopped fresh flat-leaf (Italian) parsley
- 1 teaspoon fresh thyme leaves
- 3 (5-ounce) cod fillets, or other white-fleshed, mild-flavored fish, patted dry (about 1 ¼ inches thick)
- 2 tablespoons dry white wine
- 2 teaspoons fresh lemon juice

Directions:
1. Preheat the toaster oven to 400°F. Lightly grease the baking pan with olive oil.
2. Heat the tablespoon of olive oil in a small skillet over medium-high heat. Add the onion and cook, stirring frequently, for 3 to 4 minutes, or until tender. Add the garlic and cook for 30 seconds. Remove the skillet from the heat. Stir in the bread crumbs, parsley, and thyme.
3. Place the fish in the prepared pan. Drizzle with the wine. Divide the crumb mixture evenly over the top of each fish fillet, and press onto the fillets. Roast for 20 to 25 minutes, or until the top is brown and the fish is opaque and flakes easily when tested with a fork. Sprinkle the lemon juice evenly over the fish.

Spiced Sea Bass

Servings: 4
Cooking Time: 25 Minutes

Ingredients:
- Brushing mixture:
- 2 tablespoons lemon juice
- 1 tablespoon chopped fresh parsley
- 2 garlic cloves, minced
- 2 6-ounce sea bass fillets, approximately 1 inch thick
- Spice mixture:
- 2 teaspoons paprika
- 2 teaspoons ground cumin
- 1 teaspoon allspice
- 2 teaspoons garlic powder
- Pinch of cayenne
- Salt to taste

Directions:
1. Combine the brushing mixture ingredients in a small bowl, mixing well. Place the fillets on a plate or platter.
2. Brush the fillets on both sides with the brushing mixture. Let stand at room temperature for 10 minutes.
3. Combine the spice mixture ingredients in a small bowl, mixing well. Transfer to a plate and press the fillets into the spice mixture to coat well. Transfer the fillets to an oiled or nonstick 8½ × 8½ × 2-inch square baking (cake) pan.
4. BROIL for 15 minutes, or until the fish flakes easily with a fork.

Snapper With Capers And Olives

Servings: 2
Cooking Time: 10 Minutes

Ingredients:
- 2 tablespoons capers
- ¼ cup pitted and sliced black olives
- 2 tablespoons olive oil
- ½ teaspoon dried oregano
- Salt and freshly ground black pepper to taste
- 2 6-ounce red snapper fillets
- 1 tomato, cut into wedges

Directions:
1. Combine the capers, olives, olive oil, and seasonings in a bowl.
2. Place the fillets in an oiled or nonstick 8½ × 8½ × 2-inch square baking (cake) pan and spoon the caper mixture over them.
3. BROIL for 10 minutes, or until the fish flakes easily with a fork. Serve with the tomato wedges.

Chilled Clam Cake Slices With Dijon Dill Sauce

Servings: 6
Cooking Time: 30 Minutes

Ingredients:
- 1 10-ounce can minced clams, drained
- 1 egg
- ¾ cup multigrain bread crumbs
- 1 tablespoon vegetable oil
- 1 cup skim milk
- ¼ cup chopped onions
- 2 tablespoons chopped pimientos, drained
- Salt and freshly ground black pepper to taste
- Dijon Dill Sauce (recipe follows)

Directions:
1. Preheat the toaster oven to 400° F.
2. Combine all the ingredients in a medium bowl, mixing well. Transfer to an 8½ × 8½ × 2-inch oiled or nonstick square (cake) pan.
3. BAKE for 30 minutes, or until the top is browned. Let cool, then chill the loaf in the refrigerator. Cut into thin slices or squares and serve with the sauce.

Capered Crab Cakes

Servings: 6
Cooking Time: 30 Minutes

Ingredients:
- 1 pound fresh lump crabmeat, drained and chopped, or 3 5-ounce cans good-quality lump crabmeat
- 1 cup bread crumbs
- ½ cup plain nonfat yogurt
- 1 tablespoon olive oil
- 2 tablespoons capers
- 1 tablespoon garlic powder
- 1 teaspoon hot sauce
- 1 egg, beaten
- 1 tablespoon Worcestershire sauce
- Salt and freshly ground black pepper to taste

Directions:
1. Preheat the toaster oven to 350° F.
2. Combine all the ingredients in a bowl. Shape the mixture into patties approximately 2½ inches wide, adding more bread crumbs if the mixture is too wet and sticky and more yogurt if the mixture is too dry and crumbly. Place the patties in an 8½ × 8½ × 2-inch oiled or nonstick square (cake) pan.
3. BAKE, uncovered, for 25 minutes.
4. BROIL for 5 minutes, until golden brown.

Flounder Fillets

Servings: 4
Cooking Time: 8 Minutes

Ingredients:
- 1 egg white
- 1 tablespoon water
- 1 cup panko breadcrumbs
- 2 tablespoons extra-light virgin olive oil
- 4 4-ounce flounder fillets
- salt and pepper
- oil for misting or cooking spray

Directions:
1. Preheat the toaster oven to 390°F.
2. Beat together egg white and water in shallow dish.
3. In another shallow dish, mix panko crumbs and oil until well combined and crumbly (best done by hand).
4. Season flounder fillets with salt and pepper to taste. Dip each fillet into egg mixture and then roll in panko crumbs, pressing in crumbs so that fish is nicely coated.
5. Spray air fryer oven with nonstick cooking spray and add fillets. Air-fry at 390°F for 3 minutes.
6. Spray fish fillets but do not turn. Cook 5 minutes longer or until golden brown and crispy. Using a spatula, carefully remove fish from air fryer oven and serve.

Horseradish Crusted Salmon

Servings: 2
Cooking Time: 14 Minutes

Ingredients:
- 2 (5-ounce) salmon fillets
- salt and freshly ground black pepper
- 2 teaspoons Dijon mustard
- ½ cup panko breadcrumbs
- 2 tablespoons prepared horseradish
- ½ teaspoon finely chopped lemon zest
- 1 tablespoon olive oil

- 1 tablespoon chopped fresh parsley

Directions:
1. Preheat the toaster oven to 360°F.
2. Season the salmon with salt and freshly ground black pepper. Then spread the Dijon mustard on the salmon, coating the entire surface.
3. Combine the breadcrumbs, horseradish, lemon zest and olive oil in a small bowl. Spread the mixture over the top of the salmon and press down lightly with your hands, adhering it to the salmon using the mustard as "glue".
4. Transfer the salmon to the air fryer oven and air-fry at 360°F for 14 minutes (depending on how thick your fillet is) or until the fish feels firm to the touch. Sprinkle with the parsley.

Marinated Catfish

Servings: 4
Cooking Time: 10 Minutes

Ingredients:
- Marinade:
- 1 tablespoon olive oil
- 1 tablespoon lemon juice
- ¼ dry white wine
- 1 tablespoon garlic powder
- 1 tablespoon soy sauce
- 4 6-ounce catfish fillets

Directions:
1. Combine the marinade ingredients in an 8½ × 8½ × 4-inch ovenproof baking dish. Add the fillets and let stand for 10 minutes, spooning the marinade over the fillets every 2 minutes.
2. BROIL the fillets for 15 minutes, or until the fish flakes easily with a fork.

Lemon-roasted Fish With Olives + Capers

Servings: 4
Cooking Time: 10 Minutes

Ingredients:
- Nonstick cooking spray
- 1 pound cod or white-fleshed, mild-flavored fillets, patted dry
- Kosher salt and freshly ground black pepper
- ½ teaspoon paprika
- 1 large lemon
- 3 tablespoons dry white wine
- ½ cup pitted kalamata or other variety olives, drained
- 2 tablespoons capers, drained
- 1 tablespoon olive oil

Directions:
1. Preheat the toaster oven to 425°F. Spray a 12 x 12-inch baking pan with nonstick cooking spray.
2. Place the fish fillets on the prepared pan. Season with salt, pepper, and paprika.
3. Slice the lemon in half. Slice one half crosswise into almost paper-thin slices. Arrange the slices evenly over the fish. Juice the remaining half of the lemon and drizzle over the fish. Drizzle the wine over the fish. Top with the olives and capers, then drizzle with the olive oil.
4. Roast for 10 minutes or until the fish flakes easily with a fork and a meat thermometer registers 145°F. To serve, spoon the pan drippings, olives, and capers over the fish.

Fish And "chips"

Servings: 2
Cooking Time: 10 Minutes

Ingredients:
- ½ cup flour
- ½ teaspoon paprika
- ¼ teaspoon ground white pepper (or freshly ground black pepper)
- 1 egg
- ¼ cup mayonnaise
- 2 cups salt & vinegar kettle cooked potato chips, coarsely crushed
- 12 ounces cod
- tartar sauce
- lemon wedges

Directions:
1. Set up a dredging station. Combine the flour, paprika and pepper in a shallow dish. Combine the egg

and mayonnaise in a second shallow dish. Place the crushed potato chips in a third shallow dish.
2. Cut the cod into 6 pieces. Dredge each piece of fish in the flour, then dip it into the egg mixture and then place it into the crushed potato chips. Make sure all sides of the fish are covered and pat the chips gently onto the fish so they stick well.
3. Preheat the toaster oven to 370°F.
4. Place the coated fish fillets into the air fry oven. (It is ok if a couple of pieces slightly overlap or rest on top of other fillets in order to fit everything in the air fryer oven.)
5. Air-fry for 10 minutes, gently turning the fish over halfway through the cooking time.
6. Transfer the fish to a platter and serve with tartar sauce and lemon wedges.

Roasted Garlic Shrimp

Servings: 4
Cooking Time: 12 Minutes

Ingredients:
- Nonstick cooking spray
- ¼ cup unsalted butter, melted
- 2 cloves garlic, minced
- 1 teaspoon grated lemon zest
- ½ teaspoon dried thyme leaves
- ¼ teaspoon freshly ground black pepper
- Kosher salt
- 1 pound uncooked large shrimp, fresh or frozen and thawed, peeled and deveined
- 1 ½ tablespoons fresh lemon juice
- Optional: Minced fresh flat-leaf (Italian) parsley

Directions:
1. Preheat the toaster oven to 400°F. Spray a 12 x 12-inch baking pan with nonstick cooking spray.
2. Mix the melted butter, garlic, lemon zest, thyme, and pepper in a small bowl. Season with salt. Set aside.
3. Arrange the shrimp in a single layer in the prepared pan. Pour the butter mixture over the shrimp, then stir gently to coat the shrimp.
4. Roast, uncovered, for 10 to 12 minutes or until the shrimp turn pink. Drizzle with the lemon juice. Transfer to a serving platter and spoon any collected drippings over the shrimp. Garnish, if desired, with minced parsley.

Broiled Scallops

Servings: 6
Cooking Time: 3 Minutes

Ingredients:
- Broiling sauce:
- 2 tablespoons chopped fresh parsley
- 3 shallots, finely chopped
- ¾ cup white wine
- 3 tablespoons margarine, at room
- Temperature
- ½ teaspoon dried thyme
- 3 tablespoons sesame seeds
- Salt and freshly ground black pepper
- 1½ pounds (3 cups) bay scallops, rinsed and drained

Directions:
1. Whisk together the ingredients for the broiling sauce in a small bowl and transfer to a 1-quart 8½ × 8½ × 4-inch ovenproof baking dish. Adjust the seasoning, add the scallops, and spoon the mixture over them.
2. BROIL for 3 minutes, or until all the scallops are opaque instead of translucent. Serve with the sauce.

Coconut-crusted Shrimp

Servings: 4
Cooking Time: 20 Minutes

Ingredients:
- Oil spray (hand-pumped)
- ½ cup all-purpose flour
- 2 large eggs
- ¾ cup unsweetened, shredded coconut
- ½ cup panko bread crumbs
- ¼ teaspoon sea salt
- 1 pound (26 to 30 count) raw extra-large shrimp, peeled and deveined with tails attached

Directions:
1. Preheat the toaster oven to 400°F on AIR FRY for 5 minutes.
2. Place the air-fryer basket in the baking tray and spray it generously with the oil.

3. Place the flour on a plate and set it on your work surface.
4. In a small bowl, whisk the eggs until well beaten and place next to the flour.
5. In a medium bowl, stir the coconut, bread crumbs, and salt, and place next to the eggs.
6. Pat the shrimp dry with paper towels. Working in two batches, dredge the shrimp in the flour, then egg, then coconut mixture, and place them in the basket. Do not crowd the basket.
7. Lightly spray the shrimp with the oil on both sides and in position 2, air fry for 10 minutes, turning halfway through, until golden brown.
8. Repeat with the remaining shrimp, covering the cooked shrimp loosely with foil to keep them warm. Serve.

Molasses-glazed Salmon

Servings: 4
Cooking Time: 15 Minutes

Ingredients:
- Oil spray (hand-pumped)
- 4 (5-ounce) salmon fillets
- Sea salt, for seasoning
- ¼ cup molasses
- 1 teaspoon fresh ginger, peeled and grated

Directions:
1. Preheat the toaster oven to 350°F on CONVECTION BAKE for 5 minutes.
2. Place the air-fryer basket in the baking tray. Generously spray the basket with the oil.
3. Pat the salmon dry with paper towels, season lightly with salt, and place on the baking tray.
4. In a small bowl, stir the molasses and ginger until well blended.
5. Spread the molasses mixture on the fish fillets.
6. Place the baking tray in position 2 and bake for 15 minutes until just cooked through. Serve.

Garlic And Dill Salmon

Servings: 2
Cooking Time: 8 Minutes

Ingredients:
- 12 ounces salmon filets with skin
- 2 tablespoons melted butter
- 1 tablespoon extra-virgin olive oil
- 2 garlic cloves, minced
- 1 tablespoon fresh dill
- ½ teaspoon sea salt
- ½ lemon

Directions:
1. Pat the salmon dry with paper towels.
2. In a small bowl, mix together the melted butter, olive oil, garlic, and dill.
3. Sprinkle the top of the salmon with sea salt. Brush all sides of the salmon with the garlic and dill butter.
4. Preheat the toaster oven to 350°F.
5. Place the salmon, skin side down, in the air fryer oven. Air-fry for 6 to 8 minutes, or until the fish flakes in the center.
6. Remove the salmon and plate on a serving platter. Squeeze fresh lemon over the top of the salmon. Serve immediately.

Crispy Calamari

Servings: 4
Cooking Time: 30 Minutes

Ingredients:
- Oil spray (hand-pumped)
- ¾ cup buttermilk
- 1 large egg
- 1 cup panko bread crumbs
- ¾ cup all-purpose flour
- ½ teaspoon sea salt or Old Bay seasoning
- 1 pound frozen squid rings, thawed and drained well or fresh
- 1 lemon, cut into wedges

Directions:
1. Preheat the toaster oven to 400°F on AIR FRY for 5 minutes.
2. Place the air-fryer basket in the baking tray and generously spray it with the oil.
3. In a medium bowl, whisk the buttermilk and egg.
4. In another medium bowl, stir the bread crumbs, flour, and salt until well blended.

5. Dredge the squid in the buttermilk mixture and then dredge it in the bread crumb mixture.
6. Place the breaded calamari in the basket in a single layer and lightly spray it with the oil. You will have to do several batches.
7. In position 2, air fry for 10 minutes until crispy and golden brown. Cover the cooked calamari with foil to keep it warm while you cook the remaining batches.
8. Repeat with the remaining calamari rings.
9. Serve with lemon wedges.

Fish Tacos With Jalapeño-lime Sauce

Servings: 4
Cooking Time: 7 Minutes

Ingredients:
- Fish Tacos
- 1 pound fish fillets
- ¼ teaspoon cumin
- ¼ teaspoon coriander
- ⅛ teaspoon ground red pepper
- 1 tablespoon lime zest
- ¼ teaspoon smoked paprika
- 1 teaspoon oil
- cooking spray
- 6–8 corn or flour tortillas (6-inch size)
- Jalapeño-Lime Sauce
- ½ cup sour cream
- 1 tablespoon lime juice
- ¼ teaspoon grated lime zest
- ½ teaspoon minced jalapeño (flesh only)
- ¼ teaspoon cumin
- Napa Cabbage Garnish
- 1 cup shredded Napa cabbage
- ¼ cup slivered red or green bell pepper
- ¼ cup slivered onion

Directions:
1. Slice the fish fillets into strips approximately ½-inch thick.
2. Put the strips into a sealable plastic bag along with the cumin, coriander, red pepper, lime zest, smoked paprika, and oil. Massage seasonings into the fish until evenly distributed.
3. Spray air fryer oven with nonstick cooking spray and place seasoned fish inside.
4. Air-fry at 390°F for approximately 5 minutes. Distribute fish. Cook an additional 2 minutes, until fish flakes easily.
5. While the fish is cooking, prepare the Jalapeño-Lime Sauce by mixing the sour cream, lime juice, lime zest, jalapeño, and cumin together to make a smooth sauce. Set aside.
6. Mix the cabbage, bell pepper, and onion together and set aside.
7. To warm refrigerated tortillas, wrap in damp paper towels and microwave for 30 to 60 seconds.
8. To serve, spoon some of fish into a warm tortilla. Add one or two tablespoons Napa Cabbage Garnish and drizzle with Jalapeño-Lime Sauce.

Baked Tomato Pesto Bluefish

Servings: 2
Cooking Time: 23 Minutes

Ingredients:
- 2 plum tomatoes
- 2 tablespoons tomato paste
- ¼ cup fresh basil leaves
- 1 tablespoon olive oil
- 2 garlic cloves
- 2 tablespoons pine nuts
- ¼ cup grated Parmesan cheese
- 1 teaspoon dried oregano
- Salt to taste
- 2 6-ounce bluefish fillets

Directions:
1. Preheat the toaster oven to 400° F.
2. Process the pesto ingredients in a blender or food processor until smooth.
3. Place the bluefish fillets in an oiled or nonstick 8½ × 8½ × 2-inch square baking (cake) pan.
4. BAKE, covered, for 15 minutes, or until the fish flakes with a fork. Remove from the oven, uncover, and spread the pesto mixture on both sides of the fillets.
5. BROIL, uncovered, for 8 minutes, or until the pesto is lightly browned.

Beer-breaded Halibut Fish Tacos

Servings: 4
Cooking Time: 10 Minutes

Ingredients:
- 1 pound halibut, cut into 1-inch strips
- 1 cup light beer
- 1 jalapeño, minced and divided
- 1 clove garlic, minced
- ¼ teaspoon ground cumin
- ½ cup cornmeal
- ¼ cup all-purpose flour
- 1¼ teaspoons sea salt, divided
- 2 cups shredded cabbage
- 1 lime, juiced and divided
- ¼ cup Greek yogurt
- ¼ cup mayonnaise
- 1 cup grape tomatoes, quartered
- ½ cup chopped cilantro
- ¼ cup chopped onion
- 1 egg, whisked
- 8 corn tortillas

Directions:
1. In a shallow baking dish, place the fish, the beer, 1 teaspoon of the minced jalapeño, the garlic, and the cumin. Cover and refrigerate for 30 minutes.
2. Meanwhile, in a medium bowl, mix together the cornmeal, flour, and ½ teaspoon of the salt.
3. In large bowl, mix together the shredded cabbage, 1 tablespoon of the lime juice, the Greek yogurt, the mayonnaise, and ½ teaspoon of the salt.
4. In a small bowl, make the pico de gallo by mixing together the tomatoes, cilantro, onion, ¼ teaspoon of the salt, the remaining jalapeño, and the remaining lime juice.
5. Remove the fish from the refrigerator and discard the marinade. Dredge the fish in the whisked egg; then dredge the fish in the cornmeal flour mixture, until all pieces of fish have been breaded.
6. Preheat the toaster oven to 350°F.
7. Place the fish in the air fryer oven and spray liberally with cooking spray. Air-fry for 6 minutes, flip the fish, and cook another 4 minutes.
8. While the fish is cooking, heat the tortillas in a heavy skillet for 1 to 2 minutes over high heat.
9. To assemble the tacos, place the battered fish on the heated tortillas, and top with slaw and pico de gallo. Serve immediately.

Crab Cakes

Servings: 4
Cooking Time: 9 Minutes

Ingredients:
- 1 pound lump crab meat, checked for shells
- ⅓ cup breadcrumbs
- ¼ cup finely chopped onions
- ¼ cup finely chopped red bell peppers
- ¼ cup finely chopped parsley
- ¼ teaspoon sea salt
- 2 eggs, whisked
- ¾ cup mayonnaise, divided
- ¼ cup sour cream
- 1 lemon, divided
- ¼ cup sweet pickle relish
- 1 tablespoon prepared mustard

Directions:
1. In a large bowl, mix together the crab meat, breadcrumbs, onions, bell peppers, parsley, sea salt, eggs, and ¼ cup of the mayonnaise.
2. Preheat the toaster oven to 380°F.
3. Form 8 patties with the crab cake mixture. Line the air fryer oven with parchment paper and place the crab cakes on the parchment paper. Spray with cooking spray. Air-fry for 4 minutes, turn over the crab cakes, spray with cooking spray, and air-fry for an additional 3 to 5 minutes, or until golden brown and the edges are crispy. Cook in batches as needed.
4. Meanwhile, make the sauce. In a small bowl, mix together the remaining ½ cup of mayonnaise, the sour cream, the juice from ½ of the lemon, the pickle relish, and the mustard.
5. Place the cooked crab cakes on a serving platter and serve with the remaining ½ lemon cut into wedges and the dipping sauce.

Coconut Shrimp

Servings: 4
Cooking Time: 15 Minutes

Ingredients:
- ¼ cup cassava flour
- 1 teaspoon sugar
- ¼ teaspoon black pepper
- ½ teaspoon salt
- 2 large eggs
- 1 cup shredded coconut flakes, unsweetened
- ½ pound deveined, tail-off large shrimp

Directions:
1. Preheat the toaster oven to 330°F. Spray the air fryer oven with olive oil spray. Set aside.
2. In a small bowl, mix the flour, sugar, pepper, and salt.
3. In a separate bowl, whisk the eggs.
4. In a third bowl, place the coconut flakes.
5. Place 1 shrimp at a time in the flour mixture, then wash with the eggs, and cover with coconut flakes.
6. Liberally spray the metal trivet that fits inside the air fryer oven with olive oil spray. Place the shrimp onto the metal trivet and air-fry for 15 minutes, flipping halfway through. Repeat until all shrimp are cooked.
7. Serve immediately with desired sauce.

Pecan-topped Sole

Servings: 4
Cooking Time: 12 Minutes

Ingredients:
- 4 (4-ounce) sole fillets
- Sea salt, for seasoning
- Freshly ground black pepper, for seasoning
- 1 cup crushed pecans
- ½ cup seasoned bread crumbs
- 1 large egg
- 2 tablespoons water
- Oil spray (hand-pumped)

Directions:
1. Preheat the toaster oven to 375°F on BAKE for 5 minutes.
2. Line the baking tray with parchment paper.
3. Pat the fish dry with paper towels and lightly season with salt and pepper.
4. In a small bowl, stir the pecans and bread crumbs.
5. In another small bowl, beat the egg and water until well blended.
6. Dredge the fish in the egg mixture, shaking off any excess, then in the nut mixture.
7. Place the fish in the baking sheet and repeat with the remaining fish.
8. Lightly spray the fillets with the oil on both sides.
9. In position 2, bake until golden and crispy, turning halfway, for 12 minutes in total. Serve.

Shrimp

Servings: 4
Cooking Time: 8 Minutes

Ingredients:
- 1 pound (26–30 count) shrimp, peeled, deveined, and butterflied (last tail section of shell intact)
- Marinade
- 1 5-ounce can evaporated milk
- 2 eggs, beaten
- 2 tablespoons white vinegar
- 1 tablespoon baking powder
- Coating
- 1 cup crushed panko breadcrumbs
- ½ teaspoon paprika
- ½ teaspoon Old Bay Seasoning
- ¼ teaspoon garlic powder
- oil for misting or cooking spray

Directions:
1. Stir together all marinade ingredients until well mixed. Add shrimp and stir to coat. Refrigerate for 1 hour.
2. When ready to cook, preheat the toaster oven to 390°F.
3. Combine coating ingredients in shallow dish.
4. Remove shrimp from marinade, roll in crumb mixture, and spray with olive oil or cooking spray.
5. Cooking in two batches, place shrimp in air fryer oven in single layer, close but not overlapping. Air-fry at 390°F for 8 minutes, until light golden brown and crispy.
6. Repeat step 5 to cook remaining shrimp.

Sesame-crusted Tuna Steaks

Servings: 3
Cooking Time: 13 Minutes

Ingredients:
- ½ cup Sesame seeds, preferably a blend of white and black
- 1½ tablespoons Toasted sesame oil
- 3 6-ounce skinless tuna steaks

Directions:
1. Preheat the toaster oven to 400°F.
2. Pour the sesame seeds on a dinner plate. Use ½ tablespoon of the sesame oil as a rub on both sides and the edges of a tuna steak. Set it in the sesame seeds, then turn it several times, pressing gently, to create an even coating of the seeds, including around the steak's edge. Set aside and continue coating the remaining steak(s).
3. When the machine is at temperature, set the steaks in the air fryer oven with as much air space between them as possible. Air-fry undisturbed for 10 minutes for medium-rare (not USDA-approved), or 12 to 13 minutes for cooked through (USDA-approved).
4. Use a nonstick-safe spatula to transfer the steaks to serving plates. Serve hot.

POULTRY

Pickle Brined Fried Chicken

Servings: 4
Cooking Time: 47 Minutes

Ingredients:
- 4 bone-in, skin-on chicken legs, cut into drumsticks and thighs (about 3½ pounds)
- pickle juice from a 24-ounce jar of kosher dill pickles
- ½ cup flour
- salt and freshly ground black pepper
- 2 eggs
- 1 cup fine breadcrumbs
- 1 teaspoon salt
- 1 teaspoon freshly ground black pepper
- ½ teaspoon ground paprika
- ⅛ teaspoon ground cayenne pepper
- vegetable or canola oil in a spray bottle

Directions:
1. Place the chicken in a shallow dish and pour the pickle juice over the top. Cover and transfer the chicken to the refrigerator to brine in the pickle juice for 3 to 8 hours.
2. When you are ready to cook, remove the chicken from the refrigerator to let it come to room temperature while you set up a dredging station. Place the flour in a shallow dish and season well with salt and freshly ground black pepper. Whisk the eggs in a second shallow dish. In a third shallow dish, combine the breadcrumbs, salt, pepper, paprika and cayenne pepper.
3. Preheat the toaster oven to 370°F.
4. Remove the chicken from the pickle brine and gently dry it with a clean kitchen towel. Dredge each piece of chicken in the flour, then dip it into the egg mixture, and finally press it into the breadcrumb mixture to coat all sides of the chicken. Place the breaded chicken on a plate or baking sheet and spray each piece all over with vegetable oil.
5. Air-fry the chicken in two batches. Place two chicken thighs and two drumsticks into the air fryer oven. Air-fry for 10 minutes. Then, gently turn the chicken pieces over and air-fry for another 10 minutes. Remove the chicken pieces and let them rest on plate – do not cover. Repeat with the second batch of chicken, air-frying for 20 minutes, turning the chicken over halfway through.
6. Lower the temperature of the air fryer oven to 340°F. Place the first batch of chicken on top of the second batch already in the air fryer oven and air-fry for an additional 7 minutes. Serve warm and enjoy.

Sesame Orange Chicken

Servings: 2
Cooking Time: 9 Minutes

Ingredients:
- 1 pound boneless, skinless chicken breasts, cut into cubes
- salt and freshly ground black pepper
- ¼ cup cornstarch
- 2 eggs, beaten
- 1½ cups panko breadcrumbs
- vegetable or peanut oil, in a spray bottle
- 12 ounces orange marmalade
- 1 tablespoon soy sauce
- 1 teaspoon minced ginger
- 2 tablespoons hoisin sauce
- 1 tablespoon sesame oil
- sesame seeds, toasted

Directions:
1. Season the chicken pieces with salt and pepper. Set up a dredging station. Put the cornstarch in a zipper-sealable plastic bag. Place the beaten eggs in a bowl and put the panko breadcrumbs in a shallow dish. Transfer the seasoned chicken to the bag with the cornstarch and shake well to completely coat the chicken on all sides. Remove the chicken from the bag, shaking off any excess cornstarch and dip the pieces into the egg. Let any excess egg drip from the chicken and transfer into the breadcrumbs, pressing the crumbs onto the chicken pieces with your hands. Spray the chicken pieces with vegetable or peanut oil.
2. Preheat the toaster oven to 400°F.

3. Combine the orange marmalade, soy sauce, ginger, hoisin sauce and sesame oil in a saucepan. Bring the mixture to a boil on the stovetop, lower the heat and simmer for 10 minutes, until the sauce has thickened. Set aside and keep warm.

4. Transfer the coated chicken to the air fryer oven and air-fry at 400°F for 9 minutes, rotate a few times during the cooking process to help the chicken cook evenly.

5. Right before serving, toss the browned chicken pieces with the sesame orange sauce. Serve over white rice with steamed broccoli. Sprinkle the sesame seeds on top.

Lemon Sage Roast Chicken

Servings: 4
Cooking Time: 60 Minutes

Ingredients:
- 1 (4-pound) chicken
- 1 bunch sage, divided
- 1 lemon, zest and juice
- salt and freshly ground black pepper

Directions:

1. Preheat the toaster oven to 350°F and pour a little water into the bottom of the air fryer oven. (This will help prevent the grease that drips into the bottom drawer from burning and smoking.)

2. Run your fingers between the skin and flesh of the chicken breasts and thighs. Push a couple of sage leaves up underneath the skin of the chicken on each breast and each thigh.

3. Push some of the lemon zest up under the skin of the chicken next to the sage. Sprinkle some of the zest inside the chicken cavity, and reserve any leftover zest. Squeeze the lemon juice all over the chicken and in the cavity as well.

4. Season the chicken, inside and out, with the salt and freshly ground black pepper. Set a few sage leaves aside for the final garnish. Crumple up the remaining sage leaves and push them into the cavity of the chicken, along with one of the squeezed lemon halves.

5. Place the chicken breast side up into the air fryer oven and air-fry for 20 minutes at 350°F. Flip the chicken over so that it is breast side down and continue to air-fry for another 20 minutes. Return the chicken to breast side up and finish air-frying for 20 more minutes. The internal temperature of the chicken should register 165°F in the thickest part of the thigh when fully cooked. Remove the chicken from the air fryer oven and let it rest on a cutting board for at least 5 minutes.

6. Cut the rested chicken into pieces, sprinkle with the reserved lemon zest and garnish with the reserved sage leaves.

Honey Lemon Thyme Glazed Cornish Hen

Servings: 2
Cooking Time: 20 Minutes

Ingredients:
- 1 (2-pound) Cornish game hen, split in half
- olive oil
- salt and freshly ground black pepper
- ¼ teaspoon dried thyme
- ¼ cup honey
- 1 tablespoon lemon zest
- juice of 1 lemon
- 1½ teaspoons chopped fresh thyme leaves
- ½ teaspoon soy sauce
- freshly ground black pepper

Directions:

1. Split the game hen in half by cutting down each side of the backbone and then cutting through the breast. Brush or spray both halves of the game hen with the olive oil and then season with the salt, pepper and dried thyme.

2. Preheat the toaster oven to 390°F.

3. Place the game hen, skin side down, into the air fryer oven and air-fry for 5 minutes. Turn the hen halves over and air-fry for 10 minutes.

4. While the hen is cooking, combine the honey, lemon zest and juice, fresh thyme, soy sauce and pepper in a small bowl.

5. When the air fryer oven timer rings, brush the honey glaze onto the game hen and continue to air-fry for another 3 to 5 minutes, just until the hen is nicely glazed, browned and has an internal temperature of 165°F.

6. Let the hen rest for 5 minutes and serve warm.

Buffalo Egg Rolls

Servings: 8
Cooking Time: 9 Minutes

Ingredients:
- 1 teaspoon water
- 1 tablespoon cornstarch
- 1 egg
- 2½ cups cooked chicken, diced or shredded (see opposite page)
- ⅓ cup chopped green onion
- ⅓ cup diced celery
- ⅓ cup buffalo wing sauce
- 8 egg roll wraps
- oil for misting or cooking spray
- Blue Cheese Dip
- 3 ounces cream cheese, softened
- ⅓ cup blue cheese, crumbled
- 1 teaspoon Worcestershire sauce
- ¼ teaspoon garlic powder
- ¼ cup buttermilk (or sour cream)

Directions:
1. Mix water and cornstarch in a small bowl until dissolved. Add egg, beat well, and set aside.
2. In a medium size bowl, mix together chicken, green onion, celery, and buffalo wing sauce.
3. Divide chicken mixture evenly among 8 egg roll wraps, spooning ½ inch from one edge.
4. Moisten all edges of each wrap with beaten egg wash.
5. Fold the short ends over filling, then roll up tightly and press to seal edges.
6. Brush outside of wraps with egg wash, then spritz with oil or cooking spray.
7. Place 4 egg rolls in air fryer oven.
8. Air-fry at 390°F for 9 minutes or until outside is brown and crispy.
9. While the rolls are cooking, prepare the Blue Cheese Dip. With a fork, mash together cream cheese and blue cheese.
10. Stir in remaining ingredients.
11. Dip should be just thick enough to slightly cling to egg rolls. If too thick, stir in buttermilk or milk 1 tablespoon at a time until you reach the desired consistency.
12. Cook remaining 4 egg rolls as in steps 7 and 8.
13. Serve while hot with Blue Cheese Dip, more buffalo wing sauce, or both.

Oven-crisped Chicken

Servings: 4
Cooking Time: 35 Minutes

Ingredients:
- Coating mixture:
- 1 cup cornmeal
- ¼ cup wheat germ
- 1 teaspoon paprika
- 1 teaspoon garlic powder
- Salt and butcher's pepper to taste
- 3 tablespoons olive oil
- 1 tablespoon spicy brown mustard
- 6 skinless, boneless chicken thighs

Directions:
1. Preheat the toaster oven to 375° F.
2. Combine the coating mixture ingredients in a small bowl and transfer to a plate, spreading the mixture evenly over the plate's surface. Set aside.
3. Whisk together the oil and mustard in a bowl. Add the chicken pieces and toss to coat thoroughly. Press both sides of each piece into the coating mixture to coat well. Chill in the refrigerator for 10 minutes. Transfer the chicken pieces to a broiling rack with a pan underneath.
4. BAKE, uncovered, for 35 minutes, or until the meat is tender and the coating is crisp and golden brown or browned to your preference.

Air-fried Turkey Breast With Cherry Glaze

Servings: 6
Cooking Time: 54 Minutes

Ingredients:
- 1 (5-pound) turkey breast
- 2 teaspoons olive oil
- 1 teaspoon dried thyme

- ½ teaspoon dried sage
- 1 teaspoon salt
- ½ teaspoon freshly ground black pepper
- ½ cup cherry preserves
- 1 tablespoon chopped fresh thyme leaves
- 1 teaspoon soy sauce
- freshly ground black pepper

Directions:
1. All turkeys are built differently, so depending on the turkey breast and how your butcher has prepared it, you may need to trim the bottom of the ribs in order to get the turkey to sit upright in the air fryer oven without touching the heating element. The key to this recipe is getting the right size turkey breast. Once you've managed that, the rest is easy, so make sure your turkey breast fits into the air fryer oven before you Preheat the toaster oven oven.
2. Preheat the toaster oven to 350°F.
3. Brush the turkey breast all over with the olive oil. Combine the thyme, sage, salt and pepper and rub the outside of the turkey breast with the spice mixture.
4. Transfer the seasoned turkey breast to the air fryer oven, breast side up, and air-fry at 350°F for 25 minutes. Turn the turkey breast on its side and air-fry for another 12 minutes. Turn the turkey breast on the opposite side and air-fry for 12 more minutes. The internal temperature of the turkey breast should reach 165°F when fully cooked.
5. While the turkey is air-frying, make the glaze by combining the cherry preserves, fresh thyme, soy sauce and pepper in a small bowl. When the cooking time is up, return the turkey breast to an upright position and brush the glaze all over the turkey. Air-fry for a final 5 minutes, until the skin is nicely browned and crispy. Let the turkey rest, loosely tented with foil, for at least 5 minutes before slicing and serving.

Turkey Sausage Cassoulet

Servings: 4
Cooking Time: 52 Minutes

Ingredients:
- 3 turkey sausages
- 1 teaspoon olive oil
- ½ sweet onion
- 2 celery stalks, chopped
- 1 teaspoon minced garlic
- 2 (15-ounce) cans great northern beans, drained and rinsed
- 1 (15-ounce) can fire-roasted tomatoes
- 1 small sweet potato, diced
- 1 teaspoon dried thyme
- 2 cups kale, chopped
- Sea salt, for seasoning
- Freshly ground black pepper, for seasoning

Directions:
1. Preheat the toaster oven to 375°F on AIR FRY for 5 minutes.
2. Place the air-fryer basket in the baking tray and place the sausages in the basket. Prick them all over with a fork.
3. In position 2, air fry for 12 minutes until cooked through. Set the sausages aside to cool until you can handle them. Then cut into ¼-inch slices.
4. Change the oven to BAKE at 375°F and place the rack in position 1.
5. Heat the oil in a small skillet over medium-high heat and sauté the onion, celery, and garlic until softened.
6. Transfer the cooked vegetables to a 1½-quart casserole dish and stir in the sausage, beans, tomatoes, sweet potato, and thyme. Cover with foil or a lid.
7. Bake for 35 to 40 minutes until tender and any liquid is absorbed. Take the casserole out and stir in the kale. Let it sit for 10 minutes to wilt.
8. Season with salt and pepper, and serve.

Chicken Potpie

Servings: 4
Cooking Time: 48 Minutes

Ingredients:
- Pie filling:
- 1 tablespoon unbleached flour
- ½ cup evaporated skim milk
- 4 skinless, boneless chicken thighs, cut into 1-inch cubes
- 1 cup potatoes, peeled and cut into ½-inch pieces

- ½ cup frozen green peas
- ½ cup thinly sliced carrot
- 2 tablespoons chopped onion
- ½ cup chopped celery
- 1 teaspoon garlic powder
- Salt and freshly ground black pepper to taste
- 8 sheets phyllo pastry, thawed Olive oil

Directions:
1. Preheat the toaster oven to 400° F.
2. Whisk the flour into the milk until smooth in a 1-quart 8½ × 8½ × 4-inch ovenproof baking dish. Add the remaining filling ingredients and mix well. Adjust the seasonings to taste. Cover the dish with aluminum foil.
3. BAKE for 40 minutes, or until the carrot, potatoes, and celery are tender. Remove from the oven and uncover.
4. Place one sheet of phyllo pastry on top of the baked pie-filling mixture, bending the edges to fit the shape of the baking dish. Brush the sheet with olive oil. Add another sheet on top of it and brush with oil. Continue adding the remaining sheets, brushing each one, until the crust is completed. Brush the top with oil.
5. BAKE for 6 minutes, or until the phyllo pastry is browned.

Chicken Cordon Bleu

Servings: 4
Cooking Time: 25 Minutes

Ingredients:
- Oil spray (hand-pumped)
- 4 (4-ounce) chicken breasts
- 4 teaspoons Dijon mustard
- 4 slices Gruyère cheese
- 4 slices lean ham
- 1 cup all-purpose flour
- 2 large eggs
- 1 cup bread crumbs
- ½ cup Parmesan cheese

Directions:
1. Preheat the toaster oven to 350°F on AIR FRY for 5 minutes.
2. Place the air-fryer basket in the baking tray and generously spray it with the oil.
3. Place a chicken breast flat on a clean work surface and cut along the length of the breast, almost in half, holding the knife parallel to the counter. Open the breast up like a book and place it between two pieces of plastic wrap. Pound the chicken breast to about ¼-inch thick with a rolling pin or mallet. Repeat with the remaining breasts.
4. Spread the mustard on each breast, place a piece of cheese and ham in the center, and fold the sides of the breast over the cheese and ham. Roll the breast up from the unfolded sides to form a sealed packet. Secure with a toothpick.
5. Repeat with the remaining breasts.
6. Sprinkle the flour on a plate and set it on your work surface.
7. In a small bowl, whisk the eggs until well beaten and place next to the flour.
8. In a medium bowl, stir the bread crumbs and Parmesan and place next to the eggs.
9. Dredge the chicken rolls in the flour, then egg, then the bread crumb mixture, making sure they are completely breaded.
10. Arrange the chicken in the basket and spray lightly all over with the oil.
11. In position 2, air fry for 25 minutes, turning halfway through, until golden brown. Serve.

Nacho Chicken Fries

Servings: 4
Cooking Time: 7 Minutes

Ingredients:
- 1 pound chicken tenders
- salt
- ¼ cup flour
- 2 eggs
- ¾ cup panko breadcrumbs
- ¾ cup crushed organic nacho cheese tortilla chips
- oil for misting or cooking spray
- Seasoning Mix
- 1 tablespoon chili powder
- 1 teaspoon ground cumin
- ½ teaspoon garlic powder
- ½ teaspoon onion powder

Directions:
1. Stir together all seasonings in a small cup and set aside.
2. Cut chicken tenders in half crosswise, then cut into strips no wider than about ½ inch.
3. Preheat the toaster oven to 390°F.
4. Salt chicken to taste. Place strips in large bowl and sprinkle with 1 tablespoon of the seasoning mix. Stir well to distribute seasonings.
5. Add flour to chicken and stir well to coat all sides.
6. Beat eggs together in a shallow dish.
7. In a second shallow dish, combine the panko, crushed chips, and the remaining 2 teaspoons of seasoning mix.
8. Dip chicken strips in eggs, then roll in crumbs. Mist with oil or cooking spray.
9. Chicken strips will cook best if done in two batches. They can be crowded and overlapping a little but not stacked in double or triple layers.
10. Air-fry for 4 minutes. Mist with oil, and cook 3 more minutes, until chicken juices run clear and outside is crispy.
11. Repeat step 10 to cook remaining chicken fries.

Hot Thighs

Servings: 4
Cooking Time: 40 Minutes

Ingredients:
- 6 skinless, boneless chicken thighs
- ¼ cup fresh lemon juice
- Seasonings:
- 1 teaspoon garlic powder
- ¼ teaspoon cayenne
- ½ teaspoon chili powder
- 1 teaspoon onion powder
- Salt and freshly ground black pepper to taste

Directions:
1. Preheat the toaster oven to 450° F.
2. Brush the chicken thighs liberally with the lemon juice. Set aside.
3. Combine the seasonings in a small bowl and transfer to a paper or plastic bag. Add the thighs and shake well to coat. Remove from the bag and place in an oiled or nonstick 8½ × 8½ × 2-inch square (cake) pan. Cover the pan with aluminum foil.
4. BAKE, covered, for 20 minutes. Turn the pieces with tongs and bake again for another 20 minutes, or until the meat is tender and lightly browned.

Pecan Turkey Cutlets

Servings: 4
Cooking Time: 12 Minutes

Ingredients:
- ¾ cup panko breadcrumbs
- ¼ teaspoon salt
- ¼ teaspoon pepper
- ¼ teaspoon dry mustard
- ¼ teaspoon poultry seasoning
- ½ cup pecans
- ¼ cup cornstarch
- 1 egg, beaten
- 1 pound turkey cutlets, ½-inch thick
- salt and pepper
- oil for misting or cooking spray

Directions:
1. Place the panko crumbs, ¼ teaspoon salt, ¼ teaspoon pepper, mustard, and poultry seasoning in food processor. Process until crumbs are finely crushed. Add pecans and process in short pulses just until nuts are finely chopped. Go easy so you don't overdo it!
2. Preheat the toaster oven to 360°F.
3. Place cornstarch in one shallow dish and beaten egg in another. Transfer coating mixture from food processor into a third shallow dish.
4. Sprinkle turkey cutlets with salt and pepper to taste.
5. Dip cutlets in cornstarch and shake off excess. Then dip in beaten egg and roll in crumbs, pressing to coat well. Spray both sides with oil or cooking spray.
6. Place 2 cutlets in air fryer oven in a single layer and air-fry for 12 minutes or until juices run clear.
7. Repeat step 6 to cook remaining cutlets.

Crispy Fried Onion Chicken Breasts

Servings: 2
Cooking Time: 13 Minutes

Ingredients:
- ¼ cup all-purpose flour
- salt and freshly ground black pepper
- 1 egg
- 2 tablespoons Dijon mustard
- 1½ cups crispy fried onions (like French's®)
- ½ teaspoon paprika
- 2 (5-ounce) boneless, skinless chicken breasts
- vegetable or olive oil, in a spray bottle

Directions:
1. Preheat the toaster oven to 380°F.
2. Set up a dredging station with three shallow dishes. Place the flour in the first shallow dish and season well with salt and freshly ground black pepper. Combine the egg and Dijon mustard in a second shallow dish and whisk until smooth. Place the fried onions in a sealed bag and using a rolling pin, crush them into coarse crumbs. Combine these crumbs with the paprika in the third shallow dish.
3. Dredge the chicken breasts in the flour. Shake off any excess flour and dip them into the egg mixture. Let any excess egg drip off. Then coat both sides of the chicken breasts with the crispy onions. Press the crumbs onto the chicken breasts with your hands to make sure they are well adhered.
4. Spray or brush the bottom of the air fryer oven with oil. Transfer the chicken breasts to the air fryer oven and air-fry at 380°F for 13 minutes, turning the chicken over halfway through the cooking time.
5. Serve immediately.

Rotisserie-style Chicken

Servings: 4
Cooking Time: 75 Minutes

Ingredients:
- 1 (3-pound) whole chicken
- 1 teaspoon sea salt
- 1 teaspoon paprika
- 1 teaspoon dried thyme
- 1 teaspoon dried rosemary
- ¼ teaspoon freshly ground black pepper
- 2 tablespoons olive oil

Directions:
1. Preheat the toaster oven to 375°F on CONVECTION BAKE for 5 minutes.
2. Line the baking tray with foil.
3. Pat the chicken dry with paper towels and season all over with the salt, paprika, thyme, rosemary, and pepper. Place the chicken on the baking tray and drizzle with olive oil.
4. In position 1, bake for 1 hour and 15 minutes, until golden brown and the internal temperature of a thigh reads 165°F.
5. Let the chicken rest for 10 minutes and serve.

Chicken Souvlaki Gyros

Servings: 4
Cooking Time: 18 Minutes

Ingredients:
- ¼ cup extra-virgin olive oil
- 1 clove garlic, crushed
- 1 tablespoon Italian seasoning
- ½ teaspoon paprika
- ½ lemon, sliced
- ¼ teaspoon salt
- 1 pound boneless, skinless chicken breasts
- 4 whole-grain pita breads
- 1 cup shredded lettuce
- ½ cup chopped tomatoes
- ¼ cup chopped red onion
- ¼ cup cucumber yogurt sauce

Directions:
1. In a large resealable plastic bag, combine the olive oil, garlic, Italian seasoning, paprika, lemon, and salt. Add the chicken to the bag and secure shut. Vigorously shake until all the ingredients are combined. Set in the fridge for 2 hours to marinate.
2. When ready to cook, preheat the toaster oven to 360°F.
3. Liberally spray the air fryer oven with olive oil mist. Remove the chicken from the bag and discard the leftover marinade. Place the chicken into the air fryer

oven, allowing enough room between the chicken breasts to flip.
4. Air-fry for 10 minutes, flip, and cook another 8 minutes.
5. Remove the chicken from the air fryer oven when it has cooked (or the internal temperature of the chicken reaches 165°F). Let rest 5 minutes. Then thinly slice the chicken into strips.
6. Assemble the gyros by placing the pita bread on a flat surface and topping with chicken, lettuce, tomatoes, onion, and a drizzle of yogurt sauce.
7. Serve warm.

Chicken Schnitzel Dogs

Servings: 4
Cooking Time: 10 Minutes

Ingredients:
- ½ cup flour
- ½ teaspoon salt
- 1 teaspoon marjoram
- 1 teaspoon dried parsley flakes
- ½ teaspoon thyme
- 1 egg
- 1 teaspoon lemon juice
- 1 teaspoon water
- 1 cup breadcrumbs
- 4 chicken tenders, pounded thin
- oil for misting or cooking spray
- 4 whole-grain hotdog buns
- 4 slices Gouda cheese
- 1 small Granny Smith apple, thinly sliced
- ½ cup shredded Napa cabbage
- coleslaw dressing

Directions:
1. In a shallow dish, mix together the flour, salt, marjoram, parsley, and thyme.
2. In another shallow dish, beat together egg, lemon juice, and water.
3. Place breadcrumbs in a third shallow dish.
4. Cut each of the flattened chicken tenders in half lengthwise.
5. Dip flattened chicken strips in flour mixture, then egg wash. Let excess egg drip off and roll in breadcrumbs. Spray both sides with oil or cooking spray.
6. Air-fry at 390°F for 5 minutes. Spray with oil, turn over, and spray other side.
7. Air-fry for 3 to 5 minutes more, until well done and crispy brown.
8. To serve, place 2 schnitzel strips on bottom of each hot dog bun. Top with cheese, sliced apple, and cabbage. Drizzle with coleslaw dressing and top with other half of bun.

Chicken Cutlets With Broccoli Rabe And Roasted Peppers

Servings: 2
Cooking Time: 10 Minutes

Ingredients:
- ½ bunch broccoli rabe
- olive oil, in a spray bottle
- salt and freshly ground black pepper
- ⅔ cup roasted red pepper strips
- 2 (4-ounce) boneless, skinless chicken breasts
- 2 tablespoons all-purpose flour
- 1 egg, beaten
- ⅓ cup seasoned breadcrumbs
- 2 slices aged provolone cheese

Directions:
1. Bring a medium saucepot of salted water to a boil on the stovetop. Blanch the broccoli rabe for 3 minutes in the boiling water and then drain. When it has cooled a little, squeeze out as much water as possible, drizzle a little olive oil on top, season with salt and black pepper and set aside. Dry the roasted red peppers with a clean kitchen towel and set them aside as well.
2. Place each chicken breast between 2 pieces of plastic wrap. Use a meat pounder to flatten the chicken breasts to about ½-inch thick. Season the chicken on both sides with salt and pepper.
3. Preheat the toaster oven to 400°F.
4. Set up a dredging station with three shallow dishes. Place the flour in one dish, the egg in a second dish and the breadcrumbs in a third dish. Coat the chicken on all sides with the flour. Shake off any excess flour and dip

the chicken into the egg. Let the excess egg drip off and coat both sides of the chicken in the breadcrumbs. Spray the chicken with olive oil on both sides and transfer to the air fryer oven.

5. Air-fry the chicken at 400°F for 5 minutes. Turn the chicken over and air-fry for another minute. Then, top the chicken breast with the broccoli rabe and roasted peppers. Place a slice of the provolone cheese on top and secure it with a toothpick or two.

6. Air-fry at 360° for 3 to 4 minutes to melt the cheese and warm everything together.

East Indian Chicken

Servings: 4
Cooking Time: 45 Minutes

Ingredients:
- Sauce mixture:
- ¼ cup white wine
- ¼ cup red wine
- ½ cup low-sodium vegetable broth
- ½ cup finely chopped onion
- ½ cup finely chopped bell pepper
- ½ cup finely chopped fresh tomato
- 3 garlic cloves, minced
- 1 tablespoon peeled and minced fresh ginger
- 2 teaspoons curry powder
- ¼ teaspoon ground cinnamon
- ¼ teaspoon ground cumin
- 4 small dried chilies
- Salt and freshly ground black pepper to taste
- 6 skinless, boneless chicken thighs

Directions:
1. Preheat the toaster oven to 400° F.
2. Combine the sauce mixture ingredients in a 1-quart 8½ × 8½ × 4-inch ovenproof baking dish and mix well. Add the chicken and toss together to coat well. Cover the dish with aluminum foil.
3. BAKE for 45 minutes, or until the chicken is tender. Uncover and spoon the sauce over the chicken. Remove the chilies before serving.

Teriyaki Chicken Drumsticks

Servings: 2
Cooking Time: 17 Minutes

Ingredients:
- 2 tablespoons soy sauce
- ¼ cup dry sherry
- 1 tablespoon brown sugar
- 2 tablespoons water
- 1 tablespoon rice wine vinegar
- 1 clove garlic, crushed
- 1-inch fresh ginger, peeled and sliced
- pinch crushed red pepper flakes
- 4 to 6 bone-in, skin-on chicken drumsticks
- 1 tablespoon cornstarch
- fresh cilantro leaves

Directions:
1. Make the marinade by combining the soy sauce, dry sherry, brown sugar, water, rice vinegar, garlic, ginger and crushed red pepper flakes. Pour the marinade over the chicken legs, cover and let the chicken marinate for 1 to 4 hours in the refrigerator.
2. Preheat the toaster oven to 380°F.
3. Transfer the chicken from the marinade to the air fryer oven, transferring any extra marinade to a small saucepan. Air-fry at 380°F for 8 minutes. Flip the chicken over and continue to air-fry for another 6 minutes, watching to make sure it doesn't brown too much.
4. While the chicken is cooking, bring the reserved marinade to a simmer on the stovetop. Dissolve the cornstarch in 2 tablespoons of water and stir this into the saucepan. Bring to a boil to thicken the sauce. Remove the garlic clove and slices of ginger from the sauce and set aside.
5. When the time is up on the air fryer oven, brush the thickened sauce on the chicken and air-fry for 3 more minutes. Remove the chicken from the air fryer oven and brush with the remaining sauce.
6. Serve over rice and sprinkle the cilantro leaves on top.

Harissa Lemon Whole Chicken

Servings: 6
Cooking Time: 60 Minutes

Ingredients:
- 2 teaspoons kosher salt
- ½ teaspoon freshly ground black pepper
- ½ teaspoon ground cumin
- 2 garlic cloves
- 6 tablespoons harissa paste
- ½ lemon, juiced
- 1 whole lemon, zested
- 1 (5 pound) whole chicken

Directions:
1. Place salt, pepper, cumin, garlic cloves, harissa paste, lemon juice, and lemon zest in a food processor and pulse until they form a smooth puree.
2. Rub the puree all over the chicken, especially inside the cavity, and cover with plastic wrap.
3. Marinate for 1 hour at room temperature.
4. Preheat the toaster oven to 350°F.
5. Place the marinated chicken on the food tray, then insert the tray at low position in the preheated oven.
6. Select the Roast function, then press Start/Pause.
7. Remove when done, tent chicken with foil, and allow it to rest for 20 minutes before serving.

Orange-glazed Roast Chicken

Servings: 6
Cooking Time: 100 Minutes

Ingredients:
- 1 3-pound whole chicken, rinsed and patted dry with paper towels
- Brushing mixture:
- 2 tablespoons orange juice concentrate
- 1 tablespoon soy sauce
- 1 tablespoon toasted sesame oil
- 1 teaspoon ground ginger
- Salt and freshly ground black pepper to taste

Directions:
1. Preheat the toaster oven to 400° F.
2. Place the chicken, breast side up, in an oiled or nonstick 8½ × 8½ × 2-inch square (cake) pan and brush with the mixture, which has been combined in a small bowl, reserving the remaining mixture. Cover with aluminum foil.
3. BAKE for 1 hour and 20 minutes. Uncover and brush the chicken with remaining mixture.
4. BAKE, uncovered, for 20 minutes, or until the breast is tender when pierced with a fork and golden brown.

Lemon Chicken

Servings: 4
Cooking Time: 36 Minutes

Ingredients:
- Marinade:
- Juice of 1 lemon, plus pulp (no seeds)
- ¼ cup dry white wine
- 2 tablespoons olive oil
- 1 tablespoon minced garlic
- 2 bay leaves
- 1 teaspoon dried thyme
- 1 teaspoon freshly ground black pepper
- Salt to taste
- 8 skinless, boneless chicken thighs
- Juice of 1 lemon
- 2 tablespoons olive oil

Directions:
1. Preheat the toaster oven to 400° F.
2. Blend the marinade ingredients in a bowl (reserving 3 tablespoons for basting), add the chicken thighs, cover, and chill for at least 1 hour. Transfer the chicken thighs to a 1-quart 8½ × 8½ × 4-inch ovenproof baking dish. Adjust the seasonings. Cover the dish with aluminum foil.
3. BAKE for 30 minutes, or until the chicken is tender. Uncover and spoon the reserved marinade over the chicken.
4. BROIL for 8 minutes, or until lightly browned. Remove the bay leaves before serving.

Italian Baked Chicken

Servings: 4
Cooking Time: 28 Minutes

Ingredients:
- 1 pound boneless, skinless chicken breasts
- ½ cup dry white wine
- 3 tablespoons olive oil
- 2 tablespoons white wine vinegar
- 2 tablespoons fresh lemon juice
- 2 teaspoons Italian seasoning
- 3 cloves garlic, minced
- ½ teaspoon kosher salt
- ¼ teaspoon freshly ground black pepper
- 4 slices salami, cut in half
- 3 tablespoons shredded Parmesan cheese

Directions:
1. If the chicken breasts are large and thick, slice each breast in half lengthwise. Place the chicken in a shallow baking dish.
2. Combine the white wine, olive oil, vinegar, lemon juice, Italian seasoning, garlic, salt, and pepper in a small bowl. Pour over the chicken breasts. Cover and refrigerate for 2 to 8 hours, turning the chicken occasionally to coat.
3. Preheat the toaster oven to 375 ºF.
4. Drain the chicken, discarding the marinade, and place the chicken in an ungreased 12 x 12-inch baking pan. Bake, uncovered, for 20 to 25 minutes or until the chicken is done and a meat thermometer registers 165 ºF. Place one slice salami (two pieces) on top of each piece of the chicken. Sprinkle the Parmesan evenly over the chicken breasts and broil for 2 to 3 minutes, or until the cheese is melted and starting to brown.

I Forgot To Thaw—garlic Capered Chicken Thighs

Servings: 4
Cooking Time: 50 Minutes

Ingredients:
- 6 frozen skinless, boneless chicken thighs
- Garlic mixture:
- 3 garlic cloves, minced
- ¾ cup dry white wine
- 2 tablespoons capers
- ½ teaspoon paprika
- ¼ teaspoon ground cumin
- Salt and freshly ground black pepper to taste

Directions:
1. Preheat the toaster oven to 400° F.
2. Thaw the chicken as directed. Separate the pieces and add the garlic mixture, which has been combined in a small bowl, stirring well to coat. Cover the dish with aluminum foil.
3. BAKE for 30 minutes, or until the chicken is tender. Remove the cover and turn the chicken pieces, spooning the sauce over them.
4. BROIL for 8 minutes, or until the chicken is lightly browned.

Crispy Duck With Cherry Sauce

Servings: 2
Cooking Time: 33 Minutes

Ingredients:
- 1 whole duck (up to 5 pounds), split in half, back and rib bones removed
- 1 teaspoon olive oil
- salt and freshly ground black pepper
- Cherry Sauce:
- 1 tablespoon butter
- 1 shallot, minced
- ½ cup sherry
- ¾ cup cherry preserves 1 cup chicken stock
- 1 teaspoon white wine vinegar
- 1 teaspoon fresh thyme leaves
- salt and freshly ground black pepper

Directions:
1. Preheat the toaster oven to 400°F.
2. Trim some of the fat from the duck. Rub olive oil on the duck and season with salt and pepper. Place the duck halves in the air fryer oven, breast side up and facing the center of the air fryer oven.
3. Air-fry the duck for 20 minutes. Turn the duck over and air-fry for another 6 minutes.
4. While duck is air-frying, make the cherry sauce. Melt the butter in a large sauté pan. Add the shallot and

sauté until it is just starting to brown – about 2 to 3 minutes. Add the sherry and deglaze the pan by scraping up any brown bits from the bottom of the pan. Simmer the liquid for a few minutes, until it has reduced by half. Add the cherry preserves, chicken stock and white wine vinegar. Whisk well to combine all the ingredients. Simmer the sauce until it thickens and coats the back of a spoon – about 5 to 7 minutes. Season with salt and pepper and stir in the fresh thyme leaves.

5. When the air fryer oven timer goes off, spoon some cherry sauce over the duck and continue to air-fry at 400°F for 4 more minutes. Then, turn the duck halves back over so that the breast side is facing up. Spoon more cherry sauce over the top of the duck, covering the skin completely. Air-fry for 3 more minutes and then remove the duck to a plate to rest for a few minutes.

6. Serve the duck in halves, or cut each piece in half again for a smaller serving. Spoon any additional sauce over the duck or serve it on the side.

Chicken Parmesan

Servings: 4
Cooking Time: 11 Minutes

Ingredients:
- 4 chicken tenders
- Italian seasoning
- salt
- ¼ cup cornstarch
- ½ cup Italian salad dressing
- ¼ cup panko breadcrumbs
- ¼ cup grated Parmesan cheese, plus more for serving
- oil for misting or cooking spray
- 8 ounces spaghetti, cooked
- 1 24-ounce jar marinara sauce

Directions:
1. Pound chicken tenders with meat mallet or rolling pin until about ¼-inch thick.
2. Sprinkle both sides with Italian seasoning and salt to taste.
3. Place cornstarch and salad dressing in 2 separate shallow dishes.
4. In a third shallow dish, mix together the panko crumbs and Parmesan cheese.
5. Dip flattened chicken in cornstarch, then salad dressing. Dip in the panko mixture, pressing into the chicken so the coating sticks well.
6. Spray both sides with oil or cooking spray. Place in air fryer oven in single layer.
7. Air-fry at 390°F for 5 minutes. Spray with oil again, turning chicken to coat both sides. See tip about turning.
8. Air-fry for an additional 6 minutes or until chicken juices run clear and outside is browned.
9. While chicken is cooking, heat marinara sauce and stir into cooked spaghetti.
10. To serve, divide spaghetti with sauce among 4 dinner plates, and top each with a fried chicken tender. Pass additional Parmesan at the table for those who want extra cheese.

Spice-rubbed Split Game Hen

Servings: 2
Cooking Time: 48 Minutes

Ingredients:
- Spice rub mixture:
- 1 teaspoon ground cumin
- 1 teaspoon garlic powder
- 1 teaspoon onion powder
- 1 teaspoon paprika
- 1 teaspoon ground coriander
- 1 teaspoon salt (optional)
- 1 Cornish game hen, split

Directions:
1. Preheat the toaster oven to 400° F.
2. Mix all the spices together in a small bowl and rub each half of the game hen well and on both sides to coat evenly. Place the pieces skin side down in a baking dish. Cover the dish with aluminum foil.
3. BAKE for 20 minutes. Turn the pieces over and bake, covered, for another 20 minutes, or until the meat is tender. Remove from the oven and uncover.
4. BROIL 8 minutes, or until browned to your preference.

Parmesan Crusted Chicken Cordon Bleu

Servings: 2

Cooking Time: 14 Minutes

Ingredients:
- 2 (6-ounce) boneless, skinless chicken breasts
- salt and freshly ground black pepper
- 1 tablespoon Dijon mustard
- 4 slices Swiss cheese
- 4 slices deli-sliced ham
- ¼ cup all-purpose flour
- 1 egg, beaten
- ¾ cup panko breadcrumbs
- ⅓ cup grated Parmesan cheese
- olive oil, in a spray bottle

Directions:

1. Butterfly the chicken breasts. Place the chicken breast on a cutting board and press down on the breast with the palm of your hand. Slice into the long side of the chicken breast, parallel to the cutting board, but not all the way through to the other side. Open the chicken breast like a "book". Place a piece of plastic wrap over the chicken breast and gently pound it with a meat mallet to make it evenly thick.
2. Season the chicken with salt and pepper. Spread the Dijon mustard on the inside of each chicken breast. Layer one slice of cheese on top of the mustard, then top with the 2 slices of ham and the other slice of cheese.
3. Starting with the long edge of the chicken breast, roll the chicken up to the other side. Secure it shut with 1 or 2 toothpicks.
4. Preheat the toaster oven to 350°F.
5. Set up a dredging station with three shallow dishes. Place the flour in the first dish. Place the beaten egg in the second shallow dish. Combine the panko breadcrumbs and Parmesan cheese together in the third shallow dish. Dip the stuffed and rolled chicken breasts in the flour, then the beaten egg and then roll in the breadcrumb-cheese mixture to cover on all sides. Press the crumbs onto the chicken breasts with your hands to make sure they are well adhered. Spray the chicken breasts with olive oil and transfer to the air fryer oven.
6. Air-fry at 350°F for 14 minutes, flipping the breasts over halfway through the cooking time. Let the chicken rest for a few minutes before removing the toothpicks, slicing and serving.

Chicken Pot Pie

Servings: 4

Cooking Time: 65 Minutes

Ingredients:
- ¼ cup salted butter
- 1 small sweet onion, chopped
- 1 carrot, chopped
- 1 teaspoon minced garlic
- ¼ cup all-purpose flour
- 1 cup low-sodium chicken broth
- ¼ cup heavy (whipping) cream
- 2 cups diced store-bought rotisserie chicken
- 1 cup frozen peas
- Sea salt, for seasoning
- Freshly ground black pepper, for seasoning
- 1 unbaked store-bought pie crust

Directions:

1. Place the rack in position 1 and preheat the toaster oven to 350°F on BAKE for 5 minutes.
2. Melt the butter in a large saucepan over medium-high heat. Sauté the onion, carrot, and garlic until softened, about 12 minutes. Whisk in the flour to form a thick paste and whisk for 1 minute to cook.
3. Add the broth and whisk until thickened, about 2 minutes. Add the heavy cream, whisking to combine. Add the chicken and peas, and season with salt and pepper.
4. Transfer the filling to a 1½-quart casserole dish and top with the pie crust, tucking the edges into the sides of the casserole dish to completely enclose the filling. Cut 4 or 5 slits in the top of the crust.
5. Bake for 50 minutes until the crust is golden brown and the filling is bubbly. Serve.

Coconut Chicken With Apricot-ginger Sauce

Servings: 4
Cooking Time: 8 Minutes

Ingredients:
- 1½ pounds boneless, skinless chicken tenders, cut in large chunks (about 1¼ inches)
- salt and pepper
- ½ cup cornstarch
- 2 eggs
- 1 tablespoon milk
- 3 cups shredded coconut (see below)
- oil for misting or cooking spray
- Apricot-Ginger Sauce
- ½ cup apricot preserves
- 2 tablespoons white vinegar
- ¼ teaspoon ground ginger
- ¼ teaspoon low-sodium soy sauce
- 2 teaspoons white or yellow onion, grated or finely minced

Directions:
1. Mix all ingredients for the Apricot-Ginger Sauce well and let sit for flavors to blend while you cook the chicken.
2. Season chicken chunks with salt and pepper to taste.
3. Place cornstarch in a shallow dish.
4. In another shallow dish, beat together eggs and milk.
5. Place coconut in a third shallow dish. (If also using panko breadcrumbs, as suggested below, stir them to mix well.)
6. Spray air fryer oven with oil or cooking spray.
7. Dip each chicken chunk into cornstarch, shake off excess, and dip in egg mixture.
8. Shake off excess egg mixture and roll lightly in coconut or coconut mixture. Spray with oil.
9. Place coated chicken chunks in air fryer oven in a single layer, close together but without sides touching.
10. Air-fry at 360°F for 4 minutes, stop, and turn chunks over.
11. Cook an additional 4 minutes or until chicken is done inside and coating is crispy brown.
12. Repeat steps 9 through 11 to cook remaining chicken chunks.

Chicken Fajitas

Servings: 4
Cooking Time: 15 Minutes

Ingredients:
- FOR THE FAJITAS
- ½ teaspoon ground cumin
- ½ teaspoon garlic powder
- ¼ teaspoon smoked paprika
- ¼ teaspoon onion powder
- ¼ teaspoon chili powder
- 1 pound boneless, skinless chicken breast, cut into ¼-inch strips
- 1 red bell pepper, cut into thin slices
- 1 green bell pepper, cut into thin slices
- 1 small red onion, cut into thin slices
- 2 tablespoons olive oil
- 8 (6-inch) tortillas
- OPTIONAL TOPPINGS
- Salsa
- Sour cream
- Pickled jalapeños
- Shredded lettuce

Directions:
1. Preheat the toaster oven to 375°F on AIR FRY for 5 minutes.
2. Place the air-fryer basket in the baking tray.
3. In a large bowl, stir the cumin, garlic powder, paprika, onion powder, and chili powder until well mixed. Add the chicken, bell peppers, onion, and oil, and toss to coat evenly.
4. Spread the chicken and veggies on the baking sheet.
5. In position 2, air fry for 15 minutes, tossing them halfway through, until cooked and the vegetables are lightly browned.
6. Serve tucked into the tortillas with your favorite toppings.

Chicken Chunks

Servings: 4
Cooking Time: 10 Minutes

Ingredients:

- 1 pound chicken tenders cut in large chunks, about 1½ inches
- salt and pepper
- ½ cup cornstarch
- 2 eggs, beaten
- 1 cup panko breadcrumbs
- oil for misting or cooking spray

Directions:

1. Season chicken chunks to your liking with salt and pepper.
2. Dip chicken chunks in cornstarch. Then dip in egg and shake off excess. Then roll in panko crumbs to coat well.
3. Spray all sides of chicken chunks with oil or cooking spray.
4. Place chicken in air fryer oven in single layer and air-fry at 390°F for 5 minutes. Spray with oil, turn chunks over, and spray other side.
5. Air-fry for an additional 5 minutes or until chicken juices run clear and outside is golden brown.
6. Repeat steps 4 and 5 to cook remaining chicken.

Chicken Ranch Roll-ups

Servings: 4
Cooking Time: 10 Minutes

Ingredients:

- 4 6-inch flour tortillas
- Low-fat sour cream Chili powder
- Filling mixture:
- 1 cup cooked chopped chicken breast
- 4 tablespoons canned black beans
- 2 tablespoons shredded low-fat cheddar cheese
- 2 tablespoons finely chopped green bell pepper
- 2 tablespoons finely chopped onion
- 1 finely chopped plum tomato
- 2 tablespoons tomato salsa
- 1 seeded and chopped chili pepper
- Hot sauce or Salt and pepper

Directions:

1. Preheat the toaster oven to 350°F.
2. Blend filling ingredients together well in a bowl and season to taste.
3. Fill tortillas with equal portions of mixture, roll into cylinders and lay, seam side down, in an oiled or nonstick 8½" × 8½" × 2" square (cake) pan.
4. BAKE for 20 minutes or until browned and cheese is melted.

Turkey-hummus Wraps

Servings: 4
Cooking Time: 7 Minutes

Ingredients:

- 4 large whole wheat wraps
- ½ cup hummus
- 16 thin slices deli turkey
- 8 slices provolone cheese
- 1 cup fresh baby spinach (or more to taste)

Directions:

1. To assemble, place 2 tablespoons of hummus on each wrap and spread to within about a half inch from edges. Top with 4 slices of turkey and 2 slices of provolone. Finish with ¼ cup of baby spinach—or pile on as much as you like.
2. Roll up each wrap. You don't need to fold or seal the ends.
3. Place 2 wraps in air fryer oven, seam side down.
4. Air-fry at 360°F for 4 minutes to warm filling and melt cheese. If you like, you can continue cooking for 3 more minutes, until the wrap is slightly crispy.
5. Repeat step 4 to cook remaining wraps.

Marinated Green Pepper And Pineapple Chicken

Servings: 4
Cooking Time: 20 Minutes

Ingredients:

- Marinade:
- 1 teaspoon finely chopped fresh ginger
- 2 garlic cloves, finely chopped
- 1 teaspoon toasted sesame oil

- 1 tablespoon brown sugar
- 2 tablespoons soy sauce
- ¾ cup dry white wine
- 2 skinless, boneless chicken breasts, cut into 1 × 3-inch strips
- 2 tablespoons chopped onion
- 1 bell pepper, chopped
- 1 5-ounce can pineapple chunks, drained
- 2 tablespoons grated unsweetened coconut

Directions:
1. Combine the marinade ingredients in a medium bowl and blend well. Add the chicken strips and spoon the mixture over them. Marinate in the refrigerator for at least 1 hour. Remove the strips from the marinade and place in an oiled or nonstick 8½ × 8½ × 2-inch square (cake) pan. Add the onion and pepper and mix well.
2. BROIL for 8 minutes. Then remove from the oven and, using tongs, turn the chicken, pepper, and onion pieces. (Spoon the reserved marinade over the pieces, if desired.)
3. BROIL again for 8 minutes, or until the chicken, pepper, and onion are cooked through and tender. Add the pineapple chunks and coconut and toss to mix well.
4. BROIL for another 4 minutes, or until the coconut is lightly browned.

Sweet-and-sour Chicken

Servings: 6
Cooking Time: 10 Minutes

Ingredients:
- 1 cup pineapple juice
- 1 cup plus 3 tablespoons cornstarch, divided
- ¼ cup sugar
- ¼ cup ketchup
- ¼ cup apple cider vinegar
- 2 tablespoons soy sauce or tamari
- 1 teaspoon garlic powder, divided
- ¼ cup flour
- 1 tablespoon sesame seeds
- ½ teaspoon salt
- ¼ teaspoon ground black pepper
- 2 large eggs
- 2 pounds chicken breasts, cut into 1-inch cubes
- 1 red bell pepper, cut into 1-inch pieces
- 1 carrot, sliced into ¼-inch-thick rounds

Directions:
1. In a medium saucepan, whisk together the pineapple juice, 3 tablespoons of the cornstarch, the sugar, the ketchup, the apple cider vinegar, the soy sauce or tamari, and ½ teaspoon of the garlic powder. Cook over medium-low heat, whisking occasionally as the sauce thickens, about 6 minutes. Stir and set aside while preparing the chicken.
2. Preheat the toaster oven to 370°F.
3. In a medium bowl, place the remaining 1 cup of cornstarch, the flour, the sesame seeds, the salt, the remaining ½ teaspoon of garlic powder, and the pepper.
4. In a second medium bowl, whisk the eggs.
5. Working in batches, place the cubed chicken in the cornstarch mixture to lightly coat; then dip it into the egg mixture, and return it to the cornstarch mixture. Shake off the excess and place the coated chicken in the air fryer oven. Spray with cooking spray and air-fry for 5 minutes, and spray with more cooking spray. Cook an additional 3 to 5 minutes, or until completely cooked and golden brown.
6. On the last batch of chicken, add the bell pepper and carrot to the air fryer oven and cook with the chicken.
7. Place the cooked chicken and vegetables into a serving bowl and toss with the sweet-and-sour sauce to serve.

Golden Seasoned Chicken Wings

Servings: 2
Cooking Time: 40 Minutes

Ingredients:
- Oil spray (hand-pumped)
- ¾ cup all-purpose flour
- 1 teaspoon garlic powder
- 1 teaspoon smoked paprika
- ½ teaspoon sea salt
- ¼ teaspoon freshly ground black pepper
- ¼ teaspoon onion powder
- 2 pounds chicken wing drumettes and flats

Directions:

1. Preheat the toaster oven to 400°F on AIR FRY for 5 minutes.
2. Place the air-fryer basket in the baking tray and spray it generously with the oil.
3. In a medium bowl, stir the flour, garlic powder, paprika, sea salt, pepper, and onion powder until well mixed.
4. Add half the chicken wings to the bowl and toss to coat with the flour.
5. Arrange the wings in the basket and spray both sides lightly with the oil.
6. In position 2, air fry for 20 minutes, turning halfway through, until golden brown and crispy.
7. Repeat with the remaining wings, covering the cooked wings loosely with foil to keep them warm. Serve.

Philly Chicken Cheesesteak Stromboli

Servings: 2
Cooking Time: 28 Minutes

Ingredients:
- ½ onion, sliced
- 1 teaspoon vegetable oil
- 2 boneless, skinless chicken breasts, partially frozen and sliced very thin on the bias (about 1 pound)
- 1 tablespoon Worcestershire sauce
- salt and freshly ground black pepper
- ½ recipe of Blue Jean Chef pizza dough, or 14 ounces of store-bought pizza dough
- 1½ cups grated Cheddar cheese
- ½ cup Cheese Whiz® (or other jarred cheese sauce), warmed gently in the microwave
- tomato ketchup for serving

Directions:
1. Preheat the toaster oven to 400°F.
2. Toss the sliced onion with oil and air-fry for 8 minutes, stirring halfway through the cooking time. Add the sliced chicken and Worcestershire sauce to the air fryer oven, and toss to evenly distribute the ingredients. Season the mixture with salt and freshly ground black pepper and air-fry for 8 minutes, stirring a couple of times during the cooking process. Remove the chicken and onion from the air fryer oven and let the mixture cool a little.
3. On a lightly floured surface, roll or press the pizza dough out into a 13-inch by 11-inch rectangle, with the long side closest to you. Sprinkle half of the Cheddar cheese over the dough leaving an empty 1-inch border from the edge farthest away from you. Top the cheese with the chicken and onion mixture, spreading it out evenly. Drizzle the cheese sauce over the meat and sprinkle the remaining Cheddar cheese on top.
4. Start rolling the stromboli away from you and toward the empty border. Make sure the filling stays tightly tucked inside the roll. Finally, tuck the ends of the dough in and pinch the seam shut. Place the seam side down and shape the Stromboli into a U-shape to fit in the air-fry oven. Cut 4 small slits with the tip of a sharp knife evenly in the top of the dough and lightly brush the stromboli with a little oil.
5. Preheat the toaster oven to 370°F.
6. Spray or brush the air fryer oven with oil and transfer the U-shaped stromboli to the air fryer oven. Air-fry for 12 minutes, turning the stromboli over halfway through the cooking time. (Use a plate to invert the stromboli out of the air fryer oven and then slide it back into the air fryer oven off the plate.)
7. To remove, carefully flip stromboli over onto a cutting board. Let it rest for a couple of minutes before serving. Slice the stromboli into 3-inch pieces and serve with ketchup for dipping, if desired.

Guiltless Bacon

Servings: 4
Cooking Time: 10 Minutes

Ingredients:
- 6 slices lean turkey bacon, placed on a broiling pan

Directions:
1. BROIL 5 minutes, turn the pieces, and broil again for 5 more minutes, or until done to your preference. Press the slices between paper towels and serve immediately.

Tandoori Chicken Legs

Servings: 2
Cooking Time: 30 Minutes

Ingredients:
- 1 cup plain yogurt
- 2 cloves garlic, minced
- 1 tablespoon grated fresh ginger
- 2 teaspoons paprika
- 2 teaspoons ground coriander
- 1 teaspoon ground turmeric
- 1 teaspoon salt
- ¼ teaspoon ground cayenne pepper
- juice of 1 lime
- 2 bone-in, skin-on chicken legs
- fresh cilantro leaves

Directions:
1. Make the marinade by combining the yogurt, garlic, ginger, spices and lime juice. Make slashes into the chicken legs to help the marinade penetrate the meat. Pour the marinade over the chicken legs, cover and let the chicken marinate for at least an hour or overnight in the refrigerator.
2. Preheat the toaster oven oven to 380°F.
3. Transfer the chicken legs from the marinade to the air fryer oven, reserving any extra marinade. Air-fry for 15 minutes. Flip the chicken over and pour the remaining marinade over the top. Air-fry for another 15 minutes, watching to make sure it doesn't brown too much. If it does start to get too brown, you can loosely tent the chicken with aluminum foil, tucking the ends of the foil under the chicken to stop it from blowing around.
4. Serve over rice with some fresh cilantro on top.

Chicken Adobo

Servings: 6
Cooking Time: 12 Minutes

Ingredients:
- 6 boneless chicken thighs
- ¼ cup soy sauce or tamari
- ½ cup rice wine vinegar
- 4 cloves garlic, minced
- ⅛ teaspoon crushed red pepper flakes
- ½ teaspoon black pepper

Directions:
1. Place the chicken thighs into a resealable plastic bag with the soy sauce or tamari, the rice wine vinegar, the garlic, and the crushed red pepper flakes. Seal the bag and let the chicken marinate at least 1 hour in the refrigerator.
2. Preheat the toaster oven to 400°F.
3. Drain the chicken and pat dry with a paper towel. Season the chicken with black pepper and liberally spray with cooking spray.
4. Place the chicken in the air fryer oven and air-fry for 9 minutes, turn over at 9 minutes and check for an internal temperature of 165°F, and cook another 3 minutes.

Gluten-free Nutty Chicken Fingers

Servings: 4
Cooking Time: 10 Minutes

Ingredients:
- ½ cup gluten-free flour
- ½ teaspoon garlic powder
- ¼ teaspoon onion powder
- ¼ teaspoon black pepper
- ¼ teaspoon salt
- 1 cup walnuts, pulsed into coarse flour
- ½ cup gluten-free breadcrumbs
- 2 large eggs
- 1 pound boneless, skinless chicken tenders

Directions:
1. Preheat the toaster oven to 400°F.
2. In a medium bowl, mix the flour, garlic, onion, pepper, and salt. Set aside.
3. In a separate bowl, mix the walnut flour and breadcrumbs.
4. In a third bowl, whisk the eggs.
5. Liberally spray the air fryer oven with olive oil spray.
6. Pat the chicken tenders dry with a paper towel. Dredge the tenders one at a time in the flour, then dip them in the egg, and toss them in the breadcrumb coating. Repeat until all tenders are coated.
7. Set each tender in the air fryer oven, leaving room on each side of the tender to allow for flipping.

8. When the air fryer oven is full, cook 5 minutes, flip, and cook another 5 minutes. Check the internal temperature after cooking completes; it should read 165°F. If it does not, cook another 2 to 4 minutes.
9. Remove the tenders and let cool 5 minutes before serving. Repeat until all the tenders are cooked.

Pesto-crusted Chicken

Servings: 2
Cooking Time: 31 Minutes

Ingredients:

- Pesto:
- 1 cup fresh cilantro, parsley, and basil leaves
- 3 tablespoons nonfat plain yogurt
- ¼ cup pine nuts, walnut, or pecans
- 3 tablespoons grated Parmesan cheese
- 2 peeled garlic cloves
- 1 tablespoon lemon juice
- 3 tablespoons olive oil
- Salt and freshly ground black pepper to taste
- 2 skinless, boneless chicken breast halves

Directions:

1. Preheat the toaster oven to 450° F.
2. Blend the pesto ingredients in a blender or food processor until smooth. Set aside.
3. Place the chicken breast halves in an oiled or nonstick 8½ × 8½ × 2-inch square (cake) pan. With a butter knife or spatula, spread the mixture liberally on both sides of each chicken breast. Cover the dish with aluminum foil.
4. BAKE, covered, for 25 minutes, or until the chicken is tender. Remove from the oven and uncover.
5. BROIL for 6 minutes, or until the pesto coating is lightly browned.

Apricot Glazed Chicken Thighs

Servings: 2
Cooking Time: 22 Minutes

Ingredients:

- 4 bone-in chicken thighs (about 2 pounds)
- olive oil
- 1 teaspoon salt
- ¼ teaspoon freshly ground black pepper
- ½ teaspoon onion powder
- ¾ cup apricot preserves 1½ tablespoons Dijon mustard
- ½ teaspoon dried thyme
- 1 teaspoon soy sauce
- fresh thyme leaves, for garnish

Directions:

1. Preheat the toaster oven to 380°F.
2. Brush or spray both the air fryer oven and the chicken with the olive oil. Combine the salt, pepper and onion powder and season both sides of the chicken with the spice mixture.
3. Place the seasoned chicken thighs, skin side down in the air fryer oven. Air-fry for 10 minutes.
4. While chicken is cooking, make the glaze by combining the apricot preserves, Dijon mustard, thyme and soy sauce in a small bowl.
5. When the time is up on the air fryer oven, spoon half of the apricot glaze over the chicken thighs and air-fry for 2 minutes. Then flip the chicken thighs over so that the skin side is facing up and air-fry for an additional 8 minutes. Finally, spoon and spread the rest of the glaze evenly over the chicken thighs and air-fry for a final 2 minutes. Transfer the chicken to a serving platter and sprinkle the fresh thyme leaves on top.

Southwest Gluten-free Turkey Meatloaf

Servings: 8
Cooking Time: 35 Minutes

Ingredients:

- 1 pound lean ground turkey
- ¼ cup corn grits
- ¼ cup diced onion
- 1 teaspoon minced garlic
- ½ teaspoon black pepper
- ½ teaspoon salt
- 1 large egg
- ½ cup ketchup
- 4 teaspoons chipotle hot sauce
- ⅓ cup shredded cheddar cheese

Directions:

1. Preheat the toaster oven to 350°F.

2. In a large bowl, mix together the ground turkey, corn grits, onion, garlic, black pepper, and salt.
3. In a small bowl, whisk the egg. Add the egg to the turkey mixture and combine.
4. In a small bowl, mix the ketchup and hot sauce. Set aside.
5. Liberally spray a 9-x-4-inch loaf pan with olive oil spray. Depending on the size of your air fryer oven, you may need to use 2 or 3 mini loaf pans.
6. Spoon the ground turkey mixture into the loaf pan and evenly top with half of the ketchup mixture. Cover with foil and place the meatloaf into the air fryer oven. Air-fry for 30 minutes; remove the foil and discard. Check the internal temperature (it should be nearing 165°F).
7. Coat the top of the meatloaf with the remaining ketchup mixture, and sprinkle the cheese over the top. Place the meatloaf back in the air fryer oven for the remaining 5 minutes (or until the internal temperature reaches 165°F).
8. Remove from the oven and let cool 5 minutes before serving. Serve warm with desired sides.

Jerk Turkey Meatballs

Servings: 7
Cooking Time: 8 Minutes

Ingredients:
- 1 pound lean ground turkey
- ¼ cup chopped onion
- 1 teaspoon minced garlic
- ½ teaspoon dried thyme
- ¼ teaspoon ground cinnamon
- 1 teaspoon cayenne pepper
- ½ teaspoon paprika
- ½ teaspoon salt
- ⅛ teaspoon black pepper
- ¼ teaspoon red pepper flakes
- 2 teaspoons brown sugar
- 1 large egg, whisked
- ⅓ cup panko breadcrumbs
- 2⅓ cups cooked brown Jasmine rice
- 2 green onions, chopped
- ¾ cup sweet onion dressing

Directions:
1. Preheat the toaster oven to 350°F.
2. In a medium bowl, mix the ground turkey with the onion, garlic, thyme, cinnamon, cayenne pepper, paprika, salt, pepper, red pepper flakes, and brown sugar. Add the whisked egg and stir in the breadcrumbs until the turkey starts to hold together.
3. Using a 1-ounce scoop, portion the turkey into meatballs. You should get about 28 meatballs.
4. Spray the air fryer oven with olive oil spray.
5. Place the meatballs into the air fryer oven and air-fry for 5 minutes, rotate the meatball, and cook another 2 to 4 minutes (or until the internal temperature of the meatballs reaches 165°F).
6. Remove the meatballs from the air fryer oven and repeat for the remaining meatballs.
7. Serve warm over a bed of rice with chopped green onions and spicy Caribbean jerk dressing.

Tender Chicken Meatballs

Servings: 4
Cooking Time: 30 Minutes

Ingredients:
- 1 pound lean ground chicken
- ½ cup bread crumbs
- 1 large egg
- 1 scallion, both white and green parts, finely chopped
- ¼ cup whole milk
- ¼ cup shredded, unsweetened coconut
- 1 tablespoon low-sodium soy sauce
- 1 teaspoon minced garlic
- 1 teaspoon fresh ginger, peeled and grated
- Pinch cayenne powder
- Oil spray (hand-pumped)

Directions:
1. Preheat the toaster oven to 375°F on BAKE for 5 minutes.
2. Line the baking tray with parchment and set aside.
3. In a large bowl, mix the chicken, bread crumbs, egg, scallion, milk, coconut, soy sauce, garlic, ginger, and cayenne until very well combined.

4. Shape the chicken mixture into 1½-inch balls and place them in a single layer on the baking tray. Do not overcrowd them.

5. In position 2, bake for 20 minutes, turning halfway through, until they are cooked through and evenly browned. Serve.

Tasty Meat Loaf

Servings: 4
Cooking Time: 35 Minutes

Ingredients:
- 1 to 1½ pounds ground turkey or chicken breast
- 1 egg
- 1 tablespoon chopped fresh parsley
- 2 tablespoons chopped bell pepper
- 3 tablespoons chopped canned mushrooms
- 2 tablespoons chopped onion
- 2 garlic cloves, minced
- ½ cup multigrain bread crumbs
- 1 tablespoon Worcestershire sauce
- 1 tablespoon ketchup
- Freshly ground black pepper to taste

Directions:
1. Preheat the toaster oven to 400° F.
2. Combine all the ingredients in a large bowl and press into a regular-size 4½ × 8½ × 2¼-inch loaf pan.
3. BAKE for 35 minutes, or until browned on top.

Jerk Chicken Drumsticks

Servings: 2
Cooking Time: 20 Minutes

Ingredients:
- 1 or 2 cloves garlic
- 1 inch of fresh ginger
- 2 serrano peppers, (with seeds if you like it spicy, seeds removed for less heat)
- 1 teaspoon ground allspice
- 1 teaspoon ground nutmeg
- 1 teaspoon chili powder
- ½ teaspoon dried thyme
- ½ teaspoon ground cinnamon
- ½ teaspoon paprika
- 1 tablespoon brown sugar
- 1 teaspoon soy sauce
- 2 tablespoons vegetable oil
- 6 skinless chicken drumsticks

Directions:
1. Combine all the ingredients except the chicken in a small chopper or blender and blend to a paste. Make slashes into the meat of the chicken drumsticks and rub the spice blend all over the chicken (a pair of plastic gloves makes this really easy). Transfer the rubbed chicken to a non-reactive covered container and let the chicken marinate for at least 30 minutes or overnight in the refrigerator.
2. Preheat the toaster oven to 400°F.
3. Transfer the drumsticks to the air fryer oven. Air-fry for 10 minutes. Turn the drumsticks over and air-fry for another 10 minutes. Serve warm with some rice and vegetables or a green salad.

Foiled Rosemary Chicken Breasts

Servings: 2
Cooking Time: 30 Minutes

Ingredients:
- 2 skinless, boneless chicken breast halves
- Sauce:
- 3 tablespoons dry white wine
- 1 tablespoon Dijon mustard
- 2 tablespoons nonfat plain yogurt
- Salt and freshly ground black pepper to taste
- 2 rosemary sprigs

Directions:
1. Preheat the toaster oven to 400° F.
2. Place each breast on a 12 × 12-inch square of heavy-duty aluminum foil (or regular foil doubled) and turn up the edges of the foil.
3. Mix together the sauce ingredients and spoon over the chicken breasts. Lay a rosemary sprig on each breast. Bring up the edges of the foil and fold to form a sealed packet.
4. BAKE for 25 minutes or until juices run clear when the meat is pierced with a fork. Remove the rosemary sprigs.
5. BROIL for 5 minutes, or until lightly browned. Replace the sprigs and serve.

Crispy Chicken Tenders

Servings: 4
Cooking Time: 22 Minutes

Ingredients:
- 1 pound boneless, skinless chicken breasts
- ½ cup all-purpose flour
- ½ teaspoon kosher salt
- ¼ teaspoon freshly ground black ground pepper
- 1 large egg, beaten
- 3 tablespoons whole milk
- 1 cup cornflake crumbs
- ½ cup grated Parmesan cheese
- Nonstick cooking spray

Directions:
1. Preheat the toaster oven to 375°F. Line a 12 x 12-inch baking pan with nonstick aluminum foil. (Or if lining the pan with regular foil, spray it with nonstick cooking spray.)
2. Cover the chicken with plastic wrap. Pound the chicken with the flat side of a meat pounder until it is even and about ½ inch thick. Cut the chicken into strips about 1 by 3 inches.
3. Combine the flour, salt, and pepper in a small shallow dish. Place the egg and milk in another small shallow dish and use a fork to combine. Place the cornflake crumbs and Parmesan in a third small shallow dish and combine.
4. Dredge each chicken piece in the flour, then dip in the egg mixture, and then coat with the cornflake crumb mixture. Place the chicken strips in a single layer in the prepared baking pan. Spray the chicken strips generously with nonstick cooking spray.
5. Bake for 10 minutes. Turn the chicken and spray with nonstick cooking spray. Bake for an additional 10 to 12 minutes, or until crisp and a meat thermometer registers 165 °F.

Light And Lovely Loaf

Servings: 4
Cooking Time: 30 Minutes

Ingredients:
- 2 cups ground chicken or turkey breast
- 1 egg
- ½ cup grated carrot
- ½ cup grated celery
- 1 tablespoon finely chopped onion
- ½ teaspoon garlic powder
- Salt and freshly ground black pepper to taste

Directions:
1. Preheat the toaster oven to 400° F.
2. Blend all ingredients in a bowl, mixing well, and transfer to an oiled or nonstick regular-size 4½ × 8½ × 2¼-inch loaf pan
3. BAKE, uncovered, for 30 minutes, until lightly browned.

Thai Chicken Drumsticks

Servings: 4
Cooking Time: 20 Minutes

Ingredients:
- 2 tablespoons soy sauce
- ¼ cup rice wine vinegar
- 2 tablespoons chili garlic sauce
- 2 tablespoons sesame oil
- 1 teaspoon minced fresh ginger
- 2 teaspoons sugar
- ½ teaspoon ground coriander
- juice of 1 lime
- 8 chicken drumsticks (about 2½ pounds)
- ¼ cup chopped peanuts
- chopped fresh cilantro
- lime wedges

Directions:
1. Combine the soy sauce, rice wine vinegar, chili sauce, sesame oil, ginger, sugar, coriander and lime juice in a large bowl and mix together. Add the chicken drumsticks and marinate for 30 minutes.
2. Preheat the toaster oven to 370°F.
3. Place the chicken in the air fryer oven. It's ok if the ends of the drumsticks overlap a little. Spoon half of the marinade over the chicken, and reserve the other half.
4. Air-fry for 10 minutes. Turn the chicken over and pour the rest of the marinade over the chicken. Air-fry for an additional 10 minutes.
5. Transfer the chicken to a plate to rest and cool to an edible temperature. Pour the marinade from the bottom

of the air fryer oven into a small saucepan and bring it to a simmer over medium-high heat. Simmer the liquid for 2 minutes so that it thickens enough to coat the back of a spoon.

6. Transfer the chicken to a serving platter, pour the sauce over the chicken and sprinkle the chopped peanuts on top. Garnish with chopped cilantro and lime wedges.

Chicken Breast With Chermoula Sauce

Servings: 4
Cooking Time: 15 Minutes

Ingredients:

- Chicken Ingredients
- 2 boneless skinless chicken breasts 1 tablespoon olive oil
- 1 teaspoon salt
- 1 teaspoon pepper
- Chermoula Ingredients
- 1 cup fresh cilantro
- 1 cup fresh parsley
- ¼ cup fresh mint
- ½ teaspoon red chili flakes
- ½ teaspoon cumin seeds
- ½ teaspoon coriander seeds
- 3 garlic cloves, peeled
- ½ cup extra virgin olive oil
- 1 lemon, zested and juiced
- ¾ teaspoons smoked paprika
- ¾ teaspoons salt

Directions:

1. Combine all the chermoula sauce ingredients in a blender or food processor. Pulse until smooth. Taste and add salt if needed. Place into a bowl and set aside.
2. Slice the chicken breast in half lengthwise and lightly pound with a meat tenderizer until both halves are about
3. ½-inch thick.
4. Preheat the toaster oven to 430°F.
5. Line the food tray with foil, then place the chicken breasts on the tray. Drizzle chicken with olive oil and season with salt and pepper.
6. Insert the food tray at top position in the preheated oven.
7. Select the Air Fry function, adjust time to 15 minutes, and press Start/Pause.
8. Remove when the chicken breast reaches an internal temperature of 160°F. Allow the chicken to rest for 5 minutes.
9. Brush the chermoula sauce over the chicken, or serve chicken with chermoula sauce on the side.

Fried Chicken

Servings: 4
Cooking Time: 40 Minutes

Ingredients:

- 12 skin-on chicken drumsticks
- 1 cup buttermilk
- 1½ cups all-purpose flour
- 1 tablespoon smoked paprika
- ¾ teaspoon celery salt
- ¾ teaspoon dried mustard
- ½ teaspoon garlic powder
- ½ teaspoon freshly ground black pepper
- ½ teaspoon sea salt
- ½ teaspoon dried thyme
- ¼ teaspoon dried oregano
- 4 large eggs
- Oil spray (hand-pumped)

Directions:

1. Place the chicken and buttermilk in a medium bowl, cover, and refrigerate for at least 1 hour, up to overnight.
2. Preheat the toaster oven to 375°F on AIR FRY for 5 minutes.
3. In a large bowl, stir the flour, paprika, celery salt, mustard, garlic powder, pepper, salt, thyme, and oregano until well mixed.
4. Beat the eggs until frothy in a medium bowl and set them beside the flour.
5. Place the air-fryer basket in the baking tray and generously spray it with the oil.
6. Dredge a chicken drumstick in the flour, then the eggs, and then in the flour again, thickly coating it, and place the drumstick in the basket. Repeat with 5 more

drumsticks and spray them all lightly with the oil on all sides.
7. In position 2, air fry for 20 minutes, turning halfway through, until golden brown and crispy with an internal temperature of 165°F.
8. Repeat with the remaining chicken, covering the cooked chicken loosely with foil to keep it warm. Serve.

Chicken In Mango Sauce

Servings: 2
Cooking Time: 40 Minutes

Ingredients:
- 2 skinless and boneless chicken breast halves
- 1 tablespoon capers
- 1 tablespoon raisins
- Mango mixture:
- 1 cup mango pieces
- 1 teaspoon balsamic vinegar
- ½ teaspoon garlic powder
- 1 teaspoon fresh ginger, peeled and minced
- ½ teaspoon soy sauce
- ½ teaspoon curry powder
- 1 tablespoon pimientos, minced
- Salt and pepper to taste

Directions:
1. Preheat the toaster oven to 375° F.
2. Process the mango mixture ingredients in a food processor or blender until smooth. Transfer to an oiled or nonstick 8½ × 8½ × 2-inch square (cake) pan and add the capers, raisins, and pimientos, stirring well to blend. Add the chicken breasts and spoon the mixture over the breasts to coat well.
3. BAKE for 40 minutes. Serve the breasts with the sauce.

Sticky Soy Chicken Thighs

Servings: 2
Cooking Time: 20 Minutes

Ingredients:
- 2 tablespoons less-sodium soy sauce
- 1 tablespoon olive oil
- 1 tablespoon honey
- 1 tablespoon balsamic vinegar
- 1 tablespoon chili sauce
- Juice of 1 lime
- 1 teaspoon minced garlic
- 1 teaspoon ginger, peeled and grated
- 2 bone-in, skin-on chicken thighs
- Oil spray (hand-pumped)
- 1 scallion, both white and green parts, thinly sliced, for garnish
- 2 teaspoons sesame seeds, for garnish

Directions:
1. Preheat the toaster oven to 400°F on AIR FRY for 5 minutes.
2. In a large bowl, combine the soy sauce, olive oil, honey, balsamic vinegar, chili sauce, lime juice, garlic, and ginger. Add the chicken thighs to the bowl and toss to coat. Cover the bowl and refrigerate for 30 minutes.
3. Place the air-fryer basket in the baking tray and generously spray with oil.
4. Place the thighs in the basket, and in position 2, air fry for 20 minutes until cooked through and the thighs are browned and lightly caramelized, with an internal temperature of 165°F.
5. Garnish the chicken with the scallion and sesame seeds and serve.

Chicken Nuggets

Servings: 20
Cooking Time: 14 Minutes

Ingredients:
- 1 pound boneless, skinless chicken thighs, cut into 1-inch chunks
- ¾ teaspoon salt
- ½ teaspoon black pepper
- ½ teaspoon garlic powder
- ½ teaspoon onion powder
- ½ cup flour
- 2 eggs, beaten
- ½ cup panko breadcrumbs
- 3 tablespoons plain breadcrumbs
- oil for misting or cooking spray

Directions:
1. In the bowl of a food processor, combine chicken, ½ teaspoon salt, pepper, garlic powder, and onion

powder. Process in short pulses until chicken is very finely chopped and well blended.

2. Place flour in one shallow dish and beaten eggs in another. In a third dish or plastic bag, mix together the panko crumbs, plain breadcrumbs, and ¼ teaspoon salt.

3. Shape chicken mixture into small nuggets. Dip nuggets in flour, then eggs, then panko crumb mixture.

4. Spray nuggets on both sides with oil or cooking spray and place in air fryer oven in a single layer, close but not overlapping.

5. Air-fry at 360°F for 10 minutes. Spray with oil and cook 4 minutes, until chicken is done and coating is golden brown.

6. Repeat step 5 to cook remaining nuggets.

Quick Chicken For Filling

Servings: 2
Cooking Time: 8 Minutes

Ingredients:

- 1 pound chicken tenders, skinless and boneless
- ½ teaspoon ground cumin
- ½ teaspoon garlic powder
- cooking spray

Directions:

1. Sprinkle raw chicken tenders with seasonings.
2. Spray air fryer oven lightly with cooking spray to prevent sticking.
3. Place chicken in air fryer oven in single layer.
4. Air-fry at 390°F for 4 minutes, turn chicken strips over, and air-fry for an additional 4 minutes.
5. Test for doneness. Thick tenders may require an additional minute or two.

Crispy Chicken Parmesan

Servings: 4
Cooking Time: 12 Minutes

Ingredients:

- 4 skinless, boneless chicken breasts, pounded thin to ¼-inch thickness
- 1 teaspoon salt, divided
- ½ teaspoon black pepper, divided
- 1 cup flour
- 2 eggs
- 1 cup panko breadcrumbs
- ½ teaspoon dried oregano
- ½ cup grated Parmesan cheese

Directions:

1. Pat the chicken breasts with a paper towel. Season the chicken with ½ teaspoon of the salt and ¼ teaspoon of the pepper.
2. In a medium bowl, place the flour.
3. In a second bowl, whisk the eggs.
4. In a third bowl, place the breadcrumbs, oregano, cheese, and the remaining ½ teaspoon of salt and ¼ teaspoon of pepper.
5. Dredge the chicken in the flour and shake off the excess. Dip the chicken into the eggs and then into the breadcrumbs. Set the chicken on a plate and repeat with the remaining chicken pieces.
6. Preheat the toaster oven to 360°F.
7. Place the chicken in the air fryer oven and spray liberally with cooking spray. Air-fry for 8 minutes, turn the chicken breasts over, and cook another 4 minutes. When golden brown, check for an internal temperature of 165°F.

Italian Roasted Chicken Thighs

Servings: 6
Cooking Time: 14 Minutes

Ingredients:

- 6 boneless chicken thighs
- ½ teaspoon dried oregano
- ½ teaspoon garlic powder
- ½ teaspoon sea salt
- ½ teaspoon black pepper
- ¼ teaspoon crushed red pepper flakes

Directions:

1. Pat the chicken thighs with paper towel.
2. In a small bowl, mix the oregano, garlic powder, salt, pepper, and crushed red pepper flakes. Rub the spice mixture onto the chicken thighs.
3. Preheat the toaster oven to 400°F.
4. Place the chicken thighs in the air fryer oven and spray with cooking spray. Air-fry for 10 minutes, turn over, and cook another 4 minutes. When cooking completes, the internal temperature should read 165°F.

Tandoori Chicken

Servings: 4
Cooking Time: 30 Minutes

Ingredients:
- 1 cup plain Greek yogurt
- ¼ sweet onion, finely chopped
- 2 teaspoons garam masala
- 1 teaspoon minced garlic
- 1 teaspoon fresh ginger, peeled and grated
- ½ teaspoon ground cumin
- ½ teaspoon ground coriander
- ¼ teaspoon sea salt
- ⅛ teaspoon cayenne powder
- 4 (4-ounce) skinless, boneless chicken breasts
- Oil spray (hand-pumped)

Directions:
1. Preheat the toaster oven to 375°F on AIR FRY for 5 minutes.
2. In a medium bowl, whisk the yogurt, onion, garam masala, garlic, ginger, cumin, coriander, salt, and cayenne until well blended. Add the chicken breast, turning to coat.
3. Cover the bowl and refrigerate for at least 3 hours to overnight.
4. Place the air-fryer basket in the baking tray and spray it generously with the oil.
5. Place the chicken breasts in the basket after shaking off the excess marinade. Discard the remaining marinade.
6. In position 2, air fry for 25 to 30 minutes, turning halfway through, until browned with an internal temperature of 165°F. Serve.

Roasted Game Hens With Vegetable Stuffing

Servings: 2
Cooking Time: 50 Minutes

Ingredients:
- Stuffing:
- 1 cup multigrain bread crumbs
- 2 tablespoons chopped onion
- 1 carrot, shredded
- 1 celery stalk, shredded
- 1 garlic clove, minced
- 2 tablespoons chopped fresh parsley
- Salt and freshly ground black pepper to taste
- 2 whole game hens (thawed or fresh), giblets removed, rinsed, and patted dry with paper towels

Directions:
1. Preheat the toaster oven to 350° F.
2. Combine the stuffing ingredients in a medium bowl. Stuff the cavities of the game hens and place them in a baking dish.
3. BAKE, covered, for 45 minutes, or until the meat is tender and the juices run clear when the breast is pierced with a fork.
4. BROIL, uncovered, for 8 minutes, or until lightly browned.

Chicken Hand Pies

Servings: 8
Cooking Time: 10 Minutes

Ingredients:
- ¾ cup chicken broth
- ¾ cup frozen mixed peas and carrots
- 1 cup cooked chicken, chopped
- 1 tablespoon cornstarch
- 1 tablespoon milk
- salt and pepper
- 1 8-count can organic flaky biscuits
- oil for misting or cooking spray

Directions:
1. In a medium saucepan, bring chicken broth to a boil. Stir in the frozen peas and carrots and air-fry for 5 minutes over medium heat. Stir in chicken.
2. Mix the cornstarch into the milk until it dissolves. Stir it into the simmering chicken broth mixture and cook just until thickened.
3. Remove from heat, add salt and pepper to taste, and let cool slightly.
4. Lay biscuits out on wax paper. Peel each biscuit apart in the middle to make 2 rounds so you have 16 rounds total. Using your hands or a rolling pin, flatten each biscuit round slightly to make it larger and thinner.

5. Divide chicken filling among 8 of the biscuit rounds. Place remaining biscuit rounds on top and press edges all around. Use the tines of a fork to crimp biscuit edges and make sure they are sealed well.
6. Spray both sides lightly with oil or cooking spray.
7. Cook in a single layer, 4 at a time, at 330°F for 10 minutes or until biscuit dough is cooked through and golden brown.

Peanut Butter-barbeque Chicken

Servings: 4
Cooking Time: 20 Minutes

Ingredients:
- 1 pound boneless, skinless chicken thighs
- salt and pepper
- 1 large orange
- ½ cup barbeque sauce
- 2 tablespoons smooth peanut butter
- 2 tablespoons chopped peanuts for garnish (optional)
- cooking spray

Directions:
1. Season chicken with salt and pepper to taste. Place in a shallow dish or plastic bag.
2. Grate orange peel, squeeze orange and reserve 1 tablespoon of juice for the sauce.
3. Pour remaining juice over chicken and marinate for 30 minutes.
4. Mix together the reserved 1 tablespoon of orange juice, barbeque sauce, peanut butter, and 1 teaspoon grated orange peel.
5. Place ¼ cup of sauce mixture in a small bowl for basting. Set remaining sauce aside to serve with cooked chicken.
6. Preheat the toaster oven to 360°F. Spray air fryer oven with nonstick cooking spray.
7. Remove chicken from marinade, letting excess drip off. Place in air fryer oven and air-fry for 5 minutes. Turn chicken over and cook 5 minutes longer.
8. Brush both sides of chicken lightly with sauce.
9. Cook chicken 5 minutes, then turn thighs one more time, again brushing both sides lightly with sauce. Air-fry for 5 more minutes or until chicken is done and juices run clear.
10. Serve chicken with remaining sauce on the side and garnish with chopped peanuts if you like.

Crispy Curry Chicken Tenders

Servings: 4
Cooking Time: 14 Minutes

Ingredients:
- 1 pound boneless skinless chicken tenders
- ¼ cup plain yogurt
- 2 tablespoons thai red curry paste
- 1½ teaspoons salt, divided
- ½ teaspoon pepper
- 1¾ cups panko breadcrumbs
- 1 teaspoon granulated garlic
- 1 teaspoon granulated onion
- Olive oil or avocado oil spray

Directions:
1. Whisk together the yogurt, curry paste, 1 teaspoon of salt, and pepper in a large bowl. Add the chicken tenders and toss to coat. Cover bowl with plastic wrap and marinate in the fridge for 6-8 hours.
2. Combine the panko breadcrumbs, ½ teaspoon salt, garlic, and onion. Remove chicken tenders from the marinade and coat individually in the panko mixture.
3. Preheat the toaster oven to 430°F.
4. Spray both sides of each chicken tender well with olive oil or avocado oil spray, then place into the fry basket.
5. Insert the fry basket at mid position in the preheated oven.
6. Select the Air Fry and Shake functions, adjust time to 14 minutes, and press Start/Pause.
7. Flip chicken tenders halfway through cooking. The Shake Reminder will let you know when.
8. Remove when chicken tenders are golden and crispy.

Sesame Chicken Breasts

Servings: 2
Cooking Time: 20 Minutes

Ingredients:
- Mixture:
- 2 tablespoons sesame oil
- 2 teaspoons soy sauce
- 2 teaspoons balsamic vinegar
- 2 skinless, boneless chicken breast filets
- 3 tablespoons sesame seeds

Directions:
1. Combine the mixture ingredients in a small bowl and brush the filets liberally. Reserve the mixture. Place the filets on a broiling rack with a pan underneath.
2. BROIL 15 minutes, or until the meat is tender and the juices, when the meat is pierced, run clear. Remove from the oven and brush the filets with the remaining mixture. Place the sesame seeds on a plate and press the chicken breast halves into the seeds, coating well.
3. BROIL for 5 minutes, or until the sesame seeds are browned.

BEEF PORK AND LAMB

Lime And Cumin Lamb Kebabs

Servings: 4
Cooking Time: 16 Minutes

Ingredients:
- 1 pound boneless lean lamb, trimmed and cut into 1 × 1-inch pieces
- 2 plum tomatoes, cut into 2 × 2-inch pieces
- 1 bell pepper, cut into 2 × 2-inch pieces
- 1 small onion, cut into 2 × 2-inch pieces
- Brushing mixture:
- ¼ cup lime juice
- ½ teaspoon soy sauce
- 1 tablespoon honey
- 1½ teaspoon ground cumin

Directions:
1. Skewer alternating pieces of lamb, tomato, pepper, and onion on four 9-inch skewers.
2. Combine the brushing mixture ingredients in a small bowl and brush on the kebabs. Place the skewers on a broiling rack with a pan underneath.
3. BROIL for 8 minutes. Turn the skewers, brush the kebabs with the mixture, and broil for 8 minutes, or until the meat and vegetables are cooked and browned.

Pork Taco Gorditas

Servings: 4
Cooking Time: 21 Minutes

Ingredients:
- 1 pound lean ground pork
- 2 tablespoons chili powder
- 2 tablespoons ground cumin
- 1 teaspoon dried oregano
- 2 teaspoons paprika
- 1 teaspoon garlic powder
- ½ cup water
- 1 (15-ounce) can pinto beans, drained and rinsed
- ½ cup taco sauce
- salt and freshly ground black pepper
- 2 cups grated Cheddar cheese
- 5 (12-inch) flour tortillas
- 4 (8-inch) crispy corn tortilla shells
- 4 cups shredded lettuce
- 1 tomato, diced
- ⅓ cup sliced black olives
- sour cream, for serving
- tomato salsa, for serving

Directions:
1. Preheat the toaster oven to 400°F.
2. Place the ground pork in the air fryer oven and air-fry at 400°F for 10 minutes, stirring a few times during the cooking process to gently break up the meat. Combine the chili powder, cumin, oregano, paprika, garlic powder and water in a small bowl. Stir the spice mixture into the browned pork. Stir in the beans and taco sauce and air-fry for an additional minute. Transfer the pork mixture to a bowl. Season to taste with salt and freshly ground black pepper.
3. Sprinkle ½ cup of the shredded cheese in the center of four of the flour tortillas, making sure to leave a 2-inch border around the edge free of cheese and filling. Divide the pork mixture among the four tortillas, placing it on top of the cheese. Place a crunchy corn tortilla on top of the pork and top with shredded lettuce, diced tomatoes, and black olives. Cut the remaining flour tortilla into 4 quarters. These quarters of tortilla will serve as the bottom of the gordita. Place one quarter tortilla on top of each gordita and fold the edges of the bottom flour tortilla up over the sides, enclosing the filling. While holding the seams down, brush the bottom of the gordita with olive oil and place the seam side down on the countertop while you finish the remaining three gorditas.
4. Preheat the toaster oven to 380°F.
5. Air-fry one gordita at a time. Transfer the gordita carefully to the air fryer oven, seam side down. Brush or spray the top tortilla with oil and air-fry for 5 minutes. Carefully turn the gordita over and air-fry for an additional 5 minutes, until both sides are browned. When finished air frying all four gorditas, layer them back into the air fryer oven for an additional minute to make sure they are all warm before serving with sour cream and salsa.

Crispy Smoked Pork Chops

Servings: 3
Cooking Time: 8 Minutes

Ingredients:
- ⅔ cup All-purpose flour or tapioca flour
- 1 Large egg white(s)
- 2 tablespoons Water
- 1½ cups Corn flake crumbs (gluten-free, if a concern)
- 3 ½-pound, ½-inch-thick bone-in smoked pork chops

Directions:
1. Preheat the toaster oven to 375°F.
2. Set up and fill three shallow soup plates or small pie plates on your counter: one for the flour; one for the egg white(s), whisked with the water until foamy; and one for the corn flake crumbs.
3. Set a chop in the flour and turn it several times, coating both sides and the edges. Gently shake off any excess flour, then set it in the beaten egg white mixture. Turn to coat both sides as well as the edges. Let any excess egg white slip back into the rest, then set the chop in the corn flake crumbs. Turn it several times, pressing gently to coat the chop evenly on both sides and around the edge. Set the chop aside and continue coating the remaining chop(s) in the same way.
4. Set the chops in the air fryer oven with as much air space between them as possible. Air-fry undisturbed for 8 minutes, or until the coating is crunchy and the chops are heated through.
5. Use kitchen tongs to transfer the chops to a wire rack and cool for a couple of minutes before serving.

Red Curry Flank Steak

Servings: 4
Cooking Time: 18 Minutes

Ingredients:
- 3 tablespoons red curry paste
- ¼ cup olive oil
- 2 teaspoons grated fresh ginger
- 2 tablespoons soy sauce
- 2 tablespoons rice wine vinegar
- 3 scallions, minced
- 1½ pounds flank steak
- fresh cilantro (or parsley) leaves

Directions:
1. Mix the red curry paste, olive oil, ginger, soy sauce, rice vinegar and scallions together in a bowl. Place the flank steak in a shallow glass dish and pour half the marinade over the steak. Pierce the steak several times with a fork or meat tenderizer to let the marinade penetrate the meat. Turn the steak over, pour the remaining marinade over the top and pierce the steak several times again. Cover and marinate the steak in the refrigerator for 6 to 8 hours.
2. When you are ready to cook, remove the steak from the refrigerator and let it sit at room temperature for 30 minutes.
3. Preheat the toaster oven to 400°F.
4. Cut the flank steak in half so that it fits more easily into the air fryer oven and transfer both pieces to the air fryer oven. Pour the marinade over the steak. Air-fry for 18 minutes, depending on your preferred degree of doneness of the steak (12 minutes = medium rare). Flip the steak over halfway through the cooking time.
5. When your desired degree of doneness has been reached, remove the steak to a cutting board and let it rest for 5 minutes before slicing. Thinly slice the flank steak against the grain of the meat. Transfer the slices to a serving platter, pour any juice from the bottom of the air fryer oven over the sliced flank steak and sprinkle the fresh cilantro on top.

Bourbon Broiled Steak

Servings: 2
Cooking Time: 14 Minutes

Ingredients:
- Brushing mixture:
- ¼ cup bourbon
- 1 teaspoon garlic powder
- 1 tablespoon olive oil
- 1 teaspoon soy sauce
- 2 6- to 8-ounce sirloin steaks, ¾ inch thick

Directions:
1. Combine the brushing mixture ingredients in a small bowl. Brush the steaks on both sides with the

mixture and place on the broiling rack with a pan underneath.
2. BROIL 4 minutes, remove from the oven, turn with tongs, brush the top and sides, and broil again for 4 minutes, or until done to your preference. To use the brushing mixture as a sauce or gravy, pour the mixture into a baking pan.
3. BROIL the mixture for 6 minutes, or until it begins to bubble.

Albóndigas

Servings: 4
Cooking Time: 15 Minutes

Ingredients:
- 1 pound Lean ground pork
- 3 tablespoons Very finely chopped trimmed scallions
- 3 tablespoons Finely chopped fresh cilantro leaves
- 3 tablespoons Plain panko bread crumbs (gluten-free, if a concern)
- 3 tablespoons Dry white wine, dry sherry, or unsweetened apple juice
- 1½ teaspoons Minced garlic
- 1¼ teaspoons Mild smoked paprika
- ¾ teaspoon Dried oregano
- ¾ teaspoon Table salt
- ¼ teaspoon Ground black pepper
- Olive oil spray

Directions:
1. Preheat the toaster oven to 400°F.
2. Mix the ground pork, scallions, cilantro, bread crumbs, wine or its substitute, garlic, smoked paprika, oregano, salt, and pepper in a bowl until the herbs and spices are evenly distributed in the mixture.
3. Lightly coat your clean hands with olive oil spray, then form the ground pork mixture into balls, using 2 tablespoons for each one. Spray your hands frequently so that the meat mixture doesn't stick.
4. Set the balls in the air fryer oven so that they're not touching, even if they're close together. Air-fry undisturbed for 15 minutes, or until well browned and an instant-read meat thermometer inserted into one or two balls registers 165°F.
5. Use a nonstick-safe spatula and kitchen tongs for balance to gently transfer the fragile balls to a wire rack to cool for 5 minutes before serving.

Mustard-herb Lamb Chops

Servings: 2
Cooking Time: 15 Minutes

Ingredients:
- 2 tablespoons Dijon mustard
- 1 teaspoon minced garlic
- ¼ cup bread crumbs
- 1 teaspoon dried Italian herbs
- Zest of 1 lemon
- 4 lamb loin chops (about 1 pound), room temperature
- Sea salt, for seasoning
- Freshly ground black pepper, for seasoning
- Oil spray (hand-pumped)

Directions:
1. Preheat the toaster oven to 425°F on CONVECTION BAKE for 5 minutes.
2. Line the baking tray with parchment or aluminum foil.
3. In a small bowl, stir the mustard and garlic until blended.
4. In another small bowl, stir the bread crumbs, herbs, and lemon zest until mixed.
5. Lightly season the lamb chops on both sides with salt and pepper. Brush the mustard mixture over a chop and dredge it in the bread crumb mixture to lightly bread the lamb. Set the lamb on the baking tray and repeat with the other chops.
6. Spray the chops lightly with the oil, and in position 2, bake for 15 minutes until browned and the internal temperature is 130°F for medium-rare.
7. Rest the lamb for 5 minutes, then serve.

Glazed Meatloaf

Servings: 4
Cooking Time: 60 Minutes

Ingredients:
- 2 pounds extra-lean ground beef
- ½ cup fine bread crumbs
- 1 large egg
- 1 medium carrot, shredded
- 2 teaspoons minced garlic
- ¼ cup milk
- 1 tablespoon Italian seasoning
- ½ teaspoon sea salt
- ⅛ teaspoon freshly ground black pepper
- ½ cup ketchup
- 1 tablespoon dark brown sugar
- 1 teaspoon apple cider vinegar

Directions:
1. Place the rack in position 1 and preheat the toaster oven to 375°F on BAKE for 5 minutes.
2. In a large bowl, mix the ground beef, bread crumbs, egg, carrot, garlic, milk, Italian seasoning, salt, and pepper until well combined.
3. Press the mixture into a 9-by-5-inch loaf pan.
4. In a small bowl, stir the ketchup, brown sugar, and vinegar. Set aside.
5. Bake for 40 minutes.
6. Take the meatloaf out and spread the glaze over the top. Bake an additional 20 minutes until cooked through, with an internal temperature of 165°F. Serve.

Barbecue-style London Broil

Servings: 5
Cooking Time: 17 Minutes

Ingredients:
- ¾ teaspoon Mild smoked paprika
- ¾ teaspoon Dried oregano
- ¾ teaspoon Table salt
- ¾ teaspoon Ground black pepper
- ¼ teaspoon Garlic powder
- ¼ teaspoon Onion powder
- 1½ pounds Beef London broil (in one piece)
- Olive oil spray

Directions:
1. Preheat the toaster oven to 400°F.
2. Mix the smoked paprika, oregano, salt, pepper, garlic powder, and onion powder in a small bowl until uniform.
3. Pat and rub this mixture across all surfaces of the beef. Lightly coat the beef on all sides with olive oil spray.
4. When the machine is at temperature, lay the London broil flat in the air fryer oven and air-fry undisturbed for 8 minutes for the small batch, 10 minutes for the medium batch, or 12 minutes for the large batch for medium-rare, until an instant-read meat thermometer inserted into the center of the meat registers 130°F (not USDA-approved). Add 1, 2, or 3 minutes, respectively (based on the size of the cut) for medium, until an instant-read meat thermometer registers 135°F (not USDA-approved). Or add 3, 4, or 5 minutes respectively for medium, until an instant-read meat thermometer registers 145°F (USDA-approved).
5. Use kitchen tongs to transfer the London broil to a cutting board. Let the meat rest for 10 minutes. It needs a long time for the juices to be reincorporated into the meat's fibers. Carve it against the grain into very thin (less than ¼-inch-thick) slices to serve.

Kielbasa Chunks With Pineapple & Peppers

Servings: 2
Cooking Time: 10 Minutes

Ingredients:
- ¾ pound kielbasa sausage
- 1 cup bell pepper chunks (any color)
- 1 8-ounce can pineapple chunks in juice, drained
- 1 tablespoon barbeque seasoning
- 1 tablespoon soy sauce
- cooking spray

Directions:
1. Cut sausage into ½-inch slices.
2. In a medium bowl, toss all ingredients together.
3. Spray air fryer oven with nonstick cooking spray.
4. Pour sausage mixture into the air fryer oven.
5. Air-fry at 390°F for approximately 5 minutes. Cook an additional 5 minutes.

Lime-ginger Pork Tenderloin

Servings: 4
Cooking Time: 26 Minutes

Ingredients:
- ½ cup packed dark brown sugar
- Juice of ½ lime
- 2 teaspoons fresh ginger, peeled and grated
- 1 teaspoon minced garlic
- 2 (1-pound) extra-lean pork tenderloins, trimmed of fat
- Sea salt, for seasoning
- Freshly ground black pepper, for seasoning
- 1 tablespoon olive oil

Directions:
1. Preheat the toaster oven to 400°F on CONVECTION BAKE for 5 minutes.
2. In a small bowl, stir the sugar, lime juice, ginger, and garlic together.
3. Lightly season the pork tenderloins all over with salt and pepper.
4. Heat the oil in a large skillet over medium-high heat. Brown the pork on all sides, about 6 minutes in total.
5. Place the air-fryer basket in the baking tray and place the tenderloins in the basket.
6. Brush the pork all over with the ginger-lime mixture.
7. In position 2, bake for 20 minutes, basting the pork at 10 minutes, until it reaches an internal temperature of about 145°F.
8. Let the pork rest for 10 minutes and serve.

Italian Meatballs

Servings: 4
Cooking Time: 12 Minutes

Ingredients:
- 12 ounces lean ground beef
- 4 ounces Italian sausage, casing removed
- ½ cup breadcrumbs
- 1 cup grated Parmesan cheese
- 1 egg
- 2 tablespoons milk
- 2 teaspoons Italian seasoning
- ½ teaspoon onion powder
- ½ teaspoon garlic powder
- Pinch of red pepper flakes

Directions:
1. In a large bowl, place all the ingredients and mix well. Roll out 24 meatballs.
2. Preheat the toaster oven to 360°F.
3. Place the meatballs in the air fryer oven and air-fry for 12 minutes, tossing every 4 minutes. Using a food thermometer, check to ensure the internal temperature of the meatballs is 165°F.

Beef-stuffed Bell Peppers

Servings: 4
Cooking Time: 30 Minutes

Ingredients:
- 4 medium red or yellow bell peppers
- 1 pound extra-lean ground beef
- ½ sweet onion, finely chopped
- 2 teaspoons minced garlic
- 1 cup marinara sauce
- 1 cup ready-made brown or wild rice
- 1 cup fresh kale, chopped
- 1 teaspoon dried basil
- Sea salt, for seasoning
- Freshly ground black pepper, for seasoning
- 1 cup Swiss cheese, shredded

Directions:
1. Preheat the toaster oven to 350°F on AIR FRY for 5 minutes.
2. Cut the top off the peppers and scoop the seeds and membranes out. Set the pepper tops aside.
3. Place a large skillet over medium-high heat and brown the beef, about 10 minutes.
4. Add the onion and garlic and sauté until softened, about 4 minutes.
5. Add the marinara sauce, rice, kale, and basil, stirring to combine. Remove from the heat and season with salt and pepper.
6. Place the air-fryer basket in the baking tray and place the peppers in the basket, hollow-side up.
7. Evenly divide the filling among the peppers. You can place the pepper tops cut-side up and place the

pepper bottoms in the tops to balance them, so that they do not tip over.

8. In position 1, air fry for 15 minutes until the peppers are tender. Top with the cheese and air fry for 2 more minutes more to melt the cheese. Serve.

Italian Sausage & Peppers

Servings: 6
Cooking Time: 25 Minutes

Ingredients:
- 1 6-ounce can tomato paste
- ⅔ cup water
- 1 8-ounce can tomato sauce
- 1 teaspoon dried parsley flakes
- ½ teaspoon garlic powder
- ⅛ teaspoon oregano
- ½ pound mild Italian bulk sausage
- 1 tablespoon extra virgin olive oil
- ½ large onion, cut in 1-inch chunks
- 4 ounces fresh mushrooms, sliced
- 1 large green bell pepper, cut in 1-inch chunks
- 8 ounces spaghetti, cooked
- Parmesan cheese for serving

Directions:
1. In a large saucepan or skillet, stir together the tomato paste, water, tomato sauce, parsley, garlic, and oregano. Heat on stovetop over very low heat while preparing meat and vegetables.
2. Break sausage into small chunks, about ½-inch pieces. Place in air fryer oven baking pan.
3. Air-fry at 390°F for 5 minutes. Stir. Cook 7 minutes longer or until sausage is well done. Remove from pan, drain on paper towels, and add to the sauce mixture.
4. If any sausage grease remains in baking pan, pour it off or use paper towels to soak it up. (Be careful handling that hot pan!)
5. Place olive oil, onions, and mushrooms in pan and stir. Air-fry for 5 minutes or just until tender. Using a slotted spoon, transfer onions and mushrooms from baking pan into the sauce and sausage mixture.
6. Place bell pepper chunks in air fryer oven baking pan and air-fry for 8 minutes or until tender. When done, stir into sauce with sausage and other vegetables.
7. Serve over cooked spaghetti with plenty of Parmesan cheese.

Perfect Pork Chops

Servings: 3
Cooking Time: 10 Minutes

Ingredients:
- ¾ teaspoon Mild paprika
- ¾ teaspoon Dried thyme
- ¾ teaspoon Onion powder
- ¼ teaspoon Garlic powder
- ¼ teaspoon Table salt
- ¼ teaspoon Ground black pepper
- 3 6-ounce boneless center-cut pork loin chops
- Vegetable oil spray

Directions:
1. Preheat the toaster oven to 400°F.
2. Mix the paprika, thyme, onion powder, garlic powder, salt, and pepper in a small bowl until well combined. Massage this mixture into both sides of the chops. Generously coat both sides of the chops with vegetable oil spray.
3. When the machine is at temperature, set the chops in the air fryer oven with as much air space between them as possible. Air-fry undisturbed for 10 minutes, or until an instant-read meat thermometer inserted into the thickest part of a chop registers 145°F.
4. Use kitchen tongs to transfer the chops to a cutting board or serving plates. Cool for 5 minutes before serving.

Stuffed Bell Peppers

Servings: 4
Cooking Time: 10 Minutes

Ingredients:
- ¼ pound lean ground pork
- ¾ pound lean ground beef
- ¼ cup onion, minced
- 1 15-ounce can Red Gold crushed tomatoes
- 1 teaspoon Worcestershire sauce
- 1 teaspoon barbeque seasoning
- 1 teaspoon honey
- ½ teaspoon dried basil

- ½ cup cooked brown rice
- ½ teaspoon garlic powder
- ½ teaspoon oregano
- ½ teaspoon salt
- 2 small bell peppers

Directions:

1. Place pork, beef, and onion in air fryer oven baking pan and air-fry at 360°F for 5 minutes.
2. Stir to break apart chunks and cook 3 more minutes. Continue cooking and stirring in 2-minute intervals until meat is well done. Remove from pan and drain.
3. In a small saucepan, combine the tomatoes, Worcestershire, barbeque seasoning, honey, and basil. Stir well to mix in honey and seasonings.
4. In a large bowl, combine the cooked meat mixture, rice, garlic powder, oregano, and salt. Add ¼ cup of the seasoned crushed tomatoes. Stir until well mixed.
5. Cut peppers in half and remove stems and seeds.
6. Stuff each pepper half with one fourth of the meat mixture.
7. Place the peppers in air fryer oven and air-fry for 10 minutes, until peppers are crisp tender.
8. Heat remaining tomato sauce. Serve peppers with warm sauce spooned over top.

Almond And Sun-dried Tomato Crusted Pork Chops

Servings: 4
Cooking Time: 10 Minutes

Ingredients:

- ½ cup oil-packed sun-dried tomatoes
- ½ cup toasted almonds
- ¼ cup grated Parmesan cheese
- ½ cup olive oil
- 2 tablespoons water
- ½ teaspoon salt
- freshly ground black pepper
- 4 center-cut boneless pork chops (about 1¼ pounds)

Directions:

1. Place the sun-dried tomatoes into a food processor and pulse them until they are coarsely chopped. Add the almonds, Parmesan cheese, olive oil, water, salt and pepper. Process all the ingredients into a smooth paste. Spread most of the paste (leave a little in reserve) onto both sides of the pork chops and then pierce the meat several times with a needle-style meat tenderizer or a fork. Let the pork chops sit and marinate for at least 1 hour (refrigerate if marinating for longer than 1 hour).
2. Preheat the toaster oven to 370°F.
3. Brush a little olive oil on the bottom of the air fryer oven. Transfer the pork chops into the air fryer oven, spooning a little more of the sun-dried tomato paste onto the pork chops if there are any gaps where the paste may have been rubbed off. Air-fry the pork chops at 370°F for 10 minutes, turning the chops over halfway through the cooking process.
4. When the pork chops have finished cooking, transfer them to a serving plate and serve with mashed potatoes and vegetables for a hearty meal.

Seasoned Boneless Pork Sirloin Chops

Servings: 2
Cooking Time: 16 Minutes

Ingredients:

- Seasoning mixture:
- ½ teaspoon ground cumin
- ¼ teaspoon turmeric
- Pinch of ground cardamom
- Pinch of grated nutmeg
- 1 teaspoon vegetable oil
- 1 teaspoon Pickapeppa sauce
- 2½- to ¾-pound boneless lean pork sirloin chops

Directions:

1. Combine the seasoning mixture ingredients in a small bowl and brush on both sides of the chops. Place the chops on the broiling rack with a pan underneath.
2. BROIL 8 minutes, remove the chops, turn, and brush with the mixture. Broil again for 8 minutes, or until the chops are done to your preference.

Extra Crispy Country-style Pork Riblets

Servings: 3
Cooking Time: 30 Minutes

Ingredients:
- ⅓ cup Tapioca flour
- 2½ tablespoons Chile powder
- ¾ teaspoon Table salt (optional)
- 1¼ pounds Boneless country-style pork ribs, cut into 1½-inch chunks
- Vegetable oil spray

Directions:
1. Preheat the toaster oven to 375°F.
2. Mix the tapioca flour, chile powder, and salt (if using) in a large bowl until well combined. Add the country-style rib chunks and toss well to coat thoroughly.
3. When the machine is at temperature, gently shake off any excess tapioca coating from the chunks. Generously coat them on all sides with vegetable oil spray. Arrange the chunks in the air fryer oven in one (admittedly fairly tight) layer. The pieces may touch. Air-fry for 30 minutes, rearranging the pieces at the 10- and 20-minute marks to expose any touching bits, until very crisp and well browned.
4. Gently pour the contents of the pan onto a wire rack. Cool for 5 minutes before serving.

Lamb Curry

Servings: 4
Cooking Time: 40 Minutes

Ingredients:
- 1 pound lean lamb for stewing, trimmed and cut into 1 × 1-inch pieces
- 1 small onion, chopped
- 3 garlic cloves, minced
- 2 plum tomatoes, chopped
- ½ cup dry white wine
- 2 tablespoons curry powder
- Salt and cayenne to taste

Directions:
1. Preheat the toaster oven to 400° F.
2. Combine all the ingredients in an 8½ × 8½ × 4-inch ovenproof baking dish. Adjust the seasonings.
3. BAKE, covered, for 40 minutes, or until the meat is tender and the onion is cooked.

Herbed Lamb Burgers

Servings: 4
Cooking Time: 15 Minutes

Ingredients:
- 1 pound lean ground lamb
- 1 large egg
- 1 tablespoon fresh parsley, chopped
- 2 teaspoons fresh mint, chopped
- 1 teaspoon minced garlic
- ¼ teaspoon sea salt
- ⅛ teaspoon freshly ground black pepper
- Olive oil spray (hand-pumped)
- 4 whole-wheat buns
- ¼ cup store-bought tzatziki sauce
- 1 tomato, cut into slices
- 4 thin red onion slices
- ½ cup shredded lettuce

Directions:
1. Preheat the toaster oven to 350°F on CONVECTION BROIL for 5 minutes.
2. In a large bowl, mix the lamb, egg, parsley, mint, garlic, salt, and pepper. Form the mixture into 4 patties.
3. Place the air-fryer basket in the baking tray and place the burger patties in the basket. Lightly spray the patties with the oil on both sides.
4. In position 2, broil for 15 minutes, turning halfway through.
5. Serve on the buns topped with tzatziki sauce, tomato, onion, and lettuce.

Calf's Liver

Servings: 4
Cooking Time: 5 Minutes

Ingredients:
- 1 pound sliced calf's liver
- salt and pepper
- 2 eggs
- 2 tablespoons milk

- ½ cup whole wheat flour
- 1½ cups panko breadcrumbs
- ½ cup plain breadcrumbs
- ½ teaspoon salt
- ¼ teaspoon pepper
- oil for misting or cooking spray

Directions:
1. Cut liver slices crosswise into strips about ½-inch wide. Sprinkle with salt and pepper to taste.
2. Beat together egg and milk in a shallow dish.
3. Place wheat flour in a second shallow dish.
4. In a third shallow dish, mix together panko, plain breadcrumbs, ½ teaspoon salt, and ¼ teaspoon pepper.
5. Preheat the toaster oven to 390°F.
6. Dip liver strips in flour, egg wash, and then breadcrumbs, pressing in coating slightly to make crumbs stick.
7. Cooking half the liver at a time, place strips in air fryer oven in a single layer, close but not touching. Air-fry at 390°F for 5 minutes or until done to your preference.
8. Repeat step 7 to cook remaining liver.

Orange Glazed Pork Tenderloin

Servings: 3
Cooking Time: 23 Minutes

Ingredients:
- 2 tablespoons brown sugar
- 2 teaspoons cornstarch
- 2 teaspoons Dijon mustard
- ½ cup orange juice
- ½ teaspoon soy sauce
- 2 teaspoons grated fresh ginger
- ¼ cup white wine
- zest of 1 orange
- 1 pound pork tenderloin
- salt and freshly ground black pepper
- oranges, halved (for garnish)
- fresh parsley or other green herb (for garnish)

Directions:
1. Combine the brown sugar, cornstarch, Dijon mustard, orange juice, soy sauce, ginger, white wine and orange zest in a small saucepan and bring the mixture to a boil on the stovetop. Lower the heat and simmer while you cook the pork tenderloin or until the sauce has thickened.
2. Preheat the toaster oven to 370°F.
3. Season all sides of the pork tenderloin with salt and freshly ground black pepper. Transfer the tenderloin to the air fryer oven, bending the pork into a wide "U" shape if necessary to fit in the air fryer oven. Air-fry at 370°F for 20 to 23 minutes, or until the internal temperature reaches 145°F. Flip the tenderloin over halfway through the cooking process and baste with the sauce.
4. Transfer the tenderloin to a cutting board and let it rest for 5 minutes. Slice the pork at a slight angle and serve immediately with orange halves and fresh herbs to dress it up. Drizzle any remaining glaze over the top.

Tuscan Pork Tenderloin

Servings: 4
Cooking Time: 35 Minutes

Ingredients:
- Nonstick cooking spray.
- 1 pork tenderloin (1 ¼ to 1 ½ pounds)
- Kosher salt and freshly ground black pepper
- 8 to 10 fresh basil leaves
- 1 ½ teaspoons minced garlic (about 3 cloves garlic)
- 2 slices prosciutto
- 2 ounces mozzarella cheese, cut into thin strips, or ½ cup shredded
- 1 tablespoon olive oil
- 1 teaspoon Italian seasoning

Directions:
1. Preheat the toaster oven to 400°F. Spray a 12 x 12-inch baking pan with nonstick cooking spray.
2. Cut the pork tenderloin in half lengthwise, not quite cutting through one side, and gently open it (like a book) so it lays flat. Cover the meat with plastic wrap. Pound the meat with the flat side of a meat pounder until the meat is even and about ½ inch thick.
3. Season the cut side of the meat with salt and pepper. Arrange the basil leaves evenly over the meat, then sprinkle with 1 teaspoon of the minced garlic. Top with an even layer of prosciutto and cheese. Roll the meat

from the longer side covering the cheese and other filling ingredients completely. Tie the meat shut with kitchen twine, taking care to keep the roll tight and the filling inside.

4. Rub the outside of the meat with the olive oil. Mix the Italian seasoning and the remaining ½ teaspoon garlic in a small bowl. Season with salt and pepper. Rub the seasoning mixture evenly over the meat.

5. Place the meat in the prepared pan. Roast, uncovered, for 25 to 35 minutes or until the tenderloin is brown and the pork is just slightly pink inside.

6. Let stand for 5 to 10 minutes. Slice crosswise into slices about 1 inch thick.

Air-fried Roast Beef With Rosemary Roasted Potatoes

Servings: 8
Cooking Time: 60 Minutes

Ingredients:
- 1 (5-pound) top sirloin roast
- salt and freshly ground black pepper
- 1 teaspoon dried thyme
- 2 pounds red potatoes, halved or quartered
- 2 teaspoons olive oil
- 1 teaspoon very finely chopped fresh rosemary, plus more for garnish

Directions:
1. Start by making sure your roast will fit into the air fryer oven without touching the top element. Trim it if you have to in order to get it to fit nicely in your air fryer oven. (You can always save the trimmings for another use, like a beef sandwich.)
2. Preheat the toaster oven to 360°F.
3. Season the beef all over with salt, pepper and thyme. Transfer the seasoned roast to the air fryer oven.
4. Air-fry at 360°F for 20 minutes. Turn the roast over and continue to air-fry at 360°F for another 20 minutes.
5. Toss the potatoes with the olive oil, salt, pepper and fresh rosemary. Turn the roast over again in the air fryer oven and toss the potatoes in around the sides of the roast. Air-fry the roast and potatoes at 360°F for another 20 minutes. Check the internal temperature of the roast with an instant-read thermometer, and continue to roast until the beef is 5° lower than your desired degree of doneness. (Rare – 130°F, Medium – 150°F, Well done – 170°F.) Let the roast rest for 5 to 10 minutes before slicing and serving. While the roast is resting, continue to air-fry the potatoes if desired for extra browning and crispiness.
6. Slice the roast and serve with the potatoes, adding a little more fresh rosemary if desired.

Skirt Steak Fajitas

Servings: 4
Cooking Time: 30 Minutes

Ingredients:
- 2 tablespoons olive oil
- ¼ cup lime juice
- 1 clove garlic, minced
- ½ teaspoon ground cumin
- ½ teaspoon hot sauce
- ½ teaspoon salt
- 2 tablespoons chopped fresh cilantro
- 1 pound skirt steak
- 1 onion, sliced
- 1 teaspoon chili powder
- 1 red pepper, sliced
- 1 green pepper, sliced
- salt and freshly ground black pepper
- 8 flour tortillas
- shredded lettuce, crumbled Queso Fresco (or grated Cheddar cheese), sliced black olives, diced tomatoes, sour cream and guacamole for serving

Directions:
1. Combine the olive oil, lime juice, garlic, cumin, hot sauce, salt and cilantro in a shallow dish. Add the skirt steak and turn it over several times to coat all sides. Pierce the steak with a needle-style meat tenderizer or paring knife. Marinate the steak in the refrigerator for at least 3 hours, or overnight. When you are ready to cook, remove the steak from the refrigerator and let it sit at room temperature for 30 minutes.
2. Preheat the toaster oven to 400°F.
3. Toss the onion slices with the chili powder and a little olive oil and transfer them to the air fryer oven. Air-fry at 400°F for 5 minutes. Add the red and green

peppers to the air fryer oven with the onions, season with salt and pepper and air-fry for 8 more minutes, until the onions and peppers are soft. Transfer the vegetables to a dish and cover with aluminum foil to keep warm.

4. Place the skirt steak in the air fryer oven and pour the marinade over the top. Air-fry at 400°F for 12 minutes. Flip the steak over and air-fry at 400°F for an additional 5 minutes. (The time needed for your steak will depend on the thickness of the skirt steak. 17 minutes should bring your steak to roughly medium.) Transfer the cooked steak to a cutting board and let the steak rest for a few minutes. If the peppers and onions need to be heated, return them to the air fryer oven for just 1 to 2 minutes.

5. Thinly slice the steak at an angle, cutting against the grain of the steak. Serve the steak with the onions and peppers, the warm tortillas and the fajita toppings on the side so that everyone can make their own fajita.

Spicy Little Beef Birds

Servings: 2
Cooking Time: 12 Minutes

Ingredients:
- Spicy mixture:
- 1 tablespoon olive oil
- 1 tablespoon brown mustard
- 1 teaspoon chili powder
- 1 teaspoon garlic powder
- 1 teaspoon hot sauce
- 1 tablespoon barbecue sauce or salsa
- Salt and freshly ground black pepper to taste
- ½ to ¾ pound pepper steaks, cut into 3 × 4-inch strips

Directions:
1. Blend the spicy mixture ingredients in a small bowl and brush both sides of the beef strips.
2. Roll up the strips lengthwise and fasten with toothpicks near each end. Place the beef rolls in an oiled or nonstick 8½ × 8½ × 2-inch square baking (cake) pan.
3. BROIL for 6 minutes, remove from the oven, and turn with tongs. Brush with the spicy mixture and broil again for 6 minutes, or until done to your preference.

Pretzel-coated Pork Tenderloin

Servings: 4
Cooking Time: 10 Minutes

Ingredients:
- 1 Large egg white(s)
- 2 teaspoons Dijon mustard (gluten-free, if a concern)
- 1½ cups (about 6 ounces) Crushed pretzel crumbs
- 1 pound (4 sections) Pork tenderloin, cut into ¼-pound (4-ounce) sections
- Vegetable oil spray

Directions:
1. Preheat the toaster oven to 350°F.
2. Set up and fill two shallow soup plates or small pie plates on your counter: one for the egg white(s), whisked with the mustard until foamy; and one for the pretzel crumbs.
3. Dip a section of pork tenderloin in the egg white mixture and turn it to coat well, even on the ends. Let any excess egg white mixture slip back into the rest, then set the pork in the pretzel crumbs. Roll it several times, pressing gently, until the pork is evenly coated, even on the ends. Generously coat the pork section with vegetable oil spray, set it aside, and continue coating and spraying the remaining sections.
4. Set the pork sections in the air fryer oven with at least ¼ inch between them. Air-fry undisturbed for 10 minutes, or until an instant-read meat thermometer inserted into the center of one section registers 145°F.
5. Use kitchen tongs to transfer the pieces to a wire rack. Cool for 3 to 5 minutes before serving.

Beef, Onion, And Pepper Shish Kebab

Servings: 4
Cooking Time: 20 Minutes

Ingredients:
- Marinade:
- 2 tablespoons olive oil
- ½ cup dry red wine
- 1 tablespoon soy sauce
- 1 teaspoon chili powder
- 1 teaspoon Worcestershire sauce

- 1 teaspoon garlic powder
- 1 teaspoon spicy brown mustard
- 1 teaspoon brown sugar
- 8 onion quarters, approximately 2 × 2-inch pieces
- 8 bell pepper quarters, 2 × 2-inch pieces
- 1 pound lean boneless beef (sirloin, round steak, London broil), cut into 8 2-inch cubes
- 4 8-inch metal or wooden (bamboo) skewers

Directions:
1. Combine the marinade ingredients in a large bowl. Add the onion, peppers, and beef. Refrigerate, covered, for at least 1 hour or
2. Skewer alternating beef, pepper, and onion pieces. Brush with the marinade mixture and place the skewers on a broiling rack with the pan underneath.
3. BROIL for 5 minutes, remove the pan with the skewers from the oven, turn the skewers, brush again, then broil for another 5 minutes. Repeat turning and brushing every 5 minutes, until the peppers and onions are well cooked and browned to your preference.

Perfect Strip Steaks

Servings: 2
Cooking Time: 17 Minutes

Ingredients:
- 1½ tablespoons Olive oil
- 1½ tablespoons Minced garlic
- 2 teaspoons Ground black pepper
- 1 teaspoon Table salt
- 2 ¾-pound boneless beef strip steak(s)

Directions:
1. Preheat the toaster oven to 375°F (or 380°F or 390°F, if one of these is the closest setting).
2. Mix the oil, garlic, pepper, and salt in a small bowl, then smear this mixture over both sides of the steak(s).
3. When the machine is at temperature, put the steak(s) in the air fryer oven with as much air space as possible between them for the larger batch. They should not overlap or even touch. That said, even just a ¼-inch between them will work. Air-fry for 12 minutes, turning once, until an instant-read meat thermometer inserted into the thickest part of a steak registers 127°F for rare (not USDA-approved). Or air-fry for 15 minutes, turning once, until an instant-read meat thermometer registers 145°F for medium (USDA-approved). If the machine is at 390°F, the steaks may cook 2 minutes more quickly than the stated timing.
4. Use kitchen tongs to transfer the steak(s) to a wire rack. Cool for 5 minutes before serving.

Lamb Burger With Feta And Olives

Servings: 3
Cooking Time: 16 Minutes

Ingredients:
- 2 teaspoons olive oil
- ⅓ onion, finely chopped
- 1 clove garlic, minced
- 1 pound ground lamb
- 2 tablespoons fresh parsley, finely chopped
- 1½ teaspoons fresh oregano, finely chopped
- ½ cup black olives, finely chopped
- ⅓ cup crumbled feta cheese
- ½ teaspoon salt
- freshly ground black pepper
- 4 thick pita breads
- toppings and condiments

Directions:
1. Preheat a medium skillet over medium-high heat on the stovetop. Add the olive oil and cook the onion until tender, but not browned – about 4 to 5 minutes. Add the garlic and air-fry for another minute. Transfer the onion and garlic to a mixing bowl and add the ground lamb, parsley, oregano, olives, feta cheese, salt and pepper. Gently mix the ingredients together.
2. Divide the mixture into 3 or 4 equal portions and then form the hamburgers, being careful not to over-handle the meat. One good way to do this is to throw the meat back and forth between your hands like a baseball, packing the meat each time you catch it. Flatten the balls into patties, making an indentation in the center of each patty. Flatten the sides of the patties as well to make it easier to fit them into the air fryer oven.
3. Preheat the toaster oven to 370°F.
4. If you don't have room for all four burgers, air-fry two or three burgers at a time for 8 minutes at 370°F. Flip the burgers over and air-fry for another 8 minutes.

If you cooked your burgers in batches, return the first batch of burgers to the air fryer oven for the last two minutes of cooking to re-heat. This should give you a medium-well burger. If you'd prefer a medium-rare burger, shorten the cooking time to about 13 minutes. Remove the burgers to a resting plate and let the burgers rest for a few minutes before dressing and serving.

5. While the burgers are resting, toast the pita breads in the air fryer oven for 2 minutes. Tuck the burgers into the toasted pita breads, or wrap the pitas around the burgers and serve with a tzatziki sauce or some mayonnaise.

Sloppy Joes

Servings: 4
Cooking Time: 17 Minutes

Ingredients:
- oil for misting or cooking spray
- 1 pound very lean ground beef
- 1 teaspoon onion powder
- ⅓ cup ketchup
- ¼ cup water
- ½ teaspoon celery seed
- 1 tablespoon lemon juice
- 1½ teaspoons brown sugar
- 1¼ teaspoons low-sodium Worcestershire sauce
- ½ teaspoon salt (optional)
- ½ teaspoon vinegar
- ⅛ teaspoon dry mustard
- hamburger or slider buns

Directions:
1. Spray air fryer oven with nonstick cooking spray or olive oil.
2. Break raw ground beef into small chunks and pile into air fryer oven.
3. Air-fry at 390°F for 5 minutes. Stir to break apart and cook 3 minutes. Stir and cook 4 minutes longer or until meat is well done.
4. Remove meat from air fryer oven, drain, and use a knife and fork to crumble into small pieces.
5. Give your air fryer oven a quick rinse to remove any bits of meat.
6. Place all the remaining ingredients except the buns in a 6 x 6-inch baking pan and mix together.
7. Add meat and stir well.
8. Air-fry at 330°F for 5 minutes. Stir and air-fry for 2 minutes.
9. Scoop onto buns.

Minted Lamb Chops

Servings: 4
Cooking Time: 15 Minutes

Ingredients:
- Mint mixture:
- 4 tablespoons finely chopped fresh mint
- 2 tablespoons nonfat yogurt
- 1 tablespoon olive oil
- Salt and freshly ground black pepper to taste
- 4 lean lamb chops, fat trimmed, approximately ¾ inch thick
- 1 tablespoon balsamic vinegar

Directions:
1. Combine the mint mixture ingredients in a small bowl, stirring well to blend. Set aside. Place the lamp chops on a broiling rack with a pan underneath.
2. BROIL the lamb chops for 10 minutes, or until they are slightly pink. Remove from the oven and brush one side liberally with balsamic vinegar. Turn the chops over with tongs and spread with the mint mixture, using all of the mixture.
3. BROIL again for 5 minutes, or until lightly browned.

Pork Loin

Servings: 8
Cooking Time: 50 Minutes

Ingredients:
- 1 tablespoon lime juice
- 1 tablespoon orange marmalade
- 1 teaspoon coarse brown mustard
- 1 teaspoon curry powder
- 1 teaspoon dried lemongrass
- 2-pound boneless pork loin roast
- salt and pepper
- cooking spray

Directions:
1. Mix together the lime juice, marmalade, mustard, curry powder, and lemongrass.
2. Rub mixture all over the surface of the pork loin. Season to taste with salt and pepper.
3. Spray air fryer oven with nonstick spray and place pork roast diagonally in the pan.
4. Air-fry at 360°F for approximately 50 minutes, until roast registers 130°F on a meat thermometer.
5. Wrap roast in foil and let rest for 10 minutes before slicing.

Barbecued Broiled Pork Chops

Servings: 2
Cooking Time: 16 Minutes

Ingredients:
- Barbecue sauce mixture:
- 1 tablespoon ketchup
- ¼ cup dry red wine
- 1 tablespoon vegetable oil
- ⅛ teaspoon smoked flavoring (liquid smoke)
- 1 teaspoon chili powder
- 1 teaspoon ground cumin
- 1 teaspoon brown sugar
- ¼ teaspoon butcher's pepper
- 2 large (6- to 8-ounce) lean pork chops, approximately ¾ to 1 inch thick

Directions:
1. Combine the barbecue sauce mixture ingredients in a small bowl. Brush the chops with the sauce and place on a broiling rack with a pan underneath.
2. BROIL 8 minutes, turn with tongs, and broil for another 8 minutes, or until the meat is cooked to your preference.

Cilantro-crusted Flank Steak

Servings: 2
Cooking Time: 16 Minutes

Ingredients:
- Coating:
- 2 tablespoons chopped onion
- 1 tablespoon olive oil
- 2 tablespoons plain nonfat yogurt
- 1 plum tomato
- ½ cup fresh cilantro leaves
- 2 tablespoons cooking sherry
- ¼ teaspoon hot sauce
- 1 teaspoon garlic powder
- ½ teaspoon chili powder
- Salt and freshly ground black pepper
- 2 8-ounce flank steaks

Directions:
1. Process the coating ingredients in a blender or food processor until smooth. Spread half of the coating mixture on top of the flank steaks. Place the steaks on a broiling rack with a pan underneath.
2. BROIL for 8 minutes. Turn with tongs, spread the remaining mixture on the steaks, and broil again for 8 minutes, or until done to your preference.

Beef Bourguignon

Servings: 6
Cooking Time: 240 Minutes

Ingredients:
- 4 slices bacon, chopped into ½-inch pieces
- 3 pounds chuck roast, cut into 2-inch chunks
- 1 tablespoon kosher salt, plus more to taste
- 1½ tablespoons black pepper, plus more to taste
- 4 tablespoons all purpose flour, divided
- 2 tablespoons olive oil
- 2 large carrots, cut into ½-inch thick slices
- ½ large white onion, diced
- 4 cloves garlic, minced
- 2 tablespoons tomato paste
- 3 cups red wine (Merlot, Pinot Noir, or Chianti)
- 2 cups beef stock
- 1 beef bouillon cube, crushed
- ½ teaspoon dried thyme
- ¼ teaspoon dried parsley
- 2 bay leaves
- 10 ounces fresh small white or brown mushrooms, quartered
- 2 tablespoons cornstarch (optional)
- 2 tablespoons water (optional)

Directions:

1. Render the bacon in a large pot over medium heat for 5 minutes or until crispy.
2. Drain the bacon and set aside, leaving the bacon fat in the pot.
3. Mix together chuck roast chunks, kosher salt, black pepper, and 2 tablespoons of all purpose flour until well combined.
4. Dredge the beef of any extra flour and sear in the bacon grease for about 4 minutes on each side. It is important not to overcrowd the pot, so you may need to work in batches.
5. Remove the beef when done and set aside with the bacon.
6. Add the olive oil, sliced carrots, and diced onion to the pot. Cook for 5 minutes, then add the garlic and cook for another minute.
7. Add the tomato paste and cook for 1 minute, then mix in the remaining 2 tablespoons of flour and cook on medium low for 4 minutes.
8. Pour in the wine and beef stock, scraping the bottom of the pot to make sure there aren't any bits stuck to the bottom.
9. Add the bacon and seared meat back into the pot, along with the bouillon cube, dried thyme, dried parsley, bay leaves, and mushrooms. Mix well and bring to a light boil.
10. Insert the wire rack at low position in the Air Fryer Toaster Oven.
11. Cover the pot with foil and place on the rack in the oven. Make sure the foil is secure so it doesn't lift and contact the heating elements.
12. Select the Slow Cook function, adjust time to 4 hours, and press Start/Pause.
13. Remove the pot carefully from the oven when done and place back on the stove.
14. Discard the foil, mix the stew, and season to taste with salt and pepper.
15. Thicken the stew if desired by using a cornstarch slurry of 2 tablespoons cornstarch and 2 tablespoons water. Add half, mix, and bring to a boil, stirring occasionally. If the sauce is still too thin, add the other half of the slurry.

Meatloaf With Tangy Tomato Glaze

Servings: 6
Cooking Time: 50 Minutes

Ingredients:
- 1 pound ground beef
- ½ pound ground pork
- ½ pound ground veal (or turkey)
- 1 medium onion, diced
- 1 small clove of garlic, minced
- 2 egg yolks, lightly beaten
- ½ cup tomato ketchup
- 1 tablespoon Worcestershire sauce
- ½ cup plain breadcrumbs
- 2 teaspoons salt
- freshly ground black pepper
- ½ cup chopped fresh parsley, plus more for garnish
- 6 tablespoons ketchup
- 1 tablespoon balsamic vinegar
- 2 tablespoons brown sugar

Directions:
1. Combine the meats, onion, garlic, egg yolks, ketchup, Worcestershire sauce, breadcrumbs, salt, pepper and fresh parsley in a large bowl and mix well.
2. Preheat the toaster oven to 350°F and pour a little water into the bottom of the air fryer oven. (This will help prevent the grease that drips into the bottom drawer from burning and smoking.)
3. Transfer the meatloaf mixture to the air fryer oven, packing it down gently. Run a spatula around the meatloaf to create a space about ½-inch wide between the meat and the side of the air fryer oven.
4. Air-fry at 350°F for 20 minutes. Carefully invert the meatloaf onto a plate (remember to remove the pan from the air fryer oven so you don't pour all the grease out) and slide it back into the air fryer oven to turn it over. Re-shape the meatloaf with a spatula if necessary. Air-fry for another 20 minutes at 350°F.
5. Combine the ketchup, balsamic vinegar and brown sugar in a bowl and spread the mixture over the meatloaf. Air-fry for another 10 minutes, until an instant read thermometer inserted into the center of the meatloaf registers 160°F.

6. Allow the meatloaf to rest for a few more minutes and then transfer it to a serving platter using a spatula. Slice the meatloaf, sprinkle a little chopped parsley on top if desired, and serve.

Wasabi-coated Pork Loin Chops

Servings: 3
Cooking Time: 14 Minutes

Ingredients:
- 1½ cups Wasabi peas
- ¼ cup Plain panko bread crumbs
- 1 Large egg white(s)
- 2 tablespoons Water
- 3 5- to 6-ounce boneless center-cut pork loin chops (about ½ inch thick)

Directions:
1. Preheat the toaster oven to 375°F.
2. Put the wasabi peas in a food processor. Cover and process until finely ground, about like panko bread crumbs. Add the bread crumbs and pulse a few times to blend.
3. Set up and fill two shallow soup plates or small pie plates on your counter: one for the egg white(s), whisked with the water until uniform; and one for the wasabi pea mixture.
4. Dip a pork chop in the egg white mixture, coating the chop on both sides as well as around the edge. Allow any excess egg white mixture to slip back into the rest, then set the chop in the wasabi pea mixture. Press gently and turn it several times to coat evenly on both sides and around the edge. Set aside, then dip and coat the remaining chop(s).
5. Set the chops in the air fryer oven with as much air space between them as possible. Air-fry, turning once at the 6-minute mark, for 12 minutes, or until the chops are crisp and browned and an instant-read meat thermometer inserted into the center of a chop registers 145°F. If the machine is at 360°F, you may need to add 2 minutes to the cooking time.
6. Use kitchen tongs to transfer the chops to a wire rack. Cool for a couple of minutes before serving.

Easy Tex-mex Chimichangas

Servings: 2
Cooking Time: 8 Minutes

Ingredients:
- ¼ pound Thinly sliced deli roast beef, chopped
- ½ cup (about 2 ounces) Shredded Cheddar cheese or shredded Tex-Mex cheese blend
- ¼ cup Jarred salsa verde or salsa rojo
- ½ teaspoon Ground cumin
- ½ teaspoon Dried oregano
- 2 Burrito-size (12-inch) flour tortilla(s), not corn tortillas (gluten-free, if a concern)
- ⅔ cup Canned refried beans
- Vegetable oil spray

Directions:
1. Preheat the toaster oven to 375°F.
2. Stir the roast beef, cheese, salsa, cumin, and oregano in a bowl until well mixed.
3. Lay a tortilla on a clean, dry work surface. Spread ⅓ cup of the refried beans in the center lower third of the tortilla(s), leaving an inch on either side of the spread beans.
4. For one chimichanga, spread all of the roast beef mixture on top of the beans. For two, spread half of the roast beef mixture on each tortilla.
5. At either "end" of the filling mixture, fold the sides of the tortilla up and over the filling, partially covering it. Starting with the unfolded side of the tortilla just below the filling, roll the tortilla closed. Fold and roll the second filled tortilla, as necessary.
6. Coat the exterior of the tortilla(s) with vegetable oil spray. Set the chimichanga(s) seam side down in the air fryer oven, with at least ½ inch air space between them if you're working with two. Air-fry undisturbed for 8 minutes, or until the tortilla is lightly browned and crisp.
7. Use kitchen tongs to gently transfer the chimichanga(s) to a wire rack. Cool for at last 5 minutes or up to 20 minutes before serving.

Beef And Spinach Braciole

Servings: 4
Cooking Time: 92 Minutes

Ingredients:

- 7-inch oven-safe baking pan or casserole
- ½ onion, finely chopped
- 1 teaspoon olive oil
- ⅓ cup red wine
- 2 cups crushed tomatoes
- 1 teaspoon Italian seasoning
- ½ teaspoon garlic powder
- ¼ teaspoon crushed red pepper flakes
- 2 tablespoons chopped fresh parsley
- 2 top round steaks (about 1½ pounds)
- salt and freshly ground black pepper
- 2 cups fresh spinach, chopped
- 1 clove minced garlic
- ½ cup roasted red peppers, julienned
- ½ cup grated pecorino cheese
- ¼ cup pine nuts, toasted and rough chopped
- 2 tablespoons olive oil

Directions:
1. Preheat the toaster oven to 400°F.
2. Toss the onions and olive oil together in a 7-inch metal baking pan or casserole dish. Air-fry at 400°F for 5 minutes, stirring a couple times during the cooking process. Add the red wine, crushed tomatoes, Italian seasoning, garlic powder, red pepper flakes and parsley and stir. Cover the pan tightly with aluminum foil, lower the air fryer oven temperature to 350°F and continue to air-fry for 15 minutes.
3. While the sauce is simmering, prepare the beef. Using a meat mallet, pound the beef until it is ¼-inch thick. Season both sides of the beef with salt and pepper. Combine the spinach, garlic, red peppers, pecorino cheese, pine nuts and olive oil in a medium bowl. Season with salt and freshly ground black pepper. Spread the mixture evenly over the steaks. Starting at one of the short ends, roll the beef around the filling, tucking in the sides as you roll to ensure the filling is completely enclosed. Secure the beef rolls with toothpicks.
4. Remove the baking pan with the sauce from the air fryer oven and set it aside. Preheat the toaster oven to 400°F.
5. Brush or spray the beef rolls with a little olive oil and air-fry at 400°F for 12 minutes, rotating the beef during the cooking process for even browning. When the beef is browned, submerge the rolls into the sauce in the baking pan, cover the pan with foil and return it to the air fryer oven. Air-fry at 250°F for 60 minutes.
6. Remove the beef rolls from the sauce. Cut each roll into slices and serve with pasta, ladling some of the sauce overtop.

Calzones South Of The Border

Servings: 8
Cooking Time: 8 Minutes

Ingredients:
- Filling
- ¼ pound ground pork sausage
- ½ teaspoon chile powder
- ¼ teaspoon ground cumin
- ⅛ teaspoon garlic powder
- ⅛ teaspoon onion powder
- ⅛ teaspoon oregano
- ½ cup ricotta cheese
- 1 ounce sharp Cheddar cheese, shredded
- 2 ounces Pepper Jack cheese, shredded
- 1 4-ounce can chopped green chiles, drained
- oil for misting or cooking spray
- salsa, sour cream, or guacamole
- Crust
- 2 cups white wheat flour, plus more for kneading and rolling
- 1 package (¼ ounce) RapidRise yeast
- 1 teaspoon salt
- ½ teaspoon chile powder
- ½ teaspoon ground cumin
- 1 cup warm water (115°F to 125°F)
- 2 teaspoons olive oil

Directions:
1. Crumble sausage into air fryer oven baking pan and stir in the filling seasonings: chile powder, cumin, garlic powder, onion powder, and oregano. Air-fry at 390°F for 2 minutes. Stir, breaking apart, and air-fry for 3 to 4 minutes, until well done. Remove and set aside on paper towels to drain.
2. To make dough, combine flour, yeast, salt, chile powder, and cumin. Stir in warm water and oil until soft dough forms. Turn out onto lightly floured board and knead for 3 or 4 minutes. Let dough rest for 10 minutes.

3. Place the three cheeses in a medium bowl. Add cooked sausage and chiles and stir until well mixed.
4. Cut dough into 8 pieces.
5. Working with 4 pieces of the dough, press each into a circle about 5 inches in diameter. Top each dough circle with 2 heaping tablespoons of filling. Fold over into a half-moon shape and press edges together. Seal edges firmly to prevent leakage. Spray both sides with oil or cooking spray.
6. Place 4 calzones in air fryer oven and air-fry at 360°F for 5 minutes. Mist with oil or spray and air-fry for 3 minutes, until crust is done and nicely browned.
7. While the first batch is cooking, press out the remaining dough, fill, and shape into calzones.
8. Spray both sides with oil or cooking spray and air-fry for 5 minutes. If needed, mist with oil and continue cooking for 3 minutes longer. This second batch will cook a little faster than the first because your air fryer oven is already hot.
9. Serve plain or with salsa, sour cream, or guacamole.

Chinese Pork And Vegetable Non-stir-fry

Servings: 4
Cooking Time: 30 Minutes

Ingredients:
- Seasoning sauce:
- 1 tablespoon soy sauce
- ¼ cup dry white wine
- 1 tablespoon sesame oil
- 1 tablespoon vegetable oil
- 1 teaspoon Chinese five-spice powder
- 2 6-ounce lean boneless pork chops cut into ¼ × 2-inch strips
- 1 1-pound package frozen vegetable mix or 2 cups sliced assorted fresh vegetables: broccoli, carrots, cauliflower, bell pepper, and the like
- 1 4-ounce can mushroom pieces, drained, or ½ cup cleaned and sliced fresh mushrooms
- 2 tablespoons sesame seeds
- 2 tablespoons minced fresh garlic

Directions:

1. Whisk together the seasoning sauce ingredients in a small bowl. Set aside.
2. Combine the pork, vegetables, mushrooms, sesame seeds, and garlic in an oiled or nonstick 8½ × 8½ × 2-inch square baking (cake) pan. Add the seasoning sauce ingredients and toss to coat the pork, vegetables, and mushrooms well.
3. BROIL for 30 minutes, turning with tongs every 8 minutes, until the vegetables and meat are well cooked and lightly browned.

Indian Fry Bread Tacos

Servings: 4
Cooking Time: 20 Minutes

Ingredients:
- 1 cup all-purpose flour
- 1½ teaspoons salt, divided
- 1½ teaspoons baking powder
- ¼ cup milk
- ¼ cup warm water
- ½ pound lean ground beef
- One 14.5-ounce can pinto beans, drained and rinsed
- 1 tablespoon taco seasoning
- ½ cup shredded cheddar cheese
- 2 cups shredded lettuce
- ¼ cup black olives, chopped
- 1 Roma tomato, diced
- 1 avocado, diced
- 1 lime

Directions:

1. In a large bowl, whisk together the flour, 1 teaspoon of the salt, and baking powder. Make a well in the center and add in the milk and water. Form a ball and gently knead the dough four times. Cover the bowl with a damp towel, and set aside.
2. Preheat the toaster oven to 380°F.
3. In a medium bowl, mix together the ground beef, beans, and taco seasoning. Crumble the meat mixture into the air fryer oven and air-fry for 5 minutes; toss the meat and cook an additional 2 to 3 minutes, or until cooked fully. Place the cooked meat in a bowl for taco

assembly; season with the remaining ½ teaspoon salt as desired.

4. On a floured surface, place the dough. Cut the dough into 4 equal parts. Using a rolling pin, roll out each piece of dough to 5 inches in diameter. Spray the dough with cooking spray and place in the air fryer oven, working in batches as needed. Air-fry for 3 minutes, flip over, spray with cooking spray, and air-fry for an additional 1 to 3 minutes, until golden and puffy.

5. To assemble, place the fry breads on a serving platter. Equally divide the meat and bean mixture on top of the fry bread. Divide the cheese, lettuce, olives, tomatoes, and avocado among the four tacos. Squeeze lime over the top prior to serving.

Pesto Pork Chops

Servings: 2
Cooking Time: 15 Minutes

Ingredients:
- 2 (6-ounce) boneless pork loin chops
- 2 tablespoons basil pesto

Directions:
1. Preheat the toaster oven to 375°F on AIR FRY for 5 minutes.
2. Rub the pork chops all over with the pesto and set aside for 15 minutes.
3. Place the air-fryer basket in the baking tray and arrange the pork in the basket with no overlap.
4. In position 2, air fry for 15 minutes, turning halfway through, until the chops are lightly browned and have an internal temperature of 145°F.
5. Let the meat rest for 10 minutes and serve.

Classic Pepperoni Pizza

Servings: 4
Cooking Time: 11 Minutes

Ingredients:
- Oil spray (hand-pumped)
- 1 pound premade pizza dough, or your favorite recipe
- ½ cup store-bought pizza sauce
- ¼ cup grated Parmesan cheese
- ¾ cup shredded mozzarella
- 10 to 12 slices pepperoni
- 2 tablespoons chopped fresh basil
- Pinch red pepper flakes

Directions:
1. Preheat the toaster oven to 425°F on BAKE for 5 minutes.
2. Spray the baking tray with the oil and spread the pizza dough with your fingertips so that it covers the tray. Prick the dough with a fork.
3. In position 2, bake for 8 minutes until the crust is lightly golden.
4. Take the crust out and spread with the pizza sauce, leaving a ½-inch border around the edge. Sprinkle with Parmesan and mozzarella cheeses and arrange the pepperoni on the pizza.
5. Bake for 3 minutes until the cheese is melted and bubbly.
6. Top with the basil and red pepper flakes and serve.

Beef Vegetable Stew

Servings: 4
Cooking Time: 120 Minutes

Ingredients:
- 1 pound lean stewing beef, cut into 1-inch chunks
- 2 carrots, diced
- 2 celery stalks
- 1 large potato, diced
- ½ sweet onion, chopped
- 2 teaspoons minced garlic
- 1 (15-ounce) can diced tomatoes, with juices
- 1 teaspoon sea salt
- ½ teaspoon freshly ground black pepper
- 1 cup low-sodium beef broth
- 3 tablespoons all-purpose flour
- 1 cup frozen peas

Directions:
1. Place the rack in position 1 and preheat the toaster oven to 375°F on BAKE for 5 minutes.
2. In a 1½-quart casserole dish, combine the beef, carrots, celery, potato, onion, garlic, tomatoes, salt, and pepper.
3. In a small bowl, stir the broth and flour until well combined. Add the broth mixture to the beef mixture and stir to combine.

4. Cover with foil or a lid and bake for 2 hours, stirring each time you reset the timer, until the meat is very tender.
5. Stir in the peas and let stand for 10 minutes. Serve.

Ribeye Steak With Blue Cheese Compound Butter

Servings: 2
Cooking Time: 12 Minutes

Ingredients:
- 5 tablespoons unsalted butter, softened
- ¼ cup crumbled blue cheese 2 teaspoons lemon juice
- 1 tablespoon freshly chopped chives
- Salt & freshly ground black pepper, to taste
- 2 (12 ounce) boneless ribeye steaks

Directions:
1. Mix together butter, blue cheese, lemon juice, and chives until smooth.
2. Season the butter to taste with salt and pepper.
3. Place the butter on plastic wrap and form into a 3-inch log, tying the ends of the plastic wrap together.
4. Place the butter in the fridge for 4 hours to harden.
5. Allow the steaks to sit at room temperature for 1 hour.
6. Pat the steaks dry with paper towels and season to taste with salt and pepper.
7. Insert the fry basket at top position in the Cosori Smart Air Fryer Toaster Oven.
8. Preheat the toaster Oven to 450°F.
9. Place the steaks in the fry basket in the preheated oven.
10. Select the Broil function, adjust time to 12 minutes, and press Start/Pause.
11. Remove when done and allow to rest for 5 minutes.
12. Remove the butter from the fridge, unwrap, and slice into ¾-inch pieces.
13. Serve the steak with one or two pieces of sliced compound butter.

Spanish Pork Skewers

Servings: 4
Cooking Time: 16 Minutes

Ingredients:
- 1 pound pork tenderloin, cut into ¾- to 1-inch cubes
- 2 tablespoons olive oil
- 1 teaspoon ground cumin
- ½ teaspoon smoked paprika
- ½ teaspoon dried thyme leaves
- ½ teaspoon kosher salt, plus more for seasoning
- ⅛ teaspoon red pepper flakes
- 2 cloves garlic, minced
- 1 red bell pepper, cut into ¾- to 1-inch squares
- 1 small red onion, cut into ¾- to 1-inch wedges
- Freshly ground black pepper
- Nonstick cooking spray
- 2 tablespoons unsalted butter
- 1 tablespoon sherry or balsamic vinegar
- 1 teaspoon packed dark brown sugar

Directions:
1. Place the pork cubes in a medium bowl. Drizzle 1 tablespoon of oil over the pork. Stir the cumin, paprika, thyme, ½ teaspoon salt, the pepper flakes, and garlic in a small bowl. Sprinkle the seasonings over the pork. Stir to coat the pork evenly. Cover and refrigerate for at least 4 hours or up to overnight.
2. Place the bell pepper and onion pieces in a medium bowl. Drizzle with the remaining tablespoon olive oil and season with salt and pepper. Toss to coat evenly.
3. Alternately thread the pork and vegetables onto skewers. Spray a 12 x 12-inch baking pan with nonstick cooking spray. Place the filled skewers on the prepared pan. Place the pan in the toaster oven, positioning the skewers about 3 to 4 inches below the heating element. (Depending on your oven, you may need to set the rack to the middle position.)
4. Set the toaster oven on broil. Broil for 10 minutes. Turn the skewers. Broil for an additional 5 minutes, or until the vegetables are tender and a meat thermometer registers 145°F. Do not overcook.
5. Meanwhile, combine the butter, vinegar, and brown sugar in a small, glass, microwave-safe bowl. Season with salt and pepper. Microwave on High (100 percent) power for 45 seconds or until the butter melts and the mixture begins to bubble. Stir to dissolve the sugar.
6. Lightly brush the vinegar mixture over the skewers. Broil for 1 minute or until the skewers are browned.

Beef Al Carbon (street Taco Meat)

Servings: 6
Cooking Time: 8 Minutes

Ingredients:
- 1½ pounds sirloin steak, cut into ½-inch cubes
- ¾ cup lime juice
- ½ cup extra-virgin olive oil
- 1 teaspoon ground cumin
- 2 teaspoons garlic powder
- 1 teaspoon salt

Directions:
1. In a large bowl, toss together the steak, lime juice, olive oil, cumin, garlic powder, and salt. Allow the meat to marinate for 30 minutes. Drain off all the marinade and pat the meat dry with paper towels.
2. Preheat the toaster oven to 400°F.
3. Place the meat in the air fryer oven and spray with cooking spray. Cook the meat for 5 minutes, toss the meat, and continue cooking another 3 minutes, until slightly crispy.

Smokehouse-style Beef Ribs

Servings: 3
Cooking Time: 25 Minutes

Ingredients:
- ¼ teaspoon Mild smoked paprika
- ¼ teaspoon Garlic powder
- ¼ teaspoon Onion powder
- ¼ teaspoon Table salt
- ¼ teaspoon Ground black pepper
- 3 10- to 12-ounce beef back ribs (not beef short ribs)

Directions:
1. Preheat the toaster oven to 350°F.
2. Mix the smoked paprika, garlic powder, onion powder, salt, and pepper in a small bowl until uniform. Massage and pat this mixture onto the ribs.
3. When the machine is at temperature, set the ribs in the air fryer oven in one layer, turning them on their sides if necessary, sort of like they're spooning but with at least ¼ inch air space between them. Air-fry for 25 minutes, turning once, until deep brown and sizzling.
4. Use kitchen tongs to transfer the ribs to a wire rack. Cool for 5 minutes before serving.

Pork Cutlets With Almond-lemon Crust

Servings: 3
Cooking Time: 14 Minutes

Ingredients:
- ¾ cup Almond flour
- ¾ cup Plain dried bread crumbs (gluten-free, if a concern)
- 1½ teaspoons Finely grated lemon zest
- 1¼ teaspoons Table salt
- ¾ teaspoon Garlic powder
- ¾ teaspoon Dried oregano
- 1 Large egg white(s)
- 2 tablespoons Water
- 3 6-ounce center-cut boneless pork loin chops (about ¾ inch thick)
- Olive oil spray

Directions:
1. Preheat the toaster oven to 375°F.
2. Mix the almond flour, bread crumbs, lemon zest, salt, garlic powder, and dried oregano in a large bowl until well combined.
3. Whisk the egg white(s) and water in a shallow soup plate or small pie plate until uniform.
4. Dip a chop in the egg white mixture, turning it to coat all sides, even the ends. Let any excess egg white mixture slip back into the rest, then set it in the almond flour mixture. Turn it several times, pressing gently to coat it evenly. Generously coat the chop with olive oil spray, then set aside to dip and coat the remaining chop(s).
5. Set the chops in the air fryer oven with as much air space between them as possible. Air-fry undisturbed for 12 minutes, or until browned and crunchy. You may need to add 2 minutes to the cooking time if the machine is at 360°F.
6. Use kitchen tongs to transfer the chops to a wire rack. Cool for a few minutes before serving.

Steak Pinwheels With Pepper Slaw And Minneapolis Potato Salad

Servings: 4
Cooking Time: 16 Minutes

Ingredients:
- Brushing mixture:
- ½ cup cold strong brewed coffee
- 2 tablespoons molasses
- 1 tablespoon tomato paste
- 2 garlic cloves, minced
- 1 tablespoon olive oil
- Garlic powder
- 1 teaspoon butcher's pepper
- 1 pound lean, boneless beefsteak, flattened to ⅛-inch thickness with a meat mallet or rolling pin (place steak between 2 sheets of heavy-duty plastic wrap)

Directions:
1. Combine the brushing mixture ingredients in a small bowl and set aside.
2. Cut the steak into 2 × 3-inch strips, brush with the mixture, and roll up, securing the edges with toothpicks. Brush again with the mixture and place in an oiled or nonstick 8½ × 8½ × 2-inch square baking (cake) pan.
3. BROIL for 8 minutes, then turn with tongs, brush with the mixture again, and broil for another 8 minutes, or until browned.

California Burritos

Servings: 4
Cooking Time: 17 Minutes

Ingredients:
- 1 pound sirloin steak, sliced thin
- 1 teaspoon dried oregano
- 1 teaspoon ground cumin
- ½ teaspoon garlic powder
- 16 tater tots
- ⅓ cup sour cream
- ½ lime, juiced
- 2 tablespoons hot sauce
- 1 large avocado, pitted
- 1 teaspoon salt, divided
- 4 large (8- to 10-inch) flour tortillas
- ½ cup shredded cheddar cheese or Monterey jack
- 2 tablespoons avocado oil

Directions:
1. Preheat the toaster oven to 380°F.
2. Season the steak with oregano, cumin, and garlic powder. Place the steak on one side of the air fryer oven and the tater tots on the other side. (It's okay for them to touch, because the flavors will all come together in the burrito.) Air-fry for 8 minutes, toss, and cook an additional 4 to 6 minutes.
3. Meanwhile, in a small bowl, stir together the sour cream, lime juice, and hot sauce.
4. In another small bowl, mash together the avocado and season with ½ teaspoon of the salt, to taste.
5. To assemble the burrito, lay out the tortillas, equally divide the meat amongst the tortillas. Season the steak equally with the remaining ½ teaspoon salt. Then layer the mashed avocado and sour cream mixture on top. Top each tortilla with 4 tater tots and finish each with 2 tablespoons cheese. Roll up the sides and, while holding in the sides, roll up the burrito. Place the burritos in the air fryer oven and brush with avocado oil (working in batches as needed); air-fry for 3 minutes or until lightly golden on the outside.

Chipotle-glazed Meat Loaf

Servings: 4
Cooking Time: 65 Minutes

Ingredients:
- 1 ½ pounds lean ground beef
- ¼ cup finely chopped onion
- ½ cup crushed tortilla chips
- 1 teaspoon ground cumin
- ½ teaspoon chili powder
- ½ teaspoon garlic powder
- ½ teaspoon kosher salt
- ¼ teaspoon freshly ground black pepper
- 3 tablespoons chopped pickled jalapeños
- 3 tablespoons chunky salsa
- 1 large egg
- ⅓ cup ketchup
- 3 ½ teaspoons minced chipotle chilies in adobo sauce

Directions:
1. Preheat the toaster oven to 375 °F. Line a 12 x 12-inch baking pan with aluminum foil.
2. Combine the ground beef, onion, tortilla chips, cumin, chili powder, garlic powder, salt, pepper, pickled jalapeños, salsa, and egg in a large bowl, stirring until blended well. Shape the meat mixture into a 9 x 5-inch loaf and place on the prepared pan.
3. Bake, uncovered, for 30 minutes. Carefully remove the meat loaf from the oven and spoon off any collected grease from the pan.
4. Place the ketchup in a small bowl and stir in the chipotle chilies in adobo sauce. Spread the ketchup mixture on top of the meat loaf. Continue to bake for an additional 25 to 35 minutes or until a meat thermometer registers 160 °F. Let stand for 10 minutes before slicing.

Slow Cooked Carnitas

Servings: 6
Cooking Time: 360 Minutes

Ingredients:
- 1 pork shoulder (5 pounds), bone-in
- 2½ teaspoons kosher salt
- 1½ teaspoons black pepper
- 1½ teaspoons ground cumin
- 1 teaspoon dried oregano
- ¼ teaspoon ground coriander
- 2 bay leaves
- 6 garlic cloves
- 1 small onion, quartered
- 1 cinnamon stick
- 1 full orange peel (no white)
- 2 oranges, juiced
- 1 lime, juiced

Directions:
1. Season the pork shoulder with salt, pepper, cumin, oregano, and coriander.
2. Place the seasoned pork shoulder in a large pot along with any seasoning that did not stick to the pork.
3. Add in the bay leaves, garlic cloves, onion, cinnamon stick, and orange peel.
4. Squeeze in the juice of two oranges and one lime and cover with foil.
5. Insert the wire rack at low position in the Air Fryer Toaster Oven, then place the pot on the rack.
6. Select the Slow Cook function and press Start/Pause.
7. Remove carefully when done, uncover, and remove the bone.
8. Shred the carnitas and use them in tacos, burritos, or any other way you please.

Chicken Fried Steak

Servings: 4
Cooking Time: 15 Minutes

Ingredients:
- 2 eggs
- ½ cup buttermilk
- 1½ cups flour
- ¾ teaspoon salt
- ½ teaspoon pepper
- 1 pound beef cube steaks
- salt and pepper
- oil for misting or cooking spray

Directions:
1. Beat together eggs and buttermilk in a shallow dish.
2. In another shallow dish, stir together the flour, ½ teaspoon salt, and ¼ teaspoon pepper.
3. Season cube steaks with remaining salt and pepper to taste. Dip in flour, buttermilk egg wash, and then flour again.
4. Spray both sides of steaks with oil or cooking spray.
5. Cooking in 2 batches, place steaks in air fryer oven in single layer. Air-fry at 360°F for 10 minutes. Spray tops of steaks with oil and cook 5 minutes or until meat is well done.
6. Repeat to cook remaining steaks.

Kielbasa Sausage With Pierogies And Caramelized Onions

Servings: 3
Cooking Time: 30 Minutes

Ingredients:
- 1 Vidalia or sweet onion, sliced
- olive oil
- salt and freshly ground black pepper
- 2 tablespoons butter, cut into small cubes
- 1 teaspoon sugar
- 1 pound light Polish kielbasa sausage, cut into 2-inch chunks
- 1 (13-ounce) package frozen mini pierogies
- 2 teaspoons vegetable or olive oil
- chopped scallions

Directions:
1. Preheat the toaster oven to 400°F.
2. Toss the sliced onions with a little olive oil, salt and pepper and transfer them to the air fryer oven. Dot the onions with pieces of butter and air-fry at 400°F for 2 minutes. Then sprinkle the sugar over the onions and stir. Pour any melted butter from the bottom of the air fryer oven over the onions (do this over the sink – some of the butter will spill through the pan). Continue to air-fry for another 13 minutes, stirring the pan every few minutes to cook the onions evenly.
3. Add the kielbasa chunks to the onions and toss. Air-fry for another 5 minutes. Transfer the kielbasa and onions to a bowl and cover with aluminum foil to keep warm.
4. Toss the frozen pierogies with the vegetable or olive oil and transfer them to the air fryer oven. Air-fry at 400°F for 8 minutes.
5. When the pierogies have finished cooking, return the kielbasa and onions to the air fryer oven and gently toss with the pierogies. Air-fry for 2 more minutes and then transfer everything to a serving platter. Garnish with the chopped scallions and serve hot with the spicy sour cream sauce below.
6. Kielbasa Sausage with Pierogies and Caramelized Onions

Lamb Koftas Meatballs

Servings: 3
Cooking Time: 8 Minutes

Ingredients:
- 1 pound ground lamb
- 1 teaspoon ground cumin
- 1 teaspoon ground coriander
- 2 tablespoons chopped fresh mint
- 1 egg, beaten
- ½ teaspoon salt
- freshly ground black pepper

Directions:
1. Combine all ingredients in a bowl and mix together well. Divide the mixture into 10 portions. Roll each portion into a ball and then by cupping the meatball in your hand, shape it into an oval.
2. Preheat the toaster oven to 400°F.
3. Air fry the koftas for 8 minutes.
4. Serve warm with the cucumber-yogurt dip.

Steak With Herbed Butter

Servings: 2
Cooking Time: 16 Minutes

Ingredients:
- 4 tablespoons unsalted butter, softened
- 1 tablespoon minced flat-leaf (Italian) parsley
- 1 tablespoon chopped fresh chives
- 2 cloves garlic, minced
- 1 teaspoon Worcestershire sauce
- 2 beef strip steaks, cut about 1 ½ inches thick
- 1 tablespoon olive oil
- Kosher salt and freshly ground black pepper

Directions:
1. Combine the butter, parsley, chives, garlic, and Worcestershire sauce in a small bowl until well blended; set aside.
2. Preheat the toaster oven to broil.
3. Brush the steaks with olive oil and season with salt and pepper. Place the steak on the broiler rack set over the broiler pan. Place the pan in the toaster oven, positioning the steaks about 3 to 4 inches below the heating element. (Depending on your oven and the

thickness of the steak, you may need to set the rack to the middle position.) Broil for 6 minutes, turn the steaks over, and broil for an additional 7 minutes. If necessary to reach the desired doneness, turn the steaks over again and broil for an additional 3 minutes or until you reach your desired doneness.

4. Spread the herb butter generously over the steaks. Allow the steaks to stand for 5 to 10 minutes before slicing and serving.

Crunchy Fried Pork Loin Chops

Servings: 3
Cooking Time: 12 Minutes

Ingredients:
- 1 cup All-purpose flour or tapioca flour
- 1 Large egg(s), well beaten
- 1½ cups Seasoned Italian-style dried bread crumbs (gluten-free, if a concern)
- 3 4- to 5-ounce boneless center-cut pork loin chops
- Vegetable oil spray

Directions:
1. Preheat the toaster oven to 350°F.
2. Set up and fill three shallow soup plates or small pie plates on your counter: one for the flour, one for the beaten egg(s), and one for the bread crumbs.
3. Dredge a pork chop in the flour, coating both sides as well as around the edge. Gently shake off any excess, then dip the chop in the egg(s), again coating both sides and the edge. Let any excess egg slip back into the rest, then set the chop in the bread crumbs, turning it and pressing gently to coat well on both sides and the edge. Coat the pork chop all over with vegetable oil spray and set aside so you can dredge, coat, and spray the additional chop(s).
4. Set the chops in the air fryer oven with as much air space between them as possible. Air-fry undisturbed for 12 minutes, or until brown and crunchy and an instant-read meat thermometer inserted into the center of a chop registers 145°F.
5. Use kitchen tongs to transfer the chops to a wire rack. Cool for 5 minutes before serving.

Barbeque Ribs

Servings: 4
Cooking Time: 35 Minutes

Ingredients:
- 2 pounds pork spareribs or baby back ribs, silver skin removed
- 2 tablespoons brown sugar
- 1 teaspoon chili powder
- 1 teaspoon dry mustard
- Sea salt, for seasoning
- Freshly ground black pepper, for seasoning
- Oil spray (hand-pumped)
- 1 cup barbeque sauce

Directions:
1. Preheat the toaster oven to 375°F on AIR FRY for 5 minutes.
2. Cut the ribs into 4 bone sections or to fit in the basket.
3. In a small bowl, combine the brown sugar, chili powder, and mustard, and rub it all over the ribs.
4. Season the ribs with salt and pepper.
5. Place the air-fryer basket in the baking tray and spray it generously with the oil.
6. Arrange the ribs in the basket. There can be overlap if necessary.
7. In position 2, air fry for 35 minutes, turning halfway through, until the ribs are tender, browned, and crisp.
8. Baste the ribs with the barbeque sauce and serve.

Better-than-chinese-take-out Pork Ribs

Servings: 3
Cooking Time: 35 Minutes

Ingredients:
- 1½ tablespoons Hoisin sauce (gluten-free, if a concern)
- 1½ tablespoons Regular or low-sodium soy sauce or gluten-free tamari sauce
- 1½ tablespoons Shaoxing (Chinese cooking rice wine), dry sherry, or white grape juice
- 1½ teaspoons Minced garlic
- ¾ teaspoon Ground dried ginger

- ¾ teaspoon Ground white pepper
- 1½ pounds Pork baby back rib rack(s), cut into 2-bone pieces

Directions:
1. Mix the hoisin sauce, soy or tamari sauce, Shaoxing or its substitute, garlic, ginger, and white pepper in a large bowl. Add the rib sections and stir well to coat. Cover and refrigerate for at least 2 hours or up to 24 hours, stirring the rib sections in the marinade occasionally.
2. Preheat the toaster oven to 350°F. Set the ribs in their bowl on the counter as the machine heats.
3. When the machine is at temperature, set the rib pieces on their sides in a single layer in the air fryer oven with as much air space between them as possible. Air-fry for 35 minutes, turning and rearranging the pieces once, until deeply browned and sizzling.
4. Use kitchen tongs to transfer the rib pieces to a large serving bowl or platter. Wait a minute or two before serving them so the meat can reabsorb some of its own juices.

Sweet Potato–crusted Pork Rib Chops

Servings: 2
Cooking Time: 14 Minutes

Ingredients:
- 2 Large egg white(s), well beaten
- 1½ cups (about 6 ounces) Crushed sweet potato chips (certified gluten-free, if a concern)
- 1 teaspoon Ground cinnamon
- 1 teaspoon Ground dried ginger
- 1 teaspoon Table salt (optional)
- 2 10-ounce, 1-inch-thick bone-in pork rib chop(s)

Directions:
1. Preheat the toaster oven to 375°F.
2. Set up and fill two shallow soup plates or small pie plates on your counter: one for the beaten egg white(s); and one for the crushed chips, mixed with the cinnamon, ginger, and salt (if using).
3. Dip a chop in the egg white(s), coating it on both sides as well as the edges. Let the excess egg white slip back into the rest, then set it in the crushed chip mixture. Turn it several times, pressing gently, until evenly coated on both sides and the edges. If necessary, set the chop aside and coat the remaining chop(s).
4. Set the chop(s) in the air fryer oven with as much air space between them as possible. Air-fry undisturbed for 12 minutes, or until crunchy and browned and an instant-read meat thermometer inserted into the center of a chop (without touching bone) registers 145°F. If the machine is at 360°F, you may need to add 2 minutes to the cooking time.
5. Use kitchen tongs to transfer the chop(s) to a wire rack. Cool for 2 or 3 minutes before serving.

Crispy Lamb Shoulder Chops

Servings: 3
Cooking Time: 28 Minutes

Ingredients:
- ¾ cup All-purpose flour or gluten-free all-purpose flour
- 2 teaspoons Mild paprika
- 2 teaspoons Table salt
- 1½ teaspoons Garlic powder
- 1½ teaspoons Dried sage leaves
- 3 6-ounce bone-in lamb shoulder chops, any excess fat trimmed
- Olive oil spray

Directions:
1. Whisk the flour, paprika, salt, garlic powder, and sage in a large bowl until the mixture is of a uniform color. Add the chops and toss well to coat. Transfer them to a cutting board.
2. Preheat the toaster oven to 375°F.
3. When the machine is at temperature, again dredge the chops one by one in the flour mixture. Lightly coat both sides of each chop with olive oil spray before putting it in the air fryer oven. Continue on with the remaining chop(s), leaving air space between them in the air fryer oven.
4. Air-fry, turning once, for 25 minutes, or until the chops are well browned and tender when pierced with the point of a paring knife. If the machine is at 360°F, you may need to add up to 3 minutes to the cooking time.

5. Use kitchen tongs to transfer the chops to a wire rack. Cool for 5 minutes before serving.

Zesty London Broil

Servings: 4
Cooking Time: 28 Minutes

Ingredients:

- ⅔ cup ketchup
- ¼ cup honey
- ¼ cup olive oil
- 2 tablespoons apple cider vinegar
- 2 tablespoons Worcestershire sauce
- 2 tablespoons minced onion
- ½ teaspoon paprika
- 1 teaspoon salt
- 1 teaspoon freshly ground black pepper
- 2 pounds London broil, top round or flank steak (about 1-inch thick)

Directions:

1. Combine the ketchup, honey, olive oil, apple cider vinegar, Worcestershire sauce, minced onion, paprika, salt and pepper in a small bowl and whisk together.
2. Generously pierce both sides of the meat with a fork or meat tenderizer and place it in a shallow dish. Pour the marinade mixture over the steak, making sure all sides of the meat get coated with the marinade. Cover and refrigerate overnight.
3. Preheat the toaster oven to 400°F.
4. Transfer the London broil to the air fryer oven and air-fry for 28 minutes, depending on how rare or well done you like your steak. Flip the steak over halfway through the cooking time.
5. Remove the London broil from the air fryer oven and let it rest for five minutes on a cutting board. To serve, thinly slice the meat against the grain and transfer to a serving platter.

Beer-baked Pork Tenderloin

Servings: 4
Cooking Time: 40 Minutes

Ingredients:

- 1 pound lean pork tenderloin, fat trimmed off
- 3 garlic cloves, minced
- 1 cup good-quality dark ale or beer
- 2 bay leaves
- Salt and freshly cracked black pepper
- Spiced apple slices

Directions:

1. Preheat the toaster oven to 400° F.
2. Place the tenderloin in an 8½ × 8½ × 4-inch ovenproof baking dish. Sprinkle the minced garlic over the pork, pour over the beer, add the bay leaves, and season to taste with the salt and pepper. Cover with aluminum foil.
3. BAKE, covered, for 40 minutes, or until the meat is tender. Discard the bay leaves and serve sliced with the liquid. Garnish with the spiced apple slices.

Traditional Pot Roast

Servings: 6
Cooking Time: 75 Minutes

Ingredients:

- 2 tablespoons olive oil
- 1 teaspoon garlic powder
- 1 teaspoon fresh thyme, chopped
- ¼ teaspoon sea salt
- ¼ teaspoon freshly ground black pepper
- 1 (3-pound) beef rump roast

Directions:

1. Preheat the toaster oven to 350°F on CONVECTION BAKE for 5 minutes.
2. In a small bowl, stir the oil, garlic, thyme, salt, and pepper. Spread the mixture all over the beef.
3. Place the air-fryer basket in the baking tray and place the beef in the basket.
4. In position 1, bake for 1 hour and 15 minutes until browned and the internal temperature reaches 145°F for medium.
5. Let the roast rest 10 minutes and serve.

Stuffed Pork Chops

Servings: 4
Cooking Time: 12 Minutes

Ingredients:
- 4 boneless pork chops
- ½ teaspoon salt
- ½ teaspoon black pepper
- ¼ teaspoon paprika
- 1 cup frozen spinach, defrosted and squeezed dry
- 2 cloves garlic, minced
- 2 ounces cream cheese
- ¼ cup grated Parmesan cheese
- 1 tablespoon extra-virgin olive oil

Directions:

1. Pat the pork chops with a paper towel. Make a slit in the side of each pork chop to create a pouch.
2. Season the pork chops with the salt, pepper, and paprika.
3. In a small bowl, mix together the spinach, garlic, cream cheese, and Parmesan cheese.
4. Divide the mixture into fourths and stuff the pork chop pouches. Secure the pouches with toothpicks.
5. Preheat the toaster oven to 400°F.
6. Place the stuffed pork chops in the air fryer oven and spray liberally with cooking spray. Air-fry for 6 minutes, flip and coat with more cooking spray, and cook another 6 minutes. Check to make sure the meat is cooked to an internal temperature of 145°F. Cook the pork chops in batches, as needed.

DESSERTS

Black And Blue Clafoutis

Servings: 2
Cooking Time: 15 Minutes

Ingredients:
- 6-inch pie pan
- 3 large eggs
- ½ cup sugar
- 1 teaspoon vanilla extract
- 2 tablespoons butter, melted 1 cup milk
- ½ cup all-purpose flour
- 1 cup blackberries
- 1 cup blueberries
- 2 tablespoons confectioners' sugar

Directions:
1. Preheat the toaster oven to 320°F.
2. Combine the eggs and sugar in a bowl and whisk vigorously until smooth, lighter in color and well combined. Add the vanilla extract, butter and milk and whisk together well. Add the flour and whisk just until no lumps or streaks of white remain.
3. Scatter half the blueberries and blackberries in a greased (6-inch) pie pan or cake pan. Pour half of the batter (about 1¼ cups) on top of the berries and transfer the tart pan to the air fryer oven. You can use an aluminum foil sling to help with this by taking a long piece of aluminum foil, folding it in half lengthwise twice until it is roughly 26-inches by 3-inches. Place this under the pie dish and hold the ends of the foil to move the pie dish in and out of the air fryer oven. Tuck the ends of the foil beside the pie dish while it cooks in the air fryer oven.
4. Air-fry at 320°F for 15 minutes or until the clafoutis has puffed up and is still a little jiggly in the center. Remove the clafoutis from the air fryer oven, invert it onto a plate and let it cool while you bake the second batch. Serve the clafoutis warm, dusted with confectioners' sugar on top.

Midnight Nutella® Banana Sandwich

Servings: 2
Cooking Time: 8 Minutes

Ingredients:
- butter, softened
- 4 slices white bread
- ¼ cup chocolate hazelnut spread (Nutella®)
- 1 banana

Directions:
1. Preheat the toaster oven to 370°F.
2. Spread the softened butter on one side of all the slices of bread and place the slices buttered side down on the counter. Spread the chocolate hazelnut spread on the other side of the bread slices. Cut the banana in half and then slice each half into three slices lengthwise. Place the banana slices on two slices of bread and top with the remaining slices of bread (buttered side up) to make two sandwiches. Cut the sandwiches in half (triangles or rectangles) – this will help them all fit in the air fryer oven at once. Transfer the sandwiches to the air fryer oven.
3. Air-fry at 370°F for 5 minutes. Flip the sandwiches over and air-fry for another 2 to 3 minutes, or until the top bread slices are nicely browned. Pour yourself a glass of milk or a midnight nightcap while the sandwiches cool slightly and enjoy!

Donut Holes

Servings: 13
Cooking Time: 12 Minutes

Ingredients:
- 6 tablespoons Granulated white sugar
- 1½ tablespoons Butter, melted and cooled
- 2 tablespoons (or 1 small egg, well beaten) Pasteurized egg substitute, such as Egg Beaters
- 6 tablespoons Regular or low-fat sour cream (not fat-free)
- ¾ teaspoon Vanilla extract
- 1⅔ cups All-purpose flour
- ¾ teaspoon Baking powder
- ¼ teaspoon Table salt
- Vegetable oil spray

Directions:

1. Preheat the toaster oven to 350°F.
2. Whisk the sugar and melted butter in a medium bowl until well combined. Whisk in the egg substitute or egg, then the sour cream and vanilla until smooth. Remove the whisk and stir in the flour, baking powder, and salt with a wooden spoon just until a soft dough forms.
3. Use 2 tablespoons of this dough to create a ball between your clean palms. Set it aside and continue making balls: 8 more for the small batch, 12 more for the medium batch, or 17 more for the large one.
4. Coat the balls in the vegetable oil spray, then set them in the air fryer oven with as much air space between them as possible. Even a fraction of an inch will be enough, but they should not touch. Air-fry undisturbed for 12 minutes, or until browned and cooked through. A toothpick inserted into the center of a ball should come out clean.
5. Pour the contents of the air fryer oven onto a wire rack. Cool for at least 5 minutes before serving.

Warm Chocolate Fudge Cakes

Servings: 2
Cooking Time: 35 Minutes

Ingredients:
- 6 tablespoons (1¾ ounces) all-purpose flour
- ¼ teaspoon baking powder
- ⅛ teaspoon baking soda
- ⅛ teaspoon table salt
- 2½ ounces bittersweet chocolate (2 ounces chopped, ½ ounce cut into ½-inch pieces)
- ¼ cup whole milk, room temperature
- 3 tablespoons packed light brown sugar
- 2 tablespoons vegetable oil
- 1 large egg, lightly beaten
- ¼ teaspoon vanilla extract

Directions:
1. Adjust toaster oven rack to middle position and preheat the toaster oven to 350 degrees. Grease and flour two 6-ounce ramekins. Whisk flour, baking powder, baking soda, and salt together in bowl.
2. Microwave chopped chocolate and milk in medium bowl at 50 percent power, stirring occasionally, until chocolate is melted and mixture is smooth, 1 to 3 minutes. Stir in sugar until dissolved; let cool slightly. Whisk in oil, egg, and vanilla until combined. Gently whisk in flour mixture until just combined.
3. Divide batter evenly between prepared ramekins and gently tap each ramekin on counter to release air bubbles. Wipe any drops of batter off sides of ramekins. Gently press chocolate pieces evenly into center of each ramekin to submerge in batter. Place ramekins on small rimmed baking sheet and bake cakes until tops are just firm to touch and center is gooey when pierced with toothpick, 10 to 15 minutes. Let cool for 2 to 3 minutes before serving.

Mini Gingerbread Bundt Cakes

Servings: 16
Cooking Time: 24 Minutes

Ingredients:
- 3 cups all-purpose flour
- 1/4 cup baking cocoa
- 1 tablespoon baking soda
- 1 teaspoon ground cinnamon
- 1 teaspoon ground ginger
- 1 teaspoon salt
- 1/4 teaspoon ground cloves
- 1/4 teaspoon ground nutmeg
- 1 cup butter, softened
- 1 1/4 cups milk
- 1 cup packed dark brown sugar
- 1 cup molasses
- 2 large eggs
- 1 cup mini chocolate chips Glaze: 1 package (12 oz.) semi-sweet chocolate chips
- 1/3 cup heavy cream
- 2 tablespoons butter
- 2 tablespoons light corn syrup
- Chopped crystallized ginger

Directions:
1. Preheat the toaster oven to 350°F. Spray mini bundt pans with nonstick cooking spray. Dust with flour.
2. In a medium bowl, stir together flour, cocoa, baking soda, cinnamon, ginger, salt, cloves and nutmeg.

3. In a large mixer bowl, beat butter until creamy. Gradually beat in milk, brown sugar, molasses and eggs until well blended.
4. Reduce speed to LOW. Slowly add flour mixture until blended. Stir in chocolate chips.
5. Pour into prepared bundt pans.
6. Bake 20 to 24 minutes or until toothpick inserted in center comes out clean.
7. Cool on wire rack 10 minutes. Invert onto cooling rack and cool completely.
8. In a microwavable bowl, stir together 1 cup chocolate chips, heavy cream, butter and corn syrup.
9. Microwave on MEDIUM power 1 minute or until chips are shiny. Stir until mixture is smooth.
10. Spread glaze over top of each mini bundt and sprinkle with crystallized ginger.

Buttermilk Confetti Cake

Servings: 10-12
Cooking Time: 25 Minutes

Ingredients:
- 1 1/2 cups all purpose flour
- 1/2 teaspoon baking soda
- 1/4 teaspoon salt
- 1/2 cup butter, softened
- 1 cup sugar
- 1 teaspoon vanilla extract
- 2 large eggs
- 3/4 cup buttermilk
- 1/4 cup multi-colored sprinkle
- Cream Cheese Frosting
- Multi-colored sprinkles

Directions:
1. Preheat the toaster oven to 350°F. Grease two 8-inch cake pans and line with parchment paper.
2. Stir flour, baking soda and salt in small bowl. Set mixture aside.
3. Beat butter, sugar and vanilla extract on HIGH in large bowl until blended. Add eggs, one at a time, until well blended.
4. Alternately add flour mixture and buttermilk until combined. Stir in 1/4 cup sprinkles.
5. Divide batter evenly between prepared pans. Place one pan on bottom rack and one pan on top rack, rotate halfway through baking.
6. Bake 20 to 25 minutes or until a toothpick inserted in center of cakes comes out clean. Cool 10 minutes on wire rack.
7. Remove cakes from pans and cool completely on wire racks. Frost with Cream Cheese Frosting and top with sprinkles.

Meringue Topping

Servings: 1
Cooking Time: 12 Minutes

Ingredients:
- 3 egg whites
- 1 cup sugar

Directions:
1. Beat the egg whites and sugar together in a medium bowl until the mixture is stiff. Spread on top of the pie.
2. BAKE at 375°F. for 12 minutes, or until the meringue topping is browned.

Coconut Drop Cookies

Servings: 4
Cooking Time: 12 Minutes

Ingredients:
- 1 14-ounce package shredded and sweetened coconut
- 2 eggs
- 1 tablespoon margarine
- ¾ cup unbleached flour
- 1 teaspoon baking powder
- Salt to taste

Directions:
1. Preheat the toaster oven to 250° F.
2. Combine all the ingredients in a medium bowl, mixing well. Drop in small portions with a teaspoon onto an oiled or nonstick 6½ × 10-inch baking sheet or an oiled or nonstick 8½ × 8½ × 2-inch square baking (cake) pan.
3. BAKE for 10 minutes, or until golden brown.

Orange Almond Ricotta Cookies

Servings: 24
Cooking Time: 15 Minutes

Ingredients:
- Cookie Ingredients
- ½ stick unsalted butter, room temperature
- 1 cup sugar
- 1 large egg
- 1 cup ricotta cheese, drained
- 1½ tablespoons orange juice
- 1 orange, zested
- ¼ teaspoon almond extract
- 1¼ cups all purpose flour
- ½ teaspoon baking powder
- ½ teaspoon salt
- Glaze Ingredients
- 1 cup powdered sugar
- 1½ tablespoons orange juice
- ½ orange, zested

Directions:
1. Beat together the butter and sugar for 3 minutes or until light and fluffy.
2. Add the egg, ricotta, orange juice, orange zest, and almond extract and beat until well combined. Add the flour, baking powder, and salt, then fold gently to combine. Don't overmix.
3. Preheat the toaster Oven to 350°F.
4. Line the food tray with parchment paper, then divide the dough into 1½-tablespoon pieces and place on the tray.
5. Insert the tray at mid position in the preheated oven.
6. Select the Bake function, adjust time to 15 minutes, and press Start/Pause.
7. Remove when done and allow cookies to cool completely before glazing.
8. Make the glaze by stirring together the powdered sugar, orange juice, and zest until smooth. According to your preference, add more powdered sugar to make the glaze thicker, or more orange juice to make the glaze thinner.
9. Spoon about ½-teaspoon of the glaze on each cookie and spread gently. Allow the glaze to harden before serving

Pineapple Tartlets

Servings: 4
Cooking Time: 20 Minutes

Ingredients:
- Vegetable oil
- 6 sheets phyllo pastry
- 1 8-ounce can crushed pineapple, drained
- 3 tablespoons low-fat cottage cheese
- 2 tablespoons orange or pineapple marmalade
- 6 teaspoons concentrated thawed frozen orange juice
- Vanilla frozen yogurt or nonfat whipped topping

Directions:
1. Preheat the toaster oven to 350° F.
2. Brush the pans of a 6-muffin tin with vegetable oil. Lay a phyllo sheet on a clean, flat surface and brush with oil. Fold the sheet into quarters to fit the muffin pan. Repeat the process for the remaining phyllo sheets and pans.
3. BAKE for 5 minutes, or until lightly browned. Remove from the oven and cool.
4. Combine the pineapple, cottage cheese, and marmalade in a small bowl, mixing well. Fill the phyllo shells (in the pans) with equal portions of the mixture. Drizzle 1 teaspoon orange juice concentrate over each.
5. BAKE at 400° F. for 15 minutes, or until the filling is cooked. Cool and remove the tartlets carefully from the muffin pans to dessert dishes. Top with vanilla frozen yogurt or nonfat whipped topping.

Frozen Brazo De Mercedes

Servings: 8
Cooking Time: 15 Minutes

Ingredients:
- 1 pint vanilla ice cream, softened to room temperature
- 1 (8 inch) premade graham cracker crust
- 6 large eggs, yolks and whites separated
- 7 ounces condensed milk
- ½ teaspoon vanilla extract
- ¼ teaspoon cream of tartar
- ⅓ cup granulated sugar

Directions:
1. Spread the ice cream on the bottom of the graham cracker crust in an even layer, cover with plastic wrap, and place in the freezer for 8 hours or overnight.
2. Whisk egg yolks and condensed milk over a double boiler continuously for 15 minutes or until the mixture becomes thick.
3. Whisk the vanilla extract into the egg mixture until fully combined.
4. Pass the custard through a fine sieve to remove any clumps.
5. Remove the ice cream and top with the egg yolk mixture, cover with plastic wrap, and place back into the freezer for 2 hours.
6. Beat the egg whites and cream of tartar in a stand mixer on high speed.
7. Add the sugar in slowly once the egg whites begin to foam.
8. Beat the egg whites for two minutes or until they form stiff peaks.
9. Remove the plastic wrap from the pie and top with the beaten egg whites.
10. Preheat the toaster Oven to 350°F.
11. Place the pie on the wire rack, then insert the rack at mid position in the preheated air fryer.
12. Select the Bake and Shake functions, adjust time to 15 minutes, and press Start/Pause.
13. Rotate the pie halfway through cooking for even browning. The Shake Reminder will let you know when.
14. Remove when done and place in the fridge for 1 hour, uncovered.
15. Cover the pie, then place in the freezer for 6 hours or overnight.
16. Remove the pie and allow it to rest at room temperature for 10 minutes, then slice and serve.

Blueberry Clafoutis

Servings: 6
Cooking Time: 35 Minutes

Ingredients:
- 2 tablespoons salted butter, melted, plus extra for greasing the baking dish
- ½ cup all-purpose flour, plus extra for dusting the baking dish
- 2 cups fresh blueberries
- 1 cup whole milk
- 3 large eggs
- ½ cup granulated sugar
- ¼ cup light brown sugar
- 2 teaspoons vanilla extract

Directions:
1. Place the rack in position 1 and preheat the toaster oven to 350°F on BAKE for 5 minutes.
2. Lightly grease and flour a 9-inch-square baking dish.
3. Spread the blueberries in the bottom of the baking dish.
4. In a large bowl, whisk the milk, eggs, sugar, brown sugar, butter, and vanilla until smooth.
5. Add the flour and whisk to combine.
6. Pour the batter into the baking dish and bake for 35 minutes or until light brown and a toothpick inserted into the center comes out clean. If the top starts to get too brown, cover the dish lightly with foil.
7. Cool for 10 minutes and serve.

Coconut Cake

Servings: 6
Cooking Time: 25 Minutes

Ingredients:
- 2 cups unbleached flour
- 2 teaspoons baking powder
- 1 cup skim or low-fat soy milk
- 2 tablespoons vegetable oil
- 3 1 teaspoon vanilla extract
- 1 egg, beaten
- ¾ cup sugar
- Salt to taste
- Creamy Frosting (recipe follows)

Directions:
1. Preheat the toaster oven to 350° F.
2. Combine all the ingredients in a large bowl, mixing well.
3. Pour the cake batter into an oiled or nonstick 8½ × 8½ × 2-inch square baking (cake) pan.
4. BAKE for 25 minutes, or until a toothpick inserted in the center comes out clean. Ice with Creamy Frosting and sprinkle with coconut.

White Chocolate Cranberry Blondies

Servings: 6
Cooking Time: 18 Minutes

Ingredients:
- ⅓ cup butter
- ½ cup sugar
- 1 teaspoon vanilla extract
- 1 large egg
- 1 cup all-purpose flour
- ½ teaspoon baking powder
- ⅛ teaspoon salt
- ¼ cup dried cranberries
- ¼ cup white chocolate chips

Directions:
1. Preheat the toaster oven to 320°F.
2. In a large bowl, cream the butter with the sugar and vanilla extract. Whisk in the egg and set aside.
3. In a separate bowl, mix the flour with the baking powder and salt. Then gently mix the dry ingredients into the wet. Fold in the cranberries and chocolate chips.
4. Liberally spray an oven-safe 7-inch springform pan with olive oil and pour the batter into the pan.
5. Air-fry for 17 minutes or until a toothpick inserted in the center comes out clean.
6. Remove and let cool 5 minutes before serving.

Keto Cheesecake Cups

Servings: 6
Cooking Time: 10 Minutes

Ingredients:
- 8 ounces cream cheese
- ¼ cup plain whole-milk Greek yogurt
- 1 large egg
- 1 teaspoon pure vanilla extract
- 3 tablespoons monk fruit sweetener
- ¼ teaspoon salt
- ½ cup walnuts, roughly chopped

Directions:
1. Preheat the toaster oven to 315°F.
2. In a large bowl, use a hand mixer to beat the cream cheese together with the yogurt, egg, vanilla, sweetener, and salt. When combined, fold in the chopped walnuts.
3. Set 6 silicone muffin liners inside an air-fryer-safe pan.
4. Evenly fill the cupcake liners with cheesecake batter.
5. Carefully place the pan into the air fryer oven and air-fry for about 10 minutes, or until the tops are lightly browned and firm.
6. Carefully remove the pan when done and place in the refrigerator for 3 hours to firm up before serving.

Blackberry Pie

Servings: 6
Cooking Time: 30 Minutes

Ingredients:
- Filling:
- 2 16-ounce bags frozen blackberries, thawed, or 2 cups fresh blackberries, washed and well drained
- 1 4-ounce jar baby food prunes
- 2 tablespoons cornstarch
- 3 ¼ cup brown sugar
- 1 tablespoon lemon juice
- Salt to taste
- 1 Graham Cracker Crust, baked (recipe follows)
- Meringue Topping (recipe follows)

Directions:
1. Preheat the toaster oven to 350° F.
2. Combine the filling ingredients in a large bowl, mixing well. Spoon the filling into the baked Graham Cracker Crust and spread evenly.
3. BAKE for 30 minutes. When cool, top with the Meringue Topping.

Heavenly Chocolate Cupcakes

Servings: 6
Cooking Time: 30 Minutes

Ingredients:
- 2 squares semisweet chocolate
- 2 tablespoons margarine
- 1 cup unbleached flour
- 2 teaspoons baking powder
- Salt to taste
- ¾ cup brown sugar
- ½ cup skim milk
- 1 egg, beaten

- ½ cup chopped pecans
- ½ teaspoon vanilla extract

Directions:

1. Melt the chocolate and margarine in an oiled or nonstick 8½ × 8½ × 2-inch square baking (cake) pan under the broiler for 5 minutes, or until about half melted. Remove from the oven and stir until completely melted and blended.
2. Combine the flour, baking powder, salt, and sugar in a medium bowl, mixing well. Add the melted chocolate/margarine mixture, then the milk and egg. Stir to blend well, then stir in the pecans and vanilla. Fill paper baking cups or well-oiled tins in a 6-muffin pan three-quarters full with batter.
3. BAKE at 350° F. for 25 minutes, or until a toothpick inserted in the center comes out clean.

Lemon Torte

Servings: 6
Cooking Time: 16 Minutes

Ingredients:

- First mixture:
- ¼ cup margarine, at room temperature
- ½ teaspoon grated lemon zest
- 3 egg yolks
- ¼ cup sugar
- ⅓ cup unbleached flour
- 3 tablespoons cornstarch
- Second mixture:
- 3 egg whites
- 2 tablespoons sugar
- Cream Cheese Frosting (recipe follows)

Directions:

1. Beat together the first mixture ingredients in a medium bowl with an electric mixer until the mixture is smooth. Set aside. Clean the electric mixer beaters.
2. Beat the second mixture together: Beat the egg whites into soft peaks in a medium bowl, gradually adding the sugar, and continue beating until the peaks are stiff. Fold the first mixture into the second mixture to make the torte batter.
3. Pour ½ cup torte batter into a small oiled or nonstick 3½ × 7½ × 2¼-inch loaf pan.
4. BROIL for 1 or 2 minutes, or until lightly browned. Remove from the oven.
5. Pour and spread evenly another ½ cup batter on top of the first layer. Broil again for 1 or 2 minutes, or until lightly browned. Repeat the process until all the batter is used up. When cool, run a knife around the sides to loosen and invert onto a plate. Chill. Frost with Cream Cheese Frosting and serve chilled.

Maple-glazed Pumpkin Pie

Servings: 2
Cooking Time: 10 Minutes

Ingredients:

- Filling:
- 1 15-ounce can pumpkin pie filling
- 1 12-ounce can low-fat evaporated milk
- 1 egg
- 3 tablespoons maple syrup
- ½ teaspoon grated nutmeg
- ½ teaspoon ground ginger
- 1 teaspoon ground cinnamon
- Salt to taste
- 1 Apple Juice Piecrust, baked (recipe follows)
- Dark glaze:
- 3 tablespoons maple syrup
- 2 tablespoons dark brown sugar

Directions:

1. Preheat the toaster oven to 400° F.
2. Combine all the filling ingredients in a large bowl and beat with an electric mixer until smooth. Pour into the piecrust shell.
3. BAKE for 40 minutes, or until a knife inserted in the center comes out clean.
4. Combine the dark glaze ingredients in a baking pan.
5. BROIL for 5 minutes, or until bubbling. Remove from the oven and stir to dissolve the sugar. Broil again for 3 minutes, or until the liquid is thickened and the sugar is dissolved. Spoon on top of the cooled pumpkin pie, spreading evenly, then chill for at least 1 hour before serving.

Peanut Butter Cup Doughnut Holes

Servings: 24
Cooking Time: 4 Minutes

Ingredients:
- 1½ cups bread flour
- 1 teaspoon active dry yeast
- 1 tablespoon sugar
- ¼ teaspoon salt
- ½ cup warm milk
- ½ teaspoon vanilla extract
- 2 egg yolks
- 2 tablespoons melted butter
- 24 miniature peanut butter cups, plus a few more for garnish
- vegetable oil, in a spray bottle
- Doughnut Topping
- 1 cup chocolate chips
- 2 tablespoons milk

Directions:
1. Combine the flour, yeast, sugar and salt in a bowl. Add the milk, vanilla, egg yolks and butter. Mix well until the dough starts to come together. Transfer the dough to a floured surface and knead by hand for 2 minutes. Shape the dough into a ball and transfer it to a large oiled bowl. Cover the bowl with a towel and let the dough rise in a warm place for 1 to 1½ hours, until the dough has doubled in size.
2. When the dough has risen, punch it down and roll it into a 24-inch long log. Cut the dough into 24 pieces. Push a peanut butter cup into the center of each piece of dough, pinch the dough shut and roll it into a ball. Place the dough balls on a cookie sheet and let them rise in a warm place for 30 minutes.
3. Preheat the toaster oven to 400°F.
4. Spray or brush the dough balls lightly with vegetable oil. Air-fry eight at a time, at 400°F for 4 minutes, turning them over halfway through the cooking process.
5. While the doughnuts are air frying, prepare the topping. Place the chocolate chips and milk in a microwave safe bowl. Microwave on high for 1 minute. Stir and microwave for an additional 30 seconds if necessary to get all the chips to melt. Stir until the chips are melted and smooth.
6. Dip the top half of the doughnut holes into the melted chocolate. Place them on a rack to set up for just a few minutes and watch them disappear.

Bourbon Bread Pudding

Servings: 2
Cooking Time: 120 Minutes

Ingredients:
- 6 ounces baguette, torn into 1-inch pieces (4 cups)
- ¼ cup raisins
- 2 tablespoons bourbon
- ¾ cup heavy cream
- ⅓ cup packed (2⅓ ounces) light brown sugar
- ¼ cup whole milk
- 2 large egg yolks
- 1 teaspoon vanilla extract
- ½ teaspoon ground cinnamon, divided
- ⅛ teaspoon table salt
- Pinch ground nutmeg
- 2 tablespoons unsalted butter, cut into ¼-inch pieces
- 1 tablespoon granulated sugar

Directions:
1. Adjust toaster oven rack to middle position and preheat the toaster oven to 375 degrees. Spread bread in single layer on small rimmed baking sheet and bake until golden brown and crisp, 10 to 20 minutes, tossing halfway through baking. Let bread cool completely.
2. Meanwhile, microwave raisins and bourbon in covered bowl until bubbling, 30 to 60 seconds. Let sit until softened, about 15 minutes.
3. Whisk cream, brown sugar, milk, egg yolks, vanilla, ¼ teaspoon cinnamon, salt, and nutmeg together in large bowl. Add bread and raisin mixture and toss until evenly coated. Let mixture sit, tossing occasionally, until bread begins to absorb custard and is softened, about 20 minutes.
4. Grease two 12-ounce ramekins. Divide bread mixture evenly between prepared ramekins and sprinkle with butter, granulated sugar, and remaining ¼ teaspoon cinnamon. Cover each ramekin with

aluminum foil, place on small rimmed baking sheet, and bake for 30 minutes.

5. Remove foil from bread puddings and continue to bake until tops are crisp and golden brown, 10 to 15 minutes. Let bread puddings cool for 15 minutes before serving.

Chocolate And Vanilla Swirled Pudding

Servings: 4
Cooking Time: 25 Minutes

Ingredients:
- 1 square semisweet chocolate
- 1½ cups fat-free half-and-half
- 1 tablespoon sugar
- 2 egg yolks
- ½ teaspoon vanilla extract
- Fat-free whipped topping

Directions:
1. Melt the chocolate in an oiled or nonstick 8½ × 8½ × 2-inch square baking (cake) pan under the broiler for approximately 5 minutes, removing the pan from the oven before the chocolate is completely melted. Stir until melted and smooth. Set aside.
2. Whisk together the half-and-half, sugar, egg yolks, and vanilla in a medium bowl. Divide into two portions and add the melted chocolate to one, stirring to blend well.
3. Fill four 1-cup-size ovenproof dishes with equal portions of the vanilla mixture, then top with equal portions of the chocolate mixture. With a skewer or toothpick, stir the pudding in little circles to create a swirling pattern of light and dark.
4. BAKE at 350° F. for 25 minutes, or until the pudding is firm. Chill before serving. Top with fat-free whipped topping.

Little Swedish Coffee Cakes

Servings: 4
Cooking Time: 30 Minutes

Ingredients:
- Cake batter:
- 1 cup unbleached flour
- 1 teaspoon baking powder
- ½ cup sugar
- ½ cup finely ground pecans
- ¾ cup low-fat buttermilk
- 1 tablespoon vegetable oil
- 1 egg, lightly beaten
- 1 teaspoon vanilla extract
- Salt to taste
- Sifted confectioners' sugar
- Canola oil for brushing pan

Directions:
1. Preheat the toaster oven to 350° F.
2. Combine the cake batter ingredients in a bowl, mixing well. Pour the batter into an oiled or nonstick 8½ × 8½ × 2-inch square baking (cake) pan.
3. BAKE for 30 minutes, or until a toothpick inserted in the center comes out clean. Run a knife around the edge of the pan, invert, and place on a rack to cool. Sprinkle the top with sifted confectioners' sugar and cut into small squares.

Goat Cheese–stuffed Nectarines

Servings: 4
Cooking Time: 10 Minutes

Ingredients:
- 4 ripe nectarines, halved and pitted
- 1 tablespoon olive oil
- 1 cup soft goat cheese, room temperature
- 1 tablespoon maple syrup
- ¼ teaspoon vanilla extract
- ¼ teaspoon ground cinnamon
- 2 tablespoons pecans, chopped

Directions:
1. Preheat the toaster oven to 350°F on AIR FRY for 5 minutes.
2. Place the air-fryer basket in the baking tray and place the nectarines in the basket, hollow-side up. Brush the tops and hollow of the fruit with the olive oil.
3. In position 2, air fry for 5 minutes to soften and lightly brown the fruit.

4. While the fruit is air frying, in a small bowl, stir the goat cheese, maple syrup, vanilla, and cinnamon until well blended.
5. Take the fruit out and evenly divide the cheese filling between the halves. Air fry for 5 minutes until the filling is heated through and a little melted.
6. Serve topped with pecans.

Peanut Butter S'mores

Servings: 10
Cooking Time: 1 Minutes

Ingredients:
- 10 Graham crackers (full, double-square cookies as they come out of the package)
- 5 tablespoons Natural-style creamy or crunchy peanut butter
- ½ cup Milk chocolate chips
- 10 Standard-size marshmallows (not minis and not jumbo campfire ones)

Directions:
1. Preheat the toaster oven to 350°F.
2. Break the graham crackers in half widthwise at the marked place, so the rectangle is now in two squares. Set half of the squares flat side up on your work surface. Spread each with about 1½ teaspoons peanut butter, then set 10 to 12 chocolate chips point side up into the peanut butter on each, pressing gently so the chips stick.
3. Flatten a marshmallow between your clean, dry hands and set it atop the chips. Do the same with the remaining marshmallows on the other coated graham crackers. Do not set the other half of the graham crackers on top of these coated graham crackers.
4. When the machine is at temperature, set the treats graham cracker side down in a single layer in the air fryer oven. They may touch, but even a fraction of an inch between them will provide better air flow. Air-fry undisturbed for 45 seconds.
5. Use a nonstick-safe spatula to transfer the topped graham crackers to a wire rack. Set the other graham cracker squares flat side down over the marshmallows. Cool for a couple of minutes before serving.

Make-ahead Chocolate Chip Cookies

Servings: 12
Cooking Time: 45 Minutes

Ingredients:
- 2⅛ cups (10⅔ ounces) all-purpose flour
- ½ teaspoon baking soda
- ½ teaspoon table salt
- 1 cup packed (7 ounces) light brown sugar
- ½ cup (3½ ounces) granulated sugar
- 12 tablespoons unsalted butter, melted and cooled
- 1 large egg plus 1 large yolk
- 2 teaspoons vanilla extract
- 1 cup (6 ounces) semisweet chocolate chips

Directions:
1. Adjust toaster oven rack to middle position and preheat the toaster oven to 350 degrees. Line large and small rimmed baking sheets with parchment paper. Whisk flour, baking soda, and salt together in bowl.
2. Whisk brown sugar and granulated sugar together in medium bowl. Whisk in melted butter until combined. Whisk in egg and yolk and vanilla until smooth. Gently stir in flour mixture with rubber spatula until soft dough forms. Fold in chocolate chips.
3. Working with 2 tablespoons dough at a time, roll into balls. Space desired number of dough balls at least 1½ inches apart on prepared small sheet; space remaining dough balls evenly on prepared large sheet. Using bottom of greased dry measuring cup, press each ball until 2 inches in diameter.
4. Bake small sheet of cookies until edges are just beginning to brown and centers are soft and puffy, 10 to 15 minutes. Let cookies cool slightly on sheet. Serve warm or at room temperature.
5. Freeze remaining large sheet of cookies until firm, about 1 hour. Transfer cookies to 1-gallon zipper-lock bag and freeze for up to 1 month. Bake frozen cookies as directed; do not thaw.

Blueberry Crisp

Servings: 6
Cooking Time: 13 Minutes

Ingredients:

- 3 cups Fresh or thawed frozen blueberries
- ⅓ cup Granulated white sugar
- 1 tablespoon Instant tapioca
- ⅓ cup All-purpose flour
- ⅓ cup Rolled oats (not quick-cooking or steel-cut)
- ⅓ cup Chopped walnuts or pecans
- ⅓ cup Packed light brown sugar
- 5 tablespoons plus 1 teaspoon (⅔ stick) Butter, melted and cooled
- ¾ teaspoon Ground cinnamon
- ¼ teaspoon Table salt

Directions:

1. Preheat the toaster oven to 400°F.
2. Mix the blueberries, granulated white sugar, and instant tapioca in a 6-inch round cake pan for a small batch, a 7-inch round cake pan for a medium batch, or an 8-inch round cake pan for a large batch.
3. When the machine is at temperature, set the cake pan in the air fryer oven and air-fry undisturbed for 5 minutes, or just until the blueberries begin to bubble.
4. Meanwhile, mix the flour, oats, nuts, brown sugar, butter, cinnamon, and salt in a medium bowl until well combined.
5. When the blueberries have begun to bubble, crumble this flour mixture evenly on top. Continue air-frying undisturbed for 8 minutes, or until the topping has browned a bit and the filling is bubbling.
6. Use two hot pads or silicone baking mitts to transfer the cake pan to a wire rack. Cool for at least 10 minutes or to room temperature before serving.

Sweet Potato Donut Holes

Servings: 18
Cooking Time: 4 Minutes

Ingredients:

- 1 cup flour
- ⅓ cup sugar
- ¼ teaspoon baking soda
- 1 teaspoon baking powder
- ⅛ teaspoon salt
- ½ cup cooked mashed purple sweet potatoes
- 1 egg, beaten
- 2 tablespoons butter, melted
- 1 teaspoon pure vanilla extract
- oil for misting or cooking spray

Directions:

1. Preheat the toaster oven to 390°F.
2. In a large bowl, stir together the flour, sugar, baking soda, baking powder, and salt.
3. In a separate bowl, combine the potatoes, egg, butter, and vanilla and mix well.
4. Add potato mixture to dry ingredients and stir into a soft dough.
5. Shape dough into 1½-inch balls. Mist lightly with oil or cooking spray.
6. Place 9 donut holes in air fryer oven, leaving a little space in between. Air-fry for 4 minutes, until done in center and lightly browned outside.
7. Repeat step 6 to cook remaining donut holes.

Cinnamon Sugar Rolls

Servings: 8
Cooking Time: 10 Minutes

Ingredients:

- ½ cup margarine
- Filling mixture:
- 1 tablespoon ground cinnamon
- ½ cup brown sugar
- ½ cup finely chopped walnuts
- 10 sheets phyllo pastry, thawed

Directions:

1. BROIL the margarine in an oiled or nonstick 8½ × 8½ × 2-inch square baking (cake) pan for 3 minutes, or until almost melted. Remove from the oven and stir until melted (the pan will be hot and the margarine will continue to melt). Set aside.
2. Combine the filling mixture in a small bowl, mixing well.
3. Lay a sheet of phyllo pastry on a clean flat surface. Brush with the melted margarine, sprinkle with a heaping tablespoon of the filling mixture, and spread evenly to cover the sheet of pastry. Repeat the brushing

and sprinkling procedure for each sheet, layering one on top of the other until all 10 sheets are done. Use up any remaining filling mixture on the last sheet. Starting at the 9-inch (long) edge, slowly roll all of the sheets up like a jelly roll. With a sharp knife, cut the roll into 1¼-inch slices. Place the slices on an oiled or nonstick baking sheet or baking pan.

4. BAKE at 350° F. for 10 minutes, or until golden brown.

Giant Oatmeal–peanut Butter Cookie

Servings: 4
Cooking Time: 18 Minutes

Ingredients:
- 1 cup Rolled oats (not quick-cooking or steel-cut oats)
- ½ cup All-purpose flour
- ½ teaspoon Ground cinnamon
- ½ teaspoon Baking soda
- ⅓ cup Packed light brown sugar
- ¼ cup Solid vegetable shortening
- 2 tablespoons Natural-style creamy peanut butter
- 3 tablespoons Granulated white sugar
- 2 tablespoons (or 1 small egg, well beaten) Pasteurized egg substitute, such as Egg Beaters
- ⅓ cup Roasted, salted peanuts, chopped
- Baking spray

Directions:
1. Preheat the toaster oven to 350°F..
2. Stir the oats, flour, cinnamon, and baking soda in a bowl until well combined.
3. Using an electric hand mixer at medium speed, beat the brown sugar, shortening, peanut butter, granulated white sugar, and egg substitute or egg (as applicable) until smooth and creamy, about 3 minutes, scraping down the inside of the bowl occasionally.
4. Scrape down and remove the beaters. Fold in the flour mixture and peanuts with a rubber spatula just until all the flour is moistened and the peanut bits are evenly distributed in the dough.
5. For a small air fryer oven, coat the inside of a 6-inch round cake pan with baking spray. For a medium air fryer oven, coat the inside of a 7-inch round cake pan with baking spray. And for a large air fryer oven, coat the inside of an 8-inch round cake pan with baking spray. Scrape and gently press the dough into the prepared pan, spreading it into an even layer to the perimeter.
6. Set the pan in the air fryer oven and air-fry undisturbed for 18 minutes, or until well browned.
7. Transfer the pan to a wire rack and cool for 15 minutes. Loosen the cookie from the perimeter with a spatula, then invert the pan onto a cutting board and let the cookie come free. Remove the pan and reinvert the cookie onto the wire rack. Cool for 5 minutes more before slicing into wedges to serve.

Cranapple Crisp

Servings: 6
Cooking Time: 35 Minutes

Ingredients:
- 2 apples, peeled, cored, and diced
- 3 cups chopped fresh or thawed frozen cranberries
- ¼ cup brown sugar
- ¼ cup wheat germ
- 1 tablespoon margarine
- 1 tablespoon vegetable oil
- ½ cup brown sugar
- 1 teaspoon ground cinnamon
- ¼ teaspoon grated nutmeg
- Salt to taste

Directions:
1. Preheat the toaster oven to 350° F.
2. Combine the cranberries, apples, and sugar in a large bowl, mixing well. Transfer to an oiled or nonstick 8½ × 8½ × 2-inch square baking (cake) pan. Set aside.
3. Combine the topping ingredients in a medium bowl, stirring with a fork until crumbly. Sprinkle evenly on top of the cranberry/apple mixture.
4. BAKE for 35 minutes, or until the top is golden brown.

Carrot Cake

Servings: 6
Cooking Time: 30 Minutes

Ingredients:
- FOR THE CAKE
- ½ cup canola oil, plus extra for greasing the baking dish
- 1 cup all-purpose flour, plus extra for dusting the baking dish
- 1 cup granulated sugar
- 1 teaspoon baking powder
- ½ teaspoon sea salt
- 2 teaspoons pumpkin pie spice
- 2 large eggs
- 1 cup carrot, finely shredded
- ½ cup dried apricot, chopped
- FOR THE ICING
- 4 ounces cream cheese, room temperature
- ¼ cup salted butter, room temperature
- 1 teaspoon vanilla extract
- 2 cups confectioners' sugar

Directions:
1. To make the cake
2. Place the rack in position 1 and preheat the oven to 325°F on BAKE for 5 minutes.
3. Lightly grease an 8-inch-square baking dish with oil and dust with flour.
4. Place the rack in position 1.
5. In a large bowl, stir the flour, sugar, baking powder, salt, and pumpkin pie spice.
6. Make a well in the center and add the oil and eggs, stirring until just combined. Add the carrot and apricot and stir until well mixed.
7. Transfer the batter to the baking dish and bake for about 30 minutes until golden brown and a toothpick inserted in the center comes out clean.
8. Remove the cake from the oven and cool completely in the baking dish.
9. To make the icing
10. When the cake is cool, whisk the cream cheese, butter, and vanilla until very smooth and blended. Add the confectioners' sugar and whisk until creamy and thick, about 2 minutes.
11. Ice the cake and serve.

Orange-glazed Brownies

Servings: 12
Cooking Time: 30 Minutes

Ingredients:
- 3 squares unsweetened chocolate
- 3 tablespoons margarine
- 1 cup sugar
- ½ cup orange juice
- 2 eggs
- 1½ cups unbleached flour
- 1 teaspoon baking powder
- Salt to taste
- 1 tablespoon grated orange zest
- Orange Glaze (recipe follows)

Directions:
1. BROIL the chocolate and margarine in an oiled or nonstick 8½ × 8½ × 2-inch square baking (cake) pan for 3 minutes, or until almost melted. Remove from the oven and stir until completely melted. Transfer the chocolate/margarine mixture to a medium bowl.
2. Beat in the sugar, orange juice, and eggs with an electric mixer. Stir in the flour, baking powder, salt, and orange zest and mix until well blended. Pour into the oiled or nonstick square cake pan.
3. BAKE at 350° F. for 30 minutes, or until a toothpick inserted in the center comes out clean. Make holes over the entire top by piercing with a fork or toothpick. Paint with Orange Glaze and cut into squares.

German Chocolate Cake

Servings: 6
Cooking Time: 25 Minutes

Ingredients:
- Butter, shortening, or nonstick cooking spray
- ⅔ cup whole milk
- ½ teaspoon white vinegar
- ⅔ cup all-purpose flour
- 3 tablespoons unsweetened cocoa powder
- ½ teaspoon baking soda
- ½ teaspoon baking powder
- ¼ teaspoon table salt

- ½ cup packed dark brown sugar
- 2 tablespoons canola or vegetable oil
- 1 large egg
- ½ teaspoon pure vanilla extract
- GERMAN CHOCOLATE FROSTING
- 1 large egg yolk
- ½ cup evaporated milk
- ⅓ cup granulated sugar
- 3 tablespoons unsalted butter
- ¾ cup sweetened flaked coconut
- ⅓ cup chopped pecans, toasted

Directions:
1. Preheat the toaster oven to 350°F. Line an 8-inch round cake pan with parchment paper and lightly grease the bottom and sides with butter or shortening or spray with nonstick cooking spray.
2. Pour the milk into a medium bowl and stir in the vinegar; set aside.
3. Whisk the flour, cocoa, baking soda, baking powder, and salt in a small bowl; set aside.
4. Whisk the brown sugar, oil, egg, and vanilla in a medium bowl. Add the flour mixture, in thirds, alternately with the milk mixture, beginning and ending with the flour. Blend well and scrape the sides of the bowl as needed.
5. Pour the batter into the prepared pan. Bake for 20 to 25 minutes, or until a wooden pick inserted into the center comes out clean. Let cool on a wire rack for 10 minutes. Invert onto a serving platter and allow to cool completely.
6. Make the frosting: Combine the egg yolk, evaporated milk, sugar, and butter in a small saucepan. Cook, stirring, over medium heat for about 6 minutes or until thickened and bubbly. Remove from the heat and stir in the coconut and pecans. Cover and let cool completely. Frost the top of the cake.

Soft Peanut Butter Cookies

Servings: 12
Cooking Time: 20 Minutes

Ingredients:
- 1/2 cup vegetable shortening
- 1/2 cup peanut butter
- 1 1/4 cups light brown sugar
- 1 egg
- 1 teaspoon vanilla
- 1/2 teaspoon salt
- 1 1/2 cups flour
- 1 teaspoon baking soda
- Sugar crystals

Directions:
1. Preheat the toaster oven to 275°F.
2. Using the flat beater attachment, beat shortening, peanut butter, brown sugar, egg, and vanilla at a medium setting until well blended.
3. Reduce speed to low and gradually add dry ingredients until blended. Dough will be crumbly.
4. Roll 3 tablespoon-size portions of the dough into a ball. Place on ungreased cookie sheet.
5. Press to 1/2-inch thick. Sprinkle with sugar crystals.
6. Bake 18 to 20 minutes. Do not overcook.

Wild Blueberry Sweet Empanadas

Servings: 12
Cooking Time: 8 Minutes

Ingredients:
- 2 cups frozen wild blueberries
- 5 tablespoons chia seeds
- ¼ cup honey
- 1 tablespoon lemon or lime juice
- ¼ cup water
- 1½ cups all-purpose flour
- 1 cup whole-wheat flour
- ½ teaspoon salt
- 1 tablespoon sugar
- ½ cup cold unsalted butter
- 1 egg
- ½ cup plus 2 tablespoons milk, divided
- 1 cup powdered sugar
- 1 teaspoon vanilla extract

Directions:
1. To make the wild blueberry chia jam, place the blueberries, chia seeds, honey, lemon or lime juice, and water into a blender and pulse for 2 minutes. Pour the chia jam into a glass jar or bowl and cover. Store in the

refrigerator at least 4 to 8 hours or until the jam is thickened.

2. In a food processor, place the all-purpose flour, whole-wheat flour, salt, sugar, and butter and process for 2 minutes, scraping down the sides of the food processor every 30 seconds. Add in the egg and blend for 30 seconds. Using the pulse button, add in ½ cup of the milk 1 tablespoon at a time or until the dough is moist enough to handle and be rolled into a ball. Let the dough rest at room temperature for 30 minutes.

3. On a floured surface, cut the dough in half; then form a ball and cut each ball into 6 equal pieces, totaling 12 equal pieces. Work with one piece at a time, and cover the remaining dough with a towel. Roll out the dough into a 6-inch round, much like a tortilla, with ¼ inch thickness. Place 4 tablespoons of filling in the center of round, fold over to form a half-circle. Using a fork, crimp the edges together and pierce the top with a fork for air holes. Repeat with the remaining dough and filling.

4. Preheat the toaster oven to 350°F.

5. Working in batches, place 3 to 4 empanadas in the air fryer oven and spray with cooking spray. Air-fry for 8 minutes. Repeat in batches, as needed. Allow the sweet empanadas to cool for 15 minutes. Meanwhile, in a small bowl, whisk together the powdered sugar, the remaining 2 tablespoons of milk, and the vanilla extract. Then drizzle the glaze over the surface and serve.

Mississippi Mud Brownies

Servings: 16
Cooking Time: 34 Minutes

Ingredients:
- Nonstick cooking spray
- 3 tablespoons unsweetened cocoa powder
- ¼ cup canola or vegetable oil
- ¼ cup unsalted butter, softened
- 1 cup granulated sugar
- 2 large eggs
- 1 teaspoon pure vanilla extract
- ¾ cup all-purpose flour
- ½ teaspoon table salt
- ½ cup pecan pieces, toasted
- 2 cups mini marshmallows
- FROSTING
- ¼ cup unsalted butter, melted
- 3 tablespoons unsweetened cocoa powder
- ½ teaspoon pure vanilla extract
- 2 cups confectioners' sugar
- 2 to 3 tablespoons whole milk

Directions:
1. Preheat the toaster oven to 350°F. Spray an 8-inch square baking pan with nonstick cooking spray.

2. Beat the cocoa and oil in a large bowl with a handheld mixer at medium speed. Add the butter and mix until smooth. Beat in the granulated sugar. Add the eggs, one at a time, mixing after each addition. Add the vanilla and mix. On low speed, blend in the flour and salt. Stir in the pecans.

3. Pour the batter into the prepared pan. Bake for 28 to 32 minutes, or until a wooden pick inserted into the center comes out clean.

4. Remove the brownies from the oven and sprinkle the marshmallows over the top. Return to the oven and bake for about 2 minutes or until the marshmallows are puffed. Place on a wire rack and let cool completely.

5. Meanwhile, make the frosting: Combine the butter, cocoa, vanilla, confectioners' sugar, and 2 tablespoons milk in a large bowl. Beat until smooth. If needed for the desired consistency, add additional milk. Frost the cooled brownies.

Currant Carrot Cake

Servings: 6
Cooking Time: 30 Minutes

Ingredients:
- 1 cup unbleached flour
- 1 teaspoon baking powder
- 1 teaspoon baking soda
- ½ cup evaporated skim milk
- ½ cup brown sugar
- 2 tablespoons vegetable oil
- 1 egg
- 1 cup grated carrots
- ½ cup chopped currants
- ¼ cup finely chopped pecans

- Salt to taste
- Yogurt Cream Icing (recipe follows)

Directions:
1. Preheat the toaster oven to 350° F.
2. Combine all the ingredients in a medium bowl, stirring well to mix thoroughly.
3. Spread the batter in an oiled or nonstick 8½ × 8½ × 2-inch square baking (cake) pan.
4. BAKE for 30 minutes, or until a toothpick inserted in the center comes out clean. Cool on a wire rack. Ice with Yogurt Cream Icing.

Make-ahead Oatmeal-raisin Cookies

Servings: 8
Cooking Time: 45 Minutes

Ingredients:
- 1 cup (5 ounces) all-purpose flour
- ¾ teaspoon table salt
- ½ teaspoon baking soda
- ¼ teaspoon ground cinnamon
- ¾ cup (5¼ ounces) dark brown sugar
- ½ cup (3½ ounces) granulated sugar
- ½ cup vegetable oil
- 4 tablespoons unsalted butter, melted and cooled
- 1 large egg plus 1 large yolk
- 1 teaspoon vanilla extract
- 3 cups (9 ounces) old-fashioned rolled oats
- ½ cup raisins

Directions:
1. Adjust toaster oven rack to middle position and preheat the toaster oven to 350 degrees. Line large and small rimmed baking sheets with parchment paper. Whisk flour, salt, baking soda, and cinnamon together in bowl.
2. Whisk brown sugar and granulated sugar together in medium bowl. Whisk in oil and melted butter until combined. Whisk in egg and yolk and vanilla until smooth. Gently stir in flour mixture with rubber spatula until soft dough forms. Fold in oats and raisins until evenly distributed (mixture will be stiff).
3. Working with 3 tablespoons dough at a time, roll into balls. Space desired number of dough balls at least 1½ inches apart on prepared small sheet; space remaining dough balls evenly on prepared large sheet. Using bottom of greased dry measuring cup, press each ball until 2½ inches in diameter.
4. Bake small sheet of cookies until edges are just beginning to brown and centers are still soft but not wet, 10 to 15 minutes. Let cookies cool slightly on sheet. Serve warm or at room temperature.
5. Freeze remaining large sheet of cookies until firm, about 1 hour. Transfer cookies to 1-gallon zipper-lock bag and freeze for up to 1 month. Bake frozen cookies as directed; do not thaw.

Freezer-to-oven Chocolate Chip Cookies

Servings: 6
Cooking Time: 15 Minutes

Ingredients:
- 2 ½ cups all-purpose flour
- 1 teaspoon baking soda
- ½ teaspoon table salt
- ¼ teaspoon baking powder
- 1 cup unsalted butter, softened
- 1 cup packed dark brown sugar
- ¾ cup granulated sugar
- 2 large eggs
- 2 teaspoons pure vanilla extract
- 1 (12-ounce) package semisweet chocolate chips

Directions:
1. Preheat the toaster oven to 375°F. Line a 12 x 12-inch baking sheet with parchment paper.
2. Whisk the flour, baking soda, salt, and baking powder in a medium bowl; set aside.
3. Beat the butter, brown sugar, and granulated sugar in a large bowl with a handheld mixer at medium-high speed for 2 minutes or until creamy. Beat in the eggs, one at a time, beating well after each addition. Beat in the vanilla. Mix in the dry ingredients until blended. Stir in the chocolate chips.
4. Using a 2-tablespoon scoop, shape the batter into balls about 1 ½ inches in diameter. Arrange the cookies 1 inch apart on the prepared baking sheet. Bake for 13 to 15 minutes or until golden brown. Remove from the oven and let cool for 1 minute, then transfer the cookies to a wire rack.

Fried Snickers Bars

Servings: 8
Cooking Time: 4 Minutes

Ingredients:
- ⅓ cup All-purpose flour
- 1 Large egg white(s), beaten until foamy
- 1½ cups (6 ounces) Vanilla wafer cookie crumbs
- 8 Fun-size (0.6-ounce/17-gram) Snickers bars, frozen
- Vegetable oil spray

Directions:
1. Preheat the toaster oven to 400°F.
2. Set up and fill three shallow soup plates or small pie plates on your counter: one for the flour, one for the beaten egg white(s), and one for the cookie crumbs.
3. Unwrap the frozen candy bars. Dip one in the flour, turning it to coat on all sides. Gently stir any excess, then set it in the beaten egg white(s). Turn it to coat all sides, even the ends, then let any excess egg white slip back into the rest. Set the candy bar in the cookie crumbs. Turn to coat on all sides, even the ends. Dip the candy bar back in the egg white(s) a second time, then into the cookie crumbs a second time, making sure you have an even coating all around. Coat the covered candy bar all over with vegetable oil spray. Set aside so you can dip and coat the remaining candy bars.
4. Set the coated candy bars in the pan with as much air space between them as possible. Air-fry undisturbed for 4 minutes, or until golden brown.
5. Remove the pan from the machine and let the candy bars cool in the pan for 10 minutes. Use a nonstick-safe spatula to transfer them to a wire rack and cool for 5 minutes more before chowing down.

Dark Chocolate Banana Bread

Servings: 8
Cooking Time: 60 Minutes

Ingredients:
- ½ cup salted butter, melted, plus extra for greasing the pan
- 1 cup all-purpose flour, plus extra for dusting the pan
- ¾ cup dark brown sugar
- ¼ cup cocoa powder
- 2 teaspoons baking powder
- ¼ teaspoon sea salt
- 2 large bananas, mashed
- 1 large egg
- 1½ teaspoons vanilla extract
- ½ cup dark chocolate chips

Directions:
1. Place the rack in position 1 and preheat the oven to 325°F on BAKE for 5 minutes.
2. Grease a 9-by-5-inch loaf pan with melted butter and dust with all-purpose flour. Set aside.
3. In a medium bowl, stir the flour, brown sugar, cocoa powder, baking powder, and salt together until well combined.
4. In a medium bowl, whisk the butter, bananas, egg, and vanilla until well blended.
5. Add the wet ingredients to the dry ingredients and stir until combined. Add the chocolate chips and stir until incorporated.
6. Bake for 1 hour, or until a toothpick inserted into the center of the bread comes out mostly clean. If the bread starts to get too dark, cover the top with foil and bake until done.
7. Let the bread cool for 10 minutes and then run a knife around the edge and remove the bread from the loaf pan to cool completely on a rack.
8. Serve when cool.

Sour Cream Pound Cake

Servings: 6
Cooking Time: 60 Minutes

Ingredients:
- ¾ cup unsalted butter, plus extra for greasing the baking pan
- 2½ cups all-purpose flour, sifted, plus extra for dusting the baking pan
- 1½ cups granulated sugar
- 4 large eggs
- 2 teaspoons pure vanilla extract
- ½ teaspoon baking soda
- ¾ cup sour cream

Directions:

1. Place the rack in position 1 and preheat the toaster oven to 350°F on BAKE for 5 minutes.
2. Lightly grease and dust a 9-by-5-inch loaf pan.
3. In a large bowl, cream the butter and sugar with an electric hand beater until very light and fluffy, about 4 minutes.
4. Beat in the eggs one at a time, scraping down the sides of the bowl after each addition.
5. Beat in the vanilla.
6. In a medium bowl, stir the flour and baking soda.
7. Fold the flour mixture and sour cream into the butter mixture, alternating two times each, until well combined.
8. Spoon the batter into the loaf pan and bake for 1 hour, or until a toothpick inserted in the center comes out clean.
9. Let cool completely in the pan and serve.

Cowboy Cookies

Servings: 3
Cooking Time: 14 Minutes

Ingredients:
- Recommended Hamilton Beach® Product: Stand Mixers
- 1 cup butter
- 1 cup sugar
- 1 cup light brown sugar
- 2 eggs
- 2 cups flour
- 1 teaspoon baking soda
- ½ teaspoon baking powder
- ½ teaspoon salt
- 2 cups oatmeal
- 1 tablespoon vanilla
- 12 ounces chocolate chips
- 1 ½ cups coconut

Directions:
1. Preheat the toaster oven to 350°F.
2. With flat beater attachment, cream together butter, sugar, and brown sugar at a medium setting until well blended. Mix in vanilla and eggs. Reduce speed and gradually add flour, baking soda, baking powder, and salt mix until smooth.
3. On a low setting, mix in oatmeal, chocolate chips, and coconut until well mixed. Drop rounded spoon full onto ungreased cookie sheet.
4. Bake on middle rack of oven for 12 to 14 minutes.

Mixed Berry Hand Pies

Servings: 4
Cooking Time: 15 Minutes

Ingredients:
- ¾ cup sugar
- ½ teaspoon ground cinnamon
- 1 tablespoon cornstarch
- 1 cup blueberries
- 1 cup blackberries
- 1 cup raspberries, divided
- 1 teaspoon water
- 1 package refrigerated pie dough (or your own homemade pie dough)
- 1 egg, beaten

Directions:
1. Combine the sugar, cinnamon, and cornstarch in a small saucepan. Add the blueberries, blackberries, and ½ cup of the raspberries. Toss the berries gently to coat them evenly. Add the teaspoon of water to the saucepan and turn the stovetop on to medium-high heat, stirring occasionally. Once the berries break down, release their juice and start to simmer (about 5 minutes), simmer for another couple of minutes and then transfer the mixture to a bowl, stir in the remaining ½ cup of raspberries and let it cool.
2. Preheat the toaster oven to 370°F.
3. Cut the pie dough into four 5-inch circles and four 6-inch circles.
4. Spread the 6-inch circles on a flat surface. Divide the berry filling between all four circles. Brush the perimeter of the dough circles with a little water. Place the 5-inch circles on top of the filling and press the perimeter of the dough circles together to seal. Roll the edges of the bottom circle up over the top circle to make a crust around the filling. Press a fork around the crust to make decorative indentations and to seal the crust shut. Brush the pies with egg wash and sprinkle a little

sugar on top. Poke a small hole in the center of each pie with a paring knife to vent the dough.

5. Air-fry two pies at a time. Brush or spray the air fryer oven with oil and place the pies into the air fryer oven. Air-fry for 9 minutes. Turn the pies over and air-fry for another 6 minutes. Serve warm or at room temperature.

Apple Strudel

Servings: 2
Cooking Time: 90 Minutes

Ingredients:
- 2 Golden Delicious apples (14 ounces), peeled, cored, and cut into ½-inch pieces
- 1½ tablespoons granulated sugar
- ¼ teaspoon grated lemon zest plus 1 teaspoon juice
- ⅛ teaspoon ground cinnamon
- ⅛ teaspoon ground ginger
- ⅛ teaspoon table salt, divided
- 2 tablespoons golden raisins
- 1 tablespoon panko bread crumbs
- 3½ tablespoons unsalted butter, melted
- 1½ teaspoons confectioners' sugar, plus extra for serving
- 7 (14 by 9-inch) phyllo sheets, thawed

Directions:
1. Toss apples, granulated sugar, lemon zest and juice, cinnamon, ginger, and pinch salt together in large bowl. Cover and microwave until apples are softened, 2 to 4 minutes, stirring once halfway through microwaving. Let apples sit, covered, for 5 minutes. Transfer apples to colander set in second large bowl and let drain, reserving liquid. Return apples to bowl; stir in raisins and panko.
2. Adjust toaster oven rack to middle position and preheat the toaster oven to 350 degrees. Spray small rimmed baking sheet with vegetable oil spray. Stir remaining pinch salt into melted butter.
3. Place 16½ by 12-inch sheet of parchment paper on counter with long side parallel to edge of counter. Place 1 phyllo sheet on parchment with long side parallel to edge of counter. Place confectioners' sugar in fine-mesh strainer. Lightly brush sheet with melted butter and dust sparingly with confectioners' sugar. Repeat with remaining 6 phyllo sheets, melted butter, and confectioners' sugar, stacking sheets one on top of other as you go.
4. Arrange apple mixture in 2½ by 10-inch rectangle 2 inches from bottom of phyllo and about 2 inches from each side. Using parchment, fold sides of phyllo over filling, then fold bottom edge of phyllo over filling. Brush folded portions of phyllo with reserved apple liquid. Fold top edge over filling, making sure top and bottom edges overlap by about 1 inch. (If they do not overlap, unfold, rearrange filling into slightly narrower strip, and refold.) Press firmly to seal. Using thin metal spatula, transfer strudel to prepared sheet. Lightly brush top and sides of strudel with remaining apple liquid.
5. Bake until golden brown, 25 to 30 minutes, rotating sheet halfway through baking. Using thin metal spatula, immediately transfer strudel to cutting board. Let cool for 3 minutes. Slice strudel and let cool for at least 20 minutes. Serve warm or at room temperature, dusting with extra confectioners' sugar before serving.

Individual Peach Crisps

Servings: 2
Cooking Time: 60 Minutes

Ingredients:
- 2 tablespoons granulated sugar, divided
- 1 teaspoon lemon juice
- ¼ teaspoon cornstarch
- ⅛ teaspoon table salt, divided
- 1 pound frozen sliced peaches, thawed
- ⅓ cup whole almonds or pecans, chopped fine
- ¼ cup (1¼ ounces) all-purpose flour
- 2 tablespoons packed light brown sugar
- ⅛ teaspoon ground cinnamon
- Pinch ground nutmeg
- 3 tablespoons unsalted butter, melted and cooled

Directions:
1. Adjust toaster oven rack to lowest position and preheat the toaster oven to 425 degrees. Combine 1 tablespoon granulated sugar, lemon juice, cornstarch, and pinch salt in medium bowl. Gently toss peaches with sugar mixture and divide evenly between two 12-ounce ramekins.

2. Combine almonds, flour, brown sugar, cinnamon, nutmeg, remaining pinch salt, and remaining 1 tablespoon granulated sugar in now-empty bowl. Drizzle with melted butter and toss with fork until evenly moistened and mixture forms large chunks with some pea-size pieces throughout. Sprinkle topping evenly over peaches, breaking up any large chunks.

3. Place ramekins on aluminum foil–lined small rimmed baking sheet and bake until filling is bubbling around edges and topping is deep golden brown, 25 to 30 minutes, rotating sheet halfway through baking. Let crisps cool on wire rack for 15 minutes before serving.

Orange Glaze

Servings: 1
Cooking Time: 10 Minutes

Ingredients:

- 1 cup orange juice
- ½ cup sugar

Directions:

1. Combine the orange juice and sugar in a small bowl and mix well. Transfer the mixture to a baking pan.
2. BROIL for 10 minutes, stirring after 5 minutes, or until the sugar is dissolved and the liquid is reduced. Drizzle on top of brownies and cool. Cut into squares and serve with scoops of vanilla frozen yogurt or orange sherbet.

Campfire Banana Boats

Servings: 4
Cooking Time: 20 Minutes

Ingredients:

- 4 medium, unpeeled ripe bananas
- ¼ cup dark chocolate chips
- 4 teaspoons shredded, unsweetened coconut
- ½ cup mini marshmallows
- 4 graham crackers, chopped

Directions:

1. Preheat the toaster oven to 400°F on BAKE for 5 minutes.

2. Cut the bananas lengthwise through the skin about halfway through. Open the pocket to create a space for the other ingredients.

3. Evenly divide the chocolate, coconut, marshmallows, and graham crackers among the bananas.

4. Tear off four 12-inch squares of foil and place the bananas in the center of each. Crimp the foil around the banana to form a boat.

5. Place the bananas on the baking tray, two at a time, and in position 2, bake for 10 minutes until the fillings are gooey and the banana is warmed through.

6. Repeat with the remaining two bananas and serve.

Easy Churros

Servings: 12
Cooking Time: 10 Minutes

Ingredients:

- ½ cup Water
- 4 tablespoons (¼ cup/½ stick) Butter
- ¼ teaspoon Table salt
- ½ cup All-purpose flour
- 2 Large egg(s)
- ¼ cup Granulated white sugar
- 2 teaspoons Ground cinnamon

Directions:

1. Bring the water, butter, and salt to a boil in a small saucepan set over high heat, stirring occasionally.

2. When the butter has fully melted, reduce the heat to medium and stir in the flour to form a dough. Continue cooking, stirring constantly, to dry out the dough until it coats the bottom and sides of the pan with a film, even a crust. Remove the pan from the heat, scrape the dough into a bowl, and cool for 15 minutes.

3. Using an electric hand mixer at medium speed, beat in the egg, or eggs one at a time, until the dough is smooth and firm enough to hold its shape.

4. Mix the sugar and cinnamon in a small bowl. Scoop up 1 tablespoon of the dough and roll it in the sugar mixture to form a small, coated tube about ½ inch in diameter and 2 inches long. Set it aside and make 5 more tubes for the small batch or 11 more for the large one.

5. Set the tubes on a plate and freeze for 20 minutes. Meanwhile, preheat the toaster oven to 375°F.

6. Set 3 frozen tubes in the air fryer oven for a small batch or 6 for a large one with as much air space between them as possible. Air-fry undisturbed for 10 minutes, or until puffed, brown, and set.
7. Use kitchen tongs to transfer the churros to a wire rack to cool for at least 5 minutes. Meanwhile, air-fry and cool the second batch of churros in the same way.

Baked Custard

Servings: 2
Cooking Time: 45 Minutes

Ingredients:
- 2 eggs
- ¼ cup sugar
- 1 cup low-fat evaporated milk
- ½ teaspoon vanilla extract
- Pinch of grated nutmeg
- Fat-free half-and-half

Directions:
1. Preheat the toaster oven to 350° F.
2. Beat together the eggs, sugar, milk, vanilla, and nutmeg in a small bowl with an electric mixer at medium speed. Pour equal portions of the custard mixture into 2 oiled 1-cup-size ovenproof dishes.
3. BAKE for 45 minutes, or until a toothpick inserted in the center comes out clean. Serve drizzled with warm fat-free half-and-half.

Hasselback Apple Crisp

Servings: 4
Cooking Time: 20 Minutes

Ingredients:
- 2 large Gala apples, peeled, cored and cut in half
- ¼ cup butter, melted
- ½ teaspoon ground cinnamon
- 2 tablespoons sugar
- Topping
- 3 tablespoons butter, melted
- 2 tablespoons brown sugar
- ¼ cup chopped pecans
- 2 tablespoons rolled oats
- 1 tablespoon flour
- vanilla ice cream
- caramel sauce

Directions:
1. Place the apples cut side down on a cutting board. Slicing from stem end to blossom end, make 8 to 10 slits down the apple halves but only slice three quarters of the way through the apple, not all the way through to the cutting board.
2. Preheat the toaster oven to 330°F and pour a little water into the bottom of the air fryer oven drawer. (This will help prevent the grease that drips into the bottom drawer from burning and smoking.)
3. Transfer the apples to the air fryer oven, flat side down. Combine ¼ cup of melted butter, cinnamon and sugar in a small bowl. Brush this butter mixture onto the apples and air-fry at 330°F for 15 minutes. Baste the apples several times with the butter mixture during the cooking process.
4. While the apples are air-frying, make the filling. Combine 3 tablespoons of melted butter with the brown sugar, pecans, rolled oats and flour in a bowl. Stir with a fork until the mixture resembles small crumbles.
5. When the timer on the air fryer oven is up, spoon the topping down the center of the apples. Air-fry at 330°F for an additional 5 minutes.
6. Transfer the apples to a serving plate and serve with vanilla ice cream and caramel sauce.

Vegan Swedish Cinnamon Rolls (kanelbullar)

Servings: 8
Cooking Time: 18 Minutes

Ingredients:
- Dough
- 1 cup unsweetened almond milk, slightly warm (100°-110°F)
- ¼ cup vegan butter, melted
- 2 tablespoon organic sugar
- 1 teaspoon instant dry yeast
- ½ teaspoon kosher salt
- 2¾ cups all-purpose flour, divided
- Filling
- 6 tablespoons vegan butter, room temperature
- 6 tablespoons organic dark brown sugar

- 1 tablespoon ground cinnamon
- Egg Wash
- 2 tablespoons unsweetened almond milk
- 1 teaspoon agave nectar
- Glaze
- 2 tablespoons unsweetened almond milk
- ½ cup powdered sugar
- ¼ teaspoon vanilla extract
- Swedish pearl sugar, for sprinkling

Directions:
1. Whisk together the almond milk, melted butter, and sugar from the dough ingredients in a large mixing bowl.
2. Sprinkle the yeast into the milk mixture and allow it to bloom for 5 minutes.
3. Add kosher salt and 2¼-cups of flour into the milk and yeast mixture, then mix until well combined.
4. Cover the bowl with a towel or plastic wrap and set in a warm place to rise for 1 hour, or until it doubles in size.
5. Uncover and knead ½-cup all purpose flour into the risen dough. Continue kneading until it just loses its stickiness. You may need to add additional flour.
6. Roll the dough out into a large rectangle, about ½-inch thick. Fix the corners to make sure they are sharp and even.
7. Spread the softened vegan butter from the filling ingredients over the dough and sprinkle evenly with brown sugar and cinnamon.
8. Roll up the dough, forming a log, and pinch the seam closed. Place seam-side down. Trim off any unevenness on either end.
9. Cut the log in half, then divide each half into 8 evenly sized pieces, about 1½-inches thick each.
10. Line the food tray with parchment paper, then place the cinnamon rolls on the tray.
11. Cover with plastic wrap and place in a warm place to rise for 30 minutes.
12. Preheat the toaster Oven to 375°F.
13. Whisk together egg wash ingredients and lightly brush the wash on the tops of the cinnamon rolls.
14. Insert the food tray with the cinnamon rolls at mid position in the preheated oven.
15. Select the Bake function, adjust time to 18 minutes, and press Start/Pause.
16. Remove when done.
17. Whisk together almond milk, powdered sugar, and vanilla extract from the glaze ingredients to make the icing, brush it all over the cinnamon rolls, then sprinkle the rolls with Swedish pearl sugar.
18. Cool before serving, or eat warm.

Glazed Apple Crostata

Servings: 6
Cooking Time: 35 Minutes

Ingredients:
- PASTRY
- 1 ¼ cups all-purpose flour
- 3 tablespoons granulated sugar
- ¼ teaspoon table salt
- ½ cup unsalted butter, cut into 1-inch pieces
- 2 ½ to 3 ½ tablespoons ice water
- FILLING
- ¼ cup granulated sugar
- 3 tablespoons all-purpose flour
- ½ teaspoon ground cinnamon
- ¼ teaspoon ground nutmeg
- Dash table salt
- 3 large Granny Smith apples, peeled, cored, and thinly sliced
- 1 tablespoon unsalted butter, cut into small pieces
- 1 large egg
- Coarse white sugar
- GLAZE
- ¼ cup apricot preserves or apple jelly

Directions:
1. Place the flour, sugar, and salt in the work bowl of a food processor. Pulse to combine. Add the butter and pulse until it forms coarse crumbs. With the motor running, drizzle in enough cold water that the mixture comes together and forms a dough. Shape the dough into a disk, wrap in plastic wrap, and refrigerate for at least 1 hour or until chilled.
2. Make the filling: Stir the sugar, flour, cinnamon, nutmeg, and salt in a large bowl. Add the apples and stir to coat; set aside.

3. Preheat the toaster oven to 400°F. Line a 12-inch pizza pan or 12 x 12-inch baking pan with parchment paper.
4. Roll the pastry into a 12-inch circle on a lightly floured board. Gently fold the dough into quarters and transfer to the prepared pan. Unfold the dough. Pile the filling in the center of the pastry, leaving a 1- to 2-inch border around the edges. Dot the apples with the butter. Fold the edges of the crust up around the outer edge of the apples. Whisk the egg in a small bowl, then brush the edges of the crust with the egg. Sprinkle the crust with coarse sugar.
5. Bake for 30 to 35 minutes or until golden brown and the apples are tender.
6. Set on a wire rack. For the glaze, microwave the preserves in a small, microwave-safe glass bowl on High (100 percent) power for 30 seconds or until melted. Pour the preserves through a fine mesh strainer. Brush the warm preserves over the apples (but not over the crust). Serve warm.

Coconut Rice Pudding

Servings: 6
Cooking Time: 55 Minutes

Ingredients:
- ½ cup short-grain brown rice
- Pudding mixture:
- 1 egg, beaten
- 1 tablespoon cornstarch
- ½ cup fat-free half-and-half
- ½ cup chopped raisins
- 1 teaspoon vanilla extract
- ½ teaspoon ground cinnamon
- ½ teaspoon grated nutmeg
- Salt to taste
- ¼ cup shredded sweetened coconut
- Fat-free whipped topping

Directions:
1. Preheat the toaster oven to 400° F.
2. Combine the rice and 1½ cups water in a 1-quart 8½ × 8½ × 4-inch ovenproof baking dish. Cover with aluminum foil.

3. BAKE, covered, for 45 minutes, or until the rice is tender. Remove from the oven and add the pudding mixture ingredients, mixing well.
4. BAKE, uncovered, for 10 minutes, or until the top is lightly browned. Sprinkle the top with coconut and chill before serving. Top with fat-free whipped topping.

Spice Cake

Servings: 6
Cooking Time: 25 Minutes

Ingredients:
- 1 cup applesauce or 2 4-ounce jars baby food prunes
- ¼ cup skim milk or low-fat soy milk
- 1 tablespoon vegetable oil
- ½ cup brown sugar
- 1 egg
- 1½ cups unbleached flour
- 1 teaspoon baking powder
- ½ teaspoon baking soda
- ¼ teaspoon grated nutmeg
- ½ teaspoon ground cinnamon
- ½ teaspoon grated orange zest
- Salt to taste
- Creamy Frosting

Directions:
1. Preheat the toaster oven to 350° F.
2. Stir together the applesauce, milk, oil, sugar, and egg in a small bowl. Set aside.
3. Combine the flour, baking powder, nutmeg, cinnamon, orange zest, and salt in a medium bowl. Add the applesauce mixture and stir to mix well. Pour the batter into an oiled or nonstick 8½ × 8½ × 2-inch square baking (cake) pan.
4. BAKE for 25 minutes, or until a toothpick inserted in the center comes out clean. Frost with Creamy Frosting.

Chewy Brownies

Servings: 16
Cooking Time: 60 Minutes

Ingredients:
- 3 tablespoons Dutch-processed cocoa powder
- ¾ teaspoon espresso powder (optional)
- ⅓ cup boiling water
- 1 ounce unsweetened chocolate, chopped fine
- 5 tablespoons vegetable oil
- 2 tablespoons unsalted butter, melted and cooled
- 1¼ cups (8¾ ounces) sugar
- 1 large egg plus 1 large yolk
- 1 teaspoon vanilla extract
- ¾ cup (3¾ ounces) plus 2 tablespoons all-purpose flour
- 3 ounces bittersweet chocolate, cut into ½-inch pieces
- ½ teaspoon table salt

Directions:
1. Adjust toaster oven rack to middle position and preheat the toaster oven to 350 degrees. Make foil sling for 8-inch square baking pan by folding 2 long sheets of aluminum foil so each is 8 inches wide. Lay sheets of foil in pan perpendicular to each other, with extra foil hanging over edges of pan. Push foil into corners and up sides of pan, smoothing foil flush to pan. Spray foil with vegetable oil spray.
2. Whisk cocoa; espresso powder, if using; and boiling water together in large bowl until smooth. Add unsweetened chocolate and whisk until chocolate is melted. Whisk in oil and melted butter. (Mixture may look curdled.) Whisk in sugar, egg and yolk, and vanilla until smooth. Add flour, bittersweet chocolate, and salt and mix with rubber spatula until no dry flour remains.
3. Scrape batter into prepared pan, smooth top, and bake until toothpick inserted in center comes out with few moist crumbs attached, 25 to 30 minutes, rotating dish halfway through baking. Transfer pan to wire rack and cool for 1½ hours.
4. Using foil overhang, lift brownies from pan. Return brownies to wire rack and let cool completely, about 1 hour. Cut into 2-inch squares and serve.

Raspberry Hand Pies

Servings: 6
Cooking Time: 20 Minutes

Ingredients:
- 2 cups fresh raspberries
- ¼ cup granulated sugar, plus extra for topping
- 1 tablespoon cornstarch
- 1 tablespoon freshly squeezed lemon juice
- 2 store-bought unbaked pie crusts
- 1 large egg
- 1 tablespoon water
- Oil spray (hand-pumped)

Directions:
1. Preheat the toaster oven to 350°F on AIR FRY for 5 minutes.
2. Place the air-fryer basket in the baking tray.
3. In a medium bowl, stir the raspberries, sugar, cornstarch, and lemon juice until well mixed.
4. Lay the pie crusts on a clean work surface and cut out 6 (6-inch) circles.
5. Evenly divide the raspberry mixture among the circles, placing it in the center.
6. In a small bowl, beat together the egg and water with a fork. Use the egg wash to lightly moisten the edges of the circles, then fold them over to create a half-moon shape. Use a fork to crimp around the rounded part of the pies to seal.
7. Lightly spray the pies with the oil and sprinkle with sugar. Cut 2 to 3 small slits in each pie and place three pies in the basket.
8. In position 2, air fry for 10 minutes until golden brown. Repeat with the remaining pies.
9. Cool the pies and serve.

Blueberry Crumbles

Servings: 2
Cooking Time: 60 Minutes

Ingredients:
- 2 tablespoons granulated sugar
- 1½ teaspoons cornstarch
- ⅛ teaspoon table salt, divided
- 10 ounces (2 cups) blueberries
- ½ cup (1½ ounces) old-fashioned rolled oats

- ¼ cup (1¼ ounces) all-purpose flour
- ¼ cup packed (1¾ ounces) light brown sugar
- ¼ teaspoon ground cinnamon
- 4 tablespoons unsalted butter, melted and cooled

Directions:

1. Adjust toaster oven rack to lowest position and preheat the toaster oven to 375 degrees. Combine granulated sugar, cornstarch, and pinch salt in medium bowl. Gently toss blueberries in sugar mixture, then divide between two 12-ounce ramekins.
2. Combine oats, flour, brown sugar, cinnamon, and remaining pinch salt in now-empty bowl. Drizzle with melted butter and toss with fork until evenly moistened and mixture forms large chunks with some pea-size pieces throughout. Sprinkle topping evenly over blueberries, breaking up any large chunks.
3. Place ramekins on aluminum foil–lined small rimmed baking sheet and bake until filling is bubbling around edges and topping is deep golden brown, 25 to 30 minutes, rotating sheet halfway through baking. Let crumbles cool on wire rack for 15 minutes before serving.

Pear And Almond Biscotti Crumble

Servings: 6
Cooking Time: 65 Minutes

Ingredients:

- 7-inch cake pan or ceramic dish
- 3 pears, peeled, cored and sliced
- ½ cup brown sugar
- ¼ teaspoon ground ginger
- 1 teaspoon ground cinnamon
- ⅛ teaspoon ground nutmeg
- 2 tablespoons cornstarch
- 1¼ cups (4 to 5) almond biscotti, coarsely crushed
- ¼ cup all-purpose flour
- ¼ cup sliced almonds
- ¼ cup butter, melted

Directions:

1. Combine the pears, brown sugar, ginger, cinnamon, nutmeg and cornstarch in a bowl. Toss to combine and then pour the pear mixture into a greased 7-inch cake pan or ceramic dish.
2. Combine the crushed biscotti, flour, almonds and melted butter in a medium bowl. Toss with a fork until the mixture resembles large crumbles. Sprinkle the biscotti crumble over the pears and cover the pan with aluminum foil.
3. Preheat the toaster oven to 350°F.
4. Air-fry at 350°F for 60 minutes. Remove the aluminum foil and air-fry for an additional 5 minutes to brown the crumble layer.
5. Serve warm.

Cheese Blintzes

Servings: 6
Cooking Time: 10 Minutes

Ingredients:

- 1½ 7½-ounce package(s) farmer cheese
- 3 tablespoons Regular or low-fat cream cheese (not fat-free)
- 3 tablespoons Granulated white sugar
- ¼ teaspoon Vanilla extract
- 6 Egg roll wrappers
- 3 tablespoons Butter, melted and cooled

Directions:

1. Preheat the toaster oven to 375°F.
2. Use a flatware fork to mash the farmer cheese, cream cheese, sugar, and vanilla in a small bowl until smooth.
3. Set one egg roll wrapper on a clean, dry work surface. Place ¼ cup of the filling at the edge closest to you, leaving a ½-inch gap before the edge of the wrapper. Dip your clean finger in water and wet the edges of the wrapper. Fold the perpendicular sides over the filling, then roll the wrapper closed with the filling inside. Set it aside seam side down and continue filling the remainder of the wrappers.
4. Brush the wrappers on all sides with the melted butter. Be generous. Set them seam side down in the air fryer oven with as much space between them as possible. Air-fry undisturbed for 10 minutes, or until lightly browned.
5. Use a nonstick-safe spatula to transfer the blintzes to a wire rack. Cool for at least 5 minutes or up to 20 minutes before serving.

Brown Sugar Baked Apples

Servings: 4
Cooking Time: 15 Minutes

Ingredients:
- 3 Small tart apples, preferably McIntosh
- 4 tablespoons (¼ cup/½ stick) Butter
- 6 tablespoons Light brown sugar
- Ground cinnamon
- Table salt

Directions:
1. Preheat the toaster oven to 400°F.
2. Stem the apples, then cut them in half through their "equators" (that is, not the stem ends). Use a melon baller to core the apples, taking care not to break through the flesh and skin at any point but creating a little well in the center of each half.
3. When the machine is at temperature, remove the baking pan and set it on a heat-safe work surface. Set the apple halves cut side up in the baking pan with as much air space between them as possible. Even a fraction of an inch will work. Drop 2 teaspoons of butter into the well in the center of each apple half. Sprinkle each half with 1 tablespoon brown sugar and a pinch each ground cinnamon and table salt.
4. Return the baking pan to the machine. Air-fry undisturbed for 15 minutes, or until the apple halves have softened and the brown sugar has caramelized.
5. Use a nonstick-safe spatula to transfer the apple halves cut side up to a wire rack. Cool for at least 10 minutes before serving, or serve at room temperature.

Blueberry Cheesecake Tartlets

Servings: 9
Cooking Time: 6 Minutes

Ingredients:
- 8 ounces cream cheese, softened
- ¼ cup sugar
- 1 egg
- ½ teaspoon vanilla extract
- zest of 2 lemons, divided
- 9 mini graham cracker tartlet shells
- 2 cups blueberries
- ½ teaspoon ground cinnamon
- juice of ½ lemon
- ¼ cup apricot preserves

Directions:
1. Preheat the toaster oven to 330°F.
2. Combine the cream cheese, sugar, egg, vanilla and the zest of one lemon in a medium bowl and blend until smooth by hand or with an electric hand mixer. Pour the cream cheese mixture into the tartlet shells.
3. Air-fry 3 tartlets at a time at 330°F for 6 minutes, rotating them in the air fryer oven halfway through the cooking time.
4. Combine the blueberries, cinnamon, zest of one lemon and juice of half a lemon in a bowl. Melt the apricot preserves in the microwave or over low heat in a saucepan. Pour the apricot preserves over the blueberries and gently toss to coat.
5. Allow the cheesecakes to cool completely and then top each one with some of the blueberry mixture. Garnish the tartlets with a little sugared lemon peel and refrigerate until you are ready to serve.

Key Lime Pie

Servings: 8
Cooking Time: 60 Minutes

Ingredients:
- FILLING
- 1 (14-ounce) can sweetened condensed milk
- 4 large egg yolks
- 4 teaspoons grated lime zest plus ½ cup juice (5 limes)
- CRUST
- 11 whole graham crackers, broken into 1-inch pieces
- 3 tablespoons granulated sugar
- 5 tablespoons unsalted butter, melted and cooled
- TOPPING
- ¾ cup heavy cream
- ¼ cup (1 ounce) confectioners' sugar

Directions:
1. FOR THE FILLING: Whisk condensed milk, egg yolks, and lime zest and juice together in bowl until smooth. Cover mixture and let sit at room temperature until thickened, about 30 minutes.

2. FOR THE CRUST: Adjust toaster oven rack to middle position and preheat the toaster oven to 325 degrees. Process graham cracker pieces and sugar in food processor to fine, even crumbs, about 30 seconds. Sprinkle melted butter over crumbs and pulse to incorporate, about 5 pulses.

3. Sprinkle mixture into 9-inch pie plate. Using bottom of dry measuring cup, press crumbs into even layer on bottom and up sides of pie plate. Bake until crust is fragrant and beginning to brown, 10 to 15 minutes. Transfer to wire rack and let cool slightly, about 10 minutes.

4. Pour thickened filling into warm crust and smooth top. Bake pie until center is firm but jiggles slightly when shaken, 12 to 17 minutes. Let pie cool slightly on wire rack, about 1 hour. Cover pie loosely with plastic wrap and refrigerate until filling is chilled and set, at least 3 hours or up to 24 hours.

5. For the topping Using stand mixer fitted with whisk attachment, whip cream and sugar on medium-low speed until foamy, about 1 minute. Increase speed to high and whip until soft peaks form, 1 to 3 minutes. (Topping can be refrigerated in fine-mesh strainer set over small bowl and covered with plastic wrap for up to 8 hours.) Spread whipped cream attractively over pie. Serve.

Almond Amaretto Bundt Cake

Servings: 8
Cooking Time: 37 Minutes

Ingredients:
- Nonstick baking spray with flour
- 1 (15.25- to 18-ounce) box yellow cake mix
- 1 (3.9-ounce) box vanilla instant pudding
- 1 cup sour cream
- ½ cup canola or vegetable oil
- ¼ cup amaretto or almond liqueur
- 4 large eggs
- ¼ teaspoon pure almond extract
- GLAZE
- 2 ½ cups confectioners' sugar
- 2 tablespoons amaretto
- 1 teaspoon pure vanilla extract
- 1 to 2 tablespoons milk
- Sliced almonds, toasted

Directions:
1. Preheat the toaster oven to 350°F. Spray a 12-cup Bundt pan with nonstick baking spray with flour.
2. Beat the cake mix, instant pudding, sour cream, oil, ¼ cup water, the amaretto, eggs, and almond extract in a large bowl with a handheld mixer at low speed for 30 seconds to combine the ingredients. Scrape the sides of the bowl with a rubber scraper. Beat on medium-high speed for 2 minutes.
3. Pour the batter into the prepared pan. Bake for 30 to 35 minutes, or until a wooden pick inserted into the center comes out clean.
4. Place the pan on a wire rack to cool for 10 minutes. Invert the cake onto the rack and let cool completely.
5. Meanwhile, make the glaze: Whisk the sugar, amaretto, vanilla, and 1 tablespoon milk in a small bowl. If needed, stir in the additional milk to make the desired consistency. Pour over the cake. Garnish with the sliced almonds.

Easy Peach Turnovers

Servings: 6
Cooking Time: 35 Minutes

Ingredients:
- 1 ½ tablespoons granulated sugar
- 1 teaspoon cornstarch
- ¾ cup chopped peeled peaches, fresh or frozen and thawed
- ½ teaspoon grated lemon zest
- ⅛ teaspoon ground nutmeg
- Dash table salt
- 1 sheet frozen puff pastry, about 9 inches square, thawed (½ of a 17.3-ounce package)
- 1 large egg
- Coarse white sugar
- GLAZE
- ¾ cup confectioners' sugar
- ½ teaspoon pure vanilla extract
- 1 to 2 tablespoons milk

Directions:

1. Line a 12 x 12-inch baking pan with parchment paper.
2. Stir the granulated sugar and cornstarch in a medium bowl. Stir in the peaches, lemon zest, nutmeg, and salt. Mix until the sugar-cornstarch mixture coats the peaches evenly and the sugar begins to dissolve; set aside.
3. On a lightly floured board, roll the puff pastry sheet into a 13 ½ x 9-inch rectangle. Cut the puff pastry into 6 (4 ½-inch) squares. Lightly beat the egg in a small bowl, then brush the edges of each puff pastry square with the egg. Reserve the remaining egg to brush on top of each turnover.
4. Spoon about 2 tablespoons peach mixture into the center of each square. Fold the pastry over the peaches to form a triangle, pinching to seal the edges. Using the tines of a fork, crimp the edges tightly. Lightly brush the top of each turnover with the egg. Sprinkle each with the coarse sugar.
5. Place the turnovers on the prepared pan. Freeze the turnovers for 15 minutes.
6. Preheat the toaster oven to 375°F. Bake for 15 to 20 minutes or until golden brown. Let cool 5 to 10 minutes.
7. Meanwhile make the glaze: Whisk the confectioners' sugar, vanilla, and 1 tablespoon milk in a small bowl until smooth. If needed, stir in the additional milk to reach the desired consistency. Drizzle the glaze from the tip of a teaspoon in decorative stripes over the turnovers.

Blueberry Cookies

Servings: 4
Cooking Time: 12 Minutes

Ingredients:
- 1 egg
- 1 tablespoon margarine, at room temperature
- ⅓ cup sugar
- 1¼ cups unbleached flour
- Salt to taste
- 1 teaspoon baking powder
- 1 10-ounce package frozen blueberries, well drained, or
- 1½ cups fresh blueberries, rinsed and drained

Directions:
1. Preheat the toaster oven to 400° F.
2. Beat together the egg, margarine, and sugar in a medium bowl with an electric mixer until smooth. Add the flour, salt, and baking powder, mixing thoroughly. Gently stir in the blueberries just to blend. Do not overmix.
3. Drop by teaspoonfuls on an oiled or nonstick 6½ × 10-inch baking sheet or an oiled or nonstick 8½ × 8½ × 2-inch square baking (cake) pan.
4. BAKE for 12 minutes, or until the cookies are golden brown.

Rum-glazed Roasted Pineapple

Servings: 4
Cooking Time: 45 Minutes

Ingredients:
- ½ pineapple, peeled, cored, and cut lengthwise into 4 wedges
- 2 tablespoons unsalted butter, melted
- 3 tablespoons packed dark brown sugar
- 1 tablespoon lime juice
- ½ teaspoon vanilla extract
- Pinch table salt
- 1 tablespoon white or aged rum
- 2 tablespoons unsweetened shredded coconut, toasted

Directions:
1. Adjust toaster oven rack to lowest position and preheat the toaster oven to 450 degrees. Toss pineapple with melted butter in 8-inch square baking dish or pan, then arrange in single layer. Roast until bottoms of wedges are deep golden brown and fork slips easily in and out of pineapple, 25 to 35 minutes, rotating dish halfway through roasting.
2. Remove pan from oven and transfer pineapple to serving dish. Whisk sugar, lime juice, vanilla, and salt into butter and juice in pan, scraping up any browned bits, until well combined. Return pineapple wedges to pan, browned side up, along with any accumulated juices.

Roast until sauce is reduced to syrupy consistency, 3 to 5 minutes.

3. Remove pan from oven and transfer pineapple to serving dish. Whisk rum into sauce in pan until smooth, then spoon sauce over pineapple. Sprinkle with coconut and serve.

Triple Chocolate Brownies

Servings: 16
Cooking Time: 25 Minutes

Ingredients:
- ⅓ cup salted butter, room temperature, plus extra for greasing the baking dish
- ¾ cup brown sugar
- 2 large eggs
- 1 teaspoon vanilla extract
- ½ cup all-purpose flour
- ¼ cup cocoa powder
- ¼ teaspoon baking powder
- ⅛ teaspoon salt
- ½ cup dark chocolate chips
- ¼ cup white chocolate chips

Directions:
1. Place the rack in position 1 and preheat the oven to 325°F on BAKE for 5 minutes.
2. Lightly grease a 6-inch-square baking dish with butter.
3. In a large bowl, beat together the butter and sugar with an electric hand beater or a whisk until combined. Add the eggs and vanilla and beat to combine.
4. Beat in the flour, cocoa powder, baking powder, and salt until just combined.
5. Stir in dark chocolate and white chocolate chips, then spoon the batter into the prepared dish.
6. Bake for 25 minutes or until a knife inserted in the center comes out mostly clean.
7. Cool in the baking dish and serve.

VEGETABLES AND VEGETARIAN

Cauliflower

Servings: 4
Cooking Time: 6 Minutes

Ingredients:
- ½ cup water
- 1 10-ounce package frozen cauliflower (florets)
- 1 teaspoon lemon pepper seasoning

Directions:
1. Pour the water into air fryer oven.
2. Pour the frozen cauliflower into the air fryer oven and sprinkle with lemon pepper seasoning.
3. Air-fry at 390°F for approximately 6 minutes.

Roasted Ratatouille Vegetables

Servings: 15
Cooking Time: 2 Minutes

Ingredients:
- 1 baby or Japanese eggplant, cut into 1½-inch cubes
- 1 red pepper, cut into 1-inch chunks
- 1 yellow pepper, cut into 1-inch chunks
- 1 zucchini, cut into 1-inch chunks
- 1 clove garlic, minced
- ½ teaspoon dried basil
- 1 tablespoon olive oil
- salt and freshly ground black pepper
- ¼ cup sliced sun-dried tomatoes in oil
- 2 tablespoons chopped fresh basil

Directions:
1. Preheat the toaster oven to 400°F.
2. Toss the eggplant, peppers and zucchini with the garlic, dried basil, olive oil, salt and freshly ground black pepper.
3. Air-fry the vegetables at 400°F for 15 minutes.
4. As soon as the vegetables are tender, toss them with the sliced sun-dried tomatoes and fresh basil and serve.

Baked Stuffed Acorn Squash

Servings: 2
Cooking Time: 25 Minutes

Ingredients:
- Stuffing:
- ¼ cup multigrain bread crumbs
- 1 tablespoon olive oil
- ¼ cup canned or frozen thawed corn
- 2 tablespoons chopped onion
- 1 teaspoon capers
- 1 teaspoon garlic powder
- Salt and freshly ground black pepper
- 1 medium acorn squash, halved and seeds scooped out

Directions:
1. Preheat the toaster oven to 400° F.
2. Combine the stuffing ingredients and season to taste. Fill the squash cavities with the mixture and place in an oiled or nonstick 8½ × 8½ × 2-inch square baking (cake) pan.
3. BAKE for 25 minutes, or until the squash is tender and the stuffing is lightly browned.

Crispy, Cheesy Leeks

Servings: 4
Cooking Time: 15 Minutes

Ingredients:
- 2 Medium leek(s), about 9 ounces each
- Olive oil spray
- ¼ cup Seasoned Italian-style dried bread crumbs (gluten-free, if a concern)
- ¼ cup (about ¾ ounce) Finely grated Parmesan cheese
- 2 tablespoons Olive oil

Directions:
1. Preheat the toaster oven to 350°F.
2. Trim off the root end of the leek(s) as well as the dark green top(s), leaving about a 5-inch usable section. Split the leek section(s) in half lengthwise. Set the leek halves cut side up on your work surface. Pull out and remove in one piece the semicircles that make up the inner structure of the leek, about halfway down. Set the removed "inside" next to the outer leek "shells" on your

cutting board. Generously coat them all on all sides (particularly the "bottoms") with olive oil spray.

3. Set the leeks and their insides cut side up in the air fryer oven with as much air space between them as possible. Air-fry undisturbed for 12 minutes.

4. Meanwhile, mix the bread crumbs, cheese, and olive oil in a small bowl until well combined.

5. After 12 minutes in the air fryer oven, sprinkle this mixture inside the leek shells and on top of the leek insides. Increase the machine's temperature to 375°F (or 380°F or 390°F, if one of these is the closest setting). Air-fry undisturbed for 3 minutes, or until the topping is lightly browned.

6. Use a nonstick-safe spatula to transfer the leeks to a serving platter. Cool for a few minutes before serving warm.

Sweet Potato Puffs

Servings: 18
Cooking Time: 35 Minutes

Ingredients:
- 3 8- to 10-ounce sweet potatoes
- 1 cup Seasoned Italian-style dried bread crumbs
- 3 tablespoons All-purpose flour
- 3 tablespoons Instant mashed potato flakes
- ¾ teaspoon Onion powder
- ¾ teaspoon Table salt
- Olive oil spray

Directions:
1. Preheat the toaster oven to 350°F.
2. Prick the sweet potatoes in four or five different places with the tines of a flatware fork (not in a line but all around the sweet potatoes).
3. When the machine is at temperature, set the sweet potatoes in the air fryer oven with as much air space between them as possible. Air-fry undisturbed for 20 minutes.
4. Use kitchen tongs to transfer the sweet potatoes to a wire rack. (They will still be firm; they are only partially cooked.) Cool for 10 to 15 minutes. Meanwhile, increase the machine's temperature to 400°F. Spread the bread crumbs on a dinner plate.

5. Peel the sweet potatoes. Shred them through the large holes of a box grater into a large bowl. Stir in the flour, potato flakes, onion powder, and salt until well combined.

6. Scoop up 2 tablespoons of the sweet potato mixture. Form it into a small puff, a cylinder about like a Tater Tot. Set this cylinder in the bread crumbs. Gently roll it around to coat on all sides, even the ends. Set aside on a cutting board and continue making more puffs: 11 more for a small batch, 17 more for a medium batch, or 23 more for a large batch.

7. Generously coat the puffs with olive oil spray on all sides. Set the puffs in the air fryer oven with as much air space between them as possible. They should not be touching, but even a fraction of an inch will work well. Air-fry undisturbed for 15 minutes, or until lightly browned and crunchy.

8. Gently turn the contents of the air fryer oven out onto a wire rack. Cool the puffs for a couple of minutes before serving.

Oregano Zucchini

Servings: 4
Cooking Time: 30 Minutes

Ingredients:
- Mixture:
- 3 tablespoons olive oil
- 1 tablespoon Roasted Garlic
- 2 tablespoons tomato paste
- 2 tablespoons dry white wine
- 1 tablespoon chopped fresh oregano
- Salt and freshly ground pepper to taste
- 4 small zucchini squash, rinsed well, halved, then quartered
- 3 tablespoons grated Parmesan cheese

Directions:
1. Whisk together the mixture ingredients in a small bowl, adjusting the seasonings to taste. Add the zucchini and toss gently to coat well. Transfer to an oiled or nonstick 8½ × 8½ × 2-inch square baking (cake) pan.
2. Broil, uncovered, for 20 minutes. Remove the pan from the oven, turn the pieces with tongs, and spoon the sauce over the zucchini. Broil again for 10 minutes, or until tender. Before serving, sprinkle with the grated Parmesan cheese.

Quick Broccoli Quiche

Servings: 6
Cooking Time: 35 Minutes

Ingredients:
- 12 sheets phyllo dough
- Olive oil for brushing phyllo sheets
- Filling:
- ½ cup chopped fresh broccoli or ½ cup frozen chopped broccoli, thawed and well drained
- 4 eggs, well beaten
- 2 tablespoons fat-free half-and-half
- 3 tablespoons nonfat plain yogurt
- ½ cup low-fat ricotta cheese
- 3 tablespoons finely chopped onion
- Salt and freshly ground pepper
- ¼ cup shredded part-skim mozzarella cheese

Directions:
1. Preheat the toaster oven to 300° F.
2. Layer the phyllo sheets in an oiled or nonstick 9¾-inch-diameter pie pan, brushing each sheet with olive oil and folding it to fit the pan. Bake for 5 minutes, or until lightly browned. Remove from the oven and set aside.
3. Mix together all the filling ingredients in a medium bowl and season to taste with salt and pepper. Pour the mixture into the phyllo dough crust and sprinkle with the mozzarella cheese.
4. BAKE at 400° F. for 30 minutes, or until the surface is springy to touch and browned.

Green Peas With Mint

Servings: 4
Cooking Time: 5 Minutes

Ingredients:
- 1 cup shredded lettuce
- 1 10-ounce package frozen green peas, thawed
- 1 tablespoon fresh mint, shredded
- 1 teaspoon melted butter

Directions:
1. Lay the shredded lettuce in the air fryer oven.
2. Toss together the peas, mint, and melted butter and spoon over the lettuce.
3. Air-fry at 360°F for 5 minutes, until peas are warm and lettuce wilts.

Roasted Fennel Salad

Servings: 3
Cooking Time: 20 Minutes

Ingredients:
- 3 cups (about ¾ pound) Trimmed fennel, roughly chopped
- 1½ tablespoons Olive oil
- ¼ teaspoon Table salt
- ¼ teaspoon Ground black pepper
- 1½ tablespoons White balsamic vinegar

Directions:
1. Preheat the toaster oven to 400°F.
2. Toss the fennel, olive oil, salt, and pepper in a large bowl until the fennel is well coated in the oil.
3. When the machine is at temperature, pour the fennel into the air fryer oven, spreading it out into as close to one layer as possible. Air-fry for 20 minutes, tossing and rearranging the fennel pieces twice so that any covered or touching parts get exposed to the air currents, until golden at the edges and softened.
4. Pour the fennel into a serving bowl. Add the vinegar while hot. Toss well, then cool a couple of minutes before serving. Or serve at room temperature.

Roasted Herbed Shiitake Mushrooms

Servings: 5
Cooking Time: 4 Minutes

Ingredients:
- 8 ounces shiitake mushrooms, stems removed and caps roughly chopped
- 1 tablespoon olive oil
- ½ teaspoon salt
- freshly ground black pepper
- 1 teaspoon chopped fresh thyme leaves
- 1 teaspoon chopped fresh oregano
- 1 tablespoon chopped fresh parsley

Directions:
1. Preheat the toaster oven to 400°F.

2. Toss the mushrooms with the olive oil, salt, pepper, thyme and oregano. Air-fry for 5 minutes. The mushrooms will still be somewhat chewy with a meaty texture. If you'd like them a little more tender, add a couple of minutes to this cooking time.
3. Once cooked, add the parsley to the mushrooms and toss. Season again to taste and serve.

Spicy Sweet Potatoes

Servings: 4
Cooking Time: 25 Minutes

Ingredients:
- 2 sweet potatoes, peeled and sliced into 1-inch rounds
- 1 tablespoon vegetable oil
- Seasonings:
- ½ teaspoon each: grated nutmeg, ground cinnamon, cardamom, and ginger
- Salt and freshly ground black pepper to taste

Directions:
1. Preheat the toaster oven to 400° F.
2. Brush the potato slices with oil and set aside.
3. Combine the seasonings in a 1-quart 8½ × 8½ × 4-inch ovenproof baking dish and add the potato slices. Toss to coat well and adjust the seasonings to taste. Cover the dish with aluminum foil.
4. BAKE for 25 minutes, or until the potatoes are tender.

Asparagus Fries

Servings: 4
Cooking Time: 5 Minutes

Ingredients:
- 12 ounces fresh asparagus spears with tough ends trimmed off
- 2 egg whites
- ¼ cup water
- ¾ cup panko breadcrumbs
- ¼ cup grated Parmesan cheese, plus 2 tablespoons
- ¼ teaspoon salt
- oil for misting or cooking spray

Directions:

1. Preheat the toaster oven to 390°F.
2. In a shallow dish, beat egg whites and water until slightly foamy.
3. In another shallow dish, combine panko, Parmesan, and salt.
4. Dip asparagus spears in egg, then roll in crumbs. Spray with oil or cooking spray.
5. Place a layer of asparagus in air fryer oven, leaving just a little space in between each spear. Stack another layer on top, crosswise. Air-fry at 390°F for 5 minutes, until crispy and golden brown.
6. Repeat to cook remaining asparagus.

Yellow Squash

Servings: 4
Cooking Time: 10 Minutes

Ingredients:
- 1 large yellow squash (about 1½ cups)
- 2 eggs
- ¼ cup buttermilk
- 1 cup panko breadcrumbs
- ¼ cup white cornmeal
- ½ teaspoon salt
- oil for misting or cooking spray

Directions:
1. Preheat the toaster oven to 390°F.
2. Cut the squash into ¼-inch slices.
3. In a shallow dish, beat together eggs and buttermilk.
4. In sealable plastic bag or container with lid, combine ¼ cup panko crumbs, white cornmeal, and salt. Shake to mix well.
5. Place the remaining ¾ cup panko crumbs in a separate shallow dish.
6. Dump all the squash slices into the egg/buttermilk mixture. Stir to coat.
7. Remove squash from buttermilk mixture with a slotted spoon, letting excess drip off, and transfer to the panko/cornmeal mixture. Close bag or container and shake well to coat.
8. Remove squash from crumb mixture, letting excess fall off. Return squash to egg/buttermilk mixture, stirring gently to coat. If you need more liquid to coat all the squash, add a little more buttermilk.

9. Remove each squash slice from egg wash and dip in a dish of ¾ cup panko crumbs.
10. Mist squash slices with oil or cooking spray and place in air fryer oven. Squash should be in a single layer, but it's okay if the slices crowd together and overlap a little.
11. Air-fry at 390°F for 5 minutes. Break up any that have stuck together. Mist again with oil or spray.
12. Cook 5 minutes longer and check. If necessary, mist again with oil and cook an additional two minutes, until squash slices are golden brown and crisp.

Marjoram New Potatoes

Servings: 2
Cooking Time: 40 Minutes

Ingredients:

- 6 small new red potatoes, scrubbed and halved
- 1 tablespoon olive oil
- 1 tablespoon balsamic vinegar
- 1 tablespoon fresh marjoram leaves, chopped, or 1 teaspoon dried marjoram
- Salt and freshly ground black pepper to taste

Directions:
1. Preheat the toaster oven to 400° F.
2. Combine all the ingredients in a medium bowl and mix well to coat the potatoes.
3. Place in an oiled or nonstick 8½ × 8½ × 2-inch square baking (cake) pan.
4. BAKE, covered, for 30 minutes, or until the potatoes are tender.
5. BROIL 10 minutes to brown to your preference. Serve with balsamic vinegar in a small pitcher to drizzle over.

Parmesan Garlic Fries

Servings: 4
Cooking Time: 20 Minutes

Ingredients:

- 2 medium Yukon gold potatoes, washed
- 1 tablespoon extra-virgin olive oil
- 1 garlic clove, minced
- 2 tablespoons finely grated parmesan cheese
- ¼ teaspoon black pepper
- ¼ teaspoon salt
- 1 tablespoon freshly chopped parsley

Directions:
1. Preheat the toaster oven to 400°F.
2. Slice the potatoes into long strips about ¼-inch thick. In a large bowl, toss the potatoes with the olive oil, garlic, cheese, pepper, and salt.
3. Place the fries into the air fryer oven and air-fry for 8 minutes.
4. Remove and serve warm.

Air-fried Potato Salad

Servings: 4
Cooking Time: 15 Minutes

Ingredients:

- 1⅓ pounds Yellow potatoes, such as Yukon Golds, cut into ½-inch chunks
- 1 large Sweet white onion(s), such as Vidalia, chopped into ½-inch pieces
- 1 tablespoon plus 2 teaspoons Olive oil
- ¾ cup Thinly sliced celery
- 6 tablespoons Regular or low-fat mayonnaise (gluten-free, if a concern)
- 2½ tablespoons Apple cider vinegar
- 1½ teaspoons Dijon mustard (gluten-free, if a concern)
- ¾ teaspoon Table salt
- ¼ teaspoon Ground black pepper

Directions:
1. Preheat the toaster oven to 400°F.
2. Toss the potatoes, onion(s), and oil in a large bowl until the vegetables are glistening with oil.
3. When the machine is at temperature, transfer the vegetables to the air fryer oven, spreading them out into as even a layer as you can. Air-fry for 15 minutes, tossing and rearranging the vegetables every 3 minutes so that all surfaces get exposed to the air currents, until the vegetables are tender and even browned at the edges.
4. Pour the contents of the air fryer oven into a serving bowl. Cool for at least 5 minutes or up to 30 minutes. Add the celery, mayonnaise, vinegar, mustard, salt, and pepper. Stir well to coat. The potato salad can be made in advance; cover and refrigerate for up to 4 days.

Crunchy Roasted Potatoes

Servings: 5
Cooking Time: 25 Minutes

Ingredients:
- 2 pounds Small (1- to 1½-inch-diameter) red, white, or purple potatoes
- 2 tablespoons Olive oil
- 2 teaspoons Table salt
- ¾ teaspoon Garlic powder
- ½ teaspoon Ground black pepper

Directions:
1. Preheat the toaster oven to 400°F.
2. Toss the potatoes, oil, salt, garlic powder, and pepper in a large bowl until the spuds are evenly and thoroughly coated.
3. When the machine is at temperature, pour the potatoes into the air fryer oven, spreading them into an even layer (although they may be stacked on top of each other). Air-fry for 25 minutes, tossing twice, until the potatoes are tender but crunchy.
4. Pour the contents of the air fryer oven into a serving bowl. Cool for 5 minutes before serving.

Zucchini Boats With Ham And Cheese

Servings: 4
Cooking Time: 12 Minutes

Ingredients:
- 2 6-inch-long zucchini
- 2 ounces Thinly sliced deli ham, any rind removed, meat roughly chopped
- 4 Dry-packed sun-dried tomatoes, chopped
- ⅓ cup Purchased pesto
- ¼ cup Packaged mini croutons
- ¼ cup (about 1 ounce) Shredded semi-firm mozzarella cheese

Directions:
1. Preheat the toaster oven to 375°F.
2. Split the zucchini in half lengthwise and use a flatware spoon or a serrated grapefruit spoon to scoop out the insides of the halves, leaving at least a ¼-inch border all around the zucchini half. (You can save the scooped out insides to add to soups and stews—or even freeze it for a much later use.)
3. Mix the ham, sun-dried tomatoes, pesto, croutons, and half the cheese in a bowl until well combined. Pack this mixture into the zucchini "shells." Top them with the remaining cheese.
4. Set them stuffing side up in the air fryer oven without touching (even a fraction of an inch between them is enough room). Air-fry undisturbed for 12 minutes, or until softened and browned, with the cheese melted on top.
5. Use a nonstick-safe spatula to transfer the zucchini boats stuffing side up on a wire rack. Cool for 5 or 10 minutes before serving.

Classic Baked Potatoes

Servings: 4
Cooking Time: 50 Minutes

Ingredients:
- 4 medium baking potatoes,
- scrubbed and pierced with a fork

Directions:
1. Preheat the toaster oven to 450° F.
2. BAKE the potatoes on the oven rack for 50 minutes, or until tender when pierced with a fork.

Onions

Servings: 4
Cooking Time: 18 Minutes

Ingredients:
- 2 yellow onions (Vidalia or 1015 recommended)
- salt and pepper
- ¼ teaspoon ground thyme
- ¼ teaspoon smoked paprika
- 2 teaspoons olive oil
- 1 ounce Gruyère cheese, grated

Directions:
1. Peel onions and halve lengthwise (vertically).
2. Sprinkle cut sides of onions with salt, pepper, thyme, and paprika.

3. Place each onion half, cut-surface up, on a large square of aluminum foil. Pull sides of foil up to cup around onion. Drizzle cut surface of onions with oil.
4. Crimp foil at top to seal closed.
5. Place wrapped onions in air fryer oven and air-fry at 390°F for 18 minutes. When done, onions should be soft enough to pierce with fork but still slightly firm.
6. Open foil just enough to sprinkle each onion with grated cheese.
7. Air-fry for 30 seconds to 1 minute to melt cheese.

Sesame Carrots And Sugar Snap Peas

Servings: 16
Cooking Time: 4 Minutes

Ingredients:
- 1 pound carrots, peeled sliced on the bias (½-inch slices)
- 1 teaspoon olive oil
- salt and freshly ground black pepper
- ⅓ cup honey
- 1 tablespoon sesame oil
- 1 tablespoon soy sauce
- ½ teaspoon minced fresh ginger
- 4 ounces sugar snap peas (about 1 cup)
- 1½ teaspoons sesame seeds

Directions:
1. Preheat the toaster oven to 360°F.
2. Toss the carrots with the olive oil, season with salt and pepper and air-fry for 10 minutes.
3. Combine the honey, sesame oil, soy sauce and minced ginger in a large bowl. Add the sugar snap peas and the air-fried carrots to the honey mixture, toss to coat and return everything to the air fryer oven.
4. Turn up the temperature to 400°F and air-fry for an additional 6 minutes.
5. Transfer the carrots and sugar snap peas to a serving bowl. Pour the sauce from the bottom of the cooker over the vegetables and sprinkle sesame seeds over top. Serve immediately.

Roasted Garlic Potatoes

Servings: 2
Cooking Time: 40 Minutes

Ingredients:
- 2 medium potatoes, peeled and chopped
- 6 garlic cloves, roasted
- 1 tablespoon olive oil
- Salt and freshly ground black pepper
- 1 tablespoon chopped fresh parsley

Directions:
1. Preheat the toaster oven to 400° F.
2. Place the potatoes in an oiled or nonstick 8½ × 8½ × 2-inch square baking (cake) pan. Add the garlic, oil, and salt and pepper to taste. Toss to coat well. Cover the pan with aluminum foil.
3. BAKE, covered, for 40 minutes, or until the potatoes are tender. Remove the cover.
4. BROIL 10 minutes, or until lightly browned. Garnish with fresh parsley before serving.

Rosemary Roasted Potatoes With Lemon

Servings: 12
Cooking Time: 4 Minutes

Ingredients:
- 1 pound small red-skinned potatoes, halved or cut into bite-sized chunks
- 1 tablespoon olive oil
- 1 teaspoon finely chopped fresh rosemary
- ¼ teaspoon salt
- freshly ground black pepper
- 1 tablespoon lemon zest

Directions:
1. Preheat the toaster oven to 400°F.
2. Toss the potatoes with the olive oil, rosemary, salt and freshly ground black pepper.
3. Air-fry for 12 minutes (depending on the size of the chunks), tossing the potatoes a few times throughout the cooking process.
4. As soon as the potatoes are tender to a knifepoint, toss them with the lemon zest and more salt if desired.

Mushrooms, Sautéed

Servings: 4
Cooking Time: 4 Minutes

Ingredients:

- 8 ounces sliced white mushrooms, rinsed and well drained
- ¼ teaspoon garlic powder
- 1 tablespoon Worcestershire sauce

Directions:

1. Place mushrooms in a large bowl and sprinkle with garlic powder and Worcestershire. Stir well to distribute seasonings evenly.
2. Place in air fryer oven and air-fry at 390°F for 4 minutes, until tender.

Roasted Corn Salad

Servings: 3
Cooking Time: 15 Minutes

Ingredients:

- 3 4-inch lengths husked and de-silked corn on the cob
- Olive oil spray
- 1 cup Packed baby arugula leaves
- 12 Cherry tomatoes, halved
- Up to 3 Medium scallion(s), trimmed and thinly sliced
- 2 tablespoons Lemon juice
- 1 tablespoon Olive oil
- 1½ teaspoons Honey
- ¼ teaspoon Mild paprika
- ¼ teaspoon Dried oregano
- ¼ teaspoon, plus more to taste Table salt
- ¼ teaspoon Ground black pepper

Directions:

1. Preheat the toaster oven to 400°F.
2. When the machine is at temperature, lightly coat the pieces of corn on the cob with olive oil spray. Set the pieces of corn in the air fryer oven with as much air space between them as possible. Air-fry undisturbed for 15 minutes, or until the corn is charred in a few spots.
3. Use kitchen tongs to transfer the corn to a wire rack. Cool for 15 minutes.
4. Cut the kernels off the ears by cutting the fat end off each piece so it will stand up straight on a cutting board, then running a knife down the corn. (Or you can save your fingers and buy a fancy tool to remove kernels from corn cobs. Check it out at online kitchenware stores.) Scoop the kernels into a serving bowl.
5. Chop the arugula into bite-size bits and add these to the kernels. Add the tomatoes and scallions, too. Whisk the lemon juice, olive oil, honey, paprika, oregano, salt, and pepper in a small bowl until the honey dissolves. Pour over the salad and toss well to coat, tasting for extra salt before serving.

Cheesy Potato Skins

Servings: 6
Cooking Time: 54 Minutes

Ingredients:

- 3 6- to 8-ounce small russet potatoes
- 3 Thick-cut bacon strips, halved widthwise (gluten-free, if a concern)
- ¾ teaspoon Mild paprika
- ¼ teaspoon Garlic powder
- ¼ teaspoon Table salt
- ¼ teaspoon Ground black pepper
- ½ cup plus 1 tablespoon (a little over 2 ounces) Shredded Cheddar cheese
- 3 tablespoons Thinly sliced trimmed chives
- 6 tablespoons (a little over 1 ounce) Finely grated Parmesan cheese

Directions:

1. Preheat the toaster oven to 375°F.
2. Prick each potato in four places with a fork (not four places in a line but four places all around the potato). Set the potatoes in the air fryer oven with as much air space between them as possible. Air-fry undisturbed for 45 minutes, or until the potatoes are tender when pricked with a fork.
3. Use kitchen tongs to gently transfer the potatoes to a wire rack. Cool for 15 minutes. Maintain the machine's temperature.
4. Lay the bacon strip halves in the air fryer oven in one layer. They may touch but should not overlap. Air-fry undisturbed for 5 minutes, until crisp. Use those

same tongs to transfer the bacon pieces to the wire rack. If there's a great deal of rendered bacon fat in the air fryer oven's bottom or on a tray under the pan attachment, pour this into a bowl, cool, and discard. Don't throw it down the drain!

5. Cut the potatoes in half lengthwise (not just slit them open but actually cut in half). Use a flatware spoon to scoop the hot, soft middles into a bowl, leaving ½ inch of potato all around the inside of the spud next to the skin. Sprinkle the inside of the potato "shells" evenly with paprika, garlic powder, salt, and pepper.

6. Chop the bacon pieces into small bits. Sprinkle these along with the Cheddar and chives evenly inside the potato shells. Crumble 2 to 3 tablespoons of the soft potato insides over the filling mixture. Divide the grated Parmesan evenly over the tops of the potatoes.

7. Set the stuffed potatoes in the air fryer oven with as much air space between them as possible. Air-fry undisturbed for 4 minutes, until the cheese melts and lightly browns.

8. Use kitchen tongs to gently transfer the stuffed potato halves to a wire rack. Cool for 5 minutes before serving.

Empty-the-refrigerator Roasted Vegetables

Servings: 4
Cooking Time: 35 Minutes

Ingredients:
- 3 cups assorted fresh vegetables, cut into 1 × 1-inch pieces
- 2 garlic cloves, minced
- 2 tablespoons olive oil
- 3 tablespoons dry white wine
- Salt and freshly ground black pepper to taste
- 1 tablespoon chopped fresh basil
- 1 tablespoon chopped fresh oregano
- 1 tablespoon chopped fresh parsley

Directions:
1. Preheat the toaster oven to 400° F.
2. Combine all the ingredients with 2 tablespoons water in a 1-quart 8½ × 8½ × 4-inch ovenproof baking dish, mixing well. Cover the dish with aluminum foil.

3. BAKE, covered, for 25 minutes, until the vegetables are tender. Remove from the oven and stir to blend the vegetables and sauce.

4. BROIL, uncovered, for 10 minutes, or until lightly browned.

Ratatouille

Servings: 4
Cooking Time: 60 Minutes

Ingredients:
- Oil spray (hand-pumped)
- 1 eggplant, peeled and diced into ½-inch chunks
- 2 tomatoes, diced
- 1 zucchini, diced
- 2 bell peppers (any color), diced
- ½ red onion, chopped
- ½ cup tomato paste
- 2 teaspoons minced garlic
- 1 teaspoon dried basil
- ¼ teaspoon sea salt
- ⅛ teaspoon freshly ground black pepper
- Pinch red pepper flakes
- ½ cup low-sodium vegetable broth

Directions:
1. Place the rack in position 1 and preheat oven to 350°F on CONVECTION BAKE for 5 minutes.
2. Lightly coat a 1½-quart casserole dish with oil spray.
3. In a large bowl, toss the eggplant, tomatoes, zucchini, bell peppers, onion, tomato paste, garlic, basil, salt, black pepper, and red pepper flakes until well combined.
4. Transfer the vegetable mixture to the casserole dish, pour in the vegetable broth, and cover tightly with foil or a lid.
5. Convection bake for 1 hour, stirring once at the halfway mark, until the vegetables are very tender. Serve.

Broccoli With Chinese Mushrooms And Water Chestnuts

Servings: 4
Cooking Time: 20 Minutes

Ingredients:
- 2 cups broccoli florets, cut in half
- ½ cup Chinese dried mushrooms, cooked, drained, stemmed, and sliced
- ¼ cup dry white wine
- 1 5-ounce can sliced water chestnuts, well drained
- 1 tablespoon vegetable oil
- 1 teaspoon toasted sesame oil
- 1 teaspoon oyster sauce

Directions:
1. Combine all the ingredients with ¼ cup water in an oiled or nonstick 8½ × 8½ × 2-inch square baking (cake) pan. Adjust the seasonings to taste.
2. BROIL 20 minutes, turning with tongs every 5 minutes, or until the vegetables are tender.

Roasted Heirloom Carrots With Orange And Thyme

Servings: 2
Cooking Time: 12 Minutes

Ingredients:
- 10 to 12 heirloom or rainbow carrots (about 1 pound), scrubbed but not peeled
- 1 teaspoon olive oil
- salt and freshly ground black pepper
- 1 tablespoon butter
- 1 teaspoon fresh orange zest
- 1 teaspoon chopped fresh thyme

Directions:
1. Preheat the toaster oven to 400°F.
2. Scrub the carrots and halve them lengthwise. Toss them in the olive oil, season with salt and freshly ground black pepper and transfer to the air fryer oven.
3. Air-fry at 400°F for 12 minutes.
4. As soon as the carrots have finished cooking, add the butter, orange zest and thyme and toss all the ingredients together in the air fryer oven to melt the butter and coat evenly. Serve warm.

Rosemary New Potatoes

Servings: 4
Cooking Time: 6 Minutes

Ingredients:
- 3 large red potatoes (enough to make 3 cups sliced)
- ¼ teaspoon ground rosemary
- ¼ teaspoon ground thyme
- ⅛ teaspoon salt
- ⅛ teaspoon ground black pepper
- 2 teaspoons extra-light olive oil

Directions:
1. Preheat the toaster oven to 330°F.
2. Place potatoes in large bowl and sprinkle with rosemary, thyme, salt, and pepper.
3. Stir with a spoon to distribute seasonings evenly.
4. Add oil to potatoes and stir again to coat well.
5. Air-fry at 330°F for 4 minutes. Stir and break apart any that have stuck together.
6. Cook an additional 2 minutes or until fork-tender.

Baked Stuffed Potatoes With Vegetables

Servings: 2
Cooking Time: 30 Minutes

Ingredients:
- 2 large baking potatoes, baked, cooled, and pulp scooped out to make shells
- Stuffing:
- 1 carrot, shredded
- ½ bell pepper, seeded and shredded
- 2 tablespoons broccoli, shredded
- 2 tablespoons cauliflower, shredded
- 3 tablespoons fat-free half-and-half
- 1 teaspoon paprika
- ½ teaspoon garlic powder
- ½ teaspoon caraway seeds
- Salt and butcher's pepper to taste

Directions:
1. Preheat the toaster oven to 400° F.
2. Combine the stuffing mixture ingredients, mixing well. Fill the potato shells with the mixture and place

the shells in an oiled 8½ × 8½ × 2-inch square baking (cake) pan.
3. BAKE for 25 minutes or until vegetables are cooked.
4. BROIL for 5 minutes, or until the tops are lightly browned.

Roasted Brussels Sprouts With Bacon

Servings: 20
Cooking Time: 4 Minutes

Ingredients:
- 4 slices thick-cut bacon, chopped (about ¼ pound)
- 1 pound Brussels sprouts, halved (or quartered if large)
- freshly ground black pepper

Directions:
1. Preheat the toaster oven to 380°F.
2. Air-fry the bacon for 5 minutes.
3. Add the Brussels sprouts to the air fryer oven and drizzle a little bacon fat from the pan into the air fryer oven. Toss the sprouts to coat with the bacon fat. Air-fry for an additional 15 minutes, or until the Brussels sprouts are tender to a knifepoint.
4. Season with freshly ground black pepper.

Yogurt Zucchini With Onion

Servings: 4
Cooking Time: 30 Minutes

Ingredients:
- ½ cup plain fat-free yogurt
- 1 tablespoon unbleached flour
- 4 small zucchini, scrubbed and sliced into ½-inch strips
- 3 tablespoons minced fresh onion
- 1 tablespoon olive oil
- 3 tablespoons pine nuts, ground in a blender
- Salt and freshly ground black pepper

Directions:
1. Preheat the toaster oven to 400° F.
2. Whisk together the yogurt and flour in a small bowl until smooth. Transfer to a 1-quart 8½ × 8½ × 4-inch ovenproof baking dish. Add all the remaining ingredients, mixing well. Adjust the seasonings to taste. Cover the dish with aluminum foil.
3. BAKE, covered, for 25 minutes, or until the zucchini is tender. Uncover and toss gently to blend.
4. BROIL for 5 minutes, or until the top is lightly browned.

Five-spice Roasted Sweet Potatoes

Servings: 4
Cooking Time: 12 Minutes

Ingredients:
- ½ teaspoon ground cinnamon
- ¼ teaspoon ground cumin
- ¼ teaspoon paprika
- 1 teaspoon chile powder
- ⅛ teaspoon turmeric
- ½ teaspoon salt (optional)
- freshly ground black pepper
- 2 large sweet potatoes, peeled and cut into ¾-inch cubes (about 3 cups)
- 1 tablespoon olive oil

Directions:
1. In a large bowl, mix together cinnamon, cumin, paprika, chile powder, turmeric, salt, and pepper to taste.
2. Add potatoes and stir well.
3. Drizzle the seasoned potatoes with the olive oil and stir until evenly coated.
4. Place seasoned potatoes in the air fryer oven baking pan or an ovenproof dish that fits inside your air fryer oven.
5. Air-fry for 6 minutes at 390°F, stop, and stir well.
6. Air-fry for an additional 6 minutes.

Roasted Garlic

Servings: 1
Cooking Time: 20 Minutes

Ingredients:
- 3 whole garlic buds
- 3 tablespoons olive oil
- Salt and freshly ground black pepper

Directions:
1. Preheat the toaster oven to 450° F.

2. Place the garlic buds in an oiled or nonstick 8½ × 8½ × 2-inch square baking (cake) pan.

3. BAKE, uncovered, for 20 minutes, or until the buds are tender when pierced with a skewer or sharp knife. When cool enough to handle, peel and mash the baked cloves with a fork into the olive oil. Season with salt and pepper to taste.

Golden Grilled Cheese Tomato Sandwich

Servings: 2
Cooking Time: 10 Minutes

Ingredients:
- 4 slices whole-grain bread
- 4 teaspoons salted butter at room temperature, divided
- 4 to 6 slices cheddar cheese, or your favorite cheese
- 1 large tomato, thinly sliced

Directions:
1. Preheat the toaster oven to 350°F on AIR FRY for 5 minutes.
2. Place the air-fryer basket in the baking sheet and set aside.
3. Butter all four pieces of bread, using 1 teaspoon of butter for each and place 2 pieces of bread, butter-side down, in the basket. Evenly divide the cheese between the 2 bread slices and top with tomato slices. Place the remaining 2 pieces of bread on the tomatoes, butter-side up.
4. Place the tray in position 2 and air fry for 5 minutes until golden brown. Flip the sandwiches and air fry until the cheese is melted and the other side of the bread is golden brown, about 5 minutes. Serve.

Broiled Tomatoes

Servings: 4
Cooking Time: 10 Minutes

Ingredients:
- 2 medium tomatoes
- Filling:
- 2 tablespoons grated Parmesan cheese
- 2 tablespoons bread crumbs
- 2 tablespoons olive oil
- 1 teaspoon dried oregano or 1 tablespoon chopped fresh oregano
- 1 teaspoon garlic powder or 2 garlic cloves, minced
- Salt and freshly ground black pepper to taste

Directions:
1. Slice the tomatoes in half through the stem scar (top) and carefully scoop out the seeds and flesh with a teaspoon. (Remove and discard about 1 tablespoon each.)
2. Mix together the filling ingredients in a small bowl and adjust the seasonings. Fill each tomato half cavity with equal portions of the mixture. Place the tomato halves in an oiled or nonstick 8½ × 8½ × 2-inch square baking (cake) pan.
3. BROIL for 10 minutes, or until the tomatoes are cooked and the tops are browned.

Fried Green Tomatoes With Sriracha Mayo

Servings: 4
Cooking Time: 12 Minutes

Ingredients:
- 3 green tomatoes
- salt and freshly ground black pepper
- ⅓ cup all-purpose flour
- 2 eggs
- ½ cup buttermilk
- 1 cup panko breadcrumbs
- 1 cup cornmeal
- olive oil, in a spray bottle
- fresh thyme sprigs or chopped fresh chives
- Sriracha Mayo
- ½ cup mayonnaise
- 1 to 2 tablespoons sriracha hot sauce
- 1 tablespoon milk

Directions:
1. Cut the tomatoes in ¼-inch slices. Pat them dry with a clean kitchen towel and season generously with salt and pepper.
2. Set up a dredging station using three shallow dishes. Place the flour in the first shallow dish, whisk the eggs and buttermilk together in the second dish, and combine the panko breadcrumbs and cornmeal in the third dish.

3. Preheat the toaster oven to 400°F.
4. Dredge the tomato slices in flour to coat on all sides. Then dip them into the egg mixture and finally press them into the breadcrumbs to coat all sides of the tomato.
5. Spray or brush the air-fryer oven with olive oil. Transfer 3 to 4 tomato slices into the air fryer oven and spray the top with olive oil. Air-fry the tomatoes at 400°F for 8 minutes. Flip them over, spray the other side with oil and air-fry for an additional 4 minutes until golden brown.
6. While the tomatoes are cooking, make the sriracha mayo. Combine the mayonnaise, 1 tablespoon of the sriracha hot sauce and milk in a small bowl. Stir well until the mixture is smooth. Add more sriracha sauce to taste.
7. When the tomatoes are done, transfer them to a cooling rack or a platter lined with paper towels so the bottom does not get soggy. Before serving, carefully stack the all the tomatoes into air fryer oven and air-fry at 350°F for 1 to 2 minutes to heat them back up.
8. Serve the fried green tomatoes hot with the sriracha mayo on the side. Season one last time with salt and freshly ground black pepper and garnish with sprigs of fresh thyme or chopped fresh chives.

Yellow Squash With Bell Peppers

Servings: 4
Cooking Time: 50 Minutes

Ingredients:
- Squash mixture:
- 2 cups yellow (summer) squash, thinly sliced
- ⅓ cup dry white wine
- 1 bell pepper, seeded and sliced into thin strips
- 1 6½-ounce jar marinated artichoke hearts, drained and sliced
- 1 tablespoon minced fresh garlic
- 1 5-ounce can diced pimientos, drained
- Salt and freshly ground black pepper to taste
- ¼ cup shredded part-skim mozzarella cheese
- 3 tablespoons Homemade Bread Crumbs
- 2 tablespoons chopped fresh cilantro

Directions:

1. Preheat the toaster oven to 400°F.
2. Combine the squash mixture ingredients in a 1-quart 8½ × 8½ × 4-inch ovenproof baking dish, mixing well. Adjust the seasonings.
3. BAKE, covered, for 40 minutes, or until the vegetables are tender. Uncover and sprinkle with the cheese and bread crumbs.
4. BROIL 10 minutes, or until the top is lightly browned. Garnish with the chopped cilantro before serving.

Brown Rice And Goat Cheese Croquettes

Servings: 3
Cooking Time: 8 Minutes

Ingredients:
- ¾ cup Water
- 6 tablespoons Raw medium-grain brown rice, such as brown Arborio
- ½ cup Shredded carrot
- ¼ cup Walnut pieces
- 3 tablespoons (about 1½ ounces) Soft goat cheese
- 1 tablespoon Pasteurized egg substitute, such as Egg Beaters (gluten-free, if a concern)
- ¼ teaspoon Dried thyme
- ¼ teaspoon Table salt
- ¼ teaspoon Ground black pepper
- Olive oil spray

Directions:

1. Combine the water, rice, and carrots in a small saucepan set over medium-high heat. Bring to a boil, stirring occasionally. Cover, reduce the heat to very low, and simmer very slowly for 45 minutes, or until the water has been absorbed and the rice is tender. Set aside, covered, for 10 minutes.
2. Scrape the contents of the saucepan into a food processor. Cool for 10 minutes.
3. Preheat the toaster oven to 400°F.
4. Put the nuts, cheese, egg substitute, thyme, salt, and pepper into the food processor. Cover and pulse to a coarse paste, stopping the machine at least once to scrape down the inside of the canister.

5. Uncover the food processor; scrape down and remove the blade. Using wet, clean hands, form the mixture into two 4-inch-diameter patties for a small batch, three 4-inch-diameter patties for a medium batch, or four 4-inch-diameter patties for a large one. Generously coat both sides of the patties with olive oil spray.

6. Set the patties in the air fryer oven with as much air space between them as possible. Air-fry undisturbed for 8 minutes, or until brown and crisp.

7. Use a nonstick-safe spatula to transfer the croquettes to a wire rack. Cool for 5 minutes before serving.

Panzanella Salad With Crispy Croutons

Servings: 4
Cooking Time: 3 Minutes

Ingredients:
- ½ French baguette, sliced in half lengthwise
- 2 large cloves garlic
- 2 large ripe tomatoes, divided
- 2 small Persian cucumbers, quartered and diced
- ¼ cup Kalamata olives
- 1 tablespoon chopped, fresh oregano or 1 teaspoon dried oregano
- ¼ cup chopped fresh basil
- ¼ cup chopped fresh parsley
- ½ cup sliced red onion
- 2 tablespoons red wine vinegar
- ¼ cup extra-virgin olive oil
- Salt and pepper, to taste

Directions:
1. Preheat the toaster oven to 380°F.
2. Place the baguette into the air fryer oven and toast for 3 to 5 minutes or until lightly golden brown.
3. Remove the bread from air fryer oven and immediately rub 1 raw garlic clove firmly onto the inside portion of each piece of bread, scraping the garlic onto the bread.
4. Slice 1 of the tomatoes in half and rub the cut edge of one half of the tomato onto the toasted bread. Season the rubbed bread with sea salt to taste.
5. Cut the bread into cubes and place in a large bowl. Cube the remaining 1½ tomatoes and add to the bowl. Add the cucumbers, olives, oregano, basil, parsley, and onion; stir to mix. Drizzle the red wine vinegar into the bowl, and stir. Drizzle the olive oil over the top, stir, and adjust the seasonings with salt and pepper.
6. Serve immediately or allow to sit at room temperature up to 1 hour before serving.

Classic Falafel

Servings: 4
Cooking Time: 14 Minutes

Ingredients:
- 1 (15-ounce) can low-sodium chickpeas, drained and rinsed
- 3 shallots, roughly chopped
- 3 tablespoons chickpea flour
- ¼ cup fresh parsley, roughly chopped
- 2 tablespoons cilantro, chopped
- 2 teaspoons minced garlic
- 1 teaspoon ground coriander
- 1 teaspoon ground cumin
- ½ teaspoon sea salt
- ⅛ teaspoon allspice
- Oil spray (hand-pumped)

Directions:
1. Preheat the toaster oven to 350°F on AIR FRY for 5 minutes.
2. Place the chickpeas in a food processor and pulse until roughly chopped.
3. Add the shallots, flour, parsley, cilantro, garlic, coriander, cumin, salt, and allspice, and pulse to form a thick paste.
4. Roll the chickpea mixture into 2-inch balls and flatten them slightly with the palm of your hand.
5. Place the air-fryer basket in the baking tray and coat it generously with oil spray.
6. Place the falafel in a single layer in the basket. Spray the patties with oil on both sides. You might have to work in batches.
7. Place the tray in position 2 and air fry until golden, turning halfway through, for about 14 minutes in total. Repeat with remaining patties. Serve.

Potato Skins

Servings: 4
Cooking Time: 20 Minutes

Ingredients:
- 4 potato shells

Directions:
1. Place 4 potato shells in an oiled or nonstick 8½ × 8½ × 2-inch square baking (cake) pan.
2. Brush, sprinkle, and fill with a variety of seasonings or ingredients.
3. BROIL 20 minutes, or until browned and crisped to your preference.

Fingerling Potatoes

Servings: 4
Cooking Time: 15 Minutes

Ingredients:
- 1 pound fingerling potatoes
- 1 tablespoon light olive oil
- ½ teaspoon dried parsley
- ½ teaspoon lemon juice
- coarsely ground sea salt

Directions:
1. Cut potatoes in half lengthwise.
2. In a large bowl, combine potatoes, oil, parsley, and lemon juice. Stir well to coat potatoes.
3. Place potatoes in air fryer oven and air-fry at 360°F for 15 minutes or until lightly browned and tender inside.
4. Sprinkle with sea salt before serving.

Homemade Potato Puffs

Servings: 4
Cooking Time: 15 Minutes

Ingredients:
- 1¾ cups Water
- 4 tablespoons (¼ cup/½ stick) Butter
- 2 cups plus 2 tablespoons Instant mashed potato flakes
- 1½ teaspoons Table salt
- ¾ teaspoon Ground black pepper
- ¼ teaspoon Mild paprika
- ¼ teaspoon Dried thyme
- 1¼ cups Seasoned Italian-style dried bread crumbs (gluten-free, if a concern)
- Olive oil spray

Directions:
1. Heat the water with the butter in a medium saucepan set over medium-low heat just until the butter melts. Do not bring to a boil.
2. Remove the saucepan from the heat and stir in the potato flakes, salt, pepper, paprika, and thyme until smooth. Set aside to cool for 5 minutes.
3. Preheat the toaster oven to 400°F. Spread the bread crumbs on a dinner plate.
4. Scrape up 2 tablespoons of the potato flake mixture and form it into a small, oblong puff, like a little cylinder about 1½ inches long. Gently roll the puff in the bread crumbs until coated on all sides. Set it aside and continue making more, about 12 for the small batch, 18 for the medium batch, or 24 for the large.
5. Coat the potato cylinders with olive oil spray on all sides, then arrange them in the air fryer oven in one layer with some air space between them. Air-fry undisturbed for 15 minutes, or until crisp and brown.
6. Gently dump the contents of the air fryer oven onto a wire rack. Cool for 5 minutes before serving.

Perfect Asparagus

Servings: 3
Cooking Time: 10 Minutes

Ingredients:
- 1 pound Very thin asparagus spears
- 2 tablespoons Olive oil
- 1 teaspoon Coarse sea salt or kosher salt
- ¾ teaspoon Finely grated lemon zest

Directions:
1. Preheat the toaster oven to 400°F.
2. Trim just enough off the bottom of the asparagus spears so they'll fit in the air fryer oven. Put the spears on a large plate and drizzle them with some of the olive oil. Turn them over and drizzle more olive oil, working to get all the spears coated.
3. When the machine is at temperature, place the spears in one direction in the air fryer oven. They may

be touching. Air-fry for 10 minutes, tossing and rearranging the spears twice, until tender.

4. Dump the contents of the air fryer oven on a serving platter. Spread out the spears. Sprinkle them with the salt and lemon zest while still warm. Serve at once.

Roasted Belgian Endive With Pistachios And Lemon

Servings: 2
Cooking Time: 7 Minutes

Ingredients:
- 2 Medium 3-ounce Belgian endive head(s)
- 2 tablespoons Olive oil
- ½ teaspoon Table salt
- ¼ cup Finely chopped unsalted shelled pistachios
- Up to 2 teaspoons Lemon juice

Directions:
1. Preheat the toaster oven to 325°F (or 330°F, if that's the closest setting).
2. Trim the Belgian endive head(s), removing the little bit of dried-out stem end but keeping the leaves intact. Quarter the head(s) through the stem (which will hold the leaves intact). Brush the endive quarters with oil, getting it down between the leaves. Sprinkle the quarters with salt.
3. When the machine is at temperature, set the endive quarters cut sides up in the air fryer oven with as much air space between them as possible. They should not touch. Air-fry undisturbed for 7 minutes, or until lightly browned along the edges.
4. Use kitchen tongs to transfer the endive quarters to serving plates or a platter. Sprinkle with the pistachios and lemon juice. Serve warm or at room temperature.

Salmon Salad With Steamboat Dressing

Servings: 4
Cooking Time: 18 Minutes

Ingredients:
- ¼ teaspoon salt
- 1½ teaspoons dried dill weed
- 1 tablespoon fresh lemon juice
- 8 ounces fresh or frozen salmon fillet (skin on)
- 8 cups shredded romaine, Boston, or other leaf lettuce
- 8 spears cooked asparagus, cut in 1-inch pieces
- 8 cherry tomatoes, halved or quartered

Directions:
1. Mix the salt and dill weed together. Rub the lemon juice over the salmon on both sides and sprinkle the dill and salt all over. Refrigerate for 15 to 20 minutes.
2. Make Steamboat Dressing and refrigerate while cooking salmon and preparing salad.
3. Cook salmon in air fryer oven at 330°F for 18 minutes. Cooking time will vary depending on thickness of fillets. When done, salmon should flake with fork but still be moist and tender.
4. Remove salmon from air fryer oven and cool slightly. At this point, the skin should slide off easily. Cut salmon into 4 pieces and discard skin.
5. Divide the lettuce among 4 plates. Scatter asparagus spears and tomato pieces evenly over the lettuce, allowing roughly 2 whole spears and 2 whole cherry tomatoes per plate.
6. Top each salad with one portion of the salmon and drizzle with a tablespoon of dressing. Serve with additional dressing to pass at the table.

Grits Casserole

Servings: 4
Cooking Time: 30 Minutes

Ingredients:
- 10 fresh asparagus spears, cut into 1-inch pieces
- 2 cups cooked grits, cooled to room temperature
- 1 egg, beaten
- 2 teaspoons Worcestershire sauce
- ½ teaspoon garlic powder
- ¼ teaspoon salt
- 2 slices provolone cheese (about 1½ ounces)
- oil for misting or cooking spray

Directions:
1. Mist asparagus spears with oil and air-fry at 390°F for 5 minutes, until crisp-tender.
2. In a medium bowl, mix together the grits, egg, Worcestershire, garlic powder, and salt.

3. Spoon half of grits mixture into air fryer oven baking pan and top with asparagus.
4. Tear cheese slices into pieces and layer evenly on top of asparagus.
5. Top with remaining grits.
6. Bake at 360°F for 25 minutes. The casserole will rise a little as it cooks. When done, the top will have browned lightly with just a hint of crispiness.

Steakhouse Baked Potatoes

Servings: 3
Cooking Time: 55 Minutes

Ingredients:
- 3 10-ounce russet potatoes
- 2 tablespoons Olive oil
- 1 teaspoon Table salt

Directions:
1. Preheat the toaster oven to 375°F.
2. Poke holes all over each potato with a fork. Rub the skin of each potato with 2 teaspoons of the olive oil, then sprinkle ¼ teaspoon salt all over each potato.
3. When the machine is at temperature, set the potatoes in the air fryer oven in one layer with as much air space between them as possible. Air-fry for 50 minutes, turning once, or until soft to the touch but with crunchy skins. If the machine is at 360°F, you may need to add up to 5 minutes to the cooking time.
4. Use kitchen tongs to gently transfer the baked potatoes to a wire rack. Cool for 5 or 10 minutes before serving.

Mini Hasselback Potatoes

Servings: 25
Cooking Time: 4 Minutes

Ingredients:
- 1½ pounds baby Yukon Gold potatoes (about 10)
- 5 tablespoons butter, cut into very thin slices
- salt and freshly ground black pepper
- 1 tablespoon vegetable oil
- ¼ cup grated Parmesan cheese (optional)
- chopped fresh parsley or chives

Directions:

1. Preheat the toaster oven to 400°F.
2. Make six to eight deep vertical slits across the top of each potato about three quarters of the way down. Make sure the slits are deep enough to allow the slices to spread apart a little, but don't cut all the way through the potato. Place a thin slice of butter between each of the slices and season generously with salt and pepper.
3. Transfer the potatoes to the air fryer oven. Pack them in next to each other. It's alright if some of the potatoes sit on top or rest on another potato. Air-fry for 20 minutes.
4. Spray or brush the potatoes with a little vegetable oil and sprinkle the Parmesan cheese on top. Air-fry for an additional 5 minutes. Garnish with chopped parsley or chives and serve hot.

Zucchini Fries

Servings: 3
Cooking Time: 12 Minutes

Ingredients:
- 1 large Zucchini
- ½ cup All-purpose flour or tapioca flour
- 2 Large egg(s), well beaten
- 1 cup Seasoned Italian-style dried bread crumbs (gluten-free, if a concern)
- Olive oil spray

Directions:
1. Preheat the toaster oven to 400°F.
2. Trim the zucchini into a long rectangular block, taking off the ends and four "sides" to make this shape. Cut the block lengthwise into ½-inch-thick slices. Lay these slices flat and cut in half widthwise. Slice each of these pieces into ½-inch-thick batons.
3. Set up and fill three shallow soup plates or small pie plates on your counter: one for the flour, one for the beaten egg(s), and one for the bread crumbs.
4. Set a zucchini baton in the flour and turn it several times to coat all sides. Gently stir any excess flour, then dip it in the egg(s), turning it to coat. Let any excess egg slip back into the rest, then set the baton in the bread crumbs and turn it several times, pressing gently to coat all sides, even the ends. Set aside on a cutting board and

continue coating the remainder of the batons in the same way.

5. Lightly coat the batons on all sides with olive oil spray. Set them in two flat layers in the air fryer oven, the top layer at a 90-degree angle to the bottom one, with a little air space between the batons in each layer. In the end, the whole thing will look like a crosshatch pattern. Air-fry undisturbed for 6 minutes.

6. Use kitchen tongs to gently rearrange the batons so that any covered parts are now uncovered. The batons no longer need to be in a crosshatch pattern. Continue air-frying undisturbed for 6 minutes, or until lightly browned and crisp.

7. Gently pour the contents of the air fryer oven onto a wire rack. Spread the batons out and cool for only a minute or two before serving.

Roasted Vegetables

Servings: 4
Cooking Time: 20 Minutes

Ingredients:
- 1 1-pound package frozen vegetable mixture
- 1 tablespoon olive oil
- 1 tablespoon bread crumbs
- 1 teaspoon dried oregano
- 1 teaspoon ground cumin
- Salt and freshly ground black pepper to taste
- 1 tablespoon grated Parmesan cheese
- 1 tablespoon chopped walnuts

Directions:
1. Blend all the ingredients in an oiled or nonstick 8½ × 8½ × 2-inch square baking (cake) pan, tossing to coat the vegetable pieces with the oil, bread crumbs, and seasonings. Adjust the seasonings.
2. BROIL for 10 minutes. Remove the pan from the oven and turn the pieces with tongs. Add the cheese and walnuts. Broil for another 10 minutes, or until the vegetables are lightly browned. Adjust the seasonings and serve.

Brussels Sprouts

Servings: 3
Cooking Time: 5 Minutes

Ingredients:
- 1 10-ounce package frozen brussels sprouts, thawed and halved
- 2 teaspoons olive oil
- salt and pepper

Directions:
1. Toss the brussels sprouts and olive oil together.
2. Place them in the air fryer oven and season to taste with salt and pepper.
3. Air-fry at 360°F for approximately 5 minutes, until the edges begin to brown.

Blistered Tomatoes

Servings: 20
Cooking Time: 15 Minutes

Ingredients:
- 1½ pounds Cherry or grape tomatoes
- Olive oil spray
- 1½ teaspoons Balsamic vinegar
- ¼ teaspoon Table salt
- ¼ teaspoon Ground black pepper

Directions:
1. Put the pan in a drawer-style air fryer oven, or a baking tray in the lower third of a toaster oven–style air fryer oven. Place a 6-inch round cake pan in the pan or on the tray for a small batch, a 7-inch round cake pan for a medium batch, or an 8-inch round cake pan for a large one. Heat the air fryer oven to 400°F with the pan in the air fryer oven. When the machine is at temperature, keep heating the pan for 5 minutes more.
2. Place the tomatoes in a large bowl, coat them with the olive oil spray, toss gently, then spritz a couple of times more, tossing after each spritz, until the tomatoes are glistening.
3. Pour the tomatoes into the cake pan and air-fry undisturbed for 10 minutes, or until they split and begin to brown.
4. Use kitchen tongs and a nonstick-safe spatula, or silicone baking mitts, to remove the cake pan from the air fryer oven. Toss the hot tomatoes with the vinegar, salt, and pepper. Cool in the pan for a few minutes before serving.

Lemon-glazed Baby Carrots

Servings: 4
Cooking Time: 33 Minutes

Ingredients:
- Glaze:
- 1 tablespoon margarine
- 2 tablespoons lemon juice
- 1 tablespoon honey
- 1 teaspoon garlic powder
- Salt and freshly ground black pepper to taste
- 2 cups peeled baby carrots (approximately 1 pound)
- 1 tablespoon chopped fresh parsley or cilantro

Directions:
1. Place the glaze ingredients in a 1-quart 8½ × 8½ × 4-inch ovenproof baking dish and broil for 4 minutes, or until the margarine is melted. Remove from the oven and mix well. Add the carrots and toss to coat. Cover the dish with aluminum foil.
2. BAKE, covered, at 350° F. for 30 minutes, or until the carrots are tender. Garnish with chopped parsley or cilantro and serve immediately.

Crispy Herbed Potatoes

Servings: 6
Cooking Time: 20 Minutes

Ingredients:
- 3 medium baking potatoes, washed and cubed
- ½ teaspoon dried thyme
- 1 teaspoon minced dried rosemary
- ½ teaspoon garlic powder
- 1 teaspoon sea salt
- ½ teaspoon black pepper
- 2 tablespoons extra-virgin olive oil
- ¼ cup chopped parsley

Directions:
1. Preheat the toaster oven to 390°F.
2. Pat the potatoes dry. In a large bowl, mix together the cubed potatoes, thyme, rosemary, garlic powder, sea salt, and pepper. Drizzle and toss with olive oil.
3. Pour the herbed potatoes into the air fryer oven. Air-fry for 20 minutes, stirring every 5 minutes.
4. Toss the cooked potatoes with chopped parsley and serve immediately.
5. VARY IT! Potatoes are versatile — add any spice or seasoning mixture you prefer and create your own favorite side dish.

Mushrooms

Servings: 4
Cooking Time: 12 Minutes

Ingredients:
- 8 ounces whole white button mushrooms
- ½ teaspoon salt
- ⅛ teaspoon pepper
- ¼ teaspoon garlic powder
- ¼ teaspoon onion powder
- 5 tablespoons potato starch
- 1 egg, beaten
- ¾ cup panko breadcrumbs
- oil for misting or cooking spray

Directions:
1. Place mushrooms in a large bowl. Add the salt, pepper, garlic and onion powders, and stir well to distribute seasonings.
2. Add potato starch to mushrooms and toss in bowl until well coated.
3. Dip mushrooms in beaten egg, roll in panko crumbs, and mist with oil or cooking spray.
4. Place mushrooms in air fryer oven. You can cook them all at once, and it's okay if a few are stacked.
5. Air-fry at 390°F for 5 minutes. Rotate, then continue cooking for 7 more minutes, until golden brown and crispy.

Brussels Sprout And Ham Salad

Servings: 3
Cooking Time: 12 Minutes

Ingredients:
- 1 pound 2-inch-in-length Brussels sprouts, quartered through the stem
- 6 ounces Smoked ham steak, any rind removed, diced (gluten-free, if a concern)
- ¼ teaspoon Caraway seeds
- Vegetable oil spray

- ¼ cup Brine from a jar of pickles (gluten-free, if a concern)
- ¾ teaspoon Ground black pepper

Directions:
1. Preheat the toaster oven to 375°F.
2. Toss the Brussels sprout quarters, ham, and caraway seeds in a bowl until well combined. Generously coat the top of the mixture with vegetable oil spray, toss again, spray again, and repeat a couple of times until the vegetables and ham are glistening.
3. When the machine is at temperature, scrape the contents of the bowl into the air fryer oven, spreading it into as close to one layer as you can. Air-fry for 12 minutes, tossing and rearranging the pieces at least twice so that any covered or touching parts are eventually exposed to the air currents, until the Brussels sprouts are tender and a little brown at the edges.
4. Dump the contents of the air fryer oven into a serving bowl. Scrape any caraway seeds from the bottom of the air fryer oven or the tray under the pan attachment into the bowl as well. Add the pickle brine and pepper. Toss well to coat. Serve warm.

Mashed Potato Tots

Servings: 18
Cooking Time: 10 Minutes

Ingredients:
- 1 medium potato or 1 cup cooked mashed potatoes
- 1 tablespoon real bacon bits
- 2 tablespoons chopped green onions, tops only
- ¼ teaspoon onion powder
- 1 teaspoon dried chopped chives
- salt
- 2 tablespoons flour
- 1 egg white, beaten
- ½ cup panko breadcrumbs
- oil for misting or cooking spray

Directions:
1. If using cooked mashed potatoes, jump to step 4.
2. Peel potato and cut into ½-inch cubes. (Small pieces cook more quickly.) Place in saucepan, add water to cover, and heat to boil. Lower heat slightly and continue cooking just until tender, about 10 minutes.
3. Drain potatoes and place in ice cold water. Allow to cool for a minute or two, then drain well and mash.
4. Preheat the toaster oven to 390°F.
5. In a large bowl, mix together the potatoes, bacon bits, onions, onion powder, chives, salt to taste, and flour. Add egg white and stir well.
6. Place panko crumbs on a sheet of wax paper.
7. For each tot, use about 2 teaspoons of potato mixture. To shape, drop the measure of potato mixture onto panko crumbs and push crumbs up and around potatoes to coat edges. Then turn tot over to coat other side with crumbs.
8. Mist tots with oil or cooking spray and place in air fryer oven, crowded but not stacked.
9. Air-fry at 390°F for 10 minutes, until browned and crispy.
10. Repeat steps 8 and 9 to cook remaining tots.

Sweet Potato Curly Fries

Servings: 4
Cooking Time: 10 Minutes

Ingredients:
- 2 medium sweet potatoes, washed
- 2 tablespoons avocado oil
- ¾ teaspoon salt, divided
- 1 medium avocado
- ½ teaspoon garlic powder
- ½ teaspoon paprika
- ¼ teaspoon black pepper
- ½ juice lime
- 3 tablespoons fresh cilantro

Directions:
1. Preheat the toaster oven to 400°F.
2. Using a spiralizer, create curly spirals with the sweet potatoes. Keep the pieces about 1½ inches long. Continue until all the potatoes are used.
3. In a large bowl, toss the curly sweet potatoes with the avocado oil and ½ teaspoon of the salt.
4. Place the potatoes in the air fryer oven and air-fry for 5 minutes; cook another 5 minutes.
5. While cooking, add the avocado, garlic, paprika, pepper, the remaining ¼ teaspoon of salt, lime juice, and cilantro to a blender and process until smooth. Set aside.
6. When cooking completes, remove the fries and serve warm with the lime avocado sauce.

Eggplant And Tomato Slices

Servings: 4
Cooking Time: 36 Minutes

Ingredients:
- 2 tablespoons olive oil
- ¼ teaspoon garlic powder
- 4 ½-inch-thick slices eggplant
- 4 ¼-inch-thick slices fresh tomato
- 2 tablespoons tomato sauce or salsa
- ½ cup shredded Parmesan cheese
- Salt and freshly ground black pepper to taste
- 2 tablespoons chopped fresh basil, cilantro, parsley, or oregano

Directions:
1. Whisk together the oil and garlic powder in a small bowl. Brush each eggplant slice with the mixture and place in an oiled or nonstick 8½ × 8½ × 2-inch square baking (cake) pan.
2. BROIL for 20 minutes. Remove the pan from the oven and turn the pieces with tongs. Top each with a slice of tomato and broil another 10 minutes, or until tender. Remove the pan from the oven, brush each slice with tomato sauce or salsa, and sprinkle generously with Parmesan cheese. Season to taste with salt and pepper. Broil again for 6 minutes, until the tops are browned.
3. Garnish with the fresh herb and serve.

Simple Roasted Sweet Potatoes

Servings: 2
Cooking Time: 45 Minutes

Ingredients:
- 2 10- to 12-ounce sweet potato(es)

Directions:
1. Preheat the toaster oven to 350°F.
2. Prick the sweet potato(es) in four or five different places with the tines of a flatware fork (not in a line but all around).
3. When the machine is at temperature, set the sweet potato(es) in the air fryer oven with as much air space between them as possible. Air-fry undisturbed for 45 minutes, or until soft when pricked with a fork.
4. Use kitchen tongs to transfer the sweet potato(es) to a wire rack. Cool for 5 minutes before serving.

Stuffed Onions

Servings: 6
Cooking Time: 27 Minutes

Ingredients:
- 6 Small 3½- to 4-ounce yellow or white onions
- Olive oil spray
- 6 ounces Bulk sweet Italian sausage meat (gluten-free, if a concern)
- 9 Cherry tomatoes, chopped
- 3 tablespoons Seasoned Italian-style dried bread crumbs (gluten-free, if a concern)
- 3 tablespoons (about ½ ounce) Finely grated Parmesan cheese

Directions:
1. Preheat the toaster oven to 325°F (or 330°F, if that's the closest setting).
2. Cut just enough off the root ends of the onions so they will stand up on a cutting board when this end is turned down. Carefully peel off just the brown, papery skin. Now cut the top quarter off each and place the onion back on the cutting board with this end facing up. Use a flatware spoon (preferably a serrated grapefruit spoon) or a melon baller to scoop out the "insides" (interior layers) of the onion, leaving enough of the bottom and side walls so that the onion does not collapse. Depending on the thickness of the layers in the onion, this may be one or two of those layers—or even three, if they're very thin.
3. Coat the insides and outsides of the onions with olive oil spray. Set the onion "shells" in the air fryer oven and air-fry for 15 minutes.
4. Meanwhile, make the filling. Set a medium skillet over medium heat for a couple of minutes, then crumble in the sausage meat. Cook, stirring often, until browned, about 4 minutes. Transfer the contents of the skillet to a medium bowl (leave the fat behind in the skillet or add it to the bowl, depending on your cross-trainer regimen). Stir in the tomatoes, bread crumbs, and cheese until well combined.

5. When the onions are ready, use a nonstick-safe spatula to gently transfer them to a cutting board. Increase the air fryer oven's temperature to 350°F.
6. Pack the sausage mixture into the onion shells, gently compacting the filling and mounding it up at the top.
7. When the machine is at temperature, set the onions stuffing side up in the air fryer oven with at least ¼ inch between them. Air-fry for 12 minutes, or until lightly browned and sizzling hot.
8. Use a nonstick-safe spatula, and perhaps a flatware fork for balance, to transfer the onions to a cutting board or serving platter. Cool for 5 minutes before serving.

Florentine Stuffed Tomatoes

Servings: 12
Cooking Time: 2 Minutes

Ingredients:
- 1 cup frozen spinach, thawed and squeezed dry
- ¼ cup toasted pine nuts
- ¼ cup grated mozzarella cheese
- ½ cup crumbled feta cheese
- ½ cup coarse fresh breadcrumbs
- 1 tablespoon olive oil
- salt and freshly ground black pepper
- 2 to 3 beefsteak tomatoes, halved horizontally and insides scooped out

Directions:
1. Combine the spinach, pine nuts, mozzarella and feta cheeses, breadcrumbs, olive oil, salt and freshly ground black pepper in a bowl. Spoon the mixture into the tomato halves. You should have enough filling for 2 to 3 tomatoes, depending on how big they are.
2. Preheat the toaster oven to 350°F.
3. Place three or four tomato halves (depending on whether you're using 2 or 3 tomatoes and how big they are) into the air fryer oven and air-fry for 12 minutes. The tomatoes should be soft but still manageable and the tops should be lightly browned. Repeat with second batch if necessary.
4. Let the tomatoes cool for just a minute or two before serving.

Baked Mac And Cheese

Servings: 4
Cooking Time: 45 Minutes

Ingredients:
- Oil spray (hand-pumped)
- 1½ cups whole milk, room temperature
- ½ cup heavy (whipping) cream, room temperature
- 1 cup shredded cheddar cheese
- 4 ounces cream cheese, room temperature
- ½ teaspoon dry mustard
- ⅛ teaspoon sea salt
- ⅛ teaspoon freshly ground black pepper
- 1¼ cups dried elbow macaroni
- ¼ cup bread crumbs
- 2 tablespoons grated Parmesan cheese
- 1 tablespoon salted butter, melted

Directions:
1. Place the rack in position 1 and preheat the toaster oven to 375°F on CONVECTION BAKE for 5 minutes.
2. Lightly coat an 8-inch-square baking dish with the oil spray.
3. In a large bowl, stir the milk, cream, cheddar, cream cheese, mustard, salt, and pepper until well combined.
4. Transfer the mixture to the baking dish, stir in the macaroni and cover tightly with foil.
5. Bake for 35 minutes.
6. While the macaroni is baking, in a small bowl, stir the bread crumbs, Parmesan, and butter to form coarse crumbs. Set aside.
7. Take the baking dish out of the oven, uncover, stir, and evenly cover with the bread crumb mixture.
8. Bake uncovered for an additional 10 minutes until the pasta is tender, bubbly, and golden brown. Serve.

Roasted Veggie Kebabs

Servings: 4
Cooking Time: 45 Minutes

Ingredients:
- Brushing mixture:
- 3 tablespoons olive oil
- 1 tablespoon soy sauce
- 1 teaspoon garlic powder
- 1 teaspoon ground cumin
- 2 tablespoons balsamic vinegar
- Salt and freshly ground black pepper to taste
- Cauliflower, zucchini, onion, broccoli, bell pepper, mushrooms, celery, cabbage, beets, and the like, cut into approximately 2 × 2-inch pieces

Directions:
1. Preheat the toaster oven to 400° F.
2. Combine the brushing mixture ingredients in a small bowl, mixing well. Set aside.
3. Skewer the vegetable pieces on 4 9-inch metal skewers and place the skewers lengthwise on a broiling rack with a pan underneath.
4. BAKE for 40 minutes, or until the vegetables are tender, brushing with the mixture every 10 minutes.
5. BROIL for 5 minutes, or until lightly browned.

RECIPE INDEX

A

Air-fried Potato Salad 206
Air-fried Roast Beef With Rosemary Roasted Potatoes 154
Air-fried Turkey Breast With Cherry Glaze 119
Albóndigas 147
All-purpose Cornbread 67
Almond Amaretto Bundt Cake 199
Almond And Sun-dried Tomato Crusted Pork Chops 151
Almond Crab Cakes 101
Apple Fritters 24
Apple Strudel 191
Apricot Glazed Chicken Thighs 135
Asparagus Fries 205
Autumn Berry Dessert 17
Avocado Chicken Flatbread 18
Avocado Egg Rolls 80

B

Bacon Bites 86
Bacon Chicken Ranch Sandwiches 34
Bacon, Broccoli And Swiss Cheese Bread Pudding 39
Bagel Chips 84
Baked Asparagus Fries 82
Baked Custard 193
Baked Eggs With Bacon-tomato Sauce 24
Baked French Toast With Maple Bourbon Syrup 55
Baked Grapefruit 35
Baked Mac And Cheese 223
Baked Macs 37
Baked Parsleyed Cheese Grits 56
Baked Picnic Pinto Beans 49
Baked Steel-cut Oatmeal 35
Baked Stuffed Acorn Squash 202
Baked Stuffed Potatoes With Vegetables 211
Baked Tomato Casserole 61
Baked Tomato Pesto Bluefish 113
Banana Baked Oatmeal 22
Barbecue Chicken Nachos 89
Barbecued Broiled Pork Chops 158
Barbecue-style London Broil 148
Barbeque Ribs 169
Beef Al Carbon (street Taco Meat) 165
Beef And Bean Quesadillas 29
Beef And Spinach Braciole 160
Beef Bourguignon 158
Beef Empanadas 90
Beef Satay With Peanut Dipping Sauce 86
Beef Vegetable Stew 163
Beef, Onion, And Pepper Shish Kebab 155
Beef-stuffed Bell Peppers 149
Beer-baked Pork Tenderloin 171
Beer-battered Cod 97
Beer-breaded Halibut Fish Tacos 114
Beet Chips 79
Berry Crisp 15
Better Fish Sticks 94
Better-than-chinese-take-out Pork Ribs 169
Black And Blue Clafoutis 173
Blackberry Pie 178
Blackened Catfish 104
Blistered Shishito Peppers 75
Blistered Tomatoes 219
Blueberry Cheesecake Tartlets 198
Blueberry Clafoutis 177
Blueberry Cookies 200
Blueberry Crisp 183
Blueberry Crumbles 196
Blueberry Muffins 19
Bourbon Bread Pudding 180
Bourbon Broiled Steak 146
Bread Boat Eggs 20
Breakfast Bars 37
Breakfast Blueberry Peach Crisp 19
Breakfast Pita 34
Broccoli Cornbread 28
Broccoli With Chinese Mushrooms And Water Chestnuts 211
Broiled Chipotle Tilapia With Avocado Sauce 56
Broiled Dill And Lemon Salmon 107
Broiled Lemon Coconut Shrimp 99

Broiled Scallops 111
Broiled Tomatoes 213
Brown Rice And Goat Cheese Croquettes 214
Brown Sugar Baked Apples 198
Brown Sugar Grapefruit 23
Brunch Burritos 33
Brussels Sprout And Ham Salad 220
Brussels Sprouts 219
Buffalo Cauliflower 89
Buffalo Chicken Dip 75
Buffalo Egg Rolls 119
Buttered Poppy Seed Bread 17
Buttermilk Confetti Cake 175

C

Calf's Liver 152
California Burritos 166
Calzones South Of The Border 161
Campfire Banana Boats 192
Capered Crab Cakes 109
Caramelized Onion Dip 72
Carrot Cake 185
Catfish Kebabs 107
Cauliflower "tater" Tots 83
Cauliflower 202
Cheddar Bacon Broiler 22
Cheese Arancini 91
Cheese Blintzes 197
Cheesy Chicken–stuffed Shells 44
Cheesy Potato Skins 209
Cherries Jubilee 36
Cherry Chipotle Bbq Chicken Wings 68
Chewy Brownies 196
Chicken Adobo 134
Chicken Breast With Chermoula Sauce 139
Chicken Chunks 131
Chicken Cordon Bleu 121
Chicken Cutlets With Broccoli Rabe And Roasted Peppers 124
Chicken Fajitas 130
Chicken Fried Steak 167
Chicken Gumbo 44
Chicken Hand Pies 142
Chicken In Mango Sauce 140
Chicken Marengo 56
Chicken Nuggets 140
Chicken Parmesan 128
Chicken Pot Pie 129
Chicken Potpie 120
Chicken Ranch Roll-ups 131
Chicken Schnitzel Dogs 124
Chicken Souvlaki Gyros 123
Chicken Thighs With Roasted Rosemary Root Vegetables 65
Chicken Tortilla Roll-ups 48
Chilled Clam Cake Slices With Dijon Dill Sauce 109
Chinese Pork And Vegetable Non-stir-fry 162
Chipotle-glazed Meat Loaf 166
Chocolate And Vanilla Swirled Pudding 181
Cilantro-crusted Flank Steak 158
Cinnamon Apple Chips 73
Cinnamon Biscuit Rolls 32
Cinnamon Pita Chips 66
Cinnamon Rolls 24
Cinnamon Sugar Rolls 183
Cinnamon Swirl Bread 26
Cinnamon Toast 27
Classic Baked Potatoes 207
Classic Beef Stew 43
Classic Cinnamon Rolls 15
Classic Cornbread 90
Classic Falafel 215
Classic Pepperoni Pizza 163
Classic Tuna Casserole 64
Coconut Cake 177
Coconut Chicken With Apricot-ginger Sauce 130
Coconut Drop Cookies 175
Coconut Jerk Shrimp 105
Coconut Rice Pudding 195
Coconut Shrimp 115
Coconut-crusted Shrimp 111
Coffee Cake 28
Connecticut Garden Chowder 50
Corn Dog Muffins 74
Country Bread 29
Couscous-stuffed Poblano Peppers 57
Cowboy Cookies 190
Crab Cakes 114

Crab Chowder 55
Crab-stuffed Peppers 92
Cranapple Crisp 184
Creamy Parmesan Polenta 70
Creamy Roasted Pepper Basil Soup 58
Crispy Bacon 34
Crispy Calamari 112
Crispy Chicken Parmesan 141
Crispy Chicken Tenders 138
Crispy Chili Kale Chips 74
Crispy Curry Chicken Tenders 143
Crispy Duck With Cherry Sauce 127
Crispy Fried Onion Chicken Breasts 123
Crispy Herbed Potatoes 220
Crispy Lamb Shoulder Chops 170
Crispy Pecan Fish 93
Crispy Ravioli Bites 70
Crispy Smelts 93
Crispy Smoked Pork Chops 146
Crispy Spiced Chickpeas 91
Crispy Sweet Potato Fries 73
Crispy, Cheesy Leeks 202
Crunchy And Buttery Cod With Ritz® Cracker Crust 94
Crunchy Baked Chicken Tenders 48
Crunchy Fried Pork Loin Chops 169
Crunchy Roasted Potatoes 207
Cuban Sliders 80
Currant Carrot Cake 187

D
Dark Chocolate Banana Bread 189
Dijon Salmon With Green Beans Sheet Pan Supper 62
Dill Fried Pickles With Light Ranch Dip 78
Donut Holes 173

E
East Indian Chicken 125
Easy Churros 192
Easy Oven Lasagne 53
Easy Peach Turnovers 199
Easy Tex-mex Chimichangas 160
Egg-loaded Potato Skins 14
Eggplant And Tomato Slices 222
Eggs In Avocado Halves 84

Empty-the-refrigerator Roasted Vegetables 210
Extra Crispy Country-style Pork Riblets 152

F
Family Favorite Pizza 53
Favorite Baked Ziti 63
Fingerling Potatoes 216
Firecracker Bites 74
Fish And "chips" 110
Fish Tacos With Jalapeño-lime Sauce 113
Fish With Sun-dried Tomato Pesto 92
Five-spice Roasted Sweet Potatoes 212
Florentine Stuffed Tomatoes 223
Flounder Fillets 109
Foiled Rosemary Chicken Breasts 137
Freezer-ready Breakast Burritos 31
Freezer-to-oven Chocolate Chip Cookies 188
French Bread Pizza 46
French Onion Soup 50
Fresh Herb Veggie Pizza 40
Fried Chicken 139
Fried Green Tomatoes With Sriracha Mayo 213
Fried Mozzarella Sticks 76
Fried Oysters 105
Fried Scallops 96
Fried Shrimp 102
Fried Snickers Bars 189
Fried Wontons 83
Frozen Brazo De Mercedes 176
Fry Bread 38

G
Garlic And Dill Salmon 112
Garlic Basil Bread 20
Garlic-cheese Biscuits 29
Garlic-lemon Shrimp Skewers 106
German Chocolate Cake 185
Giant Oatmeal–peanut Butter Cookie 184
Ginger Miso Calamari 103
Glazed Apple Crostata 194
Glazed Meatloaf 148
Glazed Pork Tenderloin With Carrots Sheet Pan Supper 41
Gluten-free Nutty Chicken Fingers 134
Goat Cheese–stuffed Nectarines 181

Golden Grilled Cheese Tomato Sandwich 213
Golden Seasoned Chicken Wings 132
Granola 38
Green Bean Soup 45
Green Peas With Mint 204
Grilled Dagwood 16
Grilled Ham & Muenster Cheese On Raisin Bread 79
Grits Casserole 217
Guiltless Bacon 133

H
Halibut Tacos 107
Ham And Cheese Palmiers 66
Harissa Lemon Whole Chicken 126
Hashbrown Potatoes Lyonnaise 28
Hasselback Apple Crisp 193
Healthy Southwest Stuffed Peppers 64
Heavenly Chocolate Cupcakes 178
Heavenly Hash Browns 19
Herbed Lamb Burgers 152
Homemade Beef Enchiladas 52
Homemade Biscuits 22
Homemade Harissa 85
Homemade Pizza Sauce 42
Homemade Potato Puffs 216
Honey Bourbon–glazed Pork Chops With Sweet Potatoes + Apples 46
Honey Ham And Swiss Broiler 34
Honey Lemon Thyme Glazed Cornish Hen 118
Horseradish Crusted Salmon 109
Hot Mexican Bean Dip 75
Hot Thighs 122

I
I Forgot To Thaw—garlic Capered Chicken Thighs 127
Indian Fry Bread Tacos 162
Individual Baked Eggplant Parmesan 47
Individual Overnight Omelets 15
Individual Peach Crisps 191
Italian Baked Chicken 127
Italian Baked Stuffed Tomatoes 50
Italian Bread Pizza 60
Italian Meatballs 149
Italian Rice Balls 76
Italian Roasted Chicken Thighs 141
Italian Sausage & Peppers 150
Italian Strata 21
Italian Stuffed Zucchini Boats 51

J
Jerk Chicken Drumsticks 137
Jerk Turkey Meatballs 136

K
Kasha Loaf 42
Kashaburgers 57
Keto Cheesecake Cups 178
Key Lime Pie 198
Kielbasa Chunks With Pineapple & Peppers 148
Kielbasa Sausage With Pierogies And Caramelized Onions 168
Korean "fried" Chicken Wings 77

L
Lamb Burger With Feta And Olives 156
Lamb Curry 152
Lamb Koftas Meatballs 168
Lemon Blueberry Scones 36
Lemon Chicken 126
Lemon Sage Roast Chicken 118
Lemon Torte 179
Lemon-dill Salmon Burgers 106
Lemon-glazed Baby Carrots 220
Lemon-roasted Fish With Olives + Capers 110
Lemon-roasted Salmon Fillets 102
Light And Lovely Loaf 138
Light Beef Stroganoff 61
Light Quiche Lorraine 65
Light Trout Amandine 99
Lightened-up Breaded Fish Filets 101
Lima Bean And Artichoke Casserole 41
Lime And Cumin Lamb Kebabs 145
Lime-ginger Pork Tenderloin 149
Little Swedish Coffee Cakes 181
Loaded Cauliflower Casserole 82
Loaded Potato Skins 72
Lobster Tails 95

M
Make-ahead Chocolate Chip Cookies 182

Make-ahead Currant Cream Scones 17
Make-ahead Oatmeal-raisin Cookies 188
Maple Bacon 47
Maple Balsamic Glazed Salmon 94
Maple-crusted Salmon 92
Maple-glazed Pumpkin Pie 179
Marinated Catfish 110
Marinated Green Pepper And Pineapple Chicken 131
Marjoram New Potatoes 206
Mashed Potato Tots 221
Meat Lovers Pan Pizza 60
Meatloaf With Tangy Tomato Glaze 159
Meringue Topping 175
Middle Eastern Phyllo Rolls 69
Midnight Nutella® Banana Sandwich 173
Mini Gingerbread Bundt Cakes 174
Mini Hasselback Potatoes 218
Minted Lamb Chops 157
Miso-glazed Salmon With Broccoli 40
Miso-rubbed Salmon Fillets 98
Mississippi Mud Brownies 187
Mixed Berry Hand Pies 190
Molasses-glazed Salmon 112
Morning Glory Muffins 18
Moroccan Couscous 47
Moussaka 58
Mozzarella-stuffed Arancini 87
Mushrooms 220
Mushrooms, Sautéed 209
Mustard-herb Lamb Chops 147

N
Nacho Chicken Fries 121
Nacho Chips 21
Narragansett Clam Chowder 44
New York–style Crumb Cake 31

O
Okra Chips 91
One-step Classic Goulash 54
Onion And Cheese Buttermilk Biscuits 30
Onions 207
Orange Almond Ricotta Cookies 176
Orange Glaze 192
Orange Glazed Pork Tenderloin 153
Orange-glazed Brownies 185
Orange-glazed Roast Chicken 126
Oregano Zucchini 203
Oven-baked Barley 55
Oven-baked Couscous 63
Oven-baked Reuben 30
Oven-baked Rice 61
Oven-crisped Chicken 119
Oven-crisped Fish Fillets With Salsa 103
Oysters Broiled In Wine Sauce 99

P
Pancake Muffins 33
Panko-breaded Onion Rings 88
Panzanella Salad With Crispy Croutons 215
Parmesan Crisps 68
Parmesan Crusted Chicken Cordon Bleu 129
Parmesan Garlic Fries 206
Parmesan Peas 84
Pea Soup 53
Peanut Butter Cup Doughnut Holes 180
Peanut Butter S'mores 182
Peanut Butter-barbeque Chicken 143
Pear And Almond Biscotti Crumble 197
Pecan Turkey Cutlets 122
Pecan-crusted Tilapia 100
Pecan-topped Sole 115
Perfect Asparagus 216
Perfect Pork Chops 150
Perfect Strip Steaks 156
Pesto Pizza 49
Pesto Pork Chops 163
Pesto-crusted Chicken 135
Philly Chicken Cheesesteak Stromboli 133
Pickle Brined Fried Chicken 117
Pineapple Tartlets 176
Polenta Fries With Chili-lime Mayo 68
Popcorn Crawfish 96
Pork And Brown Rice Casserole 41
Pork Belly Scallion Yakitori 66
Pork Cutlets With Almond-lemon Crust 165
Pork Loin 157
Pork Pot Stickers With Yum Yum Sauce 70
Pork Taco Gorditas 145

Portobello Burgers 37
Potato Chips 86
Potato Skins 216
Pretzel-coated Pork Tenderloin 155

Q

Quick Broccoli Quiche 204
Quick Chicken For Filling 141
Quick Pan Pizza 44
Quick Shrimp Scampi 100

R

Raspberry Hand Pies 196
Ratatouille 210
Red Curry Flank Steak 146
Ribeye Steak With Blue Cheese Compound Butter 164
Roasted Belgian Endive With Pistachios And Lemon 217
Roasted Brussels Sprouts With Bacon 212
Roasted Corn Salad 209
Roasted Fennel Salad 204
Roasted Fish With Provençal Crumb Topping 108
Roasted Game Hens With Vegetable Stuffing 142
Roasted Garlic 212
Roasted Garlic Potatoes 208
Roasted Garlic Shrimp 111
Roasted Harissa Chicken + Vegetables 59
Roasted Heirloom Carrots With Orange And Thyme 211
Roasted Herbed Shiitake Mushrooms 204
Roasted Pepper Tilapia 105
Roasted Ratatouille Vegetables 202
Roasted Vegetable Gazpacho 40
Roasted Vegetables 219
Roasted Veggie Kebabs 224
Rolled Asparagus Flounder 93
Romaine Wraps With Shrimp Filling 97
Root Vegetable Crisps 69
Rosemary Lentils 63
Rosemary New Potatoes 211
Rosemary Roasted Potatoes With Lemon 208
Rosemary-roasted Potatoes 81
Rotisserie-style Chicken 123
Rum-glazed Roasted Pineapple 200

S

Sage Butter Roasted Butternut Squash With Pepitas 79
Sage, Chicken + Mushroom Pasta Casserole 45
Salad Lentils 62
Salmon Salad With Steamboat Dressing 217
Sausage Cheese Pinwheels 77
Savory Breakfast Bread Pudding 27
Savory Sausage Balls 69
Scalloped Corn Casserole 57
Sea Bass With Potato Scales And Caper Aïoli 103
Sea Scallops 100
Seasoned Boneless Pork Sirloin Chops 151
Sesame Carrots And Sugar Snap Peas 208
Sesame Chicken Breasts 144
Sesame Orange Chicken 117
Sesame Wafers 14
Sesame-crusted Tuna Steaks 116
Sheet Pan Beef Fajitas 54
Sheet Pan Chicken Nachos 73
Sheet Pan Loaded Nachos 48
Sheet-pan Hash Browns 27
Shrimp 115
Shrimp Pirogues 71
Shrimp Po'boy With Remoulade Sauce 95
Shrimp With Jalapeño Dip 98
Shrimp, Chorizo And Fingerling Potatoes 104
Simple Holiday Stuffing 78
Simple Roasted Sweet Potatoes 222
Skewered Salsa Verde Shrimp 98
Skinny Fries 84
Skirt Steak Fajitas 154
Sloppy Joes 157
Slow Cooked Carnitas 167
Smoked Gouda Bacon Macaroni And Cheese 88
Smoked Salmon Puffs 85
Smokehouse-style Beef Ribs 165
Snapper With Capers And Olives 108
Soft Peanut Butter Cookies 186
Sour Cream Pound Cake 189
Southern-style Biscuits 14
Southwest Gluten-free Turkey Meatloaf 135
Spanish Pork Skewers 164
Spanish Rice 42

Spice Cake 195
Spiced Sea Bass 108
Spice-rubbed Split Game Hen 128
Spicy Beef Fajitas 36
Spicy Little Beef Birds 155
Spicy Oven-baked Chili 51
Spicy Pigs In A Blanket 76
Spicy Sweet Potatoes 205
Spinach And Artichoke Dip 80
Spinach, Tomato & Feta Quiche 25
Steak Pinwheels With Pepper Slaw And Minneapolis Potato Salad 166
Steak With Herbed Butter 168
Steakhouse Baked Potatoes 218
Sticky Soy Chicken Thighs 140
Strawberry Bread 38
Strawberry Pie Glaze 33
Stromboli 23
Stuffed Bell Peppers 150
Stuffed Mushrooms 81
Stuffed Onions 222
Stuffed Pork Chops 172
Stuffed Shrimp 101
Sun-dried Tomato Pizza 49
Sunny-side Up Eggs 30
Sweet And Salty Roasted Nuts 82
Sweet Or Savory Baked Sweet Potatoes 81
Sweet Potato Curly Fries 221
Sweet Potato Donut Holes 183
Sweet Potato Puffs 203
Sweet Potato–crusted Pork Rib Chops 170
Sweet-and-sour Chicken 132
Sweet-hot Pepperoni Pizza 26

T
Tandoori Chicken 142
Tandoori Chicken Legs 134
Tarragon Beef Ragout 43
Tasty Meat Loaf 137
Tender Chicken Meatballs 136
Teriyaki Chicken Drumsticks 125
Thai Chicken Drumsticks 138
Thai Chicken Pizza With Cauliflower Crust 52
Thick-crust Pepperoni Pizza 67
Tilapia Teriyaki 96
Toasted Cheese Sandwich 21
Tomato Bisque 59
Tortilla-crusted Tilapia 98
Traditional Pot Roast 171
Triple Chocolate Brownies 201
Tuna Nuggets In Hoisin Sauce 95
Turkey Bacon Dates 73
Turkey Burger Sliders 81
Turkey Sausage Cassoulet 120
Turkey-hummus Wraps 131
Tuscan Pork Tenderloin 153

V
Vegan Swedish Cinnamon Rolls (kanelbullar) 193

W
Walnut Pancake 35
Warm Chocolate Fudge Cakes 174
Wasabi-coated Pork Loin Chops 160
Western Frittata 20
White Chocolate Cranberry Blondies 178
Wild Blueberry Lemon Chia Bread 16
Wild Blueberry Sweet Empanadas 186
Wonton Cups 86

Y
Yeast Dough For Two Pizzas 43
Yellow Squash 205
Yellow Squash With Bell Peppers 214
Yogurt Bread 30

Z
Yogurt Zucchini With Onion 212
Zesty London Broil 171
Zucchini Boats With Ham And Cheese 207
Zucchini Casserole 62
Zucchini Fries 218

CPSIA information can be obtained
at www.ICGtesting.com
Printed in the USA
BVHW050415130122
625994BV00005B/271